A BUNDLE FROM BRITAIN

Also by Alistair Horne

Back into Power
The Land Is Bright
Canada and the Canadians
The Price of Glory: Verdun 1916
The Fall of Paris: The Siege and the Commune 1870–71
To Lose a Battle: France 1940
The Terrible Year: The Paris Commune 1871
Death of a Generation
Small Earthquake in Chile
Napoleon: Master of Europe 1805–1807
The French Army and Politics 1870–1970
A Savage War of Peace: Algeria 1954–1962
Macmillan: 1894–1956
Macmillan: 1957–1986

ALISTAIR HORNE

A Bundle from Britain

St. Martin's Press
New York

Library of Congress Cataloging-in-Publication Data

Horne, Alistair.
A bundle from Britain / Alistair Horne ; preface by Louis
Auchincloss.
p.   cm.
"A Thomas Dunne book."
ISBN 0-312-11136-3 (hardcover)
1. Horne, Alistair.   2. World War, 1939–1945—Children—Great
Britain.   3. World War, 1939–1945—Children—United States.
4. World War, 1939–1945—Evacuation of civilians—Great Britain.
5. World War, 1939–1945—Personal narratives, British.   6. World
War, 1939–1945—Great Britain.   7. Historians—Great Britain—
Biography.   I. Title.
D810.C4H63   1994
940.53′161—dc20   94-7144   CIP

First published in Great Britain by Macmillan London Limited.

First U.S. Edition: August 1994
10   9   8   7   6   5   4   3   2   1

For my Grandchildren
– for Za and Sig: the Special Relations continue

– and for all who lovingly remember
Julia Breese and Rossy Cutler

Contents

List of Illustrations

Great-granny, Violet Greville.

The Hon. Mrs Ronnie Greville, with future King George VI (courtesy Mary, Duchess of Buccleuch).

'Uncle Zander', Count Munster.

'Uncle Newt' in World War I.

The author with Auriol.

My father.

The author; dressed as a girl.

Sari Petrass.

Auriol, Tallulah Bankhead and Leslie Howard, rehearsing *Henry's Girl*, 1928.

The author, unknown chow, and Auriol.

Antwerp, the River Scheldt, September 1930; the fatal car.

Ropley, in the 1930s; author, a first girlfriend, my father.

Top dogs – Britain; at Ropley, 'Night', 'Rajah', Governess (Christine, *not* the seductress), and 'Terry'.

America; in Edgartown, 'Mr Salteena'.

Ludgrove; author; Robin, Commander Murray.

America; Rossy Cutler, Julia Breese, AAH; on the tennis court.

Preface

This book started, quite unashamedly, as a great big thank-you to the US of A. It was the bread-and-butter letter that I had been meaning to write for many years. In July 1940, following my father's unilateral decision, I, together with hundreds of other British schoolchildren (later they were amicably nicknamed 'Bundles from Britain'), was shipped off, protesting, to America. The aim was to preserve us, for posterity, from the clutches of Adolf Hitler. For the next three years I was imposed upon an incredibly warm-hearted – and agreeably eccentric – American family. Those three years remain more vividly etched in my memory than any other part of my life. They, the Breese–Cutler family, and the friends I made at school changed my life and launched me upon an open-ended love-affair with the United States – and Americans.

Originally *A Bundle from Britain* (the only book of mine, incidentally, where I have ever hit on the title before a word was written) was to be published to coincide with the fiftieth anniversary of that red-lettered month of July 1940, when I first touched down on American soil. Then it was rescheduled for Pearl Harbor day; and finally for the date of my return to Britain. In the jargon of my exasperated publishers, the date had slipped a bit.

The reason for this slippage was that, as with almost every one of my books (some fifteen now), the end-product turned out to be very different from what had originally been intended. On thinking through the idea, I concluded that the American adventure would make little sense to readers in the 1990s unless I could help out with some comparative pictures of my British upbringing and background. For reasons that will emerge later, but notably because both my mother and father died when I was still young, and with only one of their contemporaries who could help me still alive, I found myself engaged in a major detective work of reconstruction – almost a book in itself. Like other family biographers from Osbert Sitwell to Germaine Greer, the idiosyncracies of my own parents began to intrigue me. Out of it all I deduced that my real English (or, rather, Scottish) family – a faraway clan of whom I knew almost nothing – were infinitely more eccentric (as well as being a great deal unhappier) than that unusual one on which I fell like a bomb from a Stuka in America.

There was a further problem. Talking about his engaging autobiography, *The Ragman's Son*, Kirk Douglas remarked on the wonderful 'catharsis' of writing about oneself. I found quite the reverse – it was constipation that seemed to be my trouble. Until I could fool myself into pretending that I was writing about a totally other, external set of people – like, say, the Macmillans or the Kennedys – there were days and weeks of complete seize-up. Sometimes, too, it was depressingly like being dead, writing one's own obituary.

The material for these earlier chapters came largely from some thirty scrapbooks that survived my mother's death back in 1930, as well as several steel boxes of her writings. She threw nothing away (not even the rejection slips from the multitude of London newspapers for which she wrote). She must have been a kind of squirrel, but perhaps people of her era were. There were albums of faded postcards and photographs of people and faraway places; albums full of signatures of weekend party guests, of invitations and race-cards – and even dance-cards. There were boxes full of unpublished short stories, novels, poems and plays – and even songs. There were books of cuttings of her press articles, which were published, and even letters of rejection. And there were two macabre cuttings-books, prepared by unknown hands, of her sudden death. It is largely from this material that I set about the detective work of reconstructing an unknown family past.

I had never thoroughly sifted through these archives, and in the course of it I found what seemed to me an intriguing picture of an era – not only of my own forebears. As work went on, fortuitously I came upon (thanks to my mother's last-surviving relative, Victor Creer) scrapbooks of *her* grandmother's press-cuttings – compiled at the turn of the century, a time when 'ladies' did not write columns in the tabloids. From this untapped treasure-trove of Violet and Maggie Greville, I learnt a little more about an unusual, and somewhat wayward, clan – which took me wandering still further from that bread-and-butter letter to America.

Gradually, it grew additionally into a kind of memorandum for my children and grandchildren.

For the American sections, I was able to rely on a couple of chapters from a travel book, my second, called *The Land Is Bright* (Max Parrish, 1958) written only a short time after the events it described, and while both my memory and those of the principals were still fresh. This was reinforced by letters from my father and other members of my family that had survived the war; some partial diaries and letters of my own; contemporary issues of the Millbrook School journal, the *Silo* – most kindly provided by our old headmaster, Edward Pulling; nostalgic, juvenile photographs (some reprinted here); conversations with, and letters from, many protagonists over the years; as well as a multiplicity of cuttings I had kept from journals such as *Time* magazine. On top of all this was the constant refuelling of repeated trips back to the US over the years. There was another unanticipated source, through the bizarre turns of almost extra-sensory coincidence which fate so kindly provides at regular intervals: a letter from the daughter of my old Squadron Leader in the RAF, with whom I had lost touch these past forty-odd years, arrived out of the blue while I was working on the chapter devoted to that very period. In this way I came upon a valuable trove of wartime correspondence. For this I owe warm gratitude to Mrs Gerald Aylmer, wife of the former Master of St Peter's College, Oxford.

Human memory is a curiously irrational faculty. That Winston Churchill, in his dotage, could recall vividly events from the First World War, but not from the more recent conflict in which he had played so central a role, points to a well-known phenomenon. When I read the first volume of Patrick Leigh-Fermor's marvellous memoirs, *A Time of Gifts*, I was ungratefully suspicious of his recollection in extraordinary detail of events in his extreme youth – despite his having lost his diaries. Yet, when I started delving into my schooldays of over fifty years ago, I amazed myself by being able to recall not only the names of contemporaries, but also exactly what they looked like. It was as if data, long submerged under a mass of more recent files, had emerged from the computer, having been unknowingly 'saved' on the hard disk all those years.

Of course, at the same time there lurks the dread tiger-trap of the false memory, epitomized by that immortal duet between the two old lovers, Hermione Gingold and Maurice Chevalier, in *Gigi* ('We met at nine, No, we met at eight; I was on time, No, you were late; Yes, I remember it well . . .'). For instance, my old wartime room-mate at Millbrook School, NY, William F. Buckley Jr, equipped (as an essential part of his stock-in-trade) with a phenomenally good memory, had gone through life convinced that he had heard the cataclysmic news of Pearl Harbor on his mother's car radio, while returning from a concert performed by the great Rachmaninov. But, on reading through the old copies of the *Silo*, I discovered that he had (aged sixteen) in fact reviewed that same concert the previous month! He was astounded and dismayed. I was made doubly cautious about the insidious dangers lying in wait.

Any errors of this order, and incidental distress caused to friends, is of course my fault alone, and I apologize in advance.

But, I promise, I have done my best and have tried to be scrupulously honest. Bar a few minor liberties taken with direct speech, I would like to think I could claim this to be – in the legal phrase – 'a true and accurate record'. Though I have revisited old wartime haunts in America, seen old friends again, many times, I have assiduously tried to write only of what I remember of the period, to see things only through the eyes of a teenager in the early 1940s, with minimum resort to *ex post facto* clairvoyance.

INTRODUCTION

There are some who might argue that the bleak conditions of
Alistair Horne's British adolescence had ideally prepared him to
reap the fullest advantage of the experience of being transplanted,
at the age of fourteen, from a war-wracked England to a safe New
York. How could a lonely only child, who had lost his beautiful but
preoccupied mother in infancy and been raised by an elderly and
constantly absent father, shunted off to hostile and hazing schools,
not respond to a wonderfully welcoming Yankee family and an
academy of friendly boys run by a wise and sympathetic headmaster?
Yet an understandably embittered child might just as easily have
rejected the benefits of such a change, resenting the ease and comfort of a nation still at peace while his own was battling alone to
save the world from tyranny.

Certainly the Cutler family, which adopted the young Alistair,
was admirably warm and kind, and certainly Mr. Pulling and the
faculty of Millbrook were wise and understanding in their handling
of this "bundle from Britain," but in so difficult a situation success
could only be attained if work were done on both sides. Alistair
Horne gave himself up to this new experience with a heartiness and
curiosity which embraced not only his new family and school, but
New York, the Massachusetts Cape, and ultimately America itself.
It was not easy. His heart bled at each piece of bad news from home.
He felt the dog days of guilt at his own exemption. He had a chart
listing the principal vessels of the Royal Navy and grimly crossed
off each one that was sunk. He once even toyed with the idea of
suicide. His book represents the deepest emotion recollected in the
tranquillity of his later successful English literary life. The sad but
ultimately exhilarating story of the British children sent to our
shores to escape the bombs has at last been adequately told.

—Louis Auchincloss

ACKNOWLEDGEMENTS

In particular, my thanks – for it all – are directed to the loving memory of two great American anglophiles, Julia Fish Breese and Rosalind Fish Cutler, and of two great educators, Edward Pulling and Henry Callard; and to two lifelong friends, Judy Cutler Shinkle and William F. Buckley Jr., both still happily with us. And lastly, to my father, whom I hardly knew – for making so much possible.

Among many who helped me over specific points in the book, and over illustrations, I am particularly indebted to Comte Charles de Bernis, HE Raymond Seitz, Sir Fred Mason, Monsieur Vincent Labouret, Graf Peter Münster, Graf Hermann-Siegfried Münster, the Hon. Robin Warrender, Mr Victor Creer, Mrs Renira Horne, Mrs Jackson Shinkle, Miss Priscilla Buckley, Mrs Rosalind Michahellis, Mrs R. C. Aldrich Sr, Mrs C. K. Warner, Mrs Gerald Aylmer, Mrs George W. Cutting, Mr Bob Anthony and Millbrook School, NY, Mr Stephen England for his early support, and Mr Brian Masters (for information derived about Maggie Greville from his book, *Great Hostesses*). I owe constantly renewed gratitude to Anne Whatmore for her ever willing research and secretarial work, to Peter James, and, above all, to my new, endlessly patient editor, Roland Philipps, for his advice, suggestions – and improvements. To my wife, Sheelin, there is a debt of a different kind, as well as reading and commenting on the chapters as they emerged: stoking up the author with encouragement.

I owe special thanks to that enlightened patron of writers, and good friend, Mrs H. J. Heinz, for providing a tranquil refuge in Italy, at the most difficult moment in this book.

Above all, however, I remain conscious of my supreme debt of gratitude to, and affection for, America and Americans.

The Old Vicarage,
Turville

CHAPTER ONE

Britannic to America

It was War, with a capital W, that had me on Cunard's SS *Britannic* in July 1940, scuttling off somewhat unwillingly, bound for neutral New York. And it was War that brought me back, a little less unwillingly, as Aircraftman Second Class, aboard the SS *Mauretania*, some three years later. Like those bright-hued minerals, encrusted in rock under some enormous pressure, or – less romantically – that favourite dish of British boarding schools of the day, toad-in-the-hole, sausage set in its indigestible wadge of dough, we of my generation grew up, as it were, encrusted in war.

Born just seven years after the Armistice of 1918, I lived out my childhood constantly under the influence of the Great War, perpetually reminded of it, and, much later, found it return to invade my life as a writer. What were the symbols one can immediately recall? I remember the youngish bachelors who used to come to stay, with the staring eyes and black skullcaps ('Caught with his head up above the parapet,' volunteered Cousin Cecil, Captain, MC, of the Middlesex Regiment, 'commonest of all wounds on the Western Front').

But what impinged itself much more intimately on my childish life was the 'German' toyshop in our market town of Winchester. (I say 'German', though for all I know the proprietor may just have been one of those Jewish refugees who were already beginning to flow into England; he just happened to have a guttural accent and a square head, and traded with *der Vaterland*.) In Winchester there was Batchellor's Olde Sweetshoppe, which sold quite the best rock (rose, pineapple, peppermint and lemon –

fourpence a quarter); but, next in importance there was that toyshop. It sold motion-picture projectors that really worked and – best of all – remarkable models of field guns, miniature howitzers that actually lobbed leaden shells, and U–boats that rose and submerged with superb realism in the bath. Regrettably, they bore the fatal imprint 'Made in Germany', and, therefore, they and the 'German' remained forever out of bounds to me.

I cannot recall all that much of that trip on SS *Britannic*. I did not keep a diary, but then, who – at the tender age of fourteen – did? Yet I do seem able still to scent in my nostrils the aroma of excited expectation. There were, amid all the chaos of post-Dunkirk Britain, the tearful scenes, bravely terrible, of parting at Euston Station, that Britain had experienced the previous September during the short-lived mass evacuations. A chronic sufferer from train fever, my poor father had got me to the station one and a half hours ahead of time, which increased, rather than lessened, the tension. There were the last-minute exhortations: 'Don't forget to write,' 'Do remember you're English,' 'Don't drink the water out of the taps,' 'Do see that Gladys keeps wrapped up on the boat.' The teenagers among us, with all emotion stifled by years of British boarding school already behind us, stood looking embarrassed. Together with a number of other children 'evacuees' (shameful collective tag), I was entrusted to the surveillance of a sad-eyed German refugee, Frau Fleischmann. We barely saw her again: for reasons that, to us, were not quite comprehensible, she kept a mournful vigil in her cabin for the whole voyage. I remember shaking hands gravely with my father, then turning away as he put his arm around my shoulder. Swiftly, he was gone among the crowds – and away we went.

Once the initial gloom of homesickness had dissipated (rather rapidly), we brutal children were filled with amorally high spirits. Did any of us have an inkling of just how much anguish those hundreds of adults were going through that day? The evacuation of children the previousSeptember to the remote countryside had looked likely to be for a matter of months only. But now – at least to the parents – the worsening war news made it quite clear that separation would be for much, much longer. We children, were we a little like victims of an incurable illness, where it is always so much worse for those who survive? We, like them, had no more than a walk-on (or, rather, walk-off) part.

Somewhere between Euston and sailing from Liverpool, we handed over those cumbersome, silly little cardboard boxes containing our still virgin gas-masks. All that remained of England at war was thereby taken from us. At Liverpool docks, already battered by Göring's bombers, I half expected to board something like P & O's SS *Orion*, the luxury cruise liner on which my father had taken me off to the Baltic the previous summer – the only other big ship I'd ever seen – for the best and happiest holiday we'd ever had together, a reward for passing Common Entrance. The *Britannic* still seemed anything but warlike, her paintwork, evocative of joyous Caribbean cruises, still unsullied by naval camouflage. (Was it perhaps a way of informing attendant U-boats that she was carrying a cargo of precious British schoolchildren?) The swimming pools, alas, were empty of water, filled instead with cargo – or was it extra passengers? Every inch of deck space was filled with children, and their duennas. Portholes were sealed by blackout precautions, which in the summer heat made for a stifling night-time atmosphere. There were three of us teenagers all cramped together in our cabin. One – was he called Viney? – had deplorably smelly feet; he was larger, so we never quite dared tell him. The third boy eventually solved his nocturnal problems by falling in love with another fourteen-year-old, and thereby finding an excuse to spend much of the remaining nights on deck. I was amazed and rather envious at his precocity.

We slipped out of the Mersey at night (the record reveals that it was a Sunday, 21 July 1940). The following morning we awoke, with a couple of destroyers for company, an RAF Sunderland flying-boat circling lazily above, and the smoke of a distant convoy on the far horizon. The next day, our comforting escort had disappeared. We were alone in a vast ocean, zigzagging frantically to evade any torpedo that might be loosed at us. We must have made tremendous speed: despite all the changes of course, the log shows that we reached New York the following

Sunday – that is in seven days, compared with the five days then taken by the *Queen Mary* in peacetime.) None of us showed it, but some of us older boys at least must have had secret anxieties, that second day, half-expecting the terrible crunch of a U-boat torpedo – most likely at night. But, if we did have those anxieties, they were very soon submerged in very British certainties. We were unassailable optimists: we were *not* going to be torpedoed, we were *not* going to be killed – Britain was *not* going to lose the war. These last two credos, were – I swear it – to remain with most of us all through the next few years of menace. But the poor *Britannic* was in fact sunk some six months later, bombed on her way to Barrow.

Whenever the sleek, grey shape of a warship came into sight, we knew instinctively that it was British, and not one of those Nazi pocket battleships on the prowl. Soon, inevitably, anxiety gave way to boredom. I began to half hope that a rash U-boat would suddenly appear, only to be sunk by some invisible guardian escort. Among the adults on board was an eminent French lady journalist, with dyed red hair. (I later discovered she was Geneviève Tabouis, a star writer of the Third and Fourth Republics, who lived to a ripe old age after the war.) Every evening after dinner she would sit silently in the lounge and, on the least provocation, sing out in a cracked voice a bar or two of the 'Marseillaise', then subside into uncontrollable tears that left streaks of vermilion on her cheeks. We adolescents looked upon her misery with a mixture of pity, amusement and national superiority – 'Poor old Frog!' We were as insensitive to the reasons for the lachrymose Frenchwoman's woe as we were to those for Frau Fleischmann's sadness. Apart from the sorrowful-eyed Frau Fleischmann and Madame Tabouis, weeping her pink tears for fallen France, did any of us child evacuees consider our wider condition? Did we try to evaluate what we were leaving, and what we were heading for? Did we resemble those huddled, apprehensive emigrants in Ford Madox Brown's 'The Last of England'? I doubt it, we were far too self-confident, assured of British destiny. There were the occasional exhortations on board: we must not treat the Americans as 'colonials', the United States was not a British dominion. But it all bounced off us. We were, after all, British and profoundly superior.

It would be agreeably congruent to be able to write that, gazing out over the stern across the *Britannic's* bubbling and bilious wake, swinging first right, then left, one had profound philosophic thoughts, as the days passed and home receded ever further, about the nature of what one was leaving – and about what we were going to find at the end of the journey. But it was not like that, and to pretend that it was would hardly be honest. In so far as we thought about it at all, I suspect we all regarded the future with some equanimity: our thoughts were all of the excitement of the adventure about to begin. It was all going to be a jolly summer holiday, lasting a few months, maybe, in a glamorous land of cowboys, gangsters and Red Indians, where the fountains flowed with ice-cream sodas, but otherwise populated by fairly unenlightened people, an escape from the tedium of the blackout, the privations of rationing (and, especially, the iniquities of sweet-rationing) – and maybe, in my own case, even an escape from the rough-housing and unpleasantness of Stowe, from which I still nursed an injured arm. Certainly, we all expected to be back within the year – Germany starved out by the British blockade (as the *Illustrated London News* assured us was already happening), Hitler banished to St Helena, and the war over. Of course, I'm sure I suppressed a tear or two for life at home in Ropley Manor, for the dogs, for my father, for Aunt Ethel and Cousin Eve (probably in that order), but I doubt if any of us seriously assessed whether, in America, we were going to be happier or less happy than we had been in Britain. To most children, happiness is surely an ephemeral, daily or at most hebdomadal, affair. What child can look back on his childhood and judge whether it was happy or unhappy? What yardsticks can he possibly apply?

To modify those immortal opening words of *Anna Karenina*, all happy childhoods are more or less like one another, but an unhappy one is unhappy in its own particular way. I don't suppose I ever considered that I had had a particularly unhappy childhood – until people told me so, much later on. But certainly, after a

5

week in America, I was to realize just how *different* it was. There is little point in moaning, whining, wailing or complaining about it, but, if one is to try to set down the American experience now, from a fifty-year vantage point, then the British past could be worth exploring, just to counterpoint the difference, even strangeness, of it all. In explaining his investigation of his parents' somewhat eccentric lives, Nigel Nicolson quotes:

> Life appears to me such a curious and wonderful thing that it almost seems a pity that even such a humble and uneventful life as mine should pass altogether away without some record; and I think the record may amuse and interest some who come after me.

One of the few things we have in common with dogs and cats, and lesser animals, is that we cannot choose ancestry, any more than I had any say in my dispatch to America in 1940. In contrast to Nigel Nicolson, I have a particular disability: For reasons that the reader will soon discover, I never knew my mother and had barely begun to know my father before he died. Almost all those few relatives of earlier generations had disappeared before I seriously attempted the work of reconstruction. But they were meticulous folk, my parents – particularly my mother. Afflicted with a kind of pessimism that all was going to go up in fire, some time after my departure in 1940, my father set about 'reducing his administrative tail', as he liked to put it – selling, or giving away, all but a few of his most precious belongings, and destroying papers and letters wholesale. Yet, for some motive of sentimentality, he kept all my deceased mother's papers, several steel boxes of them.

Both my paternal and maternal families were Scots. The Hornes were lowlanders of modest bourgeois extraction, originating from Edinburgh. In fairly sharp contrast, my mother's clan, the Hays, were accurately described by one of the few surviving members as 'decadent Scottish aristocracy'. Some of them were decadent indeed. One of them, the mishapped 22nd Earl of Erroll, 'Jos' to his friends, went through the lucky ladies of Kenya's 'Happy Valley' set like the proverbial dose of salts, gave rise to one of the best, though marginally libellous, headlines ever – 'BELTED EARL BUMPED BY BART' – shortly after I reached America, and provided a hero (or villain, depending how you view it) for a book and much hyped film, *White Mischief.* My mother's family abounded in Scottish peers, the Errolls, the Grevilles, the Atholls (my godmother, Kitty, was unkindly known as the 'Red Duchess' for her rather left-of-centre views as Scotland's first woman MP), the Beauforts, the Montroses and the Kinnouls. Despite the blot of the 22nd Earl, the Errolls it seems were so grand that the title passed down through the female line, carrying with it the hereditary title of Lord High Constable of Scotland; while the grandfather of my mother, Auriol Blanche Camilla Hay, was no lesser grandee than the 12th Earl of Kinnoul. The Kinnoul Hays, so *Burke's Peerage* informs me, could trace their ancestry back to 29 April 1251.

By the end of the nineteenth century, however, the blood may have been running a bit thin.

In the introduction to his massive and marvellous autobiography, *Left Hand, Right Hand,* Osbert Sitwell – with whom the Kinnouls appear to share a Duke of Beaufort (the 7th, to be precise) in their lineage – speaks of ancestors stretching behind one 'at a gathering speed; two parents, four grandparents, eight great-grandparents, sixteen great-great-grandparents, until already in the tenth generation, a man possesses one thousand and twenty-four of them . . .' They form a 'cloud of witnesses in us . . . testifying to our physical and mental heredity', though beyond the stratum of great-grandparents they have become, simply, 'ancestors'. I don't recall meeting any of my grandparents and grew up knowing next to nothing about my ancestry – and probably caring rather less. Nor did I really ever intend writing about them. But, as Sitwell suggests, suddenly they are there, ganging up on one; curiosity mounts about those funny little genes, and, bit by bit, as research gathers pace, so pieces of information pop up from time to time, fascinating to the author – and possibly to an occasional reader.

From an old picture frame, dated 1895 and suitably embossed with coronets, my Kinnoul great-grandmother, Lady Blanche Charlotte Somerset, daughter of Henry, 7th Duke of Beaufort, and a dotty duchess, gazes at me with a beady eye and down a Hay nose of aristocratic proportions and of exceptional length and sharpness. She is wearing a white lace collar over a tight-waisted black dress – an austere-looking woman, the only concession to extravagance a narrow fur trimming to the skirt. In one photograph she is leaning on a conventional Victorian parasol, with a bizarre sprig of feathers in her hair that makes her seem faintly squaw-like; in another, she is stiffly arranging a bowl of flowers carefully posed on a polygonal inlaid Indian stool, with what looks like a *trompe-l'oeil* of a rather sumptuous conservatory. And that is about all I know of her. She strikes one as being rather a fierce old bat. I can imagine her taking a hyper-Scottish interest in whether the domestics at Balhousie Castle were overspending on the housekeeping, or whether they had been cleaning the silver properly. Already in her lineage there seems to have been a decided streak of eccentricity. According to Osbert Sitwell, her mother (his great-grandmother), the 7th Duchess of Beaufort, became 'rather vague mentally' in her latter years, taking her parrot for daily drives in the New Forest:

> she always wished to go for a new drive, but the coachman invariably took her the same way; she was too old to be aware of the deception. The parrot, too, had long been dead and stuffed, so as to give an illusion of life. . . . She was also too old, fortunately, to tell the difference between the animate and the inanimate!

The old Duchess's eccentricity seems to have been well matched on the maternal, Greville side of my mother's ancestry.

My mother's great-grandmother was yet another duchess, Caroline, wife of the 4th Duke of Montrose (descendant of the Montrose hanged, drawn and quartered after his revolt on behalf of Charles II in 1650), who was born in 1818, married three husbands and died in 1894, the year after my mother was born. Her particular eccentricty seems to have been a passion for racehorses, a field in which she was astonishingly successful.

Since it was considered 'unsuitable' for Victorian ladies to own a stable, she assumed the name of 'Mr Manton', which became quite famous in the racing world. She was reckoned to have owned and trained some of the best horses of the century, selling at least one of them for over 3000 guineas, and she won the Oaks – but never quite the Derby. An obituary published just after her death (when she still had seventeen horses in training) notes that Mr Manton's winnings over the previous five years had been 'not inconsiderable'. In fact, in 1889 alone, just five years before she died, when she was seventy-one, she won a total of £21,545 – a fantastic sum in those days, which must have gone far to help restore the coffers of a fairly impoverished Scottish dukedom. Such was her dedication to the sport that she even built a special chapel for use of jockeys and stable maids.

Mr Manton's daughter, the Lady Violet, married in 1863 an Irish peer, Algernon William Fulke Greville, the 2nd Baron Greville, a relative of the famous diarist. A groom-in-waiting to Queen Victoria, Lord of the Treasury and former captain of the Life Guards, but otherwise of no great distinction, my great-grandfather Algie gazes solemnly out of my mother's scrapbooks in old age, complete with the conventional and emulative Edwardian paint-brush beard. Violet, his wife, was anything but conventional. A contemporary journal in the year of Queen Victoria's Golden Jubilee, 1897, describes her as being 'the only titled woman journalist in Great Britain'. In those days, that was no mean distinction. As a girl she had written curtain-raisers for amateur theatricals, and remained a talented actress; on marriage (perhaps out of boredom with the worthy Algernon) she took to writing – with considerable success – plays and novels. But it was her journalism that gave her fame, writing as she did a regular, highly controversial and widely read column in the tabloid *Graphic*, something virtually unheard of, even in the more liberated times of Edward VII.

I do not know what contemporary feminists would have made of Violet Greville. Her life, in many ways, bears a resemblance to that of the remarkable Daisy Warwick, for nine years reigning mistress of Edward VIII (when he was Prince of Wales). Like her contemporary Daisy, Violet was a tremendous personality with a dull husband. She had Daisy's zest, energy, radicalism – and some of her urgency for social reform. Less indiscreet and lacking in control, she was just as compassionate, and passionate. Certainly in her time, Violet was regarded alternately as a progressive iconoclast and as a Victorian reactionary – yet, well hidden from the public eye, as with the other unhappy women of the late-Victorian era, lay another reality . . .

Described by her contemporaries as 'tall and stately-looking', she must have been striking, rather than beautiful, with a very long face and an amazingly long nose, deeply indented upper lip, quizzical, twentieth-century eyes and a hairdo in the style of Queen Alexandra. One of the first women to ride a bicycle, she was praised by the journal *Home Notes* because she 'always rode gracefully, her pretty tall figure shown to great advantage'. Barely a week went by without her *Graphic* column, syndicated across the country, being quoted elsewhere by her competitors in the press: 'Lady Violet Greville says . . .', often accompanied by an ironical cartoon. 'A woman does not wear the gifts of a man she dislikes,' she declared with a passion that said something about her own, unhappy private life; 'Women are too independent now to need or appreciate a man's arm . . .'; 'The fact of dressing for dinner, differentiates men from animals . . .'; 'Women prefer men without beards . . .' This last must have annoyed both the monarch and Algernon, the 2nd Baron Greville.

There was no topic she would not tackle. To a certain amount of residual, conservative *noblesse oblige* as a daughter of her age and of a duke, she brought a passionate and very modern-minded concern for the lot of women – plus a good deal of sharp irony.

By Edwardian standards, she would have been rated as an out-and-out feminist, fighting fearlessly for any women's cause – though often fiercely critical of the foibles of her own sex. She was bitterly opposed to the suffragettes, who were queering the pitch politically, she thought, with their raucous unfemininity. The 'true woman', according to her, 'is never unfeminine'.

Like those sturdy Swiss women of the latter part of the twentieth century, Great-granny Violet opposed universal suffrage. She wrote in that heady general election year of 1906, 'Electioneering with women becomes an obsession, and intoxication which far surpasses that of men. One trembles to think of the state of enthusiasm and excitement society would fall into had women the vote. . . .' (They did not in fact get the vote until 1919.) Women, she felt (a little like Lysistrata), had better and more effective ways of changing the world. 'The secret of a woman's power is *sympathy*' was very much her war-cry. On the other hand, she was strongly in favour of women jurors, especially in breach-of-promise cases (although she regarded that particular law as a nonsense in modern life, arguing, with perhaps just a touch of tongue-in-cheek, that a change in the law 'would certainly benefit the men, as they would at once see through the wiles of their own sex . . .'. She spoke up passionately for equality in the divorce courts (again, very probably with more than a suspicion of self-interest involved), while suggesting that women should be cautious, about how much scent they wore in the witness box, lest the judge be overcome and give a prejudiced decision.

For all her pronounced feminist sympathies, she was fierce in castigating the foibles and follies of women. 'I know no one,' declared the *Lady*, 'who seems to pursue her sex with more relentless criticism than Lady Violet Greville in *The Graphic*' – after she had had a go at the silliness of women about their dogs ('known to bury them in white satin coffins'). She criticized women for attempting to compete with men in sports (as a consequence, they were already 'growing more like men in appearance . . . taller, stronger, wider shoulders . . . and [were] gradually losing the charm of a petite and graceful individuality';

they should devote themselves to 'more womanly work'). But it was women's clubs that especially drew her ire in 1905, not least because of the reprehensible male vices that she thought they would impose on women. These she listed as gossip, idleness, disorder and stealing umbrellas. Moreover, clubs for women, she declared, had 'practically destroyed home life' and were but 'a vehicle for assignations'. This all provoked a long leader in *Vanity Fair* signed 'Rasper', accusing Lady Violet of Victorian prejudices – which she seemed to 'share with the Kaiser'. She was not, however, beyond maintaining her feminine prerogative, and a little over a year later was to be found, in a sharp volte-face, championing the cause of women's clubs. Meanwhile, for girls of the 'lower classes', she thought that a much better solution might be a 'courting hall', to be made part of the equipment of the parish, where 'They might have the same advantages as their betters . . . play games, dance, talk, and have music.'

She seems to have inherited at least some of her mother's interest in the equestrian world. In 1906 she was urging that riding sidesaddle should be adopted with 'prudence and care', for 'little girls are apt grow up one-sided'. Yet she was equally capable here of modest inconsequentiality – expressing doubts a few months later as to whether 'the new fashion of riding astride is graceful or desirable for young girls' – though she was prepared to leave the last words on 'the hygienics of the matter' to the doctors.

Always strong in her dislikes, she abhorred the Cromwell Road ('so long, and so wanting in the picturesque . . . a monotony of commonplace comfort and absence of life about it which is very distasteful . . .'), and she had some very forceful, and prophetic things to say about the dread impact of the motor car on society – even though in the early 1900s it was still a relative novelty. While it had 'absolutely transformed life, and given a new interest to many jaded votaries of pleasure', and had 'brought town and country into touch', she wrote in *The Boudoir* of November 1904, this fiendish new invention had 'destroyed the remnants of peace and quiet which the railways have left us. . . .

Now we have become tramps, without home and without associations.' It had 'killed conversation'. Driving (so *Motoring Illustrated* quoted her disapprovingly as saying the following year) was simply not for the modern woman; she did not possess 'the coolness, the nerve, the resourcefulness. . . . You need a strong, determined character'. Although the Wright brothers had hardly made their maiden flight, she added with a remarkably prophetic aside that all that was now needed was the aeroplane 'to make London as perfect an inferno as any invented by Dante's fruitful imagination'.

It was, however, the mores of women in the new century, that occupied her most – and, as far as it concerned her own life, with reason. While she persistently spoke up for equal sexual rights, she deplored the women who did the cause a disservice by the writing of 'erotic books'; 'it is a reproach for our sex', she wrote in the *Daily Graphic* of July 1907:

> that just at the moment when women are clamouring to enter political life, and claim equality with men, the novels written by women should deal chiefly with unpleasant matters, and be tinged by a decided laxity of morals. . . . Where are the Miss Austens, the George Eliots, Mrs Gaskells of today?

She also criticized them for being cynical and 'so bitter', despite the enormous improvement of their position over the last few years: 'their liberty is uncontrolled, their powers acknowledged, and yet every book a woman writes is full of jibes and cynical sneers . . .'. One of her most fervently held tenets on morality was: 'The possession of a latch key and the absence of all constraint on one's comings and goings do not make a woman a bachelor.' But what was the reality in her own life?

It was in her novels that Violet seems to have come closest to revealing her own circumstances. Her *Home for Failures* of 1897 was something of a *roman-à-clef*. Oriza has a drunken and brutal husband, from whom she cannot get divorced, and has set up on her own. To keep her house and give a purpose to her life, she advertises, offering a home for 'educated people for whom life has proved too hard'. Arriving at her hospitable door are 'a voluble actress, an unappreciated painter, a faded little seamstress, a voracious poet with a taste for whiskey, and a consumptive doctor'. Of course, Oriza and the artist fall in love, but frustrated despair forces her – crushed by society – to suicide. A long enthusiastic review in the *Woman's Signal* praised the novel's 'keen appreciation of the harshness of existence to a separated wife, young and lovable, and lonely and hungry for the love at home of which she is forbidden'.

Home for Failures (published by Hutchinson for the princely sum of 3s 6d) strikes one as an eloquent indictment both of the late Victorian scene and of Violet's own life. Her husband Algernon, my mother's grandfather, was neither drunk nor brutal, but he seems to have been short on brainpower – and just plain boring. The truth was that Violet formed an attachment with another peer of the realm, Lord North, direct descendant of the man who had lost those American colonies a hundred years previously, by whom she had an illegitimate daughter. In distress, Algernon left Violet, but would not divorce her, retreating instead to his property in Ireland. Such were the built-in restraints of the press of the time that not a word ever escaped the 'other life' of this leading commentator on the predicament of women, though it was well known within the family.

The last-surviving cousin of my mother, Victor Creer, vividly remembers being told by his mother, Veronique, about her bastard stepsister, and being taken – as a boy – to visit Grandmother Violet at Lord North's home in Oxfordshire. All his life he retained the image of the two old lovers, respectively eighty and ninety, and manifestly in love with each other. (The love-child eventually married a Cambridge bank manager.)

Although Algernon, the 2nd Baron Greville, died, age sixty-eight, in 1909, and Violet lived on until 1932, outliving both her eldest son and her granddaughter, the long-term result of Violet's 'indiscretion' was to leave her children with no proper home life, thought my cousin Victor – bequeathing in full her restlessness particularly to her daughter Camilla, which she in turn was later to pass on, in full measure, to her only daughter, my mother.

In her family life, the Lady Violet Greville seems to have been rather fenced about by bars sinister. She and Algernon had four children: Ronnie, heir to the title, Grandmother Camilla, then Great-uncle Charlie and, last, Veronique, mother of Victor Creer. Aged twenty-seven, the Hon. Ronnie married (in 1891) an heiress, on the wrong side of the blanket, who – as the Hon. Mrs Maggie Greville – in the early part of the century was to gain fame and immense power as a legendary hostess, confidante of monarchs and prime ministers. Her background was so unusual and her role in my mother's life so important as to warrant a few lines.

In Victorian Edinburgh there prospered a certain Mr Wm McEwan, born in 1829, who amassed a very considerable fortune out of the brewery which, amalgamated with Youngers, still bears his name. Starting from the humblest beginnings, through the usual Celtic combination of canniness and hard work, Mr McEwan, by the age of sixty, had created a business worth £1 million – a prodigious fortune in those days. He went into politics as a Liberal MP (1886–1900) and became a much respected pillar of Edinburgh society. Yet he too, like many another of those Victorian pillars, had his little private secret: after the death of his wife, he began to fancy the wife of a humble porter in the brewery, a Mr Anderson. The porter was called in one day and told that, since he was a likely lad, the boss was making him head of the night staff. Out of this promotion to nocturnal duties there duly arrived in 1867, a little girl, Margaret Anderson. McEwan manifestly adored her, and let it be known that she would be his heiress. In the discreet way of the press in those days, Maggie was henceforth always known as 'Mr McEwans's stepdaughter', though those pawky disciples of John Knox evidently gave both father and daughter a rough time of it, ostracizing them from Edinburgh's polite society. Both were unforgiving to the end. When McEwan died, leaving Maggie the staggering sum of

15

£1,500,000, there were only two conditions attached: she was not to invest a penny in Edinburgh or in Australia, though what the latter had done to offend Wm McEwan – apart from just being Australian – is not known.

He also made it plain that Maggie should contract a dynastic marriage, marry a peer, so that with her patrimony and his title they would attain great power. She did. In 1891, obediently she married Lady Violet Greville's elder son, the Hon. Ronnie, heir to rather a dim title, but a title all the same. In delight, her 'stepfather' handed over to her £100,000 of jewellery as a wedding present. The Hon. Ronnie, ex-captain of the Life Guards, strikingly good-looking but with cold, dead eyes, is described by one of Maggie's biographers as 'awesomely dull', and rather more kindly by Sonia Keppel as 'a charming unambitious man whom she [Maggie] moulded affectionately into any shape she pleased'. Violet herself had little to say of her son in her writings, other than that he was 'fond of steeplechasing and rode many races'. Despite, or perhaps partly on account of, the stigma of illegitimacy which they both shared, Violet seems to have had no time for her daughter-in-law, virtually ignoring her.

Poor thing, Maggie's proletarian looks were certainly against her. Photographs of the time depict her, standing with squat legs akimbo, looking more like 'a butcher's wife than a *grande dame* of society' or 'a small Chinese idol with eyes that blinked' (Sonia Keppel). Certainly the patrician, literary Violet would have had little sympathy with Maggie's vulgar, materialism ('She thought solely in terms of material gain,' declaimed Kenneth Clark – who, nevertheless, seldom missed an invitation to her dinners) and an appalling 'downstairs' style of snobbery.

Nevertheless, she and the Hon. Ronnie seem to have been very happy together. Propelled by her cash, and energy, in 1896 he fought and held a hard seat for the Tories, against Keir Hardie. Together they bought Polesden Lacey, a fabulous Regency mansion near Dorking (now belonging to the National Trust), and 16 Charles Street, in Mayfair (which later became the Guards Club). In these two grand house Maggie Anderson established herself as the legendary hostess of the glittering Edwardian era. But, sadly for her so-called stepfather's ambitions, the Hon. Ronnie died of cancer, aged only forty-three, in 1908 – and without issue. The coveted title passed to his younger brother, my great-uncle Charlie, whom I remember as a kind, sweet but not very bright Victorian survivor. Nevertheless, nothing daunted, Great-aunt Maggie, whom I never met, went on from strength to strength ('I'd rather be a beeress, than a peeress,' she was wont to say). As one of King Edward VII's closest male friends, Great-uncle Ronnie had established her and then left her pointed in the right direction.

She must have had a hide like a rhinoceros and boundless vanity; she could be brutally rude, and indefatigable in pursuit of royalty ('One uses up *so* many red carpets in the season' was one of her classic remarks). The visitor's book (still on display at Polesden Lacey) reads like a combination of the Court Circular and the *Almanach de Gotha*. In 1905, Edward VII (the husband of his longest-serving mistress, Alice Keppel, had been the Hon. Ronnie's best man) was reported to be making his second stay with the Grevilles – with the great bandsman, Sousa, in attendance. The King and Queen of Spain came dozens of times; later Edward, Prince of Wales, was a frequent visitor. At one great ball she gave in 1924, the crowds were so dense that the King and Queen of Italy had to wait in their car while the footmen cleared a way through the guests. Kenneth Clark recalled her telling him how she had had three kings sitting on her bed that morning.

Perhaps her greatest social coup was to have the young Duke and Duchess of York accept an invitation to spend their honeymoon at Polesden Lacey in 1923. Always particularly attached to the royal couple, she named a special dish, *oeufs duc d'York*, after them. When she died it was to Queen Elizabeth (now the Queen Mother) personally that she bequeathed most of her magnificent jewellery, including the famous Marie-Antoinette diamond necklace, which the Queen Mother frequently wore on State occasions.

Maggie was, clearly, not entirely a nice woman. She was mocking and insensitive, and many regarded her as 'vicious and poisonous'. To that inveterate gossip, 'Chips' Channon, there was 'no one on earth quite so skilfully malicious'. Cecil Beaton, charitably, saw her as a 'galumphing, greedy, snobbish old toad who watered her chops at the sight of royalty' (a sin of which Beaton was, of course, habitually innocent), while Harold Nicolson (who was particularly outraged by her pro-German influence in politics) damned her as a 'fat slug filled with venom'. But neither they nor her other critics were ever particularly backward in accepting her invitations.

She was unsparing of her rival great hostesses. When (in 1939) Mrs Vanderbilt declared that she wanted to live in Britain, Maggie retorted acidly, 'We have enough queens here already.' Of the relatively harmless Lady Cunard she remarked bitchily, 'I'm always telling Queen Mary that she isn't half as bad as she is painted.' When Alice Keppel, Edward VII's former mistress, escaped from France during the Second World War, Maggie scoffed, 'To hear Alice talk, you would think that she had swum the Channel, with her maid between her teeth!' – or, when Mrs Neville Chamberlain went to see Mussolini in 1940, 'It is not the first time that Rome has been saved by a goose.'

With malicious glee, stories were retailed around London about her two appalling, drunk butlers, Boles and Bacon. Bacon also had a passion for baby lambs' tongue, and was once observed by Kenneth Clark in the wings, cramming the last of the dish into his maw, while Maggie's guests gazed down reproachfully at their empty plates. As Brian Masters has recounted in *Great Hostesses*:

> Mrs Greville called out, 'Boles, what's become of the baby tongues?' Boles tactfully covered the greed of his companion. 'There were none to be had in the market this morning, Madam,' he said, as Bacon hastily put a napkin over his shirt to hide the stains, and brought in the next course.

Harsh to her peers, Maggie seemed endlessly indulgent towards her staff – perhaps it was a throwback to the days when her mother had been Mr McEwan's cook. The most famous Boles story of all was when Foreign Secretary Austen Chamberlain came to dinner (at which the Queen Mother was present). Such was Boles's manifest drunkenness that even Maggie could no longer tolerate it and swiftly scribbled on the back of her placecard, 'Get out, you fool, you're drunk!' Boles placed it on his silver salver, wobbled solemnly round the table and handed it to the Foreign Secretary, who 'sat in stupefied silence for the rest of the meal'. The irreplaceable Boles survived – as ever.

Inconceivable though it is in the 1990s, hostesses of their day – and notably Great-aunt Maggie – wielded immense political influence. In the 1930s, towards the end of her life, Maggie seriously blotted her copybook by falling under the spell of the Nazis. In common with other influential establishment figures of the time, she saw Hitler as a knight-errant who was going to save the world from Bolshevism. The odious Joachim von Ribbentrop was to be seen more and more regularly at her table, provoking cries of rage from Harold Nicolson that the Axis should not be 'under any illusion that the will-power of this country is concentrated in Mrs Ronald Greville'.

Maggie could not have been all bad, however. Of all those who had no qualms in sopping up her hospitality, then turning and rending her, Osbert Sitwell seems to have been one of the few to record anything kind about her (his loyalty was rewarded with a £10,000 legacy in her will). He noted her ability to see through people, and to detect 'qualities', particularly in the young (a faculty on which the political gadfly, Bob Boothby, himself remarked after she had perceptively told him that he would never attain high office in politics, 'because I don't think you really want it').

In 1922, Mrs Greville was made a Dame of the British Empire for her charitable works (in many of which, like the Serbian War Relief, my mother had helped her), all carried out discreetly and with the minimum of self-advertisement. In her father's old age, she devoted herself selflessly to looking after him; he had become so frail (according to Osbert Sitwell's mother) 'as to look transparent'. After he had been knocked down twice by motor cars (Maggie's mother-in-law, Violet, would have been sympathetic here), she secretly engaged a private detective to see the old man, without his ever being aware of it, over dangerous crossings.

The outbreak of war in 1939 left Maggie Greville isolated politically, and very infirm. After her death a few years later, half the nobility of England (including many of her detractors, perhaps out of a snobbish curiosity to see and be seen, rather than any desire to mourn) attended her memorial service at St Mark's, South Audley Street. Had my mother not predeceased her by some twelve years, as Maggie's only niece,* she would almost certainly have inherited a goodly portion of those famous Greville diamonds. I should not now be writing books.

What is important from the point of view of this story, however, is the role that Great-aunt Maggie must have played, at various intervals, in my own mother's life, rackety and rootless as it was for reasons that I will try to show. Without any proper home of her own, the sumptuous halls, 'the unobtrusive luxury of life', praised by Osbert Sitwell at Polesden Lacey, must have presented a haven of joy to her, not to mention the powerful and glittering 'beautiful people' she met there – and the influence that her aunt's potent personality would have had upon her.

My mother's father, the Hon. Alistair ('Atta') Hay, fourth son of the 11th Earl, died suddenly of a heart attack at a moderately early age, the day before his sixty-eighth birthday, when I was not quite three; he had, apparently, become a Catholic – a requiem mass was said for him at St Edward's Roman Catholic Church in Windsor. Born in 1861, he served as a captain in the Black Watch, and was awarded the Légion d'honneur. What services to France earned it I do not know, but it would help explain both his attachment to France and my mother's excellent command of the language. An old cutting of my mother's from the *Pall Mall Gazette* of January 1917 commented (with more than just a note of reproach; he would have been well over the age to fight – though his elder brother, the current Earl, did join up), 'One of the many people I have missed from Club Land since the war began, is the Hon.

* The Hon. Ronnie and Maggie had no children; Grandmother Camilla had only Auriol, my mother; Veronique, the youngest of Violet's children, had only Victor.

20

Alistair Hay, who is still revelling in the Mediterranean sunshine.'
In the only photograph I have of him, in middle age, wearing a
rather raffish checked suit that would have done honour to an
Edwardian bookmaker, he sports a small imperial and there is a
distinct twinkle of mischief in his eyes. The same *Pall Mall Gazette*
describes him as having 'shared with Mr Burdett-Coutts the
honour of being the best dressed man in the West End'.

Among my mother's cuttings albums, one solitary contribution by Grandpa Atta from the *Tatler* of January 1927, reminisces
cheerfully of the good old days in Monte Carlo, the roués he had
gambled with in his youth (like 'Jubilee Juggins', who broke the
bank – and then promptly lost it all), and the beauties (like Lily
Langtry) he had known. One of the great differences, he noted *en
passant*, was that, 'though the crowded nature of the tables caused
cocottes to sit next to Grand Duchesses, they were never on
bowing acquaintance outside'; and you never saw an American.
Alas, the gambling instinct seems to have run deep in Atta's
blood, family legend having it that he had 'got into serious trouble
on the Stock Exchange'. Just what this meant is not clear; possibly
it was insider trading, not taken too seriously in that rather more
generous-spirited age. Anyway, it was evidently bad enough to
lose him all his money (and, possibly, his wife) – a factor of some
significance in the life of his only child, my mother. For reasons
that are obscure, Atta inherited a legacy from the Duchess of
Cleveland, which helped keep him going through otherwise
difficult times. Nevertheless, it is clear that, financially, he was of
little help to my mother. In 1908 he was divorced by his wife
Camilla, my maternal grandmother, and married a lady with the
unpromising name of Hyacinthe (daughter, so the cuttings tell
me, of the late Captain J. Ferrer, of the Life Guards), with whom
he spent most of the rest of his life in France. The sparse references
to them among my mother's papers suggest that they were not
close and that he never provided anything resembling a home for
her. Although he was only the fourth son, Atta was the heir
presumptive; had he lived he would have inherited a crumbling
castle, Balhousie, in Perthshire – but little else.

Atta's wife, my Hay grandmother, Camilla Greville, was the

eldest of the four (legitimate) children of Violet Greville. She seems to have been a little more prone to human weakness, perhaps even eccentricity. A portrait in pastel reveals a long aristocratic nose like her mother's, and a very sensual mouth, and I have a faded recollection from distant childhood of having tea with an imposing *grande dame* with red hair and an acquired French accent, in a flat full of what seemed, to a childish eye, to be clutter. Could that not have been Camilla? Alas, I cannot be sure.

Somewhere along the line, Grandma Camilla seems to have run away from my genial-looking grandfather, the Hon. Atta Hay (or did he run away from her, with Hyacinthe, whom he married in 1909?), getting a divorce (or an annulment) – which was something rather unheard of in those days – and going off to France to marry a French nobleman, the Comte Hervé de Bernis, who therefore became my mother's stepfather. But the Bernis – in those days at any rate – may have led a rather more bucolic life than the swinging Camilla reckoned on. Buried away in the wild Ardèche down in the Massif Central, the family Château St Marcel was presided over by a widowed *maman*, described by the present successor to the title as something of 'an old terror'. In her eyes, Camilla as a divorcee was, apparently, not at all *bien vue*. The family had little Paris life, and it cannot have been altogether easy for Camilla. Hervé died in Morocco in 1918 after they had been married only a few years. In the meantime, Camilla seems to have fled as often as possible to Paris, where (according to the last-surviving nephew, Victor Creer, who remembered her well) she led a somewhat 'strange', if not positively exotic life. 'Swift Camilla scours the plain . . . and skims along the main' – Pope's lines could well have been written about Granny Hay, it seems. She was given to trotting off to 'tea parties' in certain elegant premises, *hôtels particuliers*, to meet unknown gentlemen of Parisian *haute société*. If her tea-partner did not particularly please her, she would say *au revoir* and 'I do hope we'll meet again soon', and shake hands. But if, on the contrary, some flicker of a spark passed across the tea-cups and the crooked fingers . . . then they would adjourn upstairs. Paris must have been an agreeable place in those Proustian days.

Why Camilla left the bereft Atta may well have had as much to do with pecuniary matters as with Miss Hyacinthe or the *cocu* Comte. Both my grandfathers seem to have been particularly unlucky in that direction – or, at least, their wives were, and it was a failing seemingly also inherited, much later on, by 'Wicked Uncle Henry', on my father's side. By comparison with those Hays and Grevilles, my father's humble clan must seem humdrum.

I have an image of my Horne grandfather as a worthy bourgeois lowlander, with the side-grips of the time and no particular glint of intelligence in the eye. My grandmother, born Allan, on the other hand, gazes down wistfully from my dining-room wall with a face of great, rather romantic, beauty, with dark – almost Italianate – features and a sad look in the eye. She had, it seems, plenty to be sad about, Grandfather having gambled away all the family money and, almost more important in the Scotland of those days, its social status. Her five children were said to have been 'educated privately'; which meant they were too poor to be sent to school. So what learning they had was gained at my grandmother's knee. She must have been a remarkable, strong-minded woman, keeping her large family together more or less single-handed. It must also, as witness Wicked Uncle Henry (who reacted vigorously against it), have been an austerely Presbyterian household: on Sunday, whistling was forbidden, and no books could be read but the 'Gude Book' (which was perhaps why my father, in later life, seemed to have little but borrowed copies of Arthur Bryant on his shelves).

Of the five children, there was my father, James Allan (subsequently always known as Allan), who was the eldest, Newton, Ethel and Henry – the beloved afterthought, born twenty years after my father. Oh, and there was Jean – whom I was never allowed to know about until I was grown-up and returned from the wars. There was nothing outrageous or villainous about poor Jean; she was just mad. Apparently, so I learned years later, she had been very beautiful and desperately in love, aged twenty-one. But her choice was considered disastrous by her parents. When they broke it off, something inside Jean broke with it. For the remaining sixty years of her life, she was a harmless lunatic, lodged and cared for by private families, but never spoken of. I remember her from visits, a gentle old thing with a bristly chin, living with nice people in Brighton (in the days before the Mental Health Act would have forbidden such licence), and occasionally protesting by removing all her clothes and covering herself with back-numbers of the *News of the World*.

On both sides, my forebears in my parents' generation seem to have been singularly unfecund – not helped, of course, by poor Jean. The five Hornes produced two children, myself and one first cousin, twenty years older than me, Cousin Eve (about whom more later); while my grandfather, Atta, from two wives, produced only my mother. From an Edinburgh that seemed to offer only the most limited of horizons, no less than three out of the five Hornes set forth for South-east Asia in pursuit of better things; Allan and Newton to find fortunes, Ethel a husband. Indirectly, through the most improbable of combinations, it was what brought my father and my mother together.

I return to her.

CHAPTER TWO

Auriol, My Mother

Quelle galère! Or 'What a set!', as Matthew Arnold exclaimed of the Shelleys, these Hay-Grevilles. Or at least so my staid, steadily middle-class Horne grandparents must have thought when their beloved eldest son married into the clan. And what chance could my mother have had, from the very start? Auriol Camilla Sharlie Blanche Hay* was born on 2 January 1893. From the very beginning of her life, it can't have been easy for her as an only child fourth in the row of those strong-minded, eccentric and, especially, restless women. Although she was born only three years after the marriage of her parents, Atta and Camilla, the suggestion is that already the strains were there. Virtually nowhere, in all the thirty-odd scrap albums that Auriol kept so meticulously, is there any photograph of her parents nor any reference to 'home'; there is just one photo (probably) of the Hon. Atta, wearing a trilby and raffish gloves, obviously on the Riviera. I don't even know where 'home', for the three of them, was. Perhaps, in fact, it barely existed, but I suspect it may have been an imposing house in semi-smart London. It all goes to show how little I knew of her. In the first photos of her, aged about two and a half, I see a ravishingly pretty little girl with long hair, hands hidden within a vast ermine muff or under a large Gainsborough hat, clutching a beloved chow (the first pet dog I can ever remember must have been a descendant of the same), but oh so solemn and unsmiling, her sensual mouth already showing

---

* Camilla (after her mother) and Blanche (harking back to her Kinnoul/Beaufort grandmother) were family names; where Auriol and the rather unusual name of Sharlie come from, I do not know.

hints of that unhappy down-turn at the corners. In fact, I don't think I ever found a portrait – not even those taken on her two wedding-days – in which she looked pronouncedly happy:

> The laughter of contentment, and the ease
> Of an untroubled mind, sans memory . . .
> For this I crave,

she wrote in a poem illustrative of her melancholia.

Auriol's grandfather George, 12th Earl of Kinnoul, who died when she was four, had, in that careless Victorian way, eight children – but not a monstrous amount of money with which to support them. Her happiest childhood days seem to have been spent mostly with Uncle Fitzroy, Atta's elder brother, who had inherited the earldom from his father in 1897, at the family seat of Balhousie Castle, an uncomfortable-looking, Balmoral-kind of ancestral pile in Perthshire; or with Aunt Maggie at Polesden Lacey; or with Uncle Zander and Aunt Muriel, the Münsters at Maresfield Park in East Sussex. But there was a sombre cloud, almost a curse, hanging over the Kinnouls, then as later, that must have darkened the skies over Balhousie for a sensitive girl. The Earl's first wife died in 1900, followed three years later by his heir, Edmund, Viscount Dupplin, aged only twenty-four; Uncle Fitzroy married again, but his second wife's twins, Edward and Fitzroy, died in infancy. Though nearly sixty, Uncle Fitzroy himself returned to the colours in the First World War; then, in February 1916, as the result of some unknown depression (as he was then sixty-one, and posted well behind the front, it could not have been for the 'usual reasons' – of cowardice), was found shot dead in his billet at Aylesbury, with a revolver by his side.

If Balhousie cast a heavy, darkling shadow, the glitter and grandeur of Polesden Lacey must have been daunting and uncosy to a young child, and Maggie almost certainly came more into her own as an aunt after Uncle Ronnie's death, as Auriol emerged from adolescence. Judging from the rare photos of a smiling, cheerful Auriol, it seems that her happiest childhood times were spent with Aunt Muriel, sister to Fitzroy and Atta, and her

26

German husband, Uncle Zander zu Münster, at warm and welcoming Maresfield Park. Prince (though he preferred to call himself Count rather than use the imposing, Holy Roman title of *Durchlaucht*) Alexander Münster had been largely brought up in England while his father Georg was German Ambassador to London during the years 1873–85. Georg, though very popular in England, was very unpopular with Bismarck, who constantly tried to sack him; his last post was Paris, where he got into trouble again for supporting Dreyfus. His son Alexander, having found a wife among the Scottish nobility, in the shape of the Hon. Muriel Hay, had bought Maresfield Park and had settled down to becoming almost more English than the English. Master of the Erridge Hunt, he was involved in every kind of local activity, and was genuinely much loved for it. Although he retained his German citizenship and the family estate, Waldfried at Derneburg, near Hanover (its halls encrusted with dead stags, in the best tradition of German *Adelstand*), as well as a sinecure as honorary aide to the Kaiser, England was where his heart lay. All was set fair for the Münster family, but for the looming European madness. I imagine him somehow like the heroic, anglophile Prussian nobleman so brilliantly portrayed by Erich von Stroheim in Renoir's immortal masterpiece, *La Grande Illusion*. For the time being, until the avalanche descended, Maresfield provided for Auriol the nearest thing to 'home'; rare moments of childish happiness shine through the family snaps of 'Aunt Muriel on Kipper' and so on, and notes about the musical and cultural evenings that would have been par for the course in such an Anglo–German household in Edwardian days.

Equally nostalgic are the shots of young Germans in straw boaters, and jolly-looking peasants loading hay at pre-1914 Derneburg. Through the Münsters, she also learnt German, got to know and appreciate Germany and met influential Germans – like von Kühlmann, the Kaiser's anglophile former Foreign Minister. There, the deprived only child, she also played with other children, like her cousin Paul, only a couple of years younger. And the Münsters were not the only Germans to penetrate the Hay clan; Auriol's first cousin, Marie, another talented writer, married a Hindenburg, cousin of the future Field Marshal. She travelled widely for a girl of her times: to Germany (including the Hindenburg properties in the Silesia that is now Poland), to Senlis, to the French Riviera and to Belgium with either Camilla or Atta, and even to Tunis, *chez* Madame Anthomars. But all of it was the merest *hors-d'oeuvre* to what she would achieve in her frenetic later life.

Undoubtedly thanks to the influence of her aunt and godmother Muriel, when she went away to boarding school, as her parents' marriage was in its last stages of breakdown, it was to St Bernard's in nearby Bexhill. Hitherto educated by French governesses at home, her early results were, to put it mildly, unpromising. She seems to have been a dreamy and inattentive student, gazing out of windows at the wider fields beyond; her early reports ring with a familiarity painful to filial ears – 'could do better, if concentrated more . . .'. Aged twelve she won a French essay competition (she should have done, as she was already virtually bilingual; then, as now, English girls' schools didn't teach German, otherwise doubtless she might have registered more successes). At sixteen she won the long jump and the Jack and Jill race, the prizes awarded by Princess Münster. She became a skilled pianist, and, following in the footsteps of Granny Violet Greville (who, strangly, she rarely mentioned in her writings), she was already beginning to show a distinct literary bent. By the age of ten, two romantic novels had evidently been destroyed by over-zealous French governesses, foreshadowing the repeated verdicts of subsequent literary agents. Her first effort at poetry, written while at Bexhill, a piece entitled 'To a Friend', survives (indeed, it was published in *Vanity Fair*); however inept, it speaks revealingly of all the anguish of a misprized schoolgirl's 'crush':

> Into my life you came along
> And made it like one happy song
> But rending discords swiftly came
> And life to me was not the same.
> Will you do this, dear, and forget
> That I wronged you, and love me yet?

What the 'wrong' was, the reader must be left to guess.

At fifteen her parents were divorced. When she 'graduated' from St Bernard's two years later, in 1910, however, there were gracious messages of affection from the teachers, including one from the headmistress: 'I am glad your school days were happy ones. We love to make our girls so.' But what can one deduce of her character, up to this date? Moody, with perhaps a streak of the dreaded Celtic 'Black Dog', which was obviously the scourge of self-immolated Uncle Fitzroy? Highly romantic, disorganized, lacking in self-control and, perhaps, just a touch egocentric? A letter from her godmother on her confirmation at Maresfield Church in 1909, the year after Atta and Camilla's divorce was finalized, is gently chiding: 'Do try to remember what I said to you once about growing up – because you are so sweet and generous, and it is only because I love you that I write to you like this, a little thought makes such differences, and people will love you so much more.' She quoted Tennyson's lines: '"Self-reverence, self-knowledge, self-control – These three alone lead life to sovereign power."'

From St Bernard's, Auriol went on, briefly, to finishing school in Brussels. In England in 1910, with her parents divorced and no home of her own, she seems for a while to have shared a flat (at 18 Brook Street, Mayfair) with a distant cousin, a much older woman in her late sixties, Lady Geraldine Somerset, for decades the Lady-in-Waiting and confidante to Queen Alexandra, and an acrid diarist in her own right. She would, presumably, have acted as a kind of chaperone to a seventeen-year-old 'coming-out' without the assistance of respectably married parents. This conjunction also explains the otherwise mystifying presence among my mother's papers of a number of personal notes from Queen Alexandra to Lady Geraldine (and from Queen Mary, black-edged in mourning for Edward VIII, who died that year): she presumably gave them, as mementoes, to young Auriol.

The next three years seem to have been a riot of weekend parties, race-meetings, garden-parties and dances. In the manner of the day, she collected signatures of fellow guests on the writing-paper of the house, often adorned with poems or amusing sketches and watercolours (sometimes by herself, but more often *of* herself). And so, as Auriol threw nothing away, we know who was there, what horses ran, what she ate and (from her dance cards) even with whom she waltzed. Polesden Lacey figures largely, with historic signatures like Napoleon, Hindenburg, Blücher, Henry, Prince of Prussia, alongside bekilted Highland worthies at Balhousie. In March 1913, aged twenty, she took herself off to Berlin for the first time, to fill her waltz cards with names like Bernstorff, the tragic Ambassador to London on the eve of the First World War. But she seems to have returned full of foreboding, writing in an unpublished poem (*Finality*) that November, eight months before the avalanche was to descend:

> There is a touch of finality in the air,
> A last parting, glory and vain despair.

It was perhaps also with some sixth-sense of foreboding, more than just that inherited restlessness, which took her off to Australia in the spring of 1914, as she came of age; but I look at those sensual lips with the down-turned corners, and feel she must have had a heartbreak, too, to make her want to leave England so far behind. After arriving in New South Wales, she hopped from one Government House to another. The dances, the race-meetings, the parties continued as at home, the antipodean flowers lying pressed fresh between the pages, far away from the rumble of gunfire in Flanders.

But why hurry home anyway? What could a twenty-one-year-old girl do? Besides, the newspapers said it would all be over by Christmas. Then Auriol received a letter from a friend, a Frenchman, complaining of being mobilized yet stuck away in Conakry, one of the more stagnant backwaters of the French Empire, instead of fighting 'like my friends' against 'those fat Teutons', who were already at the gates of Paris. One can well imagine what a shock of divided loyalties such a communication would have provoked. 'Those fat Teutons' – weren't they, after all, the countrymen of beloved Uncle Zander and Cousin Paul, who might at this very moment be dying with them in France? And it was her mother's, Camilla's, Paris – *la Ville Lumière* itself – that was in danger! It was simply inconceivable, too terrible for any words. The stresses within such a young woman, with her triangular Franco-German-British family tugs, epitomizing the madness of the civil war then ravaging Europe, must have been extreme. She tried to come home, but – with the ships full of Anzac soldiery on their way to the disaster of Gallipoli – it was not easy to secure a passage.

In April 1915, she returned.

Meanwhile, midway between Australia and Europe, in the sweaty heat of Calcutta the industrious, no-longer-young eldest son of a middle-class Midlothian family was toiling away to recoup the family fortunes. He was, in what I remember as one of his most favoured expressions, 'getting on with the job'. When Auriol, aged eleven, had been writing her first poems, James Allan Horne was already twenty-nine, a young man with most modest resources, striving earnestly to make his way as a clerk in the very successful trading firm of Jardine, Skinner. By the outbreak of war, he was rising forty and life had definitely begun to smile on him at last, as it frequently did upon the ambitious and hard-working under the Raj in those days. He already played polo, had his own racehorse, had shot his first tiger and was beginning to make friends among the indigenous grandees – the rajahs, maha-rajahs and begums – and generally lived the life of a happy bachelor. If anything, the coming of war and its exigencies vastly increased that prosperity, which was barely interrupted by his joining up in the Calcutta Scottish, a battalion formed to garrison this potentially turbulent city, so as to release regular troops for the Western Front. (I have a photo of him, looking self-consciously unmilitary in a glengarry and an immense, hairy sporran.) But, on reaching the rank of captain, he found himself whisked back into civilian life, into government to help organize the vast war-supply machine that had been set up in India, ending

31

the war with the almost Gilbertian title of Controller of Munitions in Bombay – and a knighthood.

Back in England in the summer of 1915, Auriol would have found life remarkably unchanged. One of the standard comments about the First World War remains how great was the contrast between life at the front and life behind the lines; how much more than in the second conflict did business (which, in a young Auriol's world, meant pleasure) go on as usual. Nutty as she was, it was not thought all that bizarre at that time for Vita Sackville-West's mother Victoria (later a rather unusual friend of Auriol's) to write to the all-powerful Lord Kitchener the following plaintive letter: 'I think perhaps you do not realize, my dear Lord K., that we employ five carpenters and four painters and two blacksmiths and two footmen, and you are taking them all from us! I do not complain about the footmen, although I must say that I had never thought I would see parlourmaids at Knole!' And Britain was fighting for her very life!

So the house-parties, maybe just a little more muted than before, continued. One by one the names of the beautiful young men, the dancing partners and lovers, disappeared from her scrapbooks – mourned by Auriol in sad little poems, full of nostalgia for life as it had once been. New names appeared: Oswald Mosley, Violet Bonham-Carter, Rosita Forbes, St Oswalds, Alice and Sonia Keppel, Loelia Ponsonby, Francis Fitzalan-Howard. But it must have seemed all very hollow, as the appalling casualty lists piled up from across the Channel. Auriol enlisted to do hospital work, and was reported as 'assiduous' in her efforts at St George's, London. Then came the double blow, in 1916, of Uncle Fitzroy's suicide and the hounding of the Münsters.

This was the not very admirable time of maximum war hatred, when even an innocent dachshund risked having a stone thrown at it. Inevitably Prince Münster, as honorary ADC to the Kaiser, had been called back to the German army, to the General Staff, but had begged (successfully) to be transferred to the International Red Cross. Young Paul had been unable to avoid call-up into the German army proper; speaking no German, he had had a miserable time at Potsdam, where he was bullied as the 'English spy' and lashed to the window bars. Yet, by special permission of the Kaiser, he contrived to serve only on the Russian front, in order to avoid any chance of killing one of his mother's kinsmen; and there he spent the rest of the war.

Maresfield Park, beautiful, happy Maresfield, had been requisitioned for a British brigade headquarters staff, and whenever reference was made to Aunt Muriel in the press there was the invariable addition: 'whose husband, unfortunately, is now to be counted among alien enemies'. Then, one day, an unpleasant question was asked in the House of Commons, by an Ulster MP: 'whether Prince Münster, Aide-de-Camp to the German Emperor, was the owner of Maresfield Park, Sussex; whether this property, with a valuable herd of cattle in the park, was being preserved intact for its enemy owner. . . ?' The MP went on to claim that the best rooms were closed to officers, who had to live in the servants' quarters. Meanwhile a newspaper leader headed 'Mares' Nests at Maresfield' declaimed:

> 'Whenever you see a German head, hit it' – may be an admirable motto to which we can all subscribe. But like most excellent rules it is subject to some exceptions. We think one of these is the case of Prince Münster of Maresfield Park. . . . Up to the outbreak of hostilities, Prince Münster, who has an English wife, lived the life of an ordinary English country gentleman at Maresfield Park, and enjoyed the esteem of his neighbours. When war was declared he returned to his own country, and is said to be rendering service in connection with Red Cross work. It is infinitely to his credit that he should remain loyal to his own people; England does not seek the loyalty of those who are traitors to their own country. It is Prince Münster's misfortune, not his fault, that he was born a German.

Given the context, the editorial could hardly have been more muted, testifying to the real respect and affection in which Münster had come to be held in Britain, but to read this about her beloved Uncle Zander could only have caused Auriol the deepest distress.

Subsequently Maresfield was ransacked during the war, its contents confiscated and compulsorily sold; it was demolished afterwards. The anglophile Alexander Münster never came back to England.

Month by month, the anguishing deaths of friends by the hecatomb, went on in France. In one of her cuttings books, Auriol kept the order of service *in memoriam* of the two Greer brothers, officers in the Irish Guards, holders of the Military Cross, both killed in 1917. Meanwhile, she herself had met (probably at Polesden Lacey, engineered by Aunt Maggie) and fallen in love with a dashing cavalryman, Lieutenant Noël Barran of the Life Guards. Barran, who came from a not very affluent family of Yorkshire yeomen (his father Roland had been MP for North Leeds since 1902), had done his time in Flanders, waiting in the trenches, like all those other cavalrymen, for the breakthrough that never came, and he was currently on General Lloyd's staff in London District. In December 1916 – the end of the terrible year of the Somme and Verdun – Auriol and Noël became officially engaged. The following year, 1917, he got transferred to the staff in Paris, and the bilingual Auriol managed to follow him there, *con brio*. On 12 March they were married in the British Embassy Church, on the Faubourg St Honoré – Auriol, then aged twenty-four (an elderly bride by the standards of those days), being given away by Aunt Olive Greville. There is no evidence that either of Auriol's Hay parents attended the wedding; difficulties of wartime travel may have played a role, but it also seems to suggest just how deep the rift within the family had become. Or were those high-born Hays simply disappointed by this war-wedding, having hoped that their only daughter would snaffle a wealthy peer, *comte* or *durchlaucht*? (Reporting the marriage widely, the British press, needless to say, did not miss the opportunity to point out the bride's relationship to 'enemy aliens'.)

A pastel portrait, painted for her wedding by Eva Sawyer, a painter with whom Auriol had previously been sharing a flat, shows Auriol very much *en plein beauté*, with a gracefully elongated, aristocratic nose, magnificent auburn hair – but still that wistful look in the eyes. A honeymoon photograph, taken on the

Croisette at Cannes, shows them with an unknown young French air-force officer; Noël is in civvies, but with a trim little military moustache, Auriol wearing an amazing hat like a Polish lancer — but, again, there is no joy in the face. Was she truly happy, even then? Noël certainly seems to have been. No correspondence between them has surfaced, though a solitary letter from Barran (presumably to a brother officer), back in the line in 1918, gives a pretty clear indication:

> training hard and doing work for the trenches. We are the first to be given mechanical transport. The Germans have been almost mysteriously quiet of late with their artillery fire . . . but . . . now I think it is known that there is going to be hard fighting, and soon. It is a great wrench after a whole year together having to leave my more than precious Auriol, whom I simply worship! Although I should have hated to remain in England.

The 'hard fighting' to which Barran referred must have been the 'last gasp' Ludendorff offensive of March 1918, the full brunt of which fell on Haig's British armies, and which came within an inch of breaking them. But, by this time, American forces were pouring into France and the turn-of-tide came with amazing speed. Promoted captain, Noël Barran managed to get through the last savage fighting of 1918 unscathed. Meanwhile Auriol's scrapbooks reveal her to be taking, suddenly, a wider interest in politics and foreign affairs. How, and where (possibly in Paris?), they greeted the Armistice in November 1918 is not known; but one can be sure that, as with millions of other surviving soldiers and their wives, on both sides of the lines, it must have been with joy, relief and optimism for the future. Possibly they would have shared the reaction of her distant kinsman, Osbert Sitwell, observing the spectacle of the lugubrious Lytton Strachey breaking into a jig on Armistice Night, that it was 'the greatest renewal of life that had come for a century. . . . The world lay open again.'

Then, the dreaded scourge of the Spanish Influenza struck the exhausted combatants. Having survived the trenches, Auriol's husband caught it. On 2 April 1919, a little more than two years after their marriage, *The Times* reported briefly the death 'on active service' from pleurisy, in Paris, of Captain R. N. Barran, 2nd Life Guards.

About all Auriol had to show for her first marriage, in 1919, was a conventional note of sympathy from King George V. Still aged only twenty-six, she – like so many millions – was a widow (without the vicarious glamour of being, strictly speaking, even a 'war widow'), just one more impoverished member of an aristocracy, with no immediate family to help, little to fall back on, and increasingly expensive tastes. Suddenly her world had collapsed; the prospects can hardly have looked very bright. What could she do? Of course, she fell back on her pen; she recalled her great coup, of eight years before, getting a childish poem published by *Vanity Fair*. Her drawers were full of unpublished poems and scribblings. But first she had to get herself out of the dark tunnel of despair in which the tragic death of Noël had left her. In a poem called 'The Vigil', she tried to describe it:

> Those fevered eyes, from which is banished sleep . . .
> . . . For now, a voice has told me he is gone.
> That, I, in black despair, and grief intense
> Am faced with Death, in emptiness alone,

and, more bitterly, in 'An Allegory' lamenting the war:

> We are the debtors, we have paid the cost.
> We are the wives and mothers who have lost.

Assisted by the bereaved Barrans (but I suspect, also, by her generous Aunt Maggie), she took off on a long sea journey, to South Africa. When she returned, she set up in a house north of the Park, 9 Portsea Place – certainly not then a particularly smart address. A note from a friend of November 1919, commenting on her habit of eating no lunch and offering 'to bring a sardine sandwich in my pocket', suggests that she was not looking after herself (or, maybe to the uncharitable mind, that he was offering to do it for her). Maggie, in her style, was constantly there with consolation: in a letter from 16 Charles Street, dated 10 November 1919:

My dear little Auriol,
    I am so sorry you are unhappy, you poor dear precious. If you feel in mood come here next Friday, the 14th, about 10 . . . small party for Queen of Spain. . . .

Perhaps it was not quite the kind of peaceful distraction most needed by a young widow. That Christmas she spent at Polesden Lacey, met Osbert Sitwell on a train and was photographed in Scotland playing golf in remarkably unflattering attire. She was under way again. The following November her childhood friend, fellow godchild of Aunt Maggie, and daughter of Edward VII's last mistress, Sonia Keppel, got married in the Guards' Chapel in a splashy society wedding. That could have been hurtful, except that by this time Auriol herself seems to have acquired at least one admirer, to judge from a bad poem scrawled on the back of an OHMS envelope, in which she compares herself to a wild mare.

In July 1920, she published a five-year collection of poems under the title *Images*, some of them written in French. Many were immature, some derivative and unoriginal, a few deeply moving; but all showed the same deep underlying melancholy, disappointment in love and restlessness. One, 'Adoration', seems to have been written to another woman:

All these things do I wish; but even more,
To be the happy man that you adore.

Another speaks, sadly and prophetically, of the quite extraordinary persistence, in the face of repeated rejection, that was to characterize her literary career:

37

How I courted success a million ways,
And failed, and failed again, yet still hoped on.

Another, 'Youth', hinted at her fidgety panacea for all ills:

the changing spell
Of new romances. . . .
There is charm in every new beginning.

But her deep pessimism seems to have returned by the last line of the last, unhappy poem, 'Oiseau Bleu':

Oiseau sacré du bonheur, à toujours adieu?

Did she really mean it?

Given the tiny space that poetry habitually commands in philistine countries, the reviews were, in general, kindly. Said the *Lady*: 'She writes in a somewhat saddened vein, which is, after all, natural, as she was very young when her husband died; but has grace and distinction in her sadness and no bitterness.' and the *Daily Sketch* remarked that she 'shows a true poetic instinct'. Less obliging was the *Westminster Gazette*, which lumped *Images* in with a group of other collections of poetry as 'not worthwhile'. One thing was clear: she could not support herself on her poetry. Her thoughts now turned towards making use of her rather exceptional German and French background, and her contacts, to find herself an entrée as a foreign correspondent and, secondarily, to exploit that restless energy as a travel writer. For a woman to break into such a virtually closed shop as was the trade of foreign correspondent in the early 1920s would have made earning a livelihood from poetry seem almost child's play by comparison. But Auriol was never to be deterred; persistence must indeed have been her middle name. Curiously enough, for reasons that I cannot fathom – perhaps they were estranged – Granny Violet Greville, the one person who might have given her a leg-up in the press jungle, or even advice, seems not to have been around at all. But they were a strange clan.

Auriol's first serious offer of work seems to have come from the *Globe*, in November 1920. They offered her £10 a week, subject to one week's notice, to write on society, gossip and fashion. It was a princely sum, by any standard. But it meant sleuthing on, and inevitably traducing, friends. An early editorial commission requested: 'Is it possible for you to write a paragraph in your notes about Lady Diana Cooper and her camouflaged Ford car?'★ But this was not at all what she really wanted; one can assume that the *Globe* contract did not last many weeks. Meanwhile, she was approaching serious papers like the *Daily Telegraph* and *Daily Express*, but they turned her down. A letter from the unfailingly courteous Lord Burnham, managing editor of the *Daily Telegraph* (the journal on which her son started life, exactly thirty years later) politely refused Auriol's proposal to become their special correspondent in Central Europe; the veteran (and heavyweight) former war correspondent of *The Times*, Colonel à Court Repington, had just been given the job. (Not for the last time, Lord Burnham must have grimaced to himself at the effrontery of this unschooled and untried young widow applying for such a key post.)

An idea for a series of articles 'dealing with the workman's budget' (what could she have known about it!) met with equal failure. She tried novels ('I cannot see any reason for publishing this novel,' read one surly reader's report of *Divina*) and even lyrics; a theatrical agent wrote, candidly, of 'Indian Eyes' (in February 1920), 'I do not like it very much. You have not quite "got it", and I think we will leave that matter over for a little while.' (Later a songwriter called Burrows was able to come up with unexpectedly good news: 'I accept your "Gardens of Aranjuez". . . . The result is one of the best [songs] I have ever written; it will become popular, I think.' But it was a one-off.)

★ Readers of Evelyn Waugh's *Scoop* will recall Mrs Stitch and her ubiquitous tiny car, relentless in its pursuit of prey – a thinly disguised caricature of Lady Diana (who was also a friend of Auriol's).

Despite the rebuffs, whether through masochism or meticulousness (just as she kept all refusals to her invitations in her later, grander life), Auriol seems never to have thrown away either a rejection or a payslip. As a result one knows exactly what she earned for almost every article – an invaluable historical record of the problems and (what's new!) underpayment of freelance journalism in the 1920s. In 1921 she made her first post-war return visit to Germany, to see the Münsters, and was deeply shocked by what she found: misery, hunger, inflation, political anarchy, despair – and intense anger against the recently victorious Allies. On return, the *Morning Post*, among others, turned down a rather perceptive piece on Berlin. Then, as now, the great British public preferred not to know about Germany and its problems.

Suddenly Auriol found a home for it in the *Sunday Times*, and a handsome cheque for £3 came in. It was her first break. She went back to Germany, in November 1921, taking in Venice and Varenna on the way, to Derneburg (where she found Uncle Zander much aged by the lost war), Breslau, Berlin and Munich. Beautiful Munich Auriol found in a state bordering on political anarchy, with mistrust and hatred particularly of the triumphant French (then insisting on German fulfilment of the impossible financial terms of the Versailles Treaty) increasing every day, with the British a close second in the hate stakes. 'Bavarians are hostile to all foreigners, but the inhabitants of other states conceal it,' she wrote. Matthias Erzberger, the respected president of the Armistice Commission, had been murdered in 1921 by nationalists; the Germans had just signed an economic co-operation treaty with the Soviets, still pariahs to most of the Western world; the nationalist Kapp *Putsch* against the Weimar Republic had just been crushed; ex-Corporal Hitler was still an unknown quantity; but almost daily there were savage street clashes between the communists and the various right-wing, nationalist *Freikorps*, composed not only of future Nazis but also, sometimes, of respectable conservative landowners, like the Münsters and the von Hindenburgs. Auriol's scrapbooks show some remarkable photographs of such typical *Freikorps* gentry, training with machine guns and dressed in hunting plus-fours and an occasional wartime coal-scuttle helmet.

Using her contacts, she pulled off for the *Morning Post* an interview with Prince Rupprecht, the last of the Wittelsbachs, a marvellous-looking, dignified gentleman of the old school, who had been one of the Kaiser's abler army commanders in 1914–18. Loath to speak to foreign journalists, the Prince let down his hair to someone he considered sympathetic, and a part-compatriot. She found him 'a pathetic figure', living on only one floor in his beautiful palace in Munich. He told her of a fellow wartime army commander he knew 'who recently confessed he was feeling weak as he had eaten no meat for a month', and spoke gloomily of Germany's future.

But even more of a story came with her interview with the gruff and surly General Erich Ludendorff. As ugly as a Bavarian *Bierstein*, looking the archetype of one of George Grosz's caricatures of German militarists of the 1920s, Ludendorff had been von Hindenburg's inspired Chief of Staff, one of the most brilliant strategists on either side of the lines, and the man who had come closest to defeating the Allies; it was against the 1918 offensive bearing his name that Auriol's late husband, Noël Barran, had taken part. A thoroughly unattractive personality, shortly to become disastrously associated with Adolf Hitler, Ludendorff (who was on the Allies' list of war criminals) had hitherto assiduously refused to give any such interview to 'enemy' journalists, let alone to a woman. (She was then almost exactly the same age I was, when, as *Daily Telegraph* correspondent in Germany thirty years later, I too found myself interviewing German ex-generals from the Second World War, some of them as reticent as Ludendorff.)

The fallen warlord struck Auriol as 'the very embodiment of energy and masterful decision'. In a long interview he damned the Versailles Treaty for opening the door 'to the Bolsheviks', vigorously denying any responsibility for sending Lenin to Russia. For the man whose recent orders had probably killed off more millions of soldiers than had any other wartime general, he produced one

fairly remarkable quote: 'War is war, and once over best forgotten.'
Less than two years later, close to where Auriol had interviewed
him in Munich, Ludendorff, with the upstart Hitler at his side,
marched at the head of a demonstration into the teeth of government machine-gun fire. Hitler threw himself to the ground, but the
indestructible General kept on marching. Hitler ended in Landsberg
Prison, where he wrote *Mein Kampf*; Ludendorff, to his rage, was
sent home. 'I consider my acquittal a disgrace for the uniform and
the decorations that I wear' was his bitter comment.

When Auriol returned to London in 1922, her proverbial cleft-
sticks were brimming over with copy; her energy seemed
inexhaustible. Apart from her interviews with Rupprecht and
Ludendorff (which the *Morning Post* now accepted with instant
enthusiasm), she had articles on 'An Englishwoman in Berlin:
War Changes'; on 'Germany at Play: The Sordid Atmosphere.
Pleasure without Gaiety'; on 'Theatreland in Berlin' (for the
Lady's Pictorial); on 'German Country Life: Plight of the Aristocracy: No Money for Travelling' (*Sunday Times*); on the Passion
Play at Oberammergau, on life in Vienna, on life in Prague, and
so on and so forth. Every editor suddenly seemed to want her.
Even Burnham of the *Daily Telegraph* had to admit (in August
1922) how delighted he was with the article they had, finally,
agreed to publish on 'The New Germany: Berlin as It Really Is'.
But it was Rothermere's *Daily Mail* of 1 December 1922 which
printed Auriol Barran's real scoop, published discreetly without
byline, but blazoned across three front-page columns as the lead
story:

GERMANY AND RUSSIA
SECRET AGREEMENT
'WAR OF REVENGE'
A TEN YEARS PROGRAMME

It continued: 'We print below a memorandum that the Daily
Mail has received from a person in close touch with informed
German circles in Berlin and Munich. It states the Germans are
planning "a war of revenge".'

The story of the Black Reichswehr, von Seeckt's army being trained surreptitiously in Lenin's Russia against all the rules of Versailles, Germany's most deadly secret, pre-Hitler, was out of the bag – courtesy of Auriol Barran. The *Mail* followed up with a savage editorial: 'Those Junkers Again!'; the German Ambassador in London protested, denying the agreement. But the story was out.

Meanwhile, Auriol was pressing her luck to get a commission to go to Russia, to cover the gory Civil War then in full swing. It provoked a classic letter from the considerate Lord Burnham, clearly anxious to avoid the complications of a foolish society lady being murdered by Soviet Reds, and fobbing her off with a caution about 'the terrible amount of disease that is rife in the Volga Basin. . .'.

So, for 1923, Auriol – the world now become her oyster – set her sights on gentler topics (Germany had, presumably, become a little too hot to handle, anyway!). She took herself off to France, to write about Cannes, about Pau, about Paris ('stern living conditions'), about fashion, about tennis, about society, about the châteaux of the Loire. Her travel articles were certainly not literary classics (nor were they of the order of Granny Violet's sharper writings), but they were perceptive and full of the human touch. That November, Lord Burnham succumbing, the *Daily Telegraph* printed a long and amusing interview with Sacha Guitry – a far cry from the grim Ludendorff of the previous year. The editor of the *Telegraph* (Paris bureau) wrote to her in November 1923, 'the DT today is practically "Auriol Barran", you will see. . .'. Auriol was made; she was at her zenith. Her striking power was now such that she could even claim underpayment; *Eve* was generous enough to send her a further half-guinea! The following year it would be Spain, then little known, and fairly savage; but it clearly struck a chord with Auriol's own passionate and morose character.

In the meantime, however, something else had happened in her life.

In the course of 1923, the signatures of J. A. Horne (in a neat, clerical hand) and Newton Horne – two eligible bachelors of a certain age, returned from making their way in India and Malaya respectively – began to appear in Auriol's house-party scrapbook. Photographs of this time show Allan wearing rather unexpected co-respondent two-tone shoes, or in a topee, killing some form of wild beast. Perhaps they had met in Pau, then very fashionable, and to which all three had independently taken a liking; but more probably they had been introduced (like Noël Barran in an earlier age) by Aunt Olive Greville, who 'knew everybody' and remained all her life an assiduous match-maker. It was, indeed – on paper – an ideal match. Here was the nabob, returned from India after twenty-two years, immensely wealthy through the usual mixture of hard work, shrewd speculation and what – in post-Raj days – might be written down as exploitation of the natives, with a title and the respectability which money, if not family, could bring in the 1920s. He wanted to settle down, and there was the widow, just entering her thirties, widely cultured and with excellent (if extravagant) taste, poor, but with 'connections' into every level of smart society – and perhaps beginning to appreciate the hardships (even in the liberated 1920s) of being a woman on her own, especially when it came to moving from one foreign hotel to another. They were mature people. She lived for writing and the arts, all of which were a blank to him, who lived for wheeling and dealing (after early retirement from India, he had started up his own enterprises in the City), for polo and for big-game hunting, and he had now discovered the allure of the grouse-moor. Their different interests should have been profitably complementary, not interfering the one with the other. So it was a natural.

Or was it? There was an eighteen-year age gap between them but, much more than that, a gap of contrasting worlds. How different their friends must have been, for a start: his, the world of the Oriental Club and City: hers, all the range of the international *beau monde*, plus Grub Street. Europe (except newly discovered Pau/Biarritz) was Outer Mongolia to him; he had no languages (save kitchen Urdu), and I recall his worse than Churchillian French. To any continental woman, his favourite opener would be: '*Quelle est votre situation?*' Either it provoked derision, or – because of the manifest warmth and good humour that accompanied it – it was hugely successful. He was reputed to have a rather special, dry and eccentric sense of humour; I suspect Auriol had little. He was enormously generous, yet – probably as a legacy of the straitened circumstances into which he had been born, followed by the hard struggle to accumulate rupees – at the same time strangely parsimonious in the face of what he considered extravagance.

Gravest of all, however, after all those years as a happy bachelor, Allan probably knew nothing whatsoever of what made women tick. Auriol's cousin, Victor Creer, is the last surviving relative to remember both of them; just seventeen years younger than her, he stood between the generations and was deeply fond of her. He observed, 'She was totally genuine. . . . There was no deceit, and whenever she came into the room it just lit up – she was always fun.' He regarded Allan as a 'cold fish with a warm heart'. Shy, withdrawn, detached maybe – I could never think of him as anything but warm. But I could see how perhaps *à la longue* this could prove unsatisfactory to a highly strung and passionate woman like Auriol. On the other hand, all that heat and curry and the numerous *chota pegs* of life in India had given Allan a fiery temper and a short fuse. She, on her side, after all those years of independence and earning her living, might possibly have been described as a little selfish.

Nevertheless, in the spring of 1924, an engagement was officially announced, Allan being widely described as 'owner of a handsome fortune made as an East India merchant'. He was forty-nine, she thirty-one. Not all Auriol's circle seem to have been thrilled; conspicuously absent from her archives are any letters of congratulation from her parents, or even from the beloved Münsters. Doubtless mindful of her own father's story of self-made success, Maggie Greville was encouraging; she had met Allan in India a year and a half before and thought him 'charming'. Aunt Olive Greville, who may or may not have introduced them, with her good American common sense where money and marriage were concerned, was equally enthusiastic, though not without apprehension. The editor of the *Sunday Times* wrote a nice letter. They were married after a short engagement, then Auriol took off to Spain and Morocco (a trip which she had been planning before Allan came along). Spain especially was a country that always gripped her imagination. In those days it bore no resemblance to the Spain of Benidorm and the Marbella Club of today. Communications were incredibly primitive; politically it was in turmoil; Primo de Rivera had established a military dictatorship; Maggie Greville's closest royal friends, the King and Queen, sat upon thrones that were now distinctly wobbly; the Rif tribes of Spanish Morocco were in revolt. Out of the trip came the usual plethora of travel-cum-political articles: 'A Description of Madrid: The Directory in Spain: Dictatorship's Rule: Some Knotty Problems', 'The Fair at Seville' and 'From Morocco by Car: Fez, the Beautiful'. They seem to have spent the rest of their honeymoon on a Perthshire grouse-moor for the Glorious Twelfth (perhaps, with her writing and his shooting, the combination was hardly the most auspiciously romantic).

Back in London, they set up temporarily at 4 Berkeley Square – a rather more chic address than Auriol had previously had (today it houses a branch of the NatWest Bank). In no time at all, the glamorous, talented and now affluent Lady Horne found herself becoming one of the most publicized young hostesses of London. The worthy ex-East India merchant, though by no means unsociable himself, remained in the shadows, to the extent of being described, somewhat inaccurately, by the *Tatler* once as 'Lord Horne, the famous gunner General, to whom was given the credit of inventing what was called "the creeping barrage" in the war'. The promotion must have amused the singularly unmilitary merchant.

For Auriol, what a sudden reversal of fortune!

It was now Allan's turn to take her off on a trip, a massive journey in February 1925 to his former stamping grounds in India and Burma, to meet his old cronies in Rajasthan and shoot a few tigers – more skins to be mutilated subsequently by the latest puppy at his house in Ropley. The journey produced some magical photographs of Rajasthan (showing towns and palaces apparently little changed to this day), and another mass of articles:

'Will the Purdah System Survive?' (to her slight irritation, a letter from the editor of the *Spectator* warned her that this article would be 'slightly cut down'; *plus ça change!*); 'The Real India: A Journey through Rajputana'; 'Pagoda Land: A Visit to Burma'; 'An Indian Ruler: Oriental Hospitality. Tiger shooting in Bhopal'. This last led to somewhat widely syndicated pieces, full of suspense (no doubt somewhat embroidered), about an overnight tiger shoot, as well as a flow of fan letters, some addressed to 'Auriol Barran Esq.'. She also seems to have made a major conquest, in the shape of the British Governor of Burma, Sir Harcourt Butler, who, over the next three years, gazing adoringly at her photograph, was to bombard her with long letters, full of fascinating (and rather accurate) details on the state of subcontinental politics.

Perhaps of more consequence to the present writer, however, is that, somewhere between India and Burma (according to the meticulous details she kept of the journey), Auriol became pregnant. Was it a mistake, a moment of unheeding passion in the heat, in a double bed in some rajah's palace? Mother, I don't wish to insult you, but did you really wish to have children? You were already thirty-two (quite an age, in those days), and nothing on the record suggests you *did* – except perhaps as an adjunct to interior décor. One child was evidently to prove enough!

So, in between travels, on 9 November 1925, at 11.25 p.m., weighing 7lb 2oz, Alistair Allan was born, privately (no nonsense about hospitals) at 6 Upper Grosvenor Street, Mayfair, just next door to where the US Embassy presently stands. Meticulous in everything in her hoarding of 'archival material', my mother had Nanny Hodgson (followed by Nanny Blackman) keep a 'Baby Days' book which, to the amusement of my children, survives to this day. It relates that, among birthday presents, was a 'white bunny from the Hon. Mrs Ronnie Greville', together with 'mug, spoon, ring and rattle from Begum of Bhopal – also squirrel and donkey'. Other vital information entered by the two valiant nannies included: 'Sir Israh Khan took Baby in his arms – first Indian to do so – 15th December 1925'. Then, a few months later, in descending scale of cosmic importance: 'Baby vaccinated. . . . National strike from 3.5.26 to 12.5.26.' It went on, after a page entitled 'Baby's Amusing Sayings' (which was left ominously blank), 'Baby's Second Party' . . . att. Princess Elizabeth!' Ho hum! If only I had learnt to be more courtly and engaging at an early age . . . The one other revealing fact recorded in this document by the obviously shocked Nanny Blackman was that 'Lady Horne went away from 26.1.'26, the first time after Baby's birth . . .' – that is, not quite three months after 'Baby was born'. Meanwhile, according to Uncle Newt in later life (not always totally reliable), Nanny B., having always secretly wanted a little girl, did her best to emasculate me by dressing me up as such – with long hair in pink bows and frocks.

And Mother was not around to correct these excesses. As noted by faithful Nanny, Auriol was off on the road again. This time it was Egypt ('Modern Egypt: The Lure of Cairo' and 'A Nubian Day's Entertainment: Native Dances in Nile Valley . . . Asswan', followed by a new theme, rather more in the style of Granny Violet Greville, 'Feminism in Egypt: Struggling for Equal Rights', 'By Lady (Allan) Horne in Cairo'), succeeded by Palestine and Syria ('Through Palestine with Suitcase and Car' was the eye-catching caption that *Vogue* attached to that one). Then it was Australia ('Christmas in the Bush'). Obviously, in snobbery-bound Fleet Street, the added cachet of that byline, 'by Lady (Allan) Horne' enhanced her striking power, though one egregious editor did complain, requesting her to drop the title and revert to common 'Barran'. She now started writing more articles on the domestic market, such as a series for *Sphere* on furniture and interior décor; and she began contemplating an assault on the New World, where she had never been.

But was any of this, professionally, what she *really* wanted to do, now that the financial immediacy had been removed by marriage to the rich merchant? Meanwhile, with astonishing industry (how she found the time, I still do not comprehend; compared to her son she seems to have been a total workaholic), she had piled up drawers full of short stories, novels, plays and lyrics – none of them, it has to be admitted, of great distinction, but perhaps the yardstick of Dr Johnson's famous female preacher could most fairly be applied. Relentlessly, and undaunted, she bombarded the agents, invariably with the same discouraging result. In December 1926, Raymond Savage is urging her not to 'be upset', but there was no market for any of the stories she had sent him: 'Journalistic work may be your *métier*, but I am afraid you will have a long and very difficult struggle to .get anywhere with the short story or the novel . . .' (and she was already thirty-three). Curtis Brown (briefly, and unhappily, my own agents) turned down her play, 'Divina', set in Venice, and quite separate from her novel of the same title; ditto a film company. Charles B. Cochrane, the great impresario with the somewhat bizarre telegraphic address of 'COCKRANUS, PICCY', who had (perhaps rashly) commended Auriol for her article on Sacha Guitry, came under constant bombardment. (He was also, later, an expensive theatrical partner of Wicked Uncle Henry Horne.) Sophie Tucker politely refused her lyrics; so did the famous Alice Delysia ('not suitable for *Prince Charming*. I can only say that personally I like the song very much, and I regret the verdict . . .').

Auriol threw herself into the social frenzy of the 1920s, with the same kind of dedicated industry she devoted to her writing. At 6 Upper Grosvenor Street, the gossip writers described her blue drawing room as 'one of the most artistic in London'; in a boudoir like the inside of an Indian temple, her typewriter 'strikes the only modern note'. It was here she gave meaningful dinner parties, musical soirées (being almost of concert-pianist standard, sometimes she would perform herself), small dances and even – courageously – Proustian poetry readings when she would recite her own poems (in French). Some said these evoked soirées given by Princesse Mathilde during the Second Empire. Like the rest of *haute société*, during the National Strike of May 1926 she was photographed by the *Tatler* (along with Edwina Mountbatten) at the barricades – stirring a vast cauldron of soup, head wrapped in a proletarian bandanna. Her scrapbooks (pages of them) of this period read like scenes out of *Point Counter Point* – or one enormous name-drop: HM the King of Greece, the Crown Princess of Rumania, Princess Marina, the Maharajah of Jaipur, the Marquis of Bute, Prince and Princess

Arthur of Connaught, His Highness the Maharajah of Jaipur, the Duchess of Westminster, the Duchess of Marlborough, the Duchess of Norfolk, Princess Vladimir Galitzine, HRHs the Duke of Gloucester and the Duchess of York, Lady Dashwood, Lady Chamberlain, HE the Bolivian Ambassador, the Egyptian Ambassador, the Italian Ambassador, and so on and on.

For reasons that I simply cannot explain, just as she kept all her journalistic and literary rejection slips, so Auriol kept her social refusals, rather than the acceptances. Why? They certainly can't *all* have snubbed her invitations! Cousin Edith Sitwell regretted that she had 'promised Virginia Woolf to go and have tea with her' (but she added that she had discovered an 'absolutely *marvellous* new artist, a Russian called Pavlich Tchelitchew. I believe he is going to be as great a painter as Picasso'. Even the Sitwells could sometimes be mistaken!). Osbert Sitwell wrote from Cap d'Ail: 'I have been ill – not actually ill, but visited with pains – for about a month, and so came to try and get well. Do send me a line here to tell me what has happened about your novel.' Noël Coward explained, 'I am terribly sorry I haven't got a minute to spare – I have got two productions coming in and am rehearsing madly.' Diana Cooper (characteristically replying too late) said, 'I spent a wet day at the Derby. It would have been pleasanter with you.' And from Czechoslovakia's Foreign Minister, Jan Masaryk: 'To have missed both the matinée and your supper – too much of bad luck. I spent last night in a boat train. I am sorry!'

Reading of Auriol's nightly flits between the Bat and Sophie Tucker's Kit Kat Club, no one could have realized from these scrapbooks that the world was on the brink of the most horrendous economic collapse. 'Hutch' (Leslie Hutchinson), the black singer, was a favourite rising star from the nightclub world, whom she shared (though probably this did not include his favours) with her contemporary socialite Edwina Mountbatten. For him she wrote a song provocatively called (cribbing Anita Loos's famous novel), 'Ladies Prefer Negroes'. Imagine producing such a title today! But Hutch evidently accepted it with delight, performing it with great gusto at his fashionable Rag-Bag Club, and across the West End in 1927 and after. It even drew Auriol praise from the *Daily Mirror* as 'a brilliant woman'.

It was probably her association with Edwina Mountbatten and the busy world of charity matinées that gave Auriol, almost as if by hazard, one of her greatest coups. On 8 November 1928, the League of Mercy was to perform a matinée, in the presence of the Queen of Spain (Aunt Maggie's friend) and Princess Mary, at St James's Theatre. Auriol was chairman, becoming involved in lengthy negotiations with Sir Gerald du Maurier, various impresarios and actors. Among others, her eccentric friend Lord Berners had offered to produce 'an effective turn . . . *Trois Petites Marches Funèbres – pour un Homme d'État – pour une Canari – pour une Tante à l'Héritage*. . . . The whole thing would last about five minutes and, I think, would be an effective turn.' For once Auriol found herself in the role of her tormentors, having to reject fellow artists; but Lord Berners's skit (aided by 'masks' designed by a young Oliver Messel) was accepted. More important, by sheer force of personality, she managed to insert into the programme a one-act play of hers, which had been turned down by C. B. Cochrane, *Henry's Girl*. It was frivolously amusing, though certainly in no way remarkable; but what *was* remarkable was its cast of three young unknown but budding young actors whom Auriol had managed to conscript: Leslie Howard, Robert Newton and Tallulah Bankhead. An engaging photo of the author, Tallulah and Leslie Howard reading the play, with the actress perched on a table, suggests they had greatest fun doing it (though what the cast thought of the script is not revealed). Later on the programme, Auriol herself took part in a skit called 'The Seven Ages of Women', modelling a magnificent opera dress. Also participating, and with significance in the tragedy ahead, was a new friend of Auriol's, a beautiful Hungarian actress, Sari Petrass, recently become the toast of London, who performed some wild Magyar dances, 'with the 'Tzigane orchestra from the Hungaria Restaurant'.

Possibly because of the author's casting, *Henry's Girl* was a huge success, netting the princely sum of £632 2s 6d (to which Miss Bankhead herself contributed 16s, as against Sir Allan

Horne's modest 10s, conceivably a token of his own growing disenchantment with Auriol's social enthusiasms), and was repeated several times. The critics were charitable; 'Playwright with a Pedigree', enthused the *Daily Chronicle*; 'Friends believe she really has talent for play-writing'. 'Lady Horne is one of the cleverest young matrons in society,' declared the *Evening Standard*. 'Not content with being clever, she is also extremely smart.' Consuela, Duchess of Marlborough, unable to attend, wrote, 'How frightfully clever of you to write one [a play]. I hear it is the most difficult feat on earth.'

Auriol had also become something of a trend-setter for fashion, hideous as that of the twenties may seem to modern eyes, constantly being pursued by the glossies. She might be at a private view of the Academy, or spotted in a huge mink at Sandown Races or 'in a wine-red ensemble, even hat and shoes matching her coat, with great fur collar and revers, a "fox"'. Or she might be at the Austrian Legation's concert for Elizabeth Schumann ('Lady Horne's black net frock was trimmed with bands of cire ribbon') or noticed at Quaglino's by the *Sunday Times* gossip columnist, resisting a new fashion of women taking off their hats at a luncheon ('those who did not [remove their hats], included Miss Nancy Mitford and Lady Horne'). In 1927, there she was, dressed up for the opera – in white socks and long velvet dress.

People so much in the public eye inevitably attract stones; an anonymous journalist, whose gossip item was cut out by Auriol, was already writing, with calculated malice, quite early in the marriage:

> A certain well-known host of elderly years has received con-gratulations on the birth of an heir. His wife is rather young, a frequenter of night clubs, a good dancer, and rather high spirited among her spirited set. The elderly man's friends hope she will settle down, and reform!

Meanwhile, how was my 'poor father' (so Uncle Newt regularly used to refer to him, after his death) faring? Not, I suspect, terribly well. After three years of marriage, those great gulfs of age, interests and temperament were raising their ugly heads. At his age, especially, he must have found the incessant pressure of Auriol's social life, as well as the frenetic travelling, quite a strain. Auriol's younger, more raffish friends can't always have been congenial to him. I remember Uncle Newt once relating how Allan had lost his temper when some youth had carelessly let a cigarette burn a hole in the Queen Anne mantelshelf at No. 6. 'Your poor father was furious, threw him out of the house. That upset your poor mother.' Victor Creer recalled my (very Scottish) father once complaining to him: '"I married a White Elephant!" I asked him what that meant, and he laughed and said, "She is so extravagant, and doesn't help my life."' (Later Auriol, in her own defence, claimed, 'It's terrible! Allan thinks I am frightfully extravagant, while I am having to cut down and write on the back side of the writing paper . . .!')

In pursuit of the quiet life, my father seems to have taken refuge increasingly in his beloved Oriental Club, or behind his desk in the City, or on the grouse-moor, or, a great new interest in his life, in discovering Kenya, a wonderful place in those days (for the rich), where he transferred his passion for big-game hunting from tigers to lions and elephants (shocking as it may seem in our green age), and where – over the next few years – he acquired four (largely unprofitable) coffee plantations. In 1927–8, to please Auriol, keep the marriage together and provide a more suitable home for a child than London, he bought Ropley Manor, near Winchester. There is no evidence that she ever went to Kenya with him; he accompanied her less and less on her travels. Instead, there was a coterie of 'walkers' (perhaps they were more, perhaps not) or, later, women friends.

It seems improbable, however, that in the later years of the marriage Auriol and Allan had any sort of amorous life. At least, so thought Cousin Victor. Here, as in so much in the life of the mother I never knew, I am largely at the mercy of what can be gleaned from those copious scrapbooks – copious, but incomplete. In the way of a world rather more private than our own, they had obviously been weeded of all embarrassing intimacies and love letters. So, in fear of getting it wrong, and with the sense of a flurry of resentful family spirits over one's shoulder, one has to use one's imagination. And how much dare one surmise? Perhaps there may be secrets best left to the grave.

Whatever, neither of them could have had a great deal of time for the pampered little heir; the green-baize door must have been firmly closed with some consistency. Of course, there were the grand childrens' parties she threw ('Never did I see such big balloons,' wrote the *Daily Sketch*; 'there was Lady (Allan) Horne's minute son staggering like Atlas beneath the weight of an enormous blue globe . . .'), but this, I suspect, is hardly what three-year-olds most desire out of life. I am not complaining, but it helps explain to me why, sadly, I grew up with so little recollection of Auriol.

Henry's Girl, I sense in retrospect, must have marked a kind of high-tide in this last phase of Auriol's life. After it, the tides of fate reversed themselves with gathering speed. Again, peripeteia set in. In the autumn of 1927, she was (uniquely for her) taken ill. She went to hospital, and there followed an unspecified operation (it could have been a hysterectomy, on the hypothesis that it would have demanded an even longer recuperation and have been even more lowering than today). Gordon Crocker, the foreign-correspondent husband of Sari Petrass, met her convalescing in a *Kurhaus* in her beloved southern Germany, and composed some not entirely kind nor very good doggerel.

> I once met a young Lady Horne
> Who was full of complexes when born.
> She studied psychology, sex and theology
> Until she was lost and forlorn
> She hastened away
> To Paris to stay
> Not to husband and duties domestic. . . .

Three months later a long letter from her admirer in Burma, Harcourt Butler, commiserating with her operation and slow recovery, suggests that she was still unwell. The following October she was back in a sanatorium in Dresden, only a matter of weeks before *Henry's Girl* was staged. This must have required quite a triumph of mind over matter – few seem to have known that she had been ill. The following spring, just after she had been to visit him in Cannes, her father, Atta, died aged sixty-eight, of a sudden heart-attack – it being revealed that he had converted to Catholicism. However estranged she may have been from him (the record suggests there may have been some reconciliation), the death of a parent inevitably leaves its mark.

In her writing, she was still up against a brick wall as far as any encouragement for her more ambitious work went. Perhaps it was that, with her frenetic social life, she never allowed herself the luxury of a week or two of total isolation – 'to stand on top of the table, and look down', as a French historian friend of mind once put it. Her journalism took on a more domestic note, her topics sometimes a little resembling Granny Violet's, but not always so punchy. She wrote about 'The English Nursery' ('a reputation in the world to sustain . . .'); it is impossible not to wonder where she found her information – certainly not from excessive acquaintance with her son's! She wrote about 'Personality in Furnishing', about 'Health Is Character'. For *Illustrated Sporting World* she wrote (shades of Violet again!) condemning sports for women, as making them ugly. She spoke up for 'Peerages for Women', though she thought 'Dame' an 'absurd and ridiculous title'. At the beginning of 1930, perhaps rather pointedly – given that neither had a particularly happy background – she wrote 'How I Envy My Mother and Grandmother!': 'Time to enjoy. . . . the war sounded the death knell of that one-time happy-go-lucky feeling.' It all seemed to show a mounting listlessness, the growth of a certain jaded feeling.

Equally pointed, for *Evening World* she was writing about 'The Kind of Man a Woman Loves' (apart from having a sense of humour, he had to be 'attentive'. I suspect that this may have been one direction in which my 'poor father' fell down). Towards the end of 1928 his name had begun to disappear from the things they did together, and then gradually from invitations, some of which now read, 'Lady Horne and Partner'. Among the steel boxes she left was the unfinished synopsis of a play, which must date from about this time, entitled 'Summer Ermine', and which may or may not have had some autobiographical content, as much of her unpublished fiction did:

> a society woman, Lady Marchmont, is married to a rich business man – who rather neglects her. Guests at dinner praise her for having a spotless reputation, and not known to have any clandestine attachment. Previously her husband had apologized for being neglectful, and given her a 'valuable diamond bracelet'. Makes her feel very bad. For she has a lover – whom she now decides to sack. (She is really a good woman, but out of *désoeuvrement* and the emptiness of her life, has drifted into this affair, believing too that her husband did not really care for her). . . . Now she has had definite proof of his affection. . . . She goes to John, the lover, to break off – but he persuades her to yield to him.

The unfinished plot becomes complicated, with John, the unpleasant lover, strangled with a telephone cord.

In 1929 Auriol went back to her beloved Spain, where, in Madrid, she met the legendary film-star Pola Negri and watched *rejoneadores* kill from horseback – the old and most skilful school of Spanish bull-fighting. Then she made her first trip to America aboard the SS *Homeric*. Like others after her, it recharged her low batteries quite marvellously. She was assailed by bootleggers (it was still Prohibition; she kept, from the Cotton Club, a printed note: 'WARNING – please do not ask for intoxicating liquors, as we have none. . . . It is illegal to transport such prohibitive beverages and the management assumes no responsibility for anyone detected doing so . . .'); danced on the St Regis Roof; watched Gershwin perform his *Rhapsody in Blue*; was amazed to discover that American bricklayers earned $8 a day; but managed to find the most beautiful Italian restaurant in New York, the Venetian Garden, where her bill came to $1.50 ('or the same as a bottle of Brylcreem!'). She was entranced, equally, by Harlem, by Newport, by American women's feet and their shoes, by American Colonial furniture – and by what wealthy New York journals paid their contributors. *Harpers* paid her $250, but *Saturday Evening Post* would go as high as $2000.

Her many articles from America sparkle with life, with renewal and with delight. One senses that the New World provided the happiest period of these last years – something her son would come to comprehend. When she returned to England, it was downhill all the way. After the initial success of her New York piece, there were more and more rejection slips in the post – or journals would try to get away with paying her less. Val Gielgud turned down her sketches for the BBC. C. B. Cochrane thanked her for 'the very entertaining items, but I don't think there will be a chance of including them in the Midnight Revue. One cannot get actors to study for these functions. . . .' There was still no market for her plays, novels or short stories. Yet, in the most admirable way, she struggled on, never taking no for an answer. She never gave up, never showed the bitter discouragement she must have felt – a lesson to all of us writers. But one begins to sense a certain staleness emerging from the frustration.

And it looked as if, very soon, she would have to face earning her living again. The Hornes had, effectively, separated. Auriol moved into a pretty little house at 16 Grove End Gardens – in unfashionable St John's Wood, traditionally the repository for mistresses and divorced women. Allan let 6 Upper Grosvenor Street to a well-known dress designer, Madame Schiaparelli, and moved into a sumptuous flat just round the corner, at 48 Grosvenor Square. I would be transported, briefly, to Grove End Gardens, or to Ropley. Auriol's avant-garde taste may be judged from her commissioning for the new house 'a room with a roof of alternate gold and red stripes, and walls covered with large sheets of tin foil, such as is used in packing chocolates'. Her own boudoir was to be fashioned like an Egyptian temple this time, while an invoice from an expensive interior decorator charged her for '1 square armchair covered with silver velvet'. It all sounds fairly drastic. At least one reader, bound for Lenin's Soviet paradise, was outraged by an article of hers at this time, 'Furnishing a House on a Tight Budget' for having been written:

when 2 million men and women are living upon weekly doles of a few shillings. . . . As an old man employed in a clothing factory, I however know your statements of prices today are utterly false. . . . Ladies moving in high society *can* purchase stylish clothes in London today, at more moderate costs.

Doubtless Sir Allan would have been the first to agree.

While work was under way at Grove End Gardens, she set forth, in January, on a long journey to South Africa (leaving a four-year-old, rapidly growing-up junior once again with Nanny), travelling on the same ship, the *Kenilworth Castle*, that was conveying the Prince of Wales on his official visit. 'Unexpectedly, I came on this ship,' she told the press. 'I was so exhausted I couldn't stand London any longer.' On returning to England, she found the going – socially, as a single woman, as well as professionally – harder than ever before. There were turndowns from the *Daily Mail*, the paper that had published her great scoop about the Black Reichswehr eight years previously ('owing to a pressure of space . . .'). The next few weeks she seemed to spend in a frenzy of meaningless travel and profitless activities.

Her youngest aunt, Veronique Creer (Camilla's younger sister), who lived near by in St John's Wood and was going through a period of unhappiness herself, visited her quite often at this time and found a great sadness about Auriol. They offered each other comfort. In later years, Veronique told her son Victor about an episode which had happened that summer, of 1930, and had haunted her ever since. Auriol had asked Veronique's Australian sister-in-law, who had clairvoyant powers, to look at tea leaves for her. She went white and pushed them away, saying, 'I'm afraid I can't look at it, it's too horrible. I see a lot of water – and disaster.' (Was there a curse on the family? Veronique told Victor that Auriol certainly felt there was.)

For the superstitious, another ominously tragic event took place that same summer. In June, Auriol had been invited to christen or launch ('blooded' was in fact the sinister expression used by the *Sphere* at the time) at Croydon Airport a German Junker plane that was about to inaugurate a new service between London and Le Touquet. She flew with the pilot afterwards. Six weeks later, the same plane crashed at Meopham in Kent. In the first Society air disaster, all the passengers were killed, each of them a friend of Auriol's, including the Marquis of Dufferin and Ava, Edward Ward and Viscountess Ednam. It was also almost the last cutting Auriol stuck in her book.

At the beginning of September, Auriol was in Le Touquet herself, where she had spent a month visiting friends and touring aimlessly in her blue Bentley, driven by her chauffeur, Gordon Preedy. Somehow everything appeared to have gone consistently wrong with the plans for the trip. A woman friend (described by the press as a 'Miss Redhead of Hallam Street') related how she had left England on 13 August, motoring through Germany and Austria. 'Throughout the journey,' she was quoted as saying, 'Lady Horne was terribly depressed. I had never seen her in such low spirits. She kept on saying, "I am sure something is going to happen. I am sure something is going to happen . . ."' (Could the last, sombre words of her poem 'Oiseau Bleu' – '*Oiseau sacré de bonheur, à toujours adieu*' – conceivably have been whispering in her ears?)

In Le Touquet she was joined by her friend, Sari Petrass, the thirty-nine-year-old Hungarian actress, wife of the foreign correspondent, Gordon Crocker, whose name appears on the programme of the *Henry's Girl* matinée. Miss Petrass was described at the time (in the *Star*) as being the 'most magnetic woman on the lyrical stage'. Mysterious legends surrounded her, to the effect that she had been rumoured shot, like Mata Hari, as a spy during the war. Sari Petrass had been a close friend of Auriol's for some years, and it is fair to conjecture that, by this time in her life, Auriol had come to feel more comfortable in the company of women. Men, all through a tormented life of seeking, and never finding, had finally seemed to disappoint her, definitively. This undated, bitter fragment of a poem found among her papers perhaps says a lot:

59

You came, you loved, you lied
Just like all lovers do.
And like other loves, yours died
And friendship too!

So the two set off, late and in a great hurry, heading for Holland — evidently a fairly rash thing to do, given the state of the roads in 1930. At Le Touquet, friends spoke of 'one chaotic muddle', and a 'sense of rush'. Mrs Claude Beddington, a well-known London hostess, observed of Auriol: 'She seemed so terribly tired. . . . She felt always that she must press on. I was told that sometimes she didn't even stop for lunch. I told her that to speed through the country was very foolish. . . .'

The following day, 8 September, the British evening press headlined:

KNIGHT'S WIFE DROWNED
AS CAR DIVES INTO RIVER

Sari Petrass had drowned too.

From the weight of evidence, it seems that Preedy, pressed on by an impatient Auriol, had — in darkness and mist, and blinded by the lights of Antwerp ahead — driven the Bentley into the River Scheldt, instead of on to the ferry. Lady Horne, he said in evidence, had told him to 'make a bee-line for the spire of the cathedral', which lay on the far side of the river. The way to the ferry, he insisted, was very poorly lit. The unhappy man, who miraculously managed to jump out of the car as it hit the water, must have been desperately over-tired. He was immediately arrested by the Belgian police, charged with manslaughter and subsequently released. The only eyewitness of the disaster, a Belgian sailor called Alphonse Deley, claimed that the car had descended 'with great speed on to the ramp, traversed the pontoon, all its length, without diminishing its speed . . .'.

The logical explanation would be that Preedy had momentarily dozed off. A visit I made to Antwerp, for the first time in my life, in June 1991, tended to confirm this. From the position of the cathedral and the river, the scene of the macabre accident was readily identifiable. Little has changed, except that the ferry exists no longer, replaced by a tunnel which – had it existed in 1930 – would have saved my mother's life. Straight as a die, the flat, boring and sleep-inducing road from Ghent, down which the fatigued Preedy had been rushing, still points directly at the high cathedral tower, an unmistakable landmark – across the water. The low river floodbank, also, could well have obscured the river from view, until too late.

The following day, terrible photographs, published all over the papers, showed the Bentley – 7857 XV – dangling like a large fish from a crane, with Antwerp cathedral in the background. According to *The Times*, the glass of the rear windows had been broken, 'evidently by a blow from the fist, and the hands of the two women were cut . . .'. Their last seconds hardly bear thinking about.

Allan, in Scotland at the time (presumably shooting grouse), hastened to the scene of the accident and brought the body home. He was fifty-five, Auriol only thirty-seven. They had been married barely six years, much of it spent apart. When her will was read, Auriol had left just £350.

CHAPTER THREE

Ropley

I was not quite five. Most children who lose a parent at a similar age retain some recollections. I have none. There remains a memory of a scent, of a beautiful, luxuriant, female, all-embracing environment. But that is about all. I cannot, with unassailable truth, describe what she looked like; had it not been for photographs, I think I would have grown up with absolutely no idea. The truth was, I had so seldom *seen* her. With conceit, I feel we could have offered each other so much. Perhaps, even, I could have brought her some joy, as I grew up, in what otherwise seems to have been so unfulfilled and sad a life. Perhaps she would have taken delight from her granddaughters – though, somehow, one senses she was never designed to be a grandmother.

I *think* I remember the setting, when I was told she had 'gone away on a long trip' – by whichever nanny happened to be reigning at the time, in September 1930. It was in the day-nursery at Ropley, with yellow walls and child's furniture painted cobalt blue. In what must probably be my first firm recollection in life, I gazed out into the branches of the vast sycamore just outside the window. It was raining. I could tell something terribly sad had happened, but felt only a sense of insubstantiality, and a vast emptiness all round. My father was not there. From what I came to know of him later, I judge that he would have found it too difficult, too painful. He must have been stricken by Auriol's death, very possibly blaming himself. Henceforth, he never mentioned it, or her name. From postcards in an old album, I now know that he had taken off to his beloved Kenya to recover, imposing his grief on wild beasts. In his funny, withdrawn way, I know he must have loved her and have been utterly miserable. The cards, addressed for Nanny to read out, of course, gave no clues. 'This is a rhinoceros which is a very dangerous animal. . . . So glad you enjoyed the circus. . . .' 'Am going to try and shoot a lion next week. . . . This is a leopard; I saw two last week but they were too far away to shoot. . . .' 'Just shot two buffaloes . . . but I missed the lion. I think I was frightened. . . . Hear you enjoyed Peter Pan. . . .' This was the first correspondence I had from him; compared even with the wartime letters to America that I kept, preciously, they were rather unnewsworthy.

Curiously enough, what my mother did leave was music. In the nursery at Ropley there was an old wind-up gramophone (with a horn like that into which the HMV terrier raptly gazed) and half-a-dozen records that must have belonged to her. They were mostly kitsch, but I love them to this day and recall the childish fantasies that I wove around them: *Scheherezade* (to me it represented not wild dancing in an Arabian souk, but a sled escaping from wolves across the Siberian tundra – how *did* I know it was composed by a Russian?); Ravel's *Bolero* (to me not a highly erotic Spanish dance, but my parents riding in a howdah atop a stately elephant); Strauss waltzes (*Voices of Spring*, I particularly remember) and Gershwin's *Rhapsody in Blue* (somehow I always associate Auriol with shades of the colour blue – my favourite too). At Ropley the only room clearly to retain her flavour was the large and elegant drawing room, carpeted in ultramarine, leading out on to a sunken terrace (once a goldfish pond, but filled in, lest the precious heir come to grief). The room was always kept locked, like a tabernacle, except at Christmas and other (rare) special occasions. In one corner stood a magnificent elephant's tusk, intricately carved to depict the triumphant entry into Delhi of the Mogul Emperor Akbar. I don't know why I should remember it, except that it was such a superlative piece of work (those were days when one did not comprehend that the world was running short of elephants). It must have been of inestimable value, and I often wonder what became of it, when, under stress of war, my father sold up, or gave away to museums, almost all the treasures that he had so painstakingly and lovingly collected during his twenty-two years in the Raj.

The Mogul tusk was the only artefact that bore the stamp of my father in a room that was otherwise, uniquely, my mother's. The rest of the house, as I remember it, had become uncompromisingly male – and bachelor at that. My father had his being and held his court during his brief weekend visits in the Smoking Room – a room like a London club, redolent with the aroma of Balkan Sobranje cigarettes (or, when Wicked Uncle Henry came to stay, with the most expensive cigars that he could, only infrequently, afford). Pretentious folk, like the Gutfreunds of New York, would, so I am told, refer to it as the *fumoir*; its walls were grained in artificial walnut ('Very clever, the fellow who did it,' my father would tell his guests), a vast table covered with every imaginable newspaper but conspicuously few books, mostly bought at bring-and-buys, and great squashy sofas so deep that ladies of limited stature would often find their little legs sticking out horizontally in front of them. Next to the Smoking Room were two small rooms, also coffee-hued and masculine. One was called the Business Room, which housed the only telephone and displayed train timetables (*Sporting Life* when Uncle Henry was visiting, *Who's Who* and *Debrett* when it was Uncle Newt's turn). The second was known, bizarrely, as the Boudoir, and was used to dispense afternoon tea when there were lady visitors. Then there was the dining room, with (supposedly) Elizabethan exposed beams, the floor covered with skins of lions and tigers, liberally urinated on by every visiting dog, the walls encrusted with bristly rhino horns that would have driven any undersexed Chinaman to a frenzy of covetousness.

Ropley was (and remains) a sprawling sort of non-village lying in Hampshire between Winchester and Alton, some fifty miles from London. It was flattish, enervating and not very exciting country, designated by Uncle Newt, rather scathingly, as chiefly inhabited by chicken-farmers and stockbrokers (he himself being one of the latter class). The Manor lay in a sleepy hollow, surrounded by gardens and vast lawns, and adjacent to the kennels of the rather chic Hampshire Hounds. The courtly sign 'HOUNDS GENTLEMEN, PLEASE!', followed by 'GENTLEMEN, THANK YOU!', was a joyous indication that one was nearing home. Occasionally a miscreant defector would creep into our gates, escaping from the gruff shouts of the men in pink, to be rewarded with an illicit ginger-biscuit, depositing a huge business (as Nanny termed it) in the middle of the lawn by way of thanks, before taking the risk of a flick around the tail as he rejoined the pack.

At the back of the house was a magnificent avenue of high beech trees, the medieval Pilgrims' Way once leading directly to Canterbury, from which came the comforting cawing of myriad crows – comforting, that is, except that their 'parliaments' usually took place in September, the month which, later, came to signal the advent of yet another grim year at boarding school. The house itself had started life as a sixteenth-century coaching inn and had grown, Topsy-like, over the centuries. It was not a big or a particularly grand house, with perhaps only six to eight principal bedrooms (in the tradition of the day, when much of the British economy was employed in private service, half of it consisted of staff quarters) but it rambled, its many corridors exciting to a child. The entrance hall, sombre in dark Elizabethan oak panelling, rose up a hideously slippery and dangerous polished wooden staircase to a large, rectangular gallery with an orange carpet, on to which light filtered from an orange skylight. All around the gallery hung priceless Chinese scrolls, life-size, of the Manchu emperors and their ladies, and the strange-hued light rendered their cruel faces (the men's not at all softened by their long wispy moustaches) and the women's tiny deformed feet especially sinister. I used to play a game with myself (and, because of the solitary nature of my upbringing, such games were generally played alone): if I could not hold my breath while I scampered from one end of the gallery to the other, the phantom of the terrible Mongoloid where I halted, panting, would leap down and get me.

The set-up at Ropley (and this during the years of the Great Depression) was like a mini-Versailles. At the base of the vast pyramid were six servants in the house, each in a strict pecking-order. Housemaids or 'tweenies' (who, according to the accounts book I still have, were paid the princely wage of fifteen shillings a week) were usually called Mavis or Edith. The cook was always Mrs Bufton, though there was no indication that there had ever been a Mr, while the grand parlourmaid responded only to her surname, Whatmore – the pun, as the dreaded brussels sprouts were piled on to one's plate, was hard to resist. In the garden there were no less than four gardeners, under a surly fellow called Maurice, with a great cut on his chin from the war and in his heart a detestation for small boys in greenhouses. He was followed by Alan, fair with pale, cold blue eyes ('Must be German', snorted Uncle Newt) and equally hostile to any small boy who dug holes among the precious nectarines to provide swimming pools for his pet tortoise.

There were two chauffeurs, Kenyon and Hall (surnames also). Kenyon, who was partly engaged driving the Rolls (never without one, he made a special point of having the smallest and cheapest model), always wore a worried look – with reason: if he ever got lost or unavoidably caught up in traffic my father's language was searing, no doubt from years of practice on Indian drivers. But Kenyon was a loyal ally of mine, wonderfully ingenious when it came to helping with Meccano, setting up toy trains or extinguishing the odd blaze occasioned by a chemistry set – or, later, by soldering awkward connections in a wireless set. 'Scranky' Hall, who spoke with a whistle and a Hampshire accent through a bewhiskered nose, always wore leather leggings and was covered in oil, except when driving Master Alistair and the reigning governess into Winchester to shop. The oil came from two amazing machines that constituted the throbbing heart of Ropley. One was a petrol-driven dynamo with an immense flywheel which, before the mains arrived, produced all the house electricity via a roomful of bubbling accumulators. The second, Heath-Robinson at his best, converted petrol into gas for the kitchen. Always fascinating to watch, a rubber bag inflated and deflated like the cheeks of 'Satchmo' Armstrong, pumping its high-explosive gas into a miniature gasometer that rose and fell as Mrs Bufton switched on the kitchen cooker. Mercury switches flashed with a blue light, and how Hall never blew himself and

Ropley to kingdom-come remains a mystery. Even with petrol at 1s 3d a gallon, it must have been an amazingly extravagant way of cooking a couple of chicken rissoles for the lunch of Master Alistair and his governess.

But, then, so was everything about Ropley. At the top of the pyramid, and responsible for the accounts and paying the army of employees, was Frederick, the secretary. Frederick was a little man, with a huge dent above one eye – not from a war wound, but from taking a corner too fast on a motorbike. He was a passionate Europhile, wore a Breton beret, flamboyant shirts and bright linen trousers, and invariably used a French *mot* when an English one would have served better. He bustled about, but what he really did, apart from rowing with the governesses and falling in love with the odd tutor, was never quite clear to me.

Always restless and, I suspect, ill at ease, my father spent as little time as possible at Ropley. For someone who could dictate his own hours, his weekends were indecently short. He would arrive on Friday night or even Saturday morning, and by Sunday evening from my bedroom I would hear the gurgle of the Rolls's exhaust and Kenyon's voice, and know that he was gone. The normal mode of transport for myself and governesses was by train. But, although the trains to Winchester left from Waterloo about every half-hour on this sixty-minute journey, it was transformed into a major operation. My father suffered from appalling train fever (a highly congenital disease, my children tell me), and standing orders were to be at Waterloo forty-five minutes ahead of time. Typewritten instructions, in triplicate, would be sent ahead to Hall, the meeting chauffeur, at Ropley, and a copy kept in my father's office just in case things went wrong. This was what was known as 'good staff work'. One enterprising French governess, who leapt into an earlier train she found standing on the platform, was mercilessly sacked on the spot.

Over weekends, I remember him clad in a raffish, checked dressing-gown and mohair bedroom slippers, long paper cigarette-holder in hand, standing outside the front door, survey-ing the scene with a happy smile on his face, then disappearing into the sanctuary of the Smoking Room for a whisky and soda. During a glum moment in the RAF, and at a time when he was closest to my thoughts, I started composing the preface to an autobiography (aged eighteen), which I rediscovered only a short while ago and in which I wrote of my father:

> Up to the age of twelve, when he began to take a deeper interest in me, I believe he was mortally terrified of me. On average, I used to see him perhaps one day in ten, and then only for a few seconds to say 'hello', 'goodnight', 'good morning' – and occasionally during a meal or two over the weekend.

I recall the cheek proffered on such occasions being as raspingly bristly as the rhino horn that graced the doorway of the dining room, and I recall the – slightly more agreeable – aroma of whisky. How I must have craved the soft tenderness of a female embrace! Doubtless he had reason to be terrified. Escaping from behind the green-baize door and anxious to make my mark in front of boring guests (so I continued in the preface), 'there were invariably those moments during the weekend when I would charge into the Smoking Room, upset my father by hurling some priceless ivory Buddha into the fire, and be marched off upstairs again, kicking and screaming . . .'. Perhaps for that reason alone, the turnover in weekend guests was rapid. There were the bachelors, with the black skullcaps and staring eyes, who had lost the tops of their craniums in the war, and the business cronies with Yorkshire accents, who laughed sycophantically at the host's jokes and patted me indulgently on the head.

Otherwise the most regular visitors to Ropley were, of course, family. First there was Uncle Newton (the 'Newt'), my father's eldest brother, who – like him – had taken the route to the colonies, to Malaya, in pursuit of a fortune. But he had not been quite so successful as my 'poor father', and I always felt that this never ceased to rankle. He too had served as a captain in the war, in Egypt and Mesopotamia, and retained the military moustache and bearing. When I was not very friendlily disposed towards Uncle Newt – which, as a child, was fairly often – I used to think of him, quite unreasonably, as one of the cruel caliphs out of the *Arabian Nights*. In later life, he reminded me a little of Jane Austen's 'Sir Walter Elliot, of Kellynch-hall' from *Persuasion*, 'who, for his own amusement, never took up any book but the Baronetage; there he found occupation for an idle hour, and consolation in a distressed one . . .'. Never without his little pocket *Debrett*, he looked like a grandee, and should have been one, preferring the company of the aristocracy and 'great swells', as he called them. I thought of him as a crashing snob, until I was grown up and began to appreciate his true worth and dry wit, realizing that it was the merriment of eccentricity as much as snobbery that attracted him to the 'upper crust'. A few months after my birth, Newt married the Lady Ursula Blackwood, who, had she been born a boy, would (so I was always told) have inherited the title of Marquis of Dufferin and Ava. Somewhere along the line (no doubt to reinforce his troops in the face of the lordly Dufferins and Kinnouls), Newt had a crackpot genealogist compile a family tree of the Hornes. Via medieval Holland, it contrived to trace the family back to Troy, and beyond – to Castor and Pollux. Surely a trumping hand. Not to be outdone by the bars sinisters among my mother's kinsmen, Uncle Newt also managed to discover descent – I do not know quite how – from Mrs Fitzherbert, George IV's mistress. Thus the unpretentious Hornes were of royal, if not heavenly, descent.

Newt's wife, Aunt Ursie, who always had the purest of white hair as far back as I can ever remember, had a devastating Irish sense of humour, replete with a certain Celtic addiction to embroidery. As a child, I was wary of her tongue. Sadly, she had no children and I always felt that they understood me even less than did my 'poor father'. Newt thought, not without reason, that I was hideously pampered, and my (rare) visits to them were, on both sides, occasions of searing *Angst*. When they came to Ropley, he would comment (quite audibly) on how useless 'those old governesses' were, and urge my father to replace them with a tutor who would, with luck, make a man of me. It was not the last time that Uncle Newt would express a view about my environment – he did so again, with moderately dire results, when I took up residence in America. Nor was he the only one of the small Horne clan to get at my father over my welfare.

Aunt Ethel, his only sister (apart from poor mad Aunt Jean), had also headed for South-east Asia, in search of her fortune (attached to a husband), where she gained a reputation as the 'Beauty of Penang'. Judging from portraits, she must have been indeed beautiful, but all it gained her was a boring and unsuccessful Scottish engineer called Sandy Buttery (whom she eventually ditched, but too late in life to improve her status). My childish memory is of rather a fussy old hen, looking like Madame Butterfly in a kimono and living in a dark house* filled with knick-knacks and orientalia, which always seemed to fall off the table whenever I came anywhere near. At Ropley, Aunt Ethel – supported by her grown-up daughter, Cousin Eve – was constantly telling my father how to run the show, and how idle and venal the servants were. It must have infuriated him, judging by the fact that Kenyon always seemed to arrive at the front door on Sunday that much earlier when the Butterys were visiting. But she was always kind to me and took my dubious health in hand. I enjoyed staying in her cottage, Little Abbots, at Bourne End in the sultry Thames Valley.

Her daughter Eve was the only first cousin I had, on either side of the family, and though twenty years older she was the nearest thing to an ally (most of the time) I possessed. She was robustly no-nonsense, with an unshockably earthy sense of humour and swinging girlfriends. The best of all childhood days (from the age of ten onwards) was when she and Aunt Ethel took a house, three summers in a row, on a wild Atlantic headland at Trebetherick in Cornwall. It is now in the middle of a housing estate, but then it had no electric light, and to cower beneath a storm, in the light of oil lamps, as the spray lashed the windows was a small boy's idea of paradise. To this day, I remain constant in my passion for those dramatic cliffs of North Cornwall, with their spongy grass and the boiling, booming seas below, the seals

* 74 Park Street, Mayfair, which my father had bought for her, and then (to her wrath) took back during the Second World War, after she had moved out of London during the Blitz.

occasionally to be spotted cavorting about, and the long sand beaches with surf exploding on to them. My only differences with Cousin Eve were twofold, and both occurred when I was about eight. First, for reasons best known to her, she persuaded my father to have me circumcised. Whether it improved my future, I have no way of telling, but all I know is that, at that age, it was pain (coupled with humiliation) beyond belief, and anybody subjected to it will begin by wishing never to have that part of his anatomy handled ever again.

Secondly, Cousin Eve married Cousin Cecil. He was a regular soldier in the Middlesex Regiment, a bluff and hearty man with not much brainpower, but a great deal of courage. He had won the Military Cross in the Great War, though in the harsh way of peacetime soldiering then (it was barely considered an honourable profession) was approaching forty without having got beyond the rank of captain. Much of his soldiering had been spent in Nigeria, and his house was filled with dark wooden elephants bearing tables on their backs. The trouble began with their wedding. Cousin Eve wanted me to be their sole page, but she also wanted me dressed up in a kilt (Hay tartan), sporran, black velvet doublet, white silk frills, jabot and all. Mindful of how those early nannies had tried to turn me into a little girl, with long hair and pink ribbons, and now aged eight, I steadfastly refused to be seen in a skirt. Eve beseeched me, tearfully. Then Cecil bribed me, with the promise of a real, live skean-dhu. I gave in. On the day of the wedding, the skean-dhu looked magical as it came out of the box, with a great amber-coloured jewel atop the hilt. But when I tried to unsheath it, perhaps to give one of the bridesmaids a friendly jab, it would not move. I tugged and tugged, and finally realized that it was a dummy. It was the first time in my life that I had been well and truly conned, and it was a long time before I trusted Eve, or Cecil, again. Perhaps there was even (I have never thought of it before) a Freudian connection between the agonizing removal of foreskin and the dagger that would not draw. As for Cecil, he and I always regarded one another with suspicion, I being able regularly to read his thoughts – 'If I had that spoilt brat in *my* regiment, I could make a man of him.'

Finally, there was Uncle Henry, 'Wicked Uncle Henry', nearly a whole generation younger than my father, and my grandmother's spoilt favourite. Usually with other more pressing priorities on his mind, other fish to fry with my father, he alone made no attempt to influence my upbringing, except perhaps to corrupt it in the nicest possible way. Henry exuded luxury and mischief. Financially, he was always either up or down. From his extraordinarily expensive voice and the longest cigars I ever saw, one never quite knew which. He gave nothing away of his circumstances. Three times a millionaire, four times a bankrupt, at an early age he had cornered the entire British cement market, only to spend the proceeds backing stage extravaganzas of the great C. B. Cochrane (the same who was constantly turning down my mother), or on such laudably patriotic (but expensive) projects as financing Henry Seagrave's exquisite *Golden Arrow*, which won back for England the world land-speed record on 11 March 1929, or on equally exotic women, like Elsa Schiaparelli, the dress designer. When, briefly, he was chairman of Seager's Gin, he all but ruined it by chartering a vast yacht in which to entertain his friends at the Spithead Coronation Review of 1937, to watch the panoply of British naval might, the like of which would never be seen again. Seager's tottered, and invited my father to take over. Henry himself evidently sailed, financially speaking, quite close to the wind: two of his associates, one of them the famous Clarence Hatry, did time in the Scrubs (fourteen years, to be precise, for an immense fraud). Unkind people talked about the 'Three H's' – one of whom had narrowly escaped. The trouble with Henry was that his charm was boundless and irresistible. He was a constant worry to my father, whose Scottish face would take on a look of anxiety as Henry would arrive grandly at Ropley, usually in a Rolls twice as grand as Kenyon's. I loved his picaresque anecdotes, and above all the parties he took to the circus (Bertram Mills and Tom Arnold were, of course, his best friends, and invariably provided a special box).

He had his own cautionary tale of the circus. As a child, he was given a precious half-sovereign by his hard-up father, to take himself off to the circus, but there were no seats. Little Henry stood weeping quietly in a corner, until 'a most distinguished gent, in a top-hat, came up and asked me what the trouble was. I told him, and he said, "Give me your money, and I'll get you a seat."' Henry waited, but he never saw the distinguished gent again. When he told his father the terrible sequence of events, he repeated over and over again, 'But he wore a top-hat!' 'Never trust men in top-hats, my boy' came the reply. 'And I never have to this day!' declared Wicked Uncle Henry. Somehow I grew up always imagining Henry himself in a topper. Among his many paramours, the most devoted was Edith Day, the great American star of Jerome Kern's *Show Boat* in the late 1920s. In old age he would remind me, nudge, nudge, 'You'll never guess what Edith and I were doing the night your father rang to say "It's a boy!"' His last, grasshopper years were sad. Returning penniless after a war spent in South Africa, with my father no longer around to help him out, he took to running a country club at Seaford, in Sussex. Now a Labour supporter, he had hitched his wagon to the Attlee administration of 1945, as representing the tide of the future. His clientele (mostly *soi-disant* friends) were a curious blend of socialist bigwigs and stars of stage and screen. Too magnanimous to ask payment of any guest claiming penury (rather like Rosa Lewis of Cavendish Hotel fame), Henry the hotelier didn't prosper. As he aged, in step with the décor of the club, his fortune declined, and so did the number of his clientele – and his friends. Eventually the bankruptcy courts claimed him one last time; he died, like King Carol of Rumania and Magda Lupescu, marrying on his deathbed a rather ginny Edith.

So that was the immediate family. Conspicuously absent from the Ropley visitors, however, were any members of my mother's Kinnoul–Hay clan. Did this mean that, after the separation, my father had broken with them? Or, perhaps rather more likely, that they had always felt the Hornes not quite grand enough? Whatever, it meant that I was to grow up knowing nothing about her or about that whole side of the family. I look back now with regrets, wishing that in later life I had tried harder to get over a natural aversion to pushing on what seemed like closed, unfriendly doors, with a view to discovering more about my mother's life.

How far removed I became from all that side of the family was perhaps illustrated by an episode which took place years later, when I was a twenty-three-old veteran, out of the army and up at Cambridge, and five years after my father had died. A typed letter arrived out of the blue, from the Dowager Duchess of Atholl, the Red Duchess Scotland's first woman MP. Very brief, it ran roughly as follows: 'I'm afraid I've been a rotten godmother all these years, but would you like to come to the Highland Ball next week?' Until then, I had had no idea even that she was my godmother, and – like the Genie in the Bottle – my immediate reaction was to say, 'After all these years, to hell with you.' But curiosity prevailed, and I accepted – hated the Highland Ball, but at once fell in love with this new-found relative. Diminutive, usually wearing grey spats over her tiny, worn shoes, she was a doughty fighter against oppression, whether from right or left. She had been the only person to spot Arthur Koestler as a secret communist agent during the Spanish Civil War, and was later to be the first to speak up (in the late 1940s) about the British repatriations of anti-Soviet Russians at the end of the war. She became a life-long friend until she died in 1960.

Without a mother, and Aunt Ethel and Cousin Eve the only maternal surrogates, my wellbeing was left in the hands of a sequence of nannies, followed by governesses, followed by tutors. The very last entry in my mother's scrapbooks, dated just the month before that fatal excursion to Belgium, describes 'Master Alistair' ('a very attractive young man') dressed up for a tea party in 'blouse of white silk, frills at the wrist, and jabot, while Lady Horne had chosen black velvet trousers for her small son'. The felony of sissification was, as noted earlier, compounded by the early nannies dressing me up as a little girl – which evidently made me the laughing stock of nursery London, and thus, by temperament, anything but 'attractive'. Indeed, I was of a surly disposition, which severely limited my field of acquaintances. Perhaps partly as a result of the nannies' perversity, I also grew up as what is known as a 'sickly child'. I was pale and scrawny, my legs didn't quite seem to point the right way, I had a 'weak' chest – and, in swift succession, adenoids, tonsilitis and appendicitis (not to mention the appalling prepuce problem). I seemed to spend half my life in Harley Street, and I have loathed doctors, as a result, ever since. But the strange thing was that, with all this fussing about, nobody bothered to discover, until I was nearly fourteen, at public school, that I had pronouncedly bad eyes.

With no brothers and sisters to take the corners off and play with, all these factors combined to make me distinctly unclubbable. As I wrote in my precocious autobiography, near enough to the events to speak with some authority, 'No other children would come near me, after a first visit, as I generally hauled off and smacked them, kicked them, pinched them, or otherwise made myself unpleasant.' I had few regular chums at Ropley, who would come round of their own accord. At parties, I would get over-excited and wet my pants – to the contemptuous delight of the other little boys. So, taking the line of least resistance, the governesses tended to adopt damage limitation by inviting fewer and fewer playmates to Ropley. The result was a vicious circle: the fewer children I met, the more fractious and less wanted I became.

Like Frederick the Great, the more I know men, the more I like my dogs. I came distinctly to prefer the company of mine. Initially, there were old Dick, a rather boring and comatose Clumber spaniel; Rajah, my father's shooting labrador, brainlessly good-natured; and Night, a black cocker of lugubrious expression with a white 'shirt' and a bald patch on his nose caused by a bad habit of getting inside the fireguard, where his exposed muzzle would catch the sparks. But the best of all was a later addition, Terry, a mongrel terrier bought by my father from the Caledonian Market for 3s 6d. Terry was a wonderful companion, of unknown age but ever youthful – boundlessly energetic, intuitively quick-witted, always ready for a joke or for the most demanding game, and endlessly forgiving. (I had to forgive him once, too, when – on one dreadful St Bartholomew's Eve – he and the others consumed my entire family of guinea-pigs.) My favourite character in literature was Dr Dolittle and, like the good doctor, I was determined that I would fill my house with dogs, and learn their sophisticated language. Not so long ago, I asked the venerable former Lord Chancellor, Lord Hailsham, why he was so attached to his series of Jack Russells, and he replied, 'Because dogs are such superior people.' I felt like that at five – and still do.

Among the more regular visitors to Ropley, there were also the occasional woman friends, the most regular of whom I remember at one time was Elsa Schiaparelli, the famous dress designer. She had a long face, like a well-bred but friendly horse, covered in beauty spots (which I didn't find very beautiful), and wore exotic clothes and scent. Until she turned nasty, I grew to like her very much indeed – partly, perhaps, on account of the excitingly sophisticated presents she would bring, like Meccano steam-engines and power-driven model boats that really worked. But I liked even more her daughter, Go-Go, mother of the beauteous Marisa Berenson, a diminutive teenager when I was a child, but always smiling and friendly. We had a beach-hut on a pebbly, seaweedy and stagnant stretch of beach an hour away at Titchfield on the Solent, a comfortless and primitive one-room affair, without even its own privy, which my father (the Midlothian peasant side of him) adored as representing what he called the 'Simple Life': 'Come the Revolution, this is how we shall all be living!' On these great excursions to simplicity, we would set off with two chauffeurs, Whatmore the parlourmaid, a governess, a primus stove and several hampers. I have photographs, that still make me giggle, of the great *couturière* partaking of Marmite sandwiches on a wicker hamper, shrouded in a heavy cloak under the skies of an English August. It can't have quite what she was accustomed to in the Rue de Berri, and I have often wondered whether she submitted to these outings of great love for my father, or whether they proved to be the last straw.

Years later I managed to piece together the grown-up's story of Madame Scap, as we used to call her, and my father. Originally, on first arriving in London, she had become the mistress of Wicked Uncle Henry, who, tiring, had then graciously passed her on to my father – as was the case, I suspect, with many of the occasional ladies who helped cheer up his widowhood, as a small *quid pro quo* for repeatedly being helped out of debt. My father then bought for her a tiny and rather unique twin cottage of Queen Anne vintage in the heart of Mayfair, 5(a) and 5(b) Lees Place – an Italianate villa (which must have made Madame Scap feel very much at home). Each had about one and a half bedrooms and a separate entrance through a handkerchief-sized courtyard with a goldfish pond. As I discovered years later, there was also a communicating door linking the two cottages, discreetly concealed in a bedroom cupboard. For an unknown number of years, Madame Scap used No. 5(b) as her *petite baise-en-ville*. As I have said, he later let her 6 Upper Grosvenor Street, a stone's throw away, to become the headquarters of Schiaparelli, London. I was, of course, the last to know the extent of this relationship, or that, in the way of the world, it had crumbled. Years later, at the end of the war, after my father's death, I happened to be in Paris on leave, and, all insouciant, called on beloved Madame Scap (who was still under something of a cloud as a *collabo*) at her sumptuous house on the Rue de Berri. Recalling all those *consommations* of hospitality at Ropley, I expected that, thrilled to see me grown into a dashing captain of the Coldstream Guards, she would kill every black-market fatted calf, and weigh me down (in place of Meccano models) with voluptuous real-live ones. Alas, all I got was a cup of tea, and a first introduction to the true meaning of Parisian *froideur*. I still wonder what they could have done to each other.

Of a very different order among the foreign lady visitors was Julia Breese, the first American I had ever met and who was to have the most profound influence on my future life. She had met my father at Pau, his favourite resort in the French Pyrenees, then very chic, when she was a war-widow in the early 1920s. Even to a child, it was fairly apparent that his relationship with Mrs Breese, a wealthy but highly religious woman of strictest ethical principles, was of a rather different order to that with Madame Scap. But they obviously had the greatest affection and respect for each other. She laughed at his jokes; he made gentle fun of

American eccentricities. She must have been a good influence, for whenever she was around he seemed at his sunniest. Very tall, wearing conspicuously dowdy clothes (as a matter of principle – unlike Madame Scap – she felt it wrong to spend money on this kind of luxury) but nonetheless always looking immensely distinguished, she had black hair generally tied back in a severe bun, a long slanting forehead and aquiline nose, which made her, in profile, look rather like a cross between George Washington and a Sioux. (In fact, I once asked her if she was a Red Indian, at which she laughed engagingly.) She had a wonderful drawl. I had never before heard an American accent, and it became forever associated in my mind with warmth and kindliness. Often, when she was on one of her trips to England (which she regarded as her second home), she would make her base at Ropley, even when my father was away in London. I felt happy when she was there.

Like Madame Scap she always came bearing wonderful and imaginative presents. Like many another hands-outstretched Briton in the years to come, I suppose I came, deplorably, to associate Americans with giving. But the difference between Madame Scap's presents and those of Mrs Breese (as I was, formally, bidden to call her) was the genuine affection that went with them. She was always asking questions about my life at home and at school, and whether I was happy. Of course I answered with true, British stiff-upper-lip evasion, but she was one of the few people in my early life whose concern seemed real and uncontrived. That concern extended to the dogs, which of course helped win my heart. I have never known anyone with such a passion for the canine race, and worry about their condition must have caused her many hours of agonizing. She fretted about the burnt patch on silly Night's nose, and whether Dick, whose walkies consisted of waddling from the kitchen to his food bowl in the yard, was getting his due pleasure out of life. Surreptitiously, when the attention of Mrs Bufton, the cook, was distracted, she would slip him a sly 'cookie'. Often she would send me postcards from foreign places, which I kept, and I always looked forward to her visits – I even, probably, behaved rather better when she was there.

Top: Great-Granny, Violet Greville;
an early woman columnist.

Bottom: The Hon. Mrs Ronnie
Greville, with the future King
George VI; a kind aunt to Auriol.

1916.

Above: 'Uncle Zander', Count Munster, my mother's favourite uncle; an anglophile German hounded out of England in the First World War, he never returned.

Right: 'Uncle Newt' in the First World War.

The author with Auriol

Right: My father; the rosette seems to suggest he is standing for politics – or has just won the local pig show.

Below: The author; dressed as a girl.

Left: Sari Petrass, the Hungarian actress, Auriol's friend who died with her.

Below: Auriol, Tallulah Bankhead and Leslie Howard, rehearsing *Henry's Girl*, 1928.

The author, unknown chow, and Auriol; probably taken the year of her death.

Antwerp, the river Scheldt, September 1930; the fatal car.

Ropley, in the 1930s; the author resentfully dressed up as a Scot, a first girl-friend, my father, in a rare moment of relaxation.

TOP DOGS

Above: Britain; at Ropley, *left to right*, Night, Rajah, Governess (*not* the seductress), and Terry.

Right: America; in Edgartown, Mr Salteena.

Above: Ludgrove; the author bottom left; Robin, of the German mother, my fellow 'escapee', behind left ear of master; Commander Murray, not as bad as he looked – rare for Ludgrove in 1934.

Right: America; Rossy Cutler, Julia Breese, AAH; on the tennis court; scene of many Isolationists v. Interventionist combats.

When there were no favoured guests, I was left in the charge of a sequence of governesses, who, succeeding the nannies came and went with swift regularity – and often for reasons not quite within my ken. The first (and the one who lasted the longest) was Miss Knight, an elderly lady with hair pulled back so severely in a bun that she looked a little like a parboiled brussels sprout. She came soon after my mother died, and was both strict and kind. I rather loved her, and think I may have prospered moderately under her reign. But Uncle Newt had it in for her ('that unfortunate old woman') and her days were numbered. After less than two years, when I went off to boarding school at seven, Miss Knight disappeared, to be succeeded by a row of governesses for the holidays only.

Some of the squadrons of these itinerant ladies were dragons, some detached and cold – and bored. A few, very few, were jolly and fun, and occasionally very pretty. In particular, there was one, a divorcee who was easy-going and treated me almost like a human being. Warm and attractive, she had a big round mouth and a caressing slow voice. When she was there, I noted, the visits of Wicked Uncle Henry seemed to assume a greater frequency. Years later I discovered that his fancy for her was rather more than just fancy. After the war, when I was at Cambridge, we met again, and happily seduced each other. I was then twenty-three, she about forty-five. She was delicious and exciting, and had an engaging way of saying at the appropriate moment, 'Was that nice?' – much as I remember her enquiring at Ropley after I had gobbled up one of Mrs Bufton's puddings. Perhaps with Colette in mind, she was gently cautioning about the dangers from my point of view, occasionally wagging a disapproving finger: 'As the nun said, you mustn't get into the habit.' Today, for any upwardly mobile young man it would have been a flattering relationship, but I was so embarrassed at the notion of being spotted by my contemporaries, out with an *old* woman of forty-five, that I used to skulk off with her to sleazy restaurants where we could be certain of total anonymity. I look back on the episode with some shame.

Few of the governesses stayed more than one holiday. Perhaps fierce Uncle Newt or bossy Aunt Ethel saw them off; or Wicked Uncle Henry corridor-crept; or they found themselves lonely in the emptiness of Ropley Manor; or, much the most likely, their tolerance of a rebarbative, spoilt small boy knew its limits.

At any rate, they left me much to my own devices: and some of these 'devices', concocted out of the chemistry set which I regularly requested for birthday and Christmas from the unwitting family, were destructive in the extreme. In those days, before busybody bureaucrats began to put the lives and limbs of small boys at a premium with all manner of repressive safety regulations, an amazing variety of highly lethal compounds could be found in these sets, and they could be readily supplemented, in bulk, through the good offices of Messrs Boots in Winchester. For example, the accompanying manuals provided the formula for chlorine gas – with which the Germans had put paid to a large portion of British soldiers in Flanders – and for gunpowder. (By extrapolation, today no doubt they would contain recipes for a simple plutonium bomb.) It was, I hoped, merely a matter of time before the deadly fluid concocted by Bulldog Drummond's arch-enemy, Carl Peterson, which dissolved his victims without trace, would be within one's grasp – an ideal solution for dealing with an unloved governess, or even Uncle Newt. But what most enticed me was the possibilities of gunpowder. I experimented first (accompanied by the ever loyal, and inquisitive, Terry) with a massive bomb detonated under a large wasps' nest in the orchard. Alas, in their manual, the manufacturers – perhaps only partially dedicated to the maiming of small boys – must have doctored the correct proportions of saltpetre, charcoal and sulphur, so that all the bomb did was to fizz merrily with a white-hot fire and lots of smoke. As a result, Terry and I were well and truly hoist with our own petard, blackened and stung mercilessly (even the poor terrier) by the outraged wasps.

My next attempt was much more sophisticated. Mixing in still more saltpetre for good measure, I filled a can of Andrews Liver Salt with the deadly explosive, then strapped a golf ball on to the top with sticky-tape, fused it and aimed it like an IRA mortar, from a great (and undetectable) range at the hated

Maurice's nectarine greenhouse. But history repeated itself. The mortar simply blazed with a hiss and a roar, and the golf ball burned with a disgusting smell. All was discovered, and I was severely punished – although my father, I learnt at a conveniently early age, had promised my mother never to inflict corporal punishment upon me, contrary to the healthy British norm of the time. (He had made her a second promise, to send me to Eton.) Then there was the conflagration in the nursery. I had devised an 'indoor firework' using my celluloid toothbrush container, which I stuffed with magnesium filings – about as potent a cocktail as the Germans would shortly be dropping by the bushel on the London docks. It burned with an unquenchable flame and, in my desperate attempts to extinguish it, it flew under the nursery ottoman, setting it alight from below. Just short of total catastrophe (though it must have left a voodoo on the nursery, because our successor Magda Eldon* subsequently managed to burn down that end of the house), I managed to get it under control, and – watched by Night with a more than usually pessimistic expression, and by Terry with ill-concealed anticipation of mischief ahead – crammed back inside the ottoman its charred entrails. The crime went undetected, but it so happened that my father, that following weekend, paid one of his rare visits to the nursery, and sank heavily on to the mortally damaged sofa. The results were predictably horrendous. I fled to the farthest reaches of the garden, and another unfortunate – and innocent – governess bit the dust.

The chemistry set was removed, and I was coaxed into more pacific pursuits of electric trains, and – later, in the extreme old age of childhood, and aided by the patient Kenyon – constructing a wireless set. Such was the concentration demanded by this last that the poor man must have begun to think that perhaps I had turned over a new leaf. I had one final attempt at destroying Ropley, on the day of departing for school in Switzerland: in the gardeners' potting shed, I found a smoke-bomb for dealing with

---

* Immortalized by Auberon Waugh as the hyper-virtuous Catholic *grande dame* in *The Foxglove Saga*.

rats and moles, and detonated it, in an experimental manner, in the wine-cellar half-an-hour before Kenyon was due to ferry me off. To my horror, great clouds of sulphurous smoke poured forth, which nothing would stop. I went upstairs, desperately trying to lure my father out of the Smoking Room before the first yellow wisps began to curl up under the skirting-boards. Fortunately I was able to play upon his chronic train fever, looking at my watch and mumbling that maybe it was time to go. To my great shame, he patted me on the back, and pressed a larger than usual tip in my hand, while remarking to Frederick (who was looking on with the utmost suspicion) 'I do believe the boy's at last getting a sense of punctuality – he must be growing up.' Kenyon and I drove off, seconds before the Smoking Room – or *Fumoir* – would have begun truly to live up to its name.

Strangely enough, this latest mischief was never mentioned. Hitler was on the move and my father had other nuisances to think about.

It must, in fact, have been the year Hitler came to power, in 1933, that I sensed something rather ominous in the air. It was a particularly hot and dull summer, spent (so my autobiographical preface reminds me) at Ropley, without the usual exodus to Frinton. Miss Knight was still valiantly hanging on in the front line, but the atmosphere seemed charged with mysterious tension. Everybody had become secretive, intense with nervous preparation. Suddenly my father arrived on a Thursday, without guests, for a long weekend – all very unusual. Shortly afterwards, Eve arrived and started telling me (in a roundabout sort of way) what fun school was – then asked me how I'd like to go to that mysterious place. My reply was frank and forceful. The grim secret was out, but it wasn't till the Sunday that my 'poor father' finally got the momentous delivery off his chest, after working himself up all weekend almost to a state of nervous prostration. I was summoned to the Smoking Room and, after a long preamble about how much the family all loved me, informed that I was to be packed off to boarding school next month. *Next month!* I was too stunned even to fly into the customary tantrum, and doubtless left my father mopping his brow and praising God that he had been saved a scene. It was not until I was outside that the tears came as I appreciated the full gravity of my position. I spent the rest of the day off in the woods, seeking the sympathy of Night, whose spaniel expression seemed appropriately doleful. We discussed running away, but Night decided the issue by heading off resolutely in the direction of the kitchen. I was still not quite eight.

Eastacre was a small pre-prep school on the edge of Winchester. The headmaster, Mr Fry, was the most enormous man I had ever encountered. A first impression was quite enough to give a seven-year-old new boy the jitters. When I was led into the small study, of which he occupied a good two-thirds, it took me some time to summon up enough courage to submit my hand to his bear-like grip. When at last a deep rumble began to shake forth from his vast depths, I realized that this imposing mountain of a man could be kind. After I had left the study, however, my apprehensions soon returned. The previous summer term, I suppose as a kind of unsuspected dummy-run, I had been invited over to Eastacre one day to play cricket. There had been an unfortunate incident when, ragged in the changing room, I had lost my cool with a bigger boy and made a fool of myself. At that first supper of the new term, my past sins were immediately visited upon me by Forrestier-Walker minor, a nine-year-old established as the school tough, who denounced me as 'the cheeky kid who had come to play cricket and had scratched Trevelyan's face' – for which heinous offence he had been severely trounced and, reduced to tears, had had to be rescued by a nanny (Miss Knight). It was nightmarish to have to sit and listen to this ghastly incrimination, and to see that devil Forrestier-Walker and his cronies rolling about in mirth at my expense. Why could I not have had the wit of later years, to remark casually that doubtless Trevelyan had richly deserved it – instead of hanging my head meekly?

I was never so glad for any meal to end as that first supper, but unfortunately it wasn't the end of the incident, by a long shot.

Soon the whole school knew, and I was singled out as the Cheekiest of all Cheeky New Kids. Is there any situation where a previous 'record' is more damning than in an English boarding school? Being a marked man seemed to typify most of my British school days. On that very first day, my fellow students were given an excuse to take it out on me – and, during all the three terms I was at Eastacre, never once did they let up. The whole school swiftly realized that, in me, they had the perfect animal for baiting. Because of my very few contacts with boys my own age at home,

> I found myself unable to understand these strange creatures at Eastacre. . . . Consequently, I treated would-be friends and bullies alike. At the slightest provocation, when I thought I was being teased, I would fly into the most violent temper, accompanied by floods of scalding tears. On these occasions I would attack all within reach, without discrimination. These tantrums of mine soon became the most popular sport at Eastacre. . . . No boys my own age could be seen appearing to be friendly to me, for fear that they too might become objects of the school's derision.

Thus, very shortly, 'I became the most "unpopular" boy in the school; not because I was particularly low, underhand or crooked, but because I was "odd", the ugly duckling, on account of my inability to take teasing and mix with my contemporaries'. Inevitably, rejection had an effect on my character, making me more introverted than ever, and something of a mental recluse. On Sunday walks in the surrounding woods, when all the others teamed off in their twos and threes, I became accustomed to always walking alone. I took to daydreaming about Ropley, about the dogs, about new chemical experiments with which to incinerate Forrestier-Walker minor and Eastacre, and about exotic voyages to distant parts of the world. For some reason, Hudson Bay and the North-West Passage of Canada particularly gripped me. As had been the case with my playmates at Ropley, a vicious circle set in:

the more I was bullied at school, the more unpopular I became; the more I brooded, then the more 'eccentric' I became. I began to resort to more underhand methods of getting my own back on my tormentors. The knotting of shoelaces, the taking of collar studs before the others got back to the changing room after games; the uncorking of ink bottles in desks, all began to seem perfectly fair methods of retaliation to me.

When excessively teased, I took to shouting so loud that a teacher would come running to discover what it was all about. My schoolfellows soon applied to me that most derogatory of all English school words: sneak.

But Eastacre wasn't all bad; there were compensations. During a football match I found myself standing near the enemy goal (no doubt dreaming about Admiral Peary and Baffin Island). Suddenly the ball appeared at my feet, and I kicked it into the goal. My stock soared, temporarily, and I was promoted to the first eleven (not the greatest of distinctions, as it comprised nearly half the tiny school!), and the following term, after being coached by a famous cricketer friend of Uncle Henry's, Ian Peebles, I found I could bowl a deadly leg-break. But cricket frankly bored me (it still does), and I dissipated this advantage by wandering off during matches, to search for rare caterpillars. This was considered to be a particularly heinous crime against 'team spirit', which, even at our tender age, was held to be a capital offence. Then I discovered I had some modest academic ability. When asked to write a first essay, 'What We Did in the Holidays', I had triumphantly completed mine in five minutes flat, running approximately as follows: 'I did lots of carpentering and built lots of Meccano and took the dogs for lots of walks.' I justly felt that it was an exact description of the holidays and that my powers of composition had been exhausted. But then I became rather fascinated by Latin, drawn chiefly by the wonderful fantasy and escapism of the myths and legends. If only I could invoke Heracles to rise up from Winchester to slaughter Forrestier-Walker minor.

Suddenly, a real hero arose, in the unexpected shape of Forrestier-Walker major, elder brother of my chief tormentor. At public school, such a relationship would plainly have been considered 'odd', but we were too young for such strictures. I think the elder boy's friendliness for me consisted in the first place of pity at the ragging I suffered at the hands of his brother and the other thugs. Later, I took him home to Ropley with me at half-term, and he was suitably impressed by my lethal prowess with the chemistry set – or was it Madame Scap's steam-engine? So the last term at Eastacre didn't end altogether badly. I was almost sorry to leave. But my time there proved to exemplify the Jacobean gloom of Webster's description of life as 'the good moments in an ague'. That September, aged eight, I went on to Ludgrove, near Barnet on the outskirts of London, supposedly Britain's most distinguished prep school, the greenhouse (still) for princes of the realm.

Out of the murk of half a passed century, I still perceive Ludgrove looming like some nightmare iceberg, the jagged pinnacles of which I can recall with painful precision. Decades previously, Osbert Sitwell had described it (lightly disguised as 'Bloodsworth') as 'a miniature model prison, with all the middle-class snobbery, but lacking the middle-class comforts'. By my day it had changed little. We all tend to be subjective about our early schooldays, and perhaps time has dramatized my memory of what – on my pampered horizon – made Dotheboys Hall seem like the Club Med. So maybe I am unfair to Ludgrove, yet those three and half years there remain unquestionably the most unpleasant of my life. Rather than simply Dotheboys Hall, Colditz is the symbol I instinctively reach for, though within that bleak wartime fortress there was at least a certain camaraderie; a Belsen of the spirit would perhaps be a more appropriate metaphor for Ludgrove, at any rate as far as I was concerned. My friend Colin Thubron once wrote in that exquisite prose of his:

> there is a feeling of slight nausea when you recognize a landscape which you associate with helplessness and vulnerability, and being on your own. When you look back on your childhood,

on being alone – and there you are never as alone as you are at a boarding school – you can never feel as vulnerable again. You don't arrange that sort of pain for yourself as an adult.

That would have been to place the gentlest interpretation upon Ludgrove. To me, in its humbug, snobbery and rampant, unchecked bullying, it came to represent everything that, all through the rest of my life, I most disliked about England. There was not a moment of those three years on which I look back with pleasure – save, possibly, my one abortive attempt to get over the camp wall.

The first term hardly began auspiciously. For repeated rowdiness in dormitory, my twelve-year-old prefect, Simon Warrender (quite reasonably), reported me to the headmaster, Mr Henley. I was called into his study and beaten – for the first, but not the last, time. (He smoked a particularly strong brand of Turkish tobacco, which I have never been able to smell since without a sense of discomfort in the nether regions.) The pain was appalling. I blubbed silently, then, composing myself, left his study and – to impress my new contemporaries with the claim that, like his namesake, the poet William Ernest Henley, I was bloody but unbowed – shouted at the top of my voice, 'I've been *swished*! Doodah, doodah, day!' Silently Mr Henley beckoned me back in and administered two more strokes. With the authorities, I was now a marked man, and, sadly, the only impression it made on the boys was to earmark me as a kind of fool, courting unnecessary trouble, and a suitable foil for ragging who could count on little support from above. F. A. H. Henley was a severe but fair man, greatly respected; however, his days were drawing to an end, and there ensued an Old-Testament-style succession. His accepted heir was the second-in-command, Mr Shaw, a large, easygoing and warm-hearted man usually to be seen shambling about in ginger-hued tweed plus-fours, accompanied by an elderly spaniel called Sammy. But the amiable 'Shawbug', as he was nicknamed, was – and remained – single. He had an attractive sister, however, whom his junior, Alan Barber, energetically wooed and married, thereby automatically giving himself – with a built-in headmistress – better odds in the succession stakes. In the best Esau-and-Jacob tradition, the popular Shawbug was passed over, and 'Ali' Barber ruled Ludgrove for the next four decades.

Ali Barber was a crashing snob, making his predilections for the various princelings and sons of magnates in the school all too plain. To that art, he added an extra dimension by being, as a former captain of Yorkshire, a cricket snob. He fawned over cricketers from that part of England, but anyone who lived in Hampshire, which had an indifferent side in those days, was beyond the pale. Not unnaturally, his snobbery percolated all the way down the school and with it went its inevitable handmaidens, humbug and hypocrisy. Clad in Edwardian knickerbockers, we all wore black ties – in mourning for George III (who let go those American colonies) and in preparation for Eton – with detachable Van Heusen collars. But the imposing façade concealed equally imposing grubbiness beneath: after sweaty games, showers in the locker rooms were non-existent; and, even in those days before wartime austerity, we were permitted only twice-weekly baths of tepid water, carefully measured at no more than five inches deep. Very occasionally, the squalor and neglect would surface: one eight-year-old classmate of mine, complaining of earache in the holidays, was found to have an orange pip in his ear that had taken root and was growing vigorously.

On Parents' Day we would be paraded for inspection in front of the school matron, a sallow-faced lady with mild elephantiasis, called Nurse Patterson (otherwise, more affectionately, 'Cow Pat'). Because of my innate weediness and poor health, I spent a fair amount of time in the sick room under Cow Pat's supervision, and she was always kind to me; but Parents' Day brought out the worst in her. Removing our Van Heusen collars, she would rub at our necks with painfully stinging methylated spirits; if the cotton wool turned an excessively dark shade of grey, we would be given a cuff on the ears. So we went to greet our parents, all pink and shining above our collars, but all filth below. To me it always epitomized all the essential sham of the school and its head.

Parents' Day was a particular nightmare. With the highly developed cruelty of small boys, we studied each other's parents like geldings in the ring, spotting and commenting on every foible. I longed, but didn't dare, to beg my father to be inconspicuous, not to wear his loudest, most raffish tweeds and a cloth cap – nor to arrive with Kenyon in the Rolls. Afterwards the comments would flow: 'I say, Horne's old man must drink a lot of port to have a red nose like that.' 'Where's your mother – why doesn't she ever come down?' To make up for their appearance, parents would strive to bring with them the most succulent and expensive sweets, to enhance the striking power of their little darlings with bigger boys, bullies or chums with grand houses. (Perhaps this was where that very English idiom, 'sucking up', originated?) Later, twice a week, the sweets would be doled out on plates, each bearing – like a lottery – a school number. The lucky numbers would then rush to offer their sweets to the nastiest and the most powerful. Regrettably, in this early lesson in competitive bribery and corruption, I did not thrive. Unaccustomed to shopping, my wifeless father would generally dispatch Frederick to buy the sweets. Always bent on economy, as the man who kept the accounts, Frederick never strayed far from Woolworth, while it was Harrods and Fortnum & Mason that bought peace for my colleagues.

By way of testing whether I had inherited any of my mother's artistic talents, it was proposed that I should take piano lessons. But the piano was in an unheated corridor, so cold that one's fingers were in constant danger of freezing to the keys. The music master, Mr Milford, a grey austere man with the face of a Cromwellian puritan and a dripping nose, repeatedly lost his patience and rapped my frost-bitten knuckles with his conductor's wand. After a few terms, I gave it up – to my everlasting sorrow. Ludgrove was not geared to what the bat-swinging headmaster clearly regarded as an effeminate pursuit. The whole ethos of the school was to prepare us for Eton, and to make men of us – by what was euphemistically known as 'competition', closely intermingled with patriotism, which in turn devolved into school and team loyalty. This, of course, was no bad thing – except for what it led to in practice.

The school was divided into six teams, named after eminent British war heroes. Rivalry between them was intense, and led to ferocious bullying, encouraged from on high. Each three 'minus marks' were accompanied by an 'extra drill'. Dreaded even more than a beating, this involved marching round and round the gym, carrying old rifles over one's head, under the eyes of a savage Great War NCO, a much hated personality called Sergeant-Major Goldie. For small boys of eight or nine, driven on to the point of collapse, it was a kind of torture never forgotten in after-life by anyone who survived Ludgrove.

What I remember with the most loathing was the bullying. Masters never intervened, which tended to confirm one's suspicion that it was deliberately encouraged, from on high, as a form of toughening up. Whether in the locker rooms, the classrooms or more often in the semi-seclusion of the dormitory, it was incessant and fed on the basest human instincts. The worst feature was that it was always the mob, led by one or two toughs, against one smaller boy (usually, it seemed, me) for whom no one – in contrast to the fiction of *Tom Brown* – ever dared speak up. For all the reasons uncovered at Eastacre, I was an ideal subject; there must have been a lot about me that was thoroughly obnoxious. The bullying was often extremely refined, whether physical or psychological, but it was always humiliating and degrading. I used to dread the nights. Worst among the ringleaders was H—, who became a great success, a brilliant scientist (about the only one produced by Ludgrove), renowned for his sexual prowess. In later years, we became good friends, but he could never recall having made my life a misery. (On the other side of the fence, some years ago a huge, balding man, six foot six inches tall, bore down on me, full of menace, at a drinks party and insisted that I, in my turn, had bullied him vilely at Ludgrove. I was quite unable to remember either his name, his face as a little boy, or the charges, and swore my innocence. Perhaps the memory is, after all, merciful in its deletions.)

At the begining of each term, at Prayers we would bellow out that sombre hymn, 'Oh God Our Help in Ages Past'. Secretly I would reproach Him for not having been much help to *me* over

the past ages of last term; I would pray for Him to afflict H—
with the Black Death or poison him with the school food (simple
expulsion was far too gentle a remedy), and for Ali Barber to be
caught by the Forty Thieves and slowly boiled in oil. Less
excessively, when we sang mournfully of a Sunday evening 'The
Day Thou Gavest, Lord, Is Ended', I would beg, mildly, that
H— might be inflicted with a headache and go to sleep early.

As no supernatural intervention ever occurred, however, one
day I hit on the ruse of 'inventing' a big brother at home, such as
so many of my fortunate contemporaries seemed to possess and
boast about. For my fantasies, I had a ready-made candidate. At
Ropley during the holidays, as I got older and was deemed to
have grown out of women, a brigade of tutors had followed Miss
Knight and the governesses. First and foremost there was Theo
Henning. Theo was German. I must have been about nine, so it
would have been shortly after Hitler came to power. Theo was
an ace. He was twenty-one, incredibly good-looking and incredibly nice. He came, I think, from Frankfurt-am-Main, stayed for
a summer and then came back again. Everybody, especially me,
adored him. Queer old Frederick was quite clearly madly in love
with him, endlessly trying to get him into the rose garden to chat
away in German. Theo was fairly scathing about Hitler, but
nervous, always referring to him in conversation with my father
as 'Mister Brown'. He did everything supremely well; he showed
me how to throw a javelin and a discus; he could long-jump like
a kangaroo; he even learnt to play cricket, with gusto; he knew
exactly how to make my (German) electric trains work, running
up inventive bits of scenery for them; and he loved animals – even
guinea-pigs. He could sing melancholic German songs; he told
marvellous fairy tales about Nordic gods. There was nothing
Theo could not or would not do, and there seemed to be no
whim of mine he would not accommodate. He was, quite simply,
fun. Suddenly, all those rooted animosities from the Great War
seemed to roll away. I was even permitted to visit the supposed
German's magical shop in Winchester.

At Ludgrove I began to weave the cautionary fantasy of Theo
as the avenging elder brother who would inflict his wrath on the

bullies. It lasted until halfway through the term, when it reached the ears of Ali, who of course gently exposed me as a liar. The bullying intensified. Then, one day, when I was about ten, as I was running after the ball in the middle of a soccer game, in mid-pitch I was suddenly stricken with a frightening breathlessness. It was the first intimation that I had contracted asthma, which thereafter was to plague me, coming and going, in bizarre cycles throughout my life. Over the immediately ensuing years of childhood, both at school and at home, in Britain and in America, in those days when you had no such miracle palliatives as Ventolin puffers, I remember night after sleepless night of panicking terror, laying awake feeling that I was going to suffocate, interspersed with painful bouts of wheezing under a towel, tearfully inhaling the sickly-sweet fumes of Friar's Balsam, which did little good. Terrible to anyone who suffers from it (and nobody outside the deadly circle can conceive quite how terrible), asthma is a mysterious affliction, often accepted as having little-understood psychosomatic origins. For instance, during four years in the armed forces, whether in freezing and damp barracks or in the insalubrious humidity of the Nile Valley, I never once suffered from it – but, the moment I was demobbed, back it came. Therefore, would it be unjust, I wonder, to blame the onset of this fearful scourge upon the miseries inflicted at Ludgrove? Certainly, I have never been able to dissociate the two.

United by a bond of common adversity with a schoolfellow who had suffered hell from the misfortune of having a German mother ('When's the Hun coming down?') and too many Christian names ('Only royalty can have six!'), we began to plot the Great Escape. For a whole term I set to embezzling money doled out each week for dropping into the collection bag at church, until I had ten of those old heavy penny pieces, sufficient to get me from Cockfosters tube station to Marble Arch, a few hundred yards from 5a Lees Place – and home. When the appointed day for the Escape came, scared and wheezing I scurried over the two miles between Ludgrove and Cockfosters. To a ten-year-old, I suppose, the adventure must have seemed no less exciting, and frightening, than escapes from the real Colditz during the war.

Alas, as I was dropping the precious, freedom-giving pennies into the ticket machine, a heavy hand descended on my shoulder. Somebody must have grassed! Fortunately my captor was the kind and warm-hearted Shawbug, but I returned expecting to be flogged unconscious, or expelled in ignominy (though at least that would have meant *escape*). To my amazement, it was an Ali Barber that I had never known who ushered me into the dread Library, a compound of puzzlement (how could anyone want to flee the elitist Elysium of Ludgrove?), of compassion even, but principally of alarm. He was clearly thinking about the school's reputation, what all those royal parents and Yorkshire grandees would think. I was released unchastised. For a while my stock rose dizzily and I was left unmolested by my fellows – even treated by the masters with some degree of respect.

About this time, in 1937, the school moved lock, stock and barrel to its present quarters at Wokingham in Berkshire, conveniently close to Windsor Castle. Almost luxurious by comparison with Cockfosters, the move represented a massive improvement in my fortunes. There was even a golf course. The hated bullies had departed to Eton, and I had developed quite a redoubtable straight-right in Sergeant-Major Goldie's boxing ring. Only the food showed little improvement. One day I found my slice of ham shared with a thriving colony of little white maggots. With a new boldness gained from the failed Great Escape, I marched up before the whole school, like Oliver Twist, presented my plate to an amazed Ali and declared in ringing tones, 'Worms in the ham, sir!' It was a tiny victory, one which would have been recognizable to Solzhenitsyn's Ivan Denisovich; nevertheless, it was the best moment of my whole career at Ludgrove. My standing in the school was now inalienable, and life became almost tolerable.

Then, one evening, during a friendly rag in the dorm, fate struck from an unexpected quarter. Playing at knights-in-armour, in what I think was called mounted wrestling, I had on my back a smaller boy who was trying to 'unhorse' another small boy from the back of a very big boy, the dorm prefect Worsley major, (in later life, a Tory MP). A heavy fellow, Worsley gave a great shove. I tripped and fell, quite unable to save myself, flat on my nose, with the combined weight of myself and 'rider'. The result was catastrophic. Pouring with blood, I was rushed off by Nurse Patterson, first to the sick room, then to hospital.

In my pain I could not anticipate at the time that this meant the end of Ludgrove, that I would never see the sanctimonious Ali or his maggotty ham again. To my father, the episode was written off as just 'messing about', and he did not claim damages on behalf of my shattered nose. But, many years later it was with considerable sympathy that I read the news that the second in line to the throne, eight-year-old Prince William, had had his skull dangerously fractured at Lugrove Preparatory School, by a friend wielding a golf club. They had been, as the communiqué put it in those familiar words, just 'messing about'.

The unfortunate, and heavily publicized, royal accident must have been no more than extremely bad luck for present-day Ludgrove, and could have happened anywhere. For it seems that, in keeping with the times, the school has become an altogether more human, happier place. And, admittedly, with my strange, lonely home background and unclubbable personality, I must have been a pretty impossible subject.

Yet, to this day, I am left wondering whether Ludgrove and its many other counterparts across the realm of King George V were really designed to rear a breed of Britons capable of administering the world's greatest empire, and, all too soon, of having to fight history's deadliest war. Or was it the Ludgroves, and the system of private education radiating upwards from them, that doomed us Britons, and still dooms us, to second-rate status? What place was there in the twentieth century for a system in which the arts and music, and foreign languages, were considered effeminate, in which science and technology were subjects fit only for a polytechnic, in which the cult of the amateur was admired and professionalism viewed with suspicion? While Old Ludgrovians of my age-group were smugly moving, after the Second World War, into comfortable slots in their fathers' banking firms, or into merchant banks or estate management or Lloyd's or the Temple, their competitors in France and Germany were dirtying their hands through the ranks of BMW, Mercedes and Rhône-Poulenc, or swotting their way through European business schools. I do not think I am alone in having these deeply rooted misgivings. In 1992 the correspondent of the *Washington Post*, departing after five years in Britain, was given a hard time for singling out the diehard snobberies still inherent in British education, which he believes made it more difficult for us to compete in today's ever tougher global market place.

If he is right, then the Ludgroves of the 1930s still have a lot to answer for.

CHAPTER FOUR

War Approaches

I had escaped Ludgrove. But at what a cost! What a Pyrrhic victory! I was an unpalatable mess. My asthma was worse than ever; my broken nose, reset with long tampons up each nostril and causing me pain comparable to the circumcision of a few years previously, looked like the battered piece of Uncle Henry's pugilist friend, Tommy Farr – and I couldn't breathe through it. Worse still, I was a jangle of complexes and inhibitions, with the instinctive snarl of the mongrel waiting to be kicked, without a shred of self-confidence or dignity. I took a whole term off, at a hotel (the Branksome Towers) in Bournemouth, with yet another governess (Christine), while my father, Aunt Ethel and Eve deliberated about the unpromising future. How on earth was my father going to fulfil his promise to my mother by getting me in shape to go to Eton? I was already twelve. Finally it was decided that I should go to school in Switzerland for a year, for health reasons. My heart leapt: Switzerland! Abroad! Few of my contemporaries at Ludgrove had ever travelled farther than a grouse-moor in Scotland. Uncle Newt cautioned me: 'There'll be foreigners there . . . probably *Germans*.' But I was thrilled.

To step down for the first time on foreign soil, at Lausanne Station from the great height of the mighty Orient Express (which seemed twice as big as any British train), accompanied by Aunt Ethel clucking at the perilous descent on to the low continental platform, with the funny square Swiss electric trains humming and moaning past, was fantastically exciting. And it still is. It was Easter 1938. Hitler has just occupied Vienna; by the time I left in June of the following year, he had marched into

Prague. Europe was tense. After a few days' acclimatization on sunny Lake Geneva, Aunt Ethel took me off to Rolle and deposited me at Le Rosey. Still a by-word for international luxury, Le Rosey was unlike any school I could ever have imagined. The *directeur* was a Monsieur Carnal, a Swiss of urbane good manners, but whose name was not inappropriate to the fleshly priorities for which Le Rosey stood – and, evidently, still stands. Madame Carnal was an American lady of great dignity, sweetness and warmth, who (I think) even kissed me on arrival. After the box of English Harrogate Toffee left with me by kind Aunt Ethel had been stolen by some small foreign fiend, the kind-hearted Madame Carnal replaced them with a huge bag of vastly superior confections from Madame Beck down in Rolle. Each time I see a packet of Suchard Sugus at the *kiosk de tabac* in Geneva Airport they still arouse lustful infantile memories.

There were other Swiss constants that have remained wonderfully unchanged over fifty-odd years – the coins, for instance, except that, since those happy days when the pound changed at approximately twenty-four Swiss francs, their value was somewhat different. Each week, from racks such as you find still in Swiss railway ticket offices, we received out precious *argent de poche*: a heavy five-franc piece for the *seniors* (seventeen-year-old grandees like the dashing Prince Radziwill of Poland); two francs for the *moyens* (like Rainier of Monaco, who – with his sophisticated bow-tie – looked rather like a croupier even aged fifteen, and received his coin with the impassivity of one), and one franc for us lowly *juniors*. The trouble was that very Swiss-like deductions were made for various minor venalities: "Orne,' Monsieur Carnal would call out, *'nonante centimes d'amende – dix centimes d'argent de poche!'* As a result, on our half-holiday sorties down to Rolle, while others gorged themselves on Madame Beck's *tartes aux fraises*, about all I could ever afford was a revolting, glutinous green jellied frog costing five centimes.

Never mind. The food at Le Rosey itself had to be the best in the world. Under the excellent tutelage of the Carnals, I learnt to acquire (my mother's son!) tastes, quite *au dessus de ma gare*, that have – alas – never since left me.

That was about all that I did learn at Le Rosey – regrettably, I did not learn to speak French (which would have pleased my dead mother), or even to ski. At regular intervals, we would be invited into Madame Carnal's *salon*, to study how to eat a chocolate éclair with one hand and make polite conversation, in French. It was a strain. As well as killing what little musical urge I might have had, Ludgrove (or one's peers there) had taught one to despise French – certainly if spoken with anything more than a Churchillian accent – as an effeminate pursuit. On dismissal from the *salon*, we Anglo-Saxons (Americans formed more than half of the school) would race off into distant corners to gabble our native tongue together. But it was a grave offence. If caught by the ubiquitous and watchful Monsieur Vuilleumier (who completed nearly fifty years at Le Rosey), one would be *consigné*, which meant sitting in a stuffy classroom on a hot Saturday afternoon, while one's friends trekked down to Madame Beck, and writing out thousands of times, '*Il faut que je parle le français, tout le temps.*' Combined with the indoctrination at Ludgrove, it was not destined to make one amorous of the language, which was perhaps why, in years to come, I always found German and even Spanish more appealing. But beating was unheard of at Le Rosey, and *la consigne* was the worst discipline that could be inflicted. There were no black ties for George III, nor Van Heusen collars to camouflage the grub, nor knickerbockers. One could wear roughly what one wanted, provided it was clean.

Despite the climate, I still suffered from asthma. Apart from the unpleasant practice of inserting a large thermometer up the wrong end, the Swiss had a strange, medieval cures. There were little glass cups, called *ventouses*, which were heated over a spirit lamp, then placed all over one's back. The ensuing vacuum painfully raised large bumps; apart from that, I can't recall that they did any good at all. Never mind – relaxed and agreeably decadent, Swiss Le Rosey was all rather different from spartan Ludgrove.

My first two room-mates, in a luxurious *chambre à trois lits*, were two princely and cosmopolitan brothers, Alfonso and 'Brownie' Hohenlohe. Although their mother was Spanish, they wore lederhosen and spoke – to my fury – German together.

Remembering my upbringing, and Uncle Newt's parting caveat, I viewed them instantly with suspicious hostility. I had heard nothing whatsoever about Franco (who was currently besieging Madrid), nor anything about the Spanish Civil War, which naturally enough greatly occupied their thoughts. But, as a matter of principle, I knew I had to be on the other side, at all costs. So, at an early age, I became a Republican. We had terrible, nationalistic rows, hammering each other on the floor, but there was never the coldly brutal ganging-up of Ludgrove and even Eastacre. Perhaps it had something to do with the diet! In later years, Alfonso, his family impoverished by world events, became famous for marrying the glamorous sixteen-year-old Ira Furstenberg and grew rich, first from selling Volkswagens to the Mexicans, then from founding the famous Marbella Club. He became a friend of mine. There was an amazing mix of nationalities and persuasions at pre-war Le Rosey. Apart from the American, whose noisy friendliness and rebellious refusal to speak French attracted me, there were Jewish refugees from Vienna, and Poles and Nazis. One wild Italian from Perugia, Coletti, who became a particular friend of mine, died in 1945 with the Italian communist partisans, probably fighting other *anciens* who had been drafted into the Wehrmacht. (There were, I suspect, fewer of Coletti's persuasion than there were fascists among the *anciens élèves* of Le Rosey.) For the first time in my life, I made several English friends, who lasted into later life.

To say I learned nothing at Le Rosey would, in fact, be an exaggeration. I learnt (very little) about sex – and about the Jews. In my English isolation I knew no more about either than I knew about the Spanish Civil War. Before reaching Le Rosey, despite having all those endlessly productive rabbits and guinea-pigs, I was sublimely ignorant of the birds and the bees; the subject seemed to be neither of interest nor of relevance to my life at Ludgrove. At Le Rosey there was much speculation and whispering about heroic *seniors*, who crept back and forth nocturnally across the sports field to the local girls' school, Lacombe. One day I overheard two of them using an unknown, monosyllabic word beginning with 'c'. I asked an English contemporary if he knew what it meant. He admitted he didn't but he had overheard his elder sister discussing it with a girlfriend, '. . . and apparently it's something that hurts like hell!' That was all he had gleaned. It didn't necessarily make one want to enquire further. In my first term I made a good friend called Karrie, a German Jew (I later discovered) with sad eyes and a sweet, unaggressive personality. But he was an irrepressible flasher, and had a habit – in prep – of unbuttoning himself and waving around a piece of diminutive gristle (circumcised like my own), until derision or the sudden advent of Monsieur Vuilleumier would cause him to retract. Then, suddenly, within two terms, it became evident that what Karrie was waving at us had miraculously grown to vast and enviable proportions. (Alas, it soon got him into trouble, causing his premature departure from the school.)

That winter there was a scandal when two boys were expelled for being found in each other's beds. Both happened to be Jewish. So someone told me – it meant nothing to me at the time. Then, in my last term, Karrie and I found ourselves sharing a room with one of the less pleasant, in fact positively uncouth, Americans, who constantly brought up the buggery scandal, coupled with the epithet 'bloody Jews'. Karrie would just go silent – and looked sadder. I was too young to be appalled, only felt bewildered, and I asked the American why he spoke of the Jews that way. 'Because my father says they're *different.*' Apart from his compulsive flashing, I couldn't see what there was that was different about Karrie, except that he was gentler. But I suppose it made me look at him with a curiosity which, though it certainly wasn't intended to be unfriendly, must have been hurtful.

At the beginning of December, the entire Le Rosey boarded that ageless little blue and white train, the MOB, and headed off to the pampered school's winter quarters at Gstaad. There we learned to ski, skate and play ice-hockey. And there I discovered something else: I was short-sighted. I couldn't understand why, learning to ski on the gentlest of slopes, I fell over clumsily when others didn't, and why, basically, I hated and feared something which was later to become the joy of my life. It was because I simply couldn't see the bumps. It may seem extraordinary to people in this health-conscious age, but nobody – either at home or at three consecutive schools – had ever bothered to have my eyes tested. It wasn't till I got to public school, aged fourteen, that I was finally tested and given spectacles – hideous wire affairs, round like two-franc pieces. At Ludgrove, without identifying it as myopia, I came to assume that it was just another peculiarity to be rather ashamed of, like bed-wetting, so I used to hide it, screw up my eyes and shuffle my way to the front of the class so as to see the blackboard. Thus it came to pass, on the nursery slopes of the Wispillen, that after endless appalling mishaps I sensed, but wasn't quite sure, that my eyes weren't like other boys'. Instead of taking the obvious course, I took evasive action, even to the extent of surreptitiously keeping attached downhill the *peaux de phoques* skins we used for climbing up mountains, which were still innocent of lifts. This slowed my descent quite miraculously. Or, on the credit side, whenever there was an option, I opted to skate instead, becoming rather a whizz at ice-hockey.* But, after ensuing decades of struggling to become a good skier, how I curse now that I missed becoming a much better one through those lost opportunities at Gstaad.

That Christmas holidays of 1938, I stayed in Gstaad, and my father and Eve came out. It was a distinctly happy time. In those far-off days before the greenhouse effect, there were actually white Christmasses in low-down Gstaad. Horse-drawn sledges with jingling bells rushed through the streets, fairy-lights twinkled on the eaves of the old chalets, carol-singers with lanterns on staves sang 'Heilige Nacht'. It was glorious. We all stayed at the little Rössli inn on the main street, full of old Bernese charm and *Gemütlichkeit*. I had never spent so much time with my father, or seen him seem so relaxed and happy. I was just old enough to be amused, in fact delighted, instead of embarrassed, by his eccentricities. Wearing the same cheerful tweed jacket and emphatic cloth-cap that he used for chasing the grouse, and

---

* A great benefit in later years. It got me into the Cambridge University ice hockey team, leading to wonderful free winter tours of Switzerland (including beloved Gstaad) in days of austerity, when a travel allowance of £25 a year imposed by the Attlee government made travel abroad all but impossible.

propped by one enormous wooden ski pole, he would amble through the streets towards the ice-rink. There, with a seraphic smile on his face, he would take up a position in mid-rink, watching the waltzers swoop past, oblivious of all danger until the ice-hockey started, when he would be ushered politely off. He was relentless in his use of his remarkable French, assured that Switzerland was entirely a francophone country, and unfazed when he was answered in *Schweitzerdeutsch*. 'They do speak French with funny accents up here,' he confided to Eve. At a fancy-dress party up at the Palace Hotel on New Year's Eve, a casual observation uttered in French – goodness knows what it was, but it was certainly meant congenially – to a gentleman of mid-Eastern appearance got up as a toreador all but provoked a fight. But he collected masses of instant friends, including several cheerful Americans, parents of my Le Rosey chums come over for Christmas. He remarked once wistfully, 'Wouldn't it be jolly if Mrs Breese would suddenly turn up here too.' It was a truly merry Christmas, the merriest I could remember, the last before the clouds of war swept in – merry perhaps for that very reason.

The following winter term I shared sumptuous quarters in a chalet overlooking Le Rosey with an agreeable Canadian, Charles Gordon, and an English newcomer, John Knatchbull. Like me, the latter had been dispatched to Le Rosey to recover from a broken nose, mashed in the Wall Game at Eton. Over us presided a delightful and humorous Welshman and his wife, the Hugheses. Mr Hughes, a marvellous teacher who became something of an institution in the school, had one caveat: 'For heaven's sake watch out for Knatchbull's nose!' It was hard not to; swollen and rubicund, it resembled Mr Punch's. Every year these days *The Times* thoughtfully reminds me that Knatchbull and I were born on exactly the same day, but he was a year older – which counted for a lot at our age. He brought with him from England some of the instincts (all too familiar to me) of the bully, and was tough and rather admirably reckless. He had a passion for smoking ten-centime Swiss *Stumpen*, which, to my tender sensibilities, looked like dogs' turds, and smelled rather worse. On collectivist principles, he reckoned that, if all three of us indulged on a verandah round the back of the chalet and were caught by the Hugheses we could not *all* be expelled. In Gordon, anxious to be adult, he had a willing accessory, but I could hardly stop myself from throwing up. One day Knatchbull pressed me too far, twisting my arm in a painful half-nelson. Quite reflexively I put out my right fist, which connected with the famous protuberance, with disastrous consequences. It burst like an over-ripe tomato. Oblivious to all traces of the *Stumpen*, Mr Hughes flew in wringing his hands: 'Oh my God, it's Knatchbull's nose!' His enraged parents gathered him back, once more to the tender care of Eton.* For the rest of the term I was regarded with a mixture of respect and aversion.

At sun-drenched Rolle, though the international situation was tense as Hitler digested Czechoslovakia and prepared to conquer Poland, while Franco conquered Madrid, the last term at Le Rosey was a cheerful one. After more painful deliberations, Cousin Eve had prevailed upon my father to risk my mother's displeasure from beyond the grave and send me – in September 1939 – to Stowe, not Eton. The nominal pretext was 'health reasons', it being reckoned that my asthma, wonderfully dormant in the dry ozone of Switzerland, would be more controllable on the heights of Buckinghamshire than down in the Slough marshes. To say that I was pleased would be an understatement in any coinage: the unknown quantity of Stowe *had* to be an improvement on Eton, where, I reckoned, I would undoubtedly find the same old mixture as before, and be met by the same old gang of bullies I had escaped from at Ludgrove. So, under the superb tuition of Mr Hughes, I worked with unprecedented fanaticism to pass my Common Entrance exam. To the amazement of all, I succeeded with flying colours, getting into the top new boys' form at Stowe, Remove C. My father was beside

---

* Years later we met in the war, in the same regiment; he was forgiving, and we became friends. But the nose, I noted with extreme guilt, still looked terrible, covering a vast expanse of his face. However, it didn't affect his future. As Lord Brabourne, he became a brilliant film producer (his films including *Murder on the Orient Express* and *A Passage to India*) and married Patricia Mountbatten. Tragically his mother and one of his twin sons were killed by the IRA bomb that murdered his father-in-law in 1979. John himself escaped with serious injuries.

himself with delight, and I was delighted that he was delighted –
it had, suddenly, come to mean a lot. As a reward, he promised
to take me ('*Deo volente* and Mr Hitler permitting') on a Baltic
cruise, in August.

For the first time, I was sad to leave a school, sad to bid
farewell to my friends, some of whom, like John Monkbretton
and several of the Americans, I would see again often in later life;
others, like Karrie, would die young or, like Coletti with his
Italian partisans, not survive the war. And I would certainly miss
the never-to-be-repeated fleshpots of Madame Carnal. To arm
myself for an uncertain future, down in unrestricted Rolle for the
princely sum of half-a-dozen Swiss francs I purchased to take
home, not a cuckoo-clock, but a knuckleduster and a tiny 7mm
pistol, capable of firing a single ball, or minute shot cartridges,
possibly lethal to a hypnotized rabbit at one yard's range, otherwise liable only to instigate hilarity-provoking stampedes among
the unfortunate pigs my father had purchased against 'Mr Hitler'.
They were to become a cause of mixed admiration and concern in
America. But I returned home on the crest of a wave, having at
last achieved, in my own right, something that seemed almost
like a success.

The euphoria lasted through that summer of 1939. Released from
school in the unEnglish month of June, it was a long one, and the
best – pre-America. I spent July and most of August engrossed in
two new hobbies at Ropley. One was pursuing the myriad gaudy
butterflies that flocked around the buddleias, as common as midges
in those pre-herbicide days, with net and cyanide bottle, and
mounting them on sheets of cork. I had an imposing collection.
Now, when one Painted Lady really does, unlike the swallow in
the proverb, 'make a summer', and with the horrible connotations
that cyanide came to assume in the war, I look back on that
particular pleasure of summer 1939 with measureless self-reproach.

More harmless, but infinitely more frustrating, was the building of a home-made wireless. Advertised in Mr F. J. Camm's
seductive (and hyperbolic) *Practical Wireless*, as being able to pick

up the four corners of the world, with its tangle of unruly wires, the name was astoundingly ill-chosen. So was its claim to be 'portable'. A bubbling accumulator slopped acid all over the place; a vast high-tension battery weighed as much as a small suitcase; another excitingly called the grid bias battery, which had a function I never quite understood, was itself bigger than most modern transistor radios. Four valves the size of light bulbs either glowed (if the accumulator was charged) or were coated with gold to keep out 'interference'. Great coppery coils glistened mysteriously. Daily I used to wait anxiously for the post to bring, COD, a new consignment of condensers, chokes, transformers, resistances and potentiometers from the ever obliging Messrs A. F. Bulgin. It was a thing of beauty in itself. Doubtless today it would be a priceless antique, or find a place of honour in the New York Gallery of Modern Art. Seven separate knobs graced its dashboard, as complex as the controls of a modern Boeing.

But, twiddling them all summer long, all I could get was howls, augmented by my own – of rage and frustration. Not one of the hundreds of exotic stations, like Hilversum, Kaunas and Fécamp, that adorned its great white escutcheon, could I receive, and I was far too diffident to write for help to the august Mr Camm, or to enquire what the hell was wrong with his blueprint.

It was a summer golden with sunshine, like those other pre-deluge days of 1914. But the shadows were closing in. My father grumbled about the increased income tax (which then stood at 5s 6d in the pound) and the cost of living. His latest mini-Rolls had set him back £2500 (why has the figure stuck in my mind all these years?). 'As much as a *new house* – it'll be the last we can afford,' he declared as Kenyon's face took on a more worried expression than usual. Cousin Cecil, now at last promoted major, came down to Ropley with grim accounts of German war-preparedness, and the superb equipment of the Wehrmacht. But the Middlesex Regiment was ready, all set to be shipped to France, 'when the balloon goes up'. Cecil made our flesh creep with prognostications of how Hitler would bring the war to Britain. There would, certainly, be mass gas attacks. Ropley would catch it – looking at me meaningfully, to see if I blanched. Cecil's terror talk was reinforced by a frighteningly realistic film, a superb piece of 'readiness' propaganda, *An Englishman's Home*, showing that archetypal Englishman, Edmund Gwenn, his semi-detached ablaze, fearlessly warding off Nazi paratroopers. But the country-side was also full of rumours of reassurance. Frederick's little Morris 8 had twice conked out near Worthy Down; it was, he declared knowingly, because the highly secret RAF installation there was experimenting (manifestly with success) on a death ray that would cause the motors of all German bombers to cut out. (In fact, as one learnt much later, experiments on a war-winning 'secret weapon' were indeed going on at Worthy Down – it was called radar.)

My father, by nature highly reactive to all bad news, remained astonishingly sanguine. He was jolly well not going to let 'Mr Hitler' interfere with our Baltic cruise. We were booked to go, for a couple of weeks, in mid-August. The itinerary was wildly exciting, and most comprehensive. Aboard the P & O *Orion*, we would take in the Scandinavian capitals, Polish ports with exotic names like Gdynia and Zoppot, the disputed Free City of Danzig (about which Hitler was already making fierce noises), and finally Helsinki and Leningrad. Had P & O adhered to this imaginative itinerary, our lives would probably have taken a different course: we would both have been interned for the duration – and there would have been no America. Then, at the last moment, wiser counsels prevailed, the inner Baltic was declared a no-go area, the cruise curtailed and redirected to Copenhagen and the Norwegian fjords. For all our disappointment, we had a splendid time. I had never seen my father in better form or funnier; we got on fabulously. He suddenly appeared to be proud of me – or perhaps he was just more able to show it. Everybody aboard the *Orion*, passengers and crew alike, seemed to sense that it was like the summer of 1914, that it was the end of something, and were deter-mined to have a good time. The band played 'Begin the Beguine' and 'Down Mexico Way' till the small hours of every night. I won a prize for collecting the largest number of teaspoons from the bottom of the swimming pool and was laden down with treats from attractive divorcees anxious to further their acquaintance with my father. (How much did my presence hamper his social life, on board ship, I wondered?) I have a photo of him in brick-red slacks, striped matelot singlet, the inevitable tweed cap, a woolly dog won from some tombola or other – and the broadest of smiles on his face. I would not see him look so happy again until, briefly, in 1943. The great fjords with their towering mountains, indigo waters, ancient wooden churches and smiling blond children, were – I thought – quite wonderful. Eight months later they would be overrun by the men in field-grey.

We got back to Ropley just before Hitler invaded Poland. During the Sunday morning, 3 September, the most exciting event of my summer occurred. With the aid of the ever patient Kenyon and a boffin in Winchester I had got the recalcitrant Colt wireless to function. Amid banshee whistles and howls I picked up a flat, melancholy voice from the BBC:

> This morning the British Ambassador in Berlin handed the German government a final Note stating that unless we heard from them by eleven o'clock that they were prepared at once to withdraw their troops from Poland a state of war would exist between us.
>
> I have to tell you now that no such undertaking has been received, and that consequently this country is at war with Germany.

Heedless of the content, I flew down to the Smoking Room to proclaim, 'Daddy, wonderful news – *it works!*' My father was sitting there, listening to his wireless, with his head between his hands, and remarked something like 'Later, old boy, later.' In the background, the London air-raid sirens sounded;* were Cecil's dire predictions about to come true? Later that day the passenger liner *Athenia* was torpedoed by a U-boat. It had begun.

*

* It was, of course, the famous false alarm.

A week later I went off to Stowe – my fourth school, already – with an expensive kit of new clothes. As I did not even complete one year, it would be easy not to be fair, but I didn't think much of it. Though infinitely preferable to Ludgrove (and what institution wouldn't be!), after Le Rosey it seemed a grey sort of place. The exquisite Palladian buildings, designed by Vanbrugh and Gibbs, were distinctly seedy inside. Through them and through the grounds, landscaped by Capability Brown (who began his career there), flitted 500 boys all clad in the school uniform of grey flannel, making them look like a ghost herd of baby elephants. For a school that was only a little older than myself, I thought it rather absurd to vest itself with traditions, like bellowing out 'Sto!' instead of 'Present!' (also rather an indifferent pun) when one's name was called out at Assembly. The dormitories were spartan and freezing, and the food terrible – certainly after the Lucullan corruption of my taste-buds at Le Rosey. The beginning of wartime rationing obviously provided the school caterers with a handy excuse. At Chandos House, my housemaster was a nice old retired major, nicknamed the 'Merch', with little inspiring about him. It was alleged of him that, badly wounded in the Great War, he had a 'rubber bum' which, if he stood near a fire, would either melt or explode. After I had released some bees in prep, a fairly innocent offence, he beat me (but without the steely dedication of Ali Barber), though prefixing the blows with 'I'm beginning to think you're a bit of a bad fellow, Horne.'

I began to resign myself at last to thinking that I must be a misfit. Years later there seemed to be something faintly relevant in the black joke about the American farmer called Axelrod who, after being visited with all the tribulations of Job, finally threw his eyes up to heaven and asked, 'Lord, Lord, why are doing this to me?' Whereupon the heavens parted with a peal of thunder, and a Voice boomed out: 'I don't know, Axelrod. I guess there's something about you that just pisses me off!' As at Ludgrove, I didn't form any particular friendships at Stowe, though in later life I acquired many close friends, like my long-time and beloved publisher Alan Maclean, and Perry Worsthorne of the *Sunday*

Telegraph, who had been Stoics then. I was plagued by one notable thug, called P—, who had eyes like Hitler's SS killer Reinhard Heydrich and made up for a low IQ by torturing his wretched pet mice. But what bullying there was at Stowe was far less institutionalized than it had been at Ludgrove. Instead, it was supplanted by the other 'B' that plagued British public school life – buggery. It came from top to bottom, in a manner of speaking. The admirable and greatly respected founding headmaster, J. F. Roxburgh, a man with a passion for the classical ethos in all aspects, was probably a sublimated homosexual (though none of us knew it at the time). So was my rather less respected form-master of Remove C, Mr Capel Cure, who was excessive in his favouritism. In my innocence, I was outraged when he regularly sent Mulligan, a pretty boy with red hair whom he nicknamed 'Becky Sharp', to the tuck-shop for an ice-cream, with the rider '. . . and buy one for yourself, Becky' – but never *me*. When, twenty-five years later, Alan Maclean let me in on the dread secret of Capel Cure's proclivities, I felt rather better. The numerous classical temples and copses of Stowe fairly vibrated with the love that dares not speak its name. I felt grateful to leave while still intact, saved by the bell, unlike my unfortunate friend Perry, 'seduced', as he told the world, 'with dispatch' by trumpeter George Melly.

Life at Stowe was of course framed by the war. Direct news was filtered down from on high, while our eyes were glued to the weekly (and highly censored) *Sphere* and *Illustrated London News*. Naturally, we acquired a distinctly optimistic view of the war. Before the weekly film show, we would sing lustily 'Run, Rabbit, Run' and 'Hang Out Your Washing on the Siegfried Line', and, after a lot of talk about an 'offensive in the Saar', wondered why we were not launching one. A film called *The Lion Has Wings* brought us a mass raid of Luftwaffe bombers turned back by the mere sight of Britain's terrifying balloon barrage. As portrayed in the *Sphere*, the latest medium artillery, the great array of the Royal Navy's battleships and, above all, the Maginot Line were comfortingly impressive, while the faces of the Tommies with the first four divisions of the British

Expeditionary Force looked smiling and purposeful. But, when I recalled Cousin Cecil twining on his leg puttees, they didn't seem quite as professional as those great phalanxes in the coal-scuttle helmets. Just before Christmas, there came the glorious boost of the first naval victory, the mighty pocket battleship, *Graf Spee*, worried to death by the three little cruisers *Ajax*, *Achilles* and *Exeter*. That was what we expected of the Royal Navy. How long could a blockaded and starving Germany hold out? Mass Observation surveys told us that only one Briton expected the war to last more than three months. Then followed the rather incomprehensible months of the Phoney War. We watched, in civic-affairs class, the valiant, but eventually tragically futile, exploits of the Finns. Then there was more good news, briefly, in April with accounts of great naval exploits off those beloved Norwegian fjords. Chamberlain assured us, 'Hitler has missed the bus.'

After a bitterly cold winter, during which – with my Le Rosey ice-hockey skates – I had briefly come into my own on Stowe's frozen lake, summer began with a vengeance in May. Never did the cow-parsley seem more luxuriant, the butterflies swarm in greater profusion. One azure day succeeded another, in what was to become historically damned as 'Göring's weather', which made us schoolboys long for the free afternoons and an escape from the classroom. On 10 May the long-awaited German offensive in the west began, striking with horrifying force against the Low Countries. In the relative, permissive freedom of Stowe, I had set up another, simpler 'wireless' in one of the many glorious Palladian temples sprinkled about the grounds, with an aerial strung from a nearby tree. It was probably only a shade less primitive than the instruments just a few miles away at Bletchley, which, in deadliest secrecy, were then picking up the Ultra intercepts from the Wehrmacht High Command – and was no great success. Distracted by the squeaks of pleasure offstage as big boys pursued smaller boys through the woods around that inappropriately named Temple of Ancient Virtue, and through the squeals and howls produced by twiddling the sensitive 'reaction control', I found it hard to pick up the BBC. But out of it I was able to glean a direr picture than that which filtered through to us via the Merch in our House. Belgium's Fort Eben-Emael, reputedly the strongest in the world, fell to Nazi stormtroops in a matter of hours; there was ominous talk of some secret weapon. Rotterdam was pulverized by Luftwaffe dive-bombers. It was alleged that 30,000 civilians had died in the attack. Enough at any rate to give a grim foretaste of what almost certainly now lay ahead for Britain.

By the end of that terrifying week, the Germans had burst across the Meuse at Sedan, and were fanning out irresistibly and at unimaginable speed over the flat plains of eastern France. I began to wonder whether Cecil, recently promoted to command his battalion of the Middlesex, was involved in the battle. Though it was concealed from all our gazes – and even that of the new Prime Minister, Winston Churchill – at the time, that battle had in fact already been lost. At Stowe, I remember the physics class suddenly being interrupted by the teacher, a man hard-of-hearing with hair sprouting liberally from his ears, whom we unkindly nicknamed 'Daddy' Dewing. He made an announcement. At Sedan, he told us, a fierce battle had been fought; we, the Allies, had lost it – but the German casualties had been so dreadful that 'they will never be able to do anything like this again'. We listened in glum disbelief. None of us were able to appreciate the full scale of the German achievement, or the slender total of their losses – a few thousand – until many years later.

Brave little Holland, then Belgium, capitulated. Next came the chilling news that France, too, was out of the war. There were photographs in the press of Hitler doing his crazy little jig outside the railway coach at Compiègne, where the great Foch had accepted the German surrender just twenty-one and half years previously, and of German cavalry riding down the Champs Élysées. It all seemed quite inconceivable. What had happened, in a bare six weeks, to the mighty French Army in its impregnable Maginot Line, about which we had read so much in the pages of the *Sphere* over the months of the Phoney War? Cousin Cecil had got out of Dunkirk with the remnants of his battalion (for which he won the DSO), but they were armed with only their rifles. I came down to London for half-term, and Uncle Henry took us all out to the Savoy Grill, in an attempt to cheer Cecil up. Gaunt and drawn, he was now wearing the red tabs of a brigadier, and gazed around the room at the guzzling, business-as-usual civilians with ill-disguised contempt. He was equally contemptuous of the French Army, whose soldiers had dropped their guns and run at the first sight of the Panzers. Some of our own troops had also not been 'very steady', and (he confided to Eve) he had come within an inch of shooting several with his own revolver. In between the terseness of his words, one could read the horror of the endless dive-bombing by screaming Stukas, of the shock troops, unstoppable with their portable flame-throwers, of unspecified 'secret weapons' – and of the devastating efficiency of Hitler's military machine. Suddenly the world seemed a dangerous and lonely place.

Stowe, however, was buckling down to the dangers with a remarkable degree of calm resolution. Every night sixth-formers would go out to drag tree-trunks across the cricket pitches, to prevent the landing of German parachutists; boys aged over fifteen in the Officers' Training Corps would join up with the Local Defence Volunteers (recently created by Anthony Eden) on night patrols, hunting down rumoured fifth columnists. Signposts to Buckingham and Brackley disappeared. There were gas-alerts and first-aid practice. The bacon ration sank to four ounces; sugar and sweet rationing began. A grim-faced Merch summoned the House to announce details of elaborate evacuation plans to be implemented in the event of invasion, and warned us gravely of the evils of rumour-mongering. The lines of A. P. Herbert that we had read in May –

> Do not believe the tale the milkman tells;
> No troops have mutinied at Potters Bar,
> Nor are there submarines at Tunbridge Wells –
> The BBC will warn us when there are

– no longer seemed quite so funny. Lying in bed at night, one could hear the curiously unsynchronized notes of the German bombers heading for the midlands airfields, like nearby Upper Heyford. I thought of the heroic little Edmund Gwenn, defending his blazing house, put my head under the blankets and tried to swallow down any tell-tale signs of the rising tide of fear. But we were vastly comforted by the stirring words of Winston Churchill, on the House wireless: 'This was their finest hour.' Stowe was supremely ready.

As of September 1939, the biggest *Völkerwanderung* in British history had taken place. Though not accompanied by anything approaching panic, it had been spurred on by the RAF's grossly inflated pre-war estimates of air-raid losses, in turn underscored by the grimly realistic scenes of *An Englishman's Home*, which were being so horrifyingly re-enacted on the wretched Poles during the first days of the war. Although the zest for evacuating children was less than it had been at the time of Munich the previous year, amid scenes of mass tearful chaos, main-line stations were flooded out as the official evacuation of over 3.5 million mothers and children clutching teddy bears and their cardboard gas-mask boxes got under way from London. The not-always-eager billetees received the princely sum of 10s 6d for the first child (compared with the wages of fifteen shillings a week that the 'tweenies' at Ropley received). Before the end of September, a quarter of the whole population had – incredibly enough – changed its address. It was, by any standard, a quite extraordinary achievement of logistics. But, in the deceiving calm of the Phoney War, by the beginning of 1940 four out of ten of the children had returned home, and nearly nine-tenths of the mothers with children under five. With May, however, the stampede had begun again – a further 230,000 unaccompanied children were evacuated over the ensuing three months. Following Dunkirk, offers to take in British children poured in from the Dominions and the USA. Under the aegis of the energetic Geoffrey Shakespeare, Under-Secretary of State for the Dominions, the Childrens' Overseas Reception Board (or CORB) was set up to marshal children between the ages of five and sixteen, attending grant-aided schools, whose parents wished them to seek safety abroad – for the duration.

Working night and day, by 4 July Shakespeare and his staff had sifted through over 210,000 applications and were obliged to close down the lists. Parents were expected to subscribe a nominal five shillings a week and – under attack – Shakespeare claimed that 94 per cent of the children dealt with by CORB came from working-class families. But, unfortunately for the scheme, rumours began to circulate that the rich were grabbing the shipboard places, and ugly questions were asked by Labour MPs in the Commons about the children of 'moneyed classes' enjoying luxury and safety in the US while the under-privileged languished. Whatever the truth of the allegations, CORB (which, whether as an acronym of some sort or as a comment on the efficiency of its operation, prefixed all telegrams with the letters CRAWL) never got off more than 3000 children before evacuations were suspended by a disaster in the autumn of 1940.

On 2 July, a Dutch-registered ship, the *Arandora Star*, carrying 1190 'enemy aliens' under armed guard to internment in Canada, was torpedoed. She also contained the Italian waiters from the Savoy Hotel. Seven hundred and fourteen of the deportees (including most of the unfortunate waiters) were drowned. No evacuee children were lost, but the sinking forced on a grudging and hard-pressed Admiralty a change in the rules of the game: henceforth the evacuee ships were placed in slow convoys. On 30 August, another Dutch vessel, the *Volendam*, was torpedoed 215 miles from the Clyde, with 321 CORB children on board. All were rescued, lustily singing 'There'll Always Be an England' – except for one nine-year-old boy, who slept through it all, came up calmly on to the deck of the sinking ship as daylight came, waved to a British warship and was rescued. But the sinking of the *Volendam* had caused a powerful reaction in Britain against the evacuations, in support of the view held by Churchill, who back in July had growled, 'I entirely deprecate any stampede from this country at the present time.' Then, on 17 September, came the real heartbreak tragedy. Bound for Canada, 600 miles out from

Liverpool, the *City of Benares* was sunk. Out of 406 people on board, 256 died, of whom 77 were children – in heavy seas and under dreadful circumstances. That marked the end of CORB – and, in fact, of virtually all evacuations.

Meanwhile, however, the freelance evacuations across the Atlantic had been gathering pace. Two days after Britain's declaration of war, Janet Davis, a Welshwoman living in Washington DC, had cabled the Foreign Office, offering her home to evacuated children. Whitehall reacted with uncharacteristic speed, accepting her proposal, which was given suitable publicity by her son Alec, a Washington-based journalist. According to Carlton Jackson, author of *Who Will Take Our Children?*, this initial pump-priming was then followed by offers of accommodation from tens of thousands of warm-hearted, anonymous and mostly middle-class Americans, simply out of a desire 'to do well by the Mother Country'. The vast majority were what would today be called Wasps, living in the eastern-seaboard states. Their early initiatives were backed up by the founding of the Committee for the Care of European Children, under the honorary chairmanship of Eleanor Roosevelt, the First Lady herself, while bodies like the American Red Cross joined hands with the Quakers to bring over as many as 20,000 children. On the West Coast, that great anglophile Douglas Fairbanks Jr planned to set up a large colony in Hollywood, composed entirely of British actors' children. Such was the pressure of demand that, in the States, one of the chief organizers, Mrs August Richards of Long Island, suffered a major nervous breakdown.

At the higher levels, not all motivations were entirely altruistic, it appears. At Westminster there were those who, evidently, saw in the well-marked American mercy ships a challenge to German U-boat commanders to 'sink an American ship sent over to fetch the children', which, if the challenge were accepted, would tilt world opinion decisively against the Germans, and possibly even bring the US into the war. In Washington, the British Ambassador, Lord Lothian, cherished the belief that the children would help the war cause, while, even more cynically, that most astute of politicians, Franklin D. Roosevelt, saw the evacuees as useful pawns. In the dreadful event of Britain falling to Hitler, the presence of thousands of her precious children in the US would also render it much more certain that Churchill would fulfil his promise to send the Royal Navy over to America.

By the time the various schemes had come to an end, with the torpedoing of the *City of Benares*, in addition to the 3000 children sent off by CORB, some 14,000 had been dispatched 'by private arrangement', of whom 5000 had gone to America.

It must have been early in July that the Merch sent for me. I hadn't let any bees out in prep recently, and wondered, nervously, what I could have done to cause his displeasure. With undisguised disapproval, he told me, 'Your father has decided to send you off to America. You're to go to down to London, today, to make the necessary preparations.' I joined my father at 5a Lees Place, the half-house he had once shared with Madame Scap. He was looking more careworn than I had ever seen him. The *Financial Times* share index had hit an all-time low of 49.4, while income tax had soared to the unprecedented level of 8s 6d in the pound, with additional surtax rates reaching 18s, or 90 per cent. He was deeply pessimistic. 'We'll surely defeat Mr Hitler, old boy, but we'll be ruined. Everything's going to be smashed up.' As a man who had created everything that he owned in his own lifetime, and by his own efforts, he was – perhaps understandably – more stricken than possibly a man of inherited wealth might have been by what the destructive consequences of total war would inevitably do to private property. 'We're going to lose everything, old boy. But you're my only son – and my most cherished possession, and I just want you to come through it, even if I don't.' I sat in silence, not quite knowing what to say. He went on, 'Mrs Breese – you like her, don't you? – has offered to have you live with her, as a member of her own family, just for the next few months – until it's all over.'

There was no question of 'Do you want to go?' It had all been decided. Some fifty years later, Quentin Crewe told me how his somewhat eccentric father had put a similar proposition to him that grim summer, but had added, 'You are old enough to decide'. At thirteen, a year younger than me, Quentin thought it all sounded marvellous and replied, 'Oh yes, Father, I'll go. I'll go.' 'What?' his father exclaimed. 'Have you no patriotism, boy? You'd run away from your country in its hour of need? You're a little coward, that's what you are.' In fact, the option was not even on offer: he was just being tested out by his bizarrely unpleasant father. (Quentin subsequently recounted the story in his engaging and deeply moving memoirs, *Well I Forget the Rest*.) I had mixed feelings. America sounded terribly exciting, I *did* like Mrs Breese and I wouldn't have minded getting away from Stowe – if nothing else, before I lost my virginity there. But, with the first tentative rounds in the Battle of Britain already being fought overhead, it seemed only a matter of time before Hitler would invade – and I didn't want to be a rat. My father read my thoughts: 'You're only fourteen, old boy, there's really not much you can do to help.' He did not actually say, quite as brutally as he might have done, 'You're just another mouth', but I knew that that was what he meant. I shrugged my shoulders and felt confused. It had all been decided, unilaterally, as my father had always decided things. I was going, and that was that.

We spent a tedious day in Grosvenor House, waiting to fill in the necessary forms. The whole of the great ballroom had been turned into an *ad hoc* briefing extension of the US Consulate. Platoons of Americans, locally conscripted for the task, strained but friendly, sat at card-tables asking hundreds of unhappy-looking parents the same questions, and writing down the answers. It was a matter of wait and shuffle, shuffle and wait, along barriers of white tapes all that long, boring day. There was at least one air-raid warning in the course of it. I suddenly decided, miserably, that I didn't want to go. It was too late – it was my turn. I answered the questionnaire, and my father paid up (I think about £25 for the rail passage and boat tickets). Handed an identity tag to attach to my lapel, I was told that I was to be ready at a moment's notice and that I could take only two suitcases with me. We had a solemn, silent meal in a nearby restaurant. Cecil (now wearing the ribbon of the DSO he had won on the Dunkirk retreat) and Cousin Eve were there, their disapproval all too evident. All at once I felt a million miles from them all, and I wanted to cry. The closeness I had at last begun to establish with my father the previous golden summer had evaporated. It was all too irrevocable. Uncle Newt, his white moustache droopier than usual, filled my ears with gloomy forebodings. The Americans! They hadn't joined in the last war until it was all but won, and then they had let us down afterwards. They were perfidious. They were sloppy, and they chewed gum. They were not quite like other people. . . . But it was up to me to show the flag.

I went back to Stowe, to pack up. In the dormitory I was ragged about running out, and the ragging turned nasty. P—, with the Gauleiter eyes, twisted my arm so badly I thought he had broken it. I said goodbye to the few friends I had made in the House and went home to Ropley, with my arm in a sling. My father appeared not to notice – but I wondered what he thought. I dismantled my wirelesses, painfully wrapped the valves in newspaper and packed them in my Stowe tuckbox. Did I have a moment to record – with joy and gratitude – the cooing of the white fantails, the cawing of rooks on the Pilgrims' Way behind the house, the lunchtime baying of the Hampshire Hounds across the meadow, the fragrance of the box-hedges on a hot summer's day, the myriad butterflies fluttering on the buddleias, and the sheer beauty of every aspect of Ropley – despite all the past loneliness? Could I take any of it to America with me? I said goodbye to Kenyon and Frederick (he, of course, had been to America, and told me that all the roads were six lanes wide and that the second 'c' in Connecticut was silent), and – more morosely – I bid farewell to Night, Rajah (old Dick had long since been gathered) and, especially, to Terry. I somehow knew I would never see any of them, or Ropley, again.

Almost immediately, I was in that tearful crowd at Euston Station, appropriately tagged and carrying the inevitable gas-mask, which was soon to be collected from me. I don't recollect my father's last words, but they were something about being your country's ambassador: be thoughtful, work hard, give my love to Mrs Breese – and you'll soon be back. Please write every week; I shall look forward to your letters. And then we were off on the *Britannic*.

CHAPTER FIVE

A Brave New World

We all became more silent, pensive, as we came closer to New York. Perhaps we were getting bored with the long voyage, with each other. The weather was becoming markedly hotter and my cabin-mate's feet, in our stuffy quarters, increasingly offensive. Tempers were strained. Spending more and more time on deck, I gazed back over the swirling, zigzagging wake, hundreds of miles of it in the empty Atlantic desert, and thought of Cornwall – watching with Terry the fierce seas as they pounded relentlessly up against Pentire Point hundreds of feet below, or the great surf rollers that thundered in across the sand of Polzeath beach, exhilarated by the ozone the spray brought with it. Suddenly when we awoke one morning (the ship's log of the lost *Britannic* reminds me that it was 28 July 1940, a Sunday) there was America: the great backdrop of the skyscrapers, of which we had all seen so many photographs, like unreal piles of Lego bricks; then the dignified Statue of Liberty, all pale green and waving its welcoming torch at us, as it had at so many other millions of hopeful arrivals from Europe. Amid much hooting and tooting, and churning propellers, little tugs shoved and cajoled us to a berth, among a seemingly endless row reaching up the Hudson River. Sad thoughts and homesickness abruptly disappeared – the great adventure had begun. Stevedores and self-important US customs officers were teeming aboard. Somewhere in the vast crowd, I hoped, would be Mrs Breese's welcoming face, that George Washington profile. Shepherded by Mrs Fleischmann of the sorrowful eyes, we were led in orderly lines into one of the ship's restaurants, which had been converted into an *ad hoc* customs shed.

It was searingly hot. None of us had ever experienced anything quite like it. Little English girls, specially got up for the occasion in their best party frocks, crumpled tearfully in the heat like melting candles. Air-conditioning simply did not exist in those far-off days. We were segregated by more of those parallel barriers of white tape (each time I arrive at JFK Airport, I still recall, and always will, that opprobrious day of July 1940), and the wait seemed even more protracted – and deliberate – than it had a few weeks previously in Grosvenor House. Frantic 'sponsors' rushed hither and thither in search of their swooning new charges. The officials, if not actually hostile, were definitely not friendly. They were, one thought, perhaps resentful at having to spend their Sunday dealing with a motley group of British evacuees. ('Probably all Irish,' explained Mrs Breese later, by way of filling the lacunae in my historical knowledge. 'They do *hate* the English.') Were any of us children, I wondered subsequently, turned back home – or transferred to the dreaded Ellis Island? An official looked at my imposing wooden Stowe tuckbox: what was in it? Bits of a wireless, said I. 'A *what*?' I explained. 'Oh, you mean a *radio*. Will it transmit? If so, you'll have to have a licence.' I assured him that it couldn't possibly transmit. He looked mistrustful. For a dreadful moment I thought I was going to lose all Messrs A. F. Bulgin's lovingly assembled parts, all last summer's work. Had I anything else to declare? Years later, I rather wished I had had the wit to make a declaration of the genes of all those eccentric, unsought and distinctly unAmerican forebears that I was bringing with me into 'God's Country'.

Then, all of a sudden, somewhere in the course of that suffocating morning, there appeared the saintly Julia Breese, as warm and compassionate as I always remembered her. She gave me the biggest of hugs, was adorably sympathetic about the day's ordeal, apologetic about the heat (even by New York standards it was, she explained, something of an unusual heatwave) and whirled me off in a large, grey, streamlined Dodge that moved as noiselessly as a whisper and as gracefully as Ginger Rogers. At the wheel was a grave and dignified Negro, the first I had ever set eyes on, called Thurman, with a gentle southern voice. As we pulled away from the turmoil of dockland (today, it seems hard to remember that this dead area was once one of the greatest ports in the world, with over one hundred berths in a row), I felt bewildered and stunned by the strangeness of New York – and a little frightened. And the devastating, stifling heat seemed to come up at one from all sides. Passing through a poor area, I spotted that time-honoured 'neighbourhood' custom, small black children dancing round an open fire hydrant, having an uproarious time and cooling themselves down. Wishing I was with them, my wilting spirits momentarily raised, I roared with laughter and exclaimed to Mrs Breese, 'Oh, look at the little piccaninnies!' She went red, poked me gently in the ribs, frowned and touched her lips. I couldn't see what I had said wrong, till later she gave a little lecture on usage and certain taboos. Thurman's face in the car mirror remained grave and dignified.

With warmth and concern, Mrs Breese asked me about England, my father, Ropley – and the dogs. I answered, in the desultory, noncommittal manner of an English fourteen-year-old of the 1940s. She did everything to break down my reserve, but, to her natural American openness, the conversation must have seemed formal and difficult. I suppose we shared the same thoughts: how were we going to cohabit together, for the indefinite period ahead? (Neither of us, of course, ever foresaw that it was to last over three years.) To begin with, what was I going to call her? For me, there was no question – it just had to be 'Mrs Breese'. And so it stuck, for the duration.

We arrived at the Chatham, a marvellously old-fashioned (by New York standards) hotel on East 48th Street where she had booked rooms – she lived permanently down south and had just come up to New York to collect me off the ship. She appraised me, sweltering in my sodden and by now shapelessly drooping Stowe grey flannels, and remarked that the next day when the shops opened, we would have to go off and buy some cool summer clothes. Then, manifestly by way of cheering up this lost little evacuee, and perhaps mistaking my suffering from the unEnglish heat for homesickness, she said, 'If you're not too tired, I thought I might take you out to the World's Fair this evening, when it's cooler.'

The World's Fair! It suddenly woke me out of my stupor. Here was a striking, but somewhat indigestible, first glimpse of America. The vastness and the dazzling splendour of its many pavilions out at Flushing Meadows numbed the senses. Inside a copper-clad building I gaped at the man-made lightning where millions of volts jumped between two great metal globes; ogled at the Aquacade where hundreds of wildly pretty girls with long slim legs (including the famous Esther Williams) swam in precisioned unison, forming giant living stars and flowers in the water, in time to languorous music. This was indeed a brave new world, different from anything I had ever seen or imagined before. I felt a million miles from England. Yet, as we drove back to New York, the picture of the great evil cloud of black smoke that had hung over Dunkirk kept thrusting itself back into my mind.

Quite awed by all that I had seen, on returning to the stifling city that night I found that Mrs Breese's thirty-year-old and only son Billy and his recently married Canadian wife Nora were there at the Chatham to greet us. Immensely tall and good-looking, with a drawl that sounded even sleepier than his mother's, very reserved and shy, Billy asked me what I had thought of the World's Fair. With typical English schoolboy's understatement, and having been brought up to eschew any display of excessive enthusiasm, I replied that it was 'not bad' or 'quite nice'. Billy looked disappointed, if not dismayed. For the second time already that day I felt I had perhaps not come up to scratch, but couldn't quite think why. For a long time afterwards, I was oblivious to how such a display of 'British phlegm' infuriated Billy, and indeed most of his countrymen. Eventually, he could bear it no longer and wrote me a long polemic on the importance of enthusiasm.

The next day, Mrs Breese marched me down the great canyon of Madison Avenue to fit me out, as promised, with some 'suitable' clothes. I wasn't sure of the image, but at least I felt almost cool for the first time. I came out of Wallachs with a racy straw hat (everybody, men and women, in New York all seemed to wear hats in those days), looking – I felt – like a 1920s film gangster. Equally I wasn't sure of the loquacious salesmen, affecting, in their impenetrable Brooklynese, not to understand my English. Why, I wondered, was it also so difficult to buy a simple comb? 'Oh, you mean a *coooomb*,' said the girl in the drugstore, irritatingly. My ruffled feelings were soothed by the introduction to a velvety, scrumptious raspberry ice-cream soda – the beginning of a long addiction. Our next stop was to the Liberty Music Shop on midtown Madison Avenue. There, among other marvels of American modernity, was the latest wonder – a tiny, truly portable radio by RCA Victor, the smallest produced to date, a masterpiece of miniaturization with four minute valves ('tubes' they called them) and tiny batteries, that made my poor, dismembered Colt seem like a dinosaur. Seeing my wide-eyed amazement, Mrs Breese, with the typical generosity I remembered from Ropley days, promptly bought it for me. I was overwhelmed, but once again felt gagged in my appreciation. It was a wonderful present. The tiny set went with me everywhere, keeping me in touch not only with the war, but with the latest Tommy Dorsey hits as well, came back to England with me in my RAF kitbag and survived the war to be the envy of my friends at Cambridge years later.

Bit by bit I began to get to know this generous, saintly but quite (by American standards) reserved lady on whom I had been foisted. Having come, subsequently, to regard her and all her family as part of my own over the long years that were to succeed the war, I find it now not easy to describe that first encounter. In her late fifties, she had not had an altogether happy life, which showed in the lines on her face. Her husband, Lawrence Breese, whom she had adored, had been an American by birth on both sides, but – following his father's death – his mother had married an Englishman and had gone to live in England. Lawrence had been brought up and educated there, acquiring as a result a passionate love for England. Aged nineteen, he set off to make his fortune as a miner in Alaska. Four years later, he met Julia Fish in the States and married her. In 1914 they were living in a mining community in California. Immediately he left for Europe, to volunteer to fight for England. In order to join the British army, he had to abandon his nationality, but, 'Had he lived, he would have taken back his American citizenship,' Mrs Breese explained to me. 'So you see, he was really not an Englishman, but just an unusually brave man.' Lawrence was killed in France, in March 1915 – one of the very first Americans to die in that war. Widowed, with two small boys, Billy and Hamilton, Julia herself volunteered to drive an ambulance in France. The stoicism of the wounded prisoners of war whom she tended left her with great respect, if not liking, for the Germans. This was not accompanied by any parallel affection for the French allies. She had once seen a Frenchman spit in the face of one of the German wounded, lying on a stretcher, who had been in her care, an incident which she had never forgotten – nor forgiven. She felt that the French lacked generosity, of which she was so full herself. Worse still, they were not kind to dogs – in the way the British were.

Billy and Ham were sent to a prep school in Sussex, but the tragedy of Lawrence's death in Julia's young life was soon compounded when little Ham died of pneumonia there, aged nine, shortly after the war ended. Heartbroken, she returned to America. But she never lost any of the deep affection for Britain that she had shared with her husband, returning whenever she could – which was how she became such a regular visitor to Ropley. In America she led a secluded and rather lonely life, between a little house in Aiken, South Carolina and an apartment in Washington DC (she found the northern winters hard to come to terms with), where she worked tirelessly for the British War Relief – or 'Bundles for Britain'. She was, I suppose, one of the very few people I have known who came near to being a saint. Certainly it would have been impossible to find a kinder, more sympathetic 'foster-parent' for an uprooted British child. But saints are not always easy to live with; they have such high standards. The previous year, in 1939, after years of assiduous match-making by his mother, Billy had finally married a pretty blonde pixie of a Canadian, Nora Magee, as tiny as he was tall, as vital, funny and quick-witted as he was gentle and slow-moving. They too lived in Washington, with one small baby, Belinda. An enthralled Mrs Breese constantly referred to Nora as 'the perfect daughter-in-law' and was determined to reciprocate by being the perfect mother-in-law – and keeping at a distance. In her loneliness she did not always succeed, and life could not always have been easy for the young couple.

Beyond her compassion for human beings, however, it was dogs that Julia Breese really loved, and suffered for, to the point of eccentricity. Her house was constantly occupied by strays she had picked up, or, as often as not, high-bred pets that had slipped away temporarily from their owners – leading often to some unfriendly words. She collected dogs as other American women collected shoes, and could never pass one on the street without speculating critically about its home life, however well favoured and prosperous-looking, convincing herself of its maltreatment. Walking down Park Avenue, even, could be quite an embarrassment (I discovered) as she would loudly question the wellbeing of the most corpulent, pampered creature with a fur-coated dowager on the other end of the lead. It was even said, in the family, that she would never eat a hot-dog – just in case. She bore the cross of every dog in the world on her shoulders, and it must have led to much unhappiness. But, reared on Dr Dolittle, I loved her for it.

The cheering-up process, to which blessed Mrs Breese dedicated herself selflessly, went on for two or three days. In between intermittent ice-cream sodas to assuage the heat, she rushed me round Manhattan on a boat and up the Empire State Building. I couldn't believe the rocket-like propulsion of the elevators up its 102 floors, or the staggering view – the like of which I had only seen once before from the ramshackle aeroplane that flew me out to school at Le Rosey one term – gazing down at mile upon square mile of the strangely shaped stalactites thrusting erratically upwards at me. Naturally I thought of King Kong, clasping the pinnacle that had once been used as a tethering post for zeppelins, and felt vertiginously sick when they told me (erroneously) that, in a high wind, the great skyscraper could sway as much as nine feet. Not quite ten years old, the world's tallest building seemed to me then to epitomize all that was modern and fantastic about America. Now, thrusting up from an otherwise slightly seedy area, it is old-fashioned and rather conservative.

We went to have tea in the little plaza that crouches under the soaring basalt columns of Rockefeller Center (somehow they reminded me of the cliffs of Cornwall), then into the vast auditorium of Radio City Music Hall – also the world's largest – to see the legendary Rockettes. Staggered by their precision, and by the length of their glorious legs, I still can't believe that, according to Jan Morris's wonderfully evocative book, *Manhattan '45*, to qualify as a Rockette a girl could be no more than five foot seven – but Jan never errs). Already a childhood Astaire addict, I half hoped for Fred and Ginger to come bounding on to the stage, clad in top-hats. It was entirely their city, and for that reason it began to grip me. The same day, Mrs Breese took me into the display rooms of the British War Relief, housed in one of the Plaza buildings. There was the fuselage of a downed Messerschmitt, a facsimile German bomb with a slit cut in it for collecting donations, and photographs of the Battle of Britain – which was just beginning – with Churchill's voice recorded in the background. It was all superbly and excitingly laid out. Mrs Breese introduced me as 'a little English boy who's just arrived'. I bridled at the 'little', but grew a foot with pride as those good and dedicated ladies treated me with gentle curiosity – and respect.

A few days later, still befuddled by the glamour of the World's Fair, the wonders of New York and its devastating heat, I left steamy, stupefying Manhattan. With Thurman at the wheel, we headed for Garrison-on-Hudson, to stay with Mrs Breese's younger sister, Rosalind Cutler. It was upon her that half the burden of my wartime sojourn in the States was to fall, they had decided between them. Because she lived close to the school in New York State where I was going to be sent, while Mrs Breese moved between Washington DC and far-off South Carolina, and also because she had children roughly my own age, it was with her unsuspecting family that I was to spend most of my time when not actually at school. Even though she had met my father only once, briefly, in England, in a very American way she had accepted the deal unquestioningly.

Garrison sits on the broad Hudson, some sixty miles out of New York, named because of the role it had filled during the War of Independence – alias the Revolution. Its picturesque old station was tarted up and used for the film set of *Hello Dolly!*, many years after the war. As Mrs Breese and I drove up into the wild countryside surrounding it, the July heatwave reached and passed its peak, and I had my first experience of America's climatic whims. A thunderstorm of tremendous force suddenly burst upon us. Trees were brought crashing down on either side of the road, frightened deer came bounding out of the forest and the car was finally driven to a standstill by the power of the rain and the hail. Then, as abruptly as it had started, the storm left off. Our ears still ringing with the thunder, we arrived at the Post Road Farm, perched high on a hill looking over wild wooded ridges down to the famous military academy of West Point, on the far side of the river. Above it all brooded a sky still full of angry-looking colours, such as only the Hudson can produce. Out of this faintly Wagnerian scene emerged a large lady with a shock of slightly greying hair – in a dress which seemed to begin nowhere and end nowhere, with great loose sleeves covering arms out-stretched like the prophet Elijah. I viewed her approach with some concern.

'So this is little Alistair. Well, I'm just going to call you Ally and you're going to be my sixth child.'

And so indeed it was. For all the three years of my stay in America, ungrateful, ungracious and pompous little English boy that I was, never for a moment was I allowed to feel that I was anything but the most wanted youngest addition to the five Cutler children. As an only child with one first cousin, it was my first experience of living in a large and noisy family, with endless equally noisy cousins constantly dropping in – and at first it was decidedly daunting. It was also very soon apparent that this big lady was the centre, the fulcrum and the focus of this vast clan. Although from the photographs and busts of her as a young woman I judged she must once have been a great beauty, with a classical American profile, she had become blissfully unaware of external trappings. To her, clothes were for basic propriety and comfort only (as I later discovered in New York, her one concession on especially chic occasions was an elderly fox, brought out of the closet, with its paw clenched between its teeth – a source of much merriment among the children). This disdain for 'dressing up' was something shared with her sisters, Janet and Helena as well as Julia – though, by comparison with Rossy, all three might have been clad by Madame Scap. Although they were as close and fond of each other as two middle-aged sisters possibly could be, she and Mrs Breese could hardly have been more different: while Julia Breese was essentially introvert, gentle and shy, almost ascetic, suffering daily from contact with the many things that distressed her in the outside world, and instinctively pessimistic, Rossy Cutler was the reverse. Extrovert, noisy, with unshakeably robust nerves, she loved life and especially its dramas. She was a total optimist; neither world catastrophes nor personal disasters ever made her downhearted – in fact, the worse things went, the more she seemed to thrive. (After the war, for example, when a favourite grandson had illegitimate twins at a tender age, something then unheard of within the confines of the *Social Register*, Rossy Cutler was positively delighted – not least for the special standing it afforded her among her smart bridge-playing friends at the New York Colony Club.)

To Rossy Cutler the external world, and all its dramas, was really all that mattered. I question whether she ever had a moment of self-doubt or depression. If she did, she hid it miraculously well. As of 1940, her passion for Britain's cause was something she shared to the full with her elder sister Julia, but to Rossy it attained an extra pitch of excitement. Clarissa Avon, widow of the late Anthony Eden, remarked that, while the 1956 Suez Crisis lasted, the Canal itself had flowed through her drawing room. As I was soon to discover, the war truly seethed and boiled through the Cutlers'. For kindness and exuberant warm-heartedness, Rossy Cutler surely had few peers – even in big-hearted America. But, as I discovered with equal rapidity, she was also a terrible tease. Hardly had I spent one night at historic Garrison than I was told of the exploits of the wicked British Tories in the Revolutionary War; I was taken to see an ancient (hardly by English standards) house where (reputedly) lodged a musket ball fired by a brutal Lobster-Back; I was shown the bend on the river at Trophy Point where the kinsmen of those 'embattled farmers' had stretched a chain to keep out the British fleet;* I was shown where Benedict Arnold had betrayed Washington, and where a British spy, Major André, had been hanged. I was drawn again and again into heated defence of my country. I rose splendidly and never ceased to rise – and how the teasing went on!

In the Cutler household it was impossible to maintain a low profile, hide behind a book, keep one's thoughts to oneself at meals, or remain neutral in the face of the arguments and controversies that seethed through the house. Rossy was a demon at drawing the shyest creature out of its shell, enticing one into some provocative remark, twisting it around, and then throwing it like a bone to the room at large. It was all too easy to fall into the trap. 'How do you like our American food, Ally?' she would ask, so innocently. Frankly, I was finding it pretty terrible, after the first raptures of a paradise without rationing had faded. The bread was tasteless and had the texture of cotton wool; ditto the much vaunted chocolate Hershey Bars; 'squash' was like a marrow gone wrong, with frightful fibres that straggled down one's throat, like trying to eat a dishcloth; peanut-butter, staple diet to every young American, looked terrible and tasted worse, and had to be emulsified with great quaffs of liquid. I longed for Mrs Bufton's tasty, simple English country cooking. It seemed bizarre beyond belief to eat, as a vegetable with meat, sweet potatoes in marshmallow sauce (though, with an insatiably sweet tooth, I later came to love it). As for apple pie with *cheese*! I had never seen corn-on-the-cob before, and it irritated me by the way it stuck between the front teeth.

---

* In her will she left me a Currier & Ives print of the very place. I felt the tease continued beyond the grave, but prized it all the more.

My ignorance provoked roars of laughter down the Cutler table: 'Oh, Ally, why, have you never seen corn before?' Bridling, I retorted, 'No, in England we feed it to the cattle.' The fat was in the fire, seized upon with mock outrage by Rossy, the remark echoed endlessly across the Hudson Valley to the bridge tables of the Colony Club. 'So what kind of food *do* they eat in England, Ally?' Pining for Mrs Bufton's cooking, I mentioned rabbit and steak-and-kidney pie. Again, there were roars of laughter. 'But rabbits are vermin. They have tularaemia – nobody *eats* them.' What about steak-and-kidney pie, then? I suggested nervously. More laughter. 'Why, that's *offal!*' they exclaimed. 'Nobody eats *that* in America!' Pronounced roughly the same, 'awful offal' became a family slogan.

Involuntarily, under Cutler teasing I found myself criticizing the language (surely it wasn't good grammar to say, when setting off in a car, 'Ally, get in back'?), the noisiness of American families, the cheeky brattishness of their young children, and the opulent size of the cars that wallowed grotesquely down the country lanes. And I felt genuinely shocked (and probably said so) by the affluence and waste, compared with the wartime Britain from which I had just come. Then there was the affair of my 'sitting room'. Bunked in with nineteen-year-old Peter Cutler in a cosy but tiny twin-bedded attic, I was alleged to have demanded querulously, 'But where's my sitting room?' I don't recall the episode, yet, fifty years later, it remains embedded in the family archives, retailed on all suitable occasions.

It was not long before, to all friends and family, and shamelessly in my hearing, Rossy Cutler would be remarking, 'I think little Ally really *hates* America!' It was all part of the tease, I realized, but there were times in those first months when I couldn't disagree with her. Even when I had sprouted to a gangly six feet two and was about to depart for the RAF, I would still be introduced, to my huge embarrassment, as 'This is Ally, our little Bundle from Britain.' The question was, what to call her? Her own children called her 'Mootsie'; to hundreds of adoring nephews, cousins and friends, she was just '*Ant* Rossy'. But, with true British formality, as with Julia Breese, for the duration she was to remain just plain 'Mrs Cutler'. In any case – although for the next three and a half decades, until her death, she was to be forever 'Aunt Rossy' and one of the leading influences in my life – as of 1940, I wasn't at all sure just how close I wanted to let this vast, exuberant and mocking lady get to me.

Apart from the teasing, I gradually came to realize that Rossy Cutler's boisterous, uncomplicated affection, enthusiasms and sense of fun were simply not to be repelled. Above all, in those lonely, terrible days of 1940 when from afar it seemed as if all England were being razed by the Nazi Blitz and as if there would be no end to the despairing retreats – from Greece, then Crete, then Cyrenaica, and finally all South-east Asia – there were times when one looked desperately for a rock to which to secure one's faith that the war would yet be won. And so often it was Rossy Cutler who provided that rock. When she was around, with her unshakeable optimism, one somehow knew that all would be well, sooner or later. It wasn't Pearl Harbor or the strategy of Churchill that *really* brought the irresistible weight of America on to our side – it was women like Rossy Cutler. In spite of her teasing, from the word go England's cause was her cause, the war her war. On the personal plane, the war was food and drink to Rossy Cutler. She read every war book at immense speed, ten pages at a time, she hung upon the words of the commentators: 'Ally, do turn on the radio – I must hear what Elmer Davis says about Tobruk.' On the putting green at Garrison, and in her New York drawing room at 80th Street, the war was fought anew. Excitement was an essential part of her life: where it was, she would be. And if there was no excitement, she would create it. A challenging remark, an outrageous statement, and a sanguinary political battle would be launched – Rossy Cutler, Cadmus-like, standing aside to watch the armed men knock each other down.

From photographs in the house at Garrison, dating back to 1907 I judged that John and Rossy must once have been an incredibly good-looking couple. He still was. In his late fifties, with wavy silver hair, a give-away pink complexion and a clipped Boston accent, still with the robust figure of a Crimson team football player, his charm was immense. It was less so on those occasions when he managed to slip across the stone wall (dodging the rattlers that were reputed to lodge there) to spend the afternoon with his hen-pecked brother-in-law, Harry Forster, and the two would emerge from the secret hut in the wilderness, in which numerous bottles had been carefully hidden, with a skinful. Then he would tend to be somewhat irascible. 'Aunt Helena' Forster, Rossy's younger sister, an angular, leathery lady who shared little of Rossy's sense of humour and ran the not very profitable farm, would look forbidding and disapproving. Rossy would appear to notice nothing. John (who from the start always treated me as if I had been part of the family forever, and would often rally to my support when Rossy's teasing got out of hand) was an investment banker who had lost much of his capital in the 1929 Crash. This had left the family, in 1940, just comfortably off, but certainly not rich by American standards. At Post Road Farm, there was barely room for the seven, large grown-ups to squeeze in. In New York, at 58 East 80th Street, they owned one of the classical brownstone houses that today would be worth a fortune, but then was regarded as rather far uptown, a bit near the 'frontier' – meaning Harlem.

The unity of the Cutlers as a family was imposing. No Highlanders could be more fiercely clannish than these Bostonians, who originated, many years before, from humble English yeoman stock. The family name had become almost synonymous with Harvard. There can rarely have been a time in living memory when there had not been one or more Cutlers attending that most ancient of all the Ivy League colleges. And to be a Cutler and to have been to Harvard *without* having been elected to the exclusive Porcellian Club was nearly as bad as having been sent down from Oxford for 'gross and continued immorality'. Strong men had been known to throw themselves in the Charles River if they did not make election. You could be sure that on entering a Cutler house the first thing you would see would be a pig, the PC emblem: a pig door-knocker, a pig doormat, pig salt-cellars, pig footrests and pig hairbrushes. (Indeed, when a Cutler once visited me at Cambridge, I had great difficulty in dissuading him from making off with the huge effigy of the Blue Boar to add to the family collection.) In John's generation of Cutlers, there were five brothers all bursting with vitality and all successful in their various fields. There was John the eldest; Elliot, one of America's top surgeons and who, in the Second World War, became general in charge of all SHAEF's medical services (and now has a Professorship at Harvard Medical School named after him); Roger, the Commodore; George, the lawyer and banker; and Bobby, later President Eisenhower's special assistant for National Security and one of the inner circle of White House advisers. All except Bobby had large families, and when all of them came together at some Cutler reunion, the noise and rowdy warmth generated was astounding – almost like a college club or football team itself.

Rossy Cutler's marriage provided a bridge between two of the old east's more distinguished families – the Fishes of New York and the Cutlers of Boston. But her own family (and Julia Breese's), the Fishes, were considerably the grander, going back as far as the United States themselves. They had somewhere along the line crossed with the Stuyvesants, descendants of old one-legged Peter Stuyvesant, the Dutch first Mayor of New Amsterdam – alias New York City). A lady who combined these two illustrious names, the wonderfully eccentric Mrs Stuyvesant Fish, was a source of some amused embarrassment to the Cutler-Breeses. As a great hostess in the last years of the past century (Mr Fish had become immensely rich, president of the Illinois Central Railroad while still in his twenties), she was America's answer to Maggie Greville – but infinitely more eccentric – and left her niche in history as the true founder of Café Society. 'Mamie' Fish evidently specialized in the gentle art of shocking people – decreeing that, at her table, cigarettes could be smoked with the soup. She hated the opera, which she decried as 'caterwauling in the street', and expelled from her soirées waltz-playing orchestras in favour of jazz musicians. A practical joker as well as something of a counter-snob, she once gave a dinner, in Newport, for Grand Duke Boris of Russia, then upstaged him by announcing that the Tsar himself was coming. In fact, it was a local humorist in disguise. But her greatest eccentricity, *épater les bourgeois,* was to deride her rival Newport hostesses by throwing a Dogs' Dinner, where the pampered pets made themselves revoltingly sick on plates of pâté de foie gras. What Julia Breese thought about Cousin Mamie's dinner party and all those dogs stuffed like Strasbourg geese, I never knew.

On a rather more elevated level, an illustrious Fish ancestor, Nicholas, had been the close friend of America's first financial wizard, Alexander Hamilton. In memory of this brilliant patrician, killed in his prime in a duel with one of American history's more controversial characters, Aaron Burr, nearly every generation of Fishes – down to the present day – has christened a son Hamilton. Perhaps the most famous was the Hamilton Fish who had been General Ulysses Grant's Secretary of State – sometimes described as the only honest man in that Cabinet. In 1940 the senior bearer of the name, the only brother of Julia Breese and Rossy Cutler, was also achieving a measure of notoriety. Congressman Ham Fish of Duchess County, NY, was the son of another Hamilton Fish who had served in Congress, and was in turn the son of yet another, also a Congressman (and Governor of New York State) – he who had served under Ulysses Grant. He liked to claim that he had 'shaken the hand that had shaken the hand of Lafayette'.

At fifty-one, Ham Fish was a huge, dominating man with craggy eyebrows, a former All-American football player who had captained Harvard (the family spoke of him in some awe as having once killed an opponent in a match), where he had been in the same class of 1910 as John Culter – to whom he had introduced his sister Rosalind. He was endowed with immense personal attraction – but not, in the eyes of most members of the family, with an equally immense amount of political good sense. As an officer with the famous US Rainbow Division in France in 1918, he came back with four decorations, including the US Silver Star and the French Croix de Guerre, and the rank of major – determined that 'foreign wars' were not for America. This was later reinforced by a healthy respect for the Germans. In August 1939 he outraged his anglophile sisters (as well as many constituents) by having tea with Hitler's Foreign Minister, Joachim von Ribbentrop, in Nazi Germany, and then availing himself of von Ribbentrop's plane to fly on a jaunt to Oslo. After twenty years as a Republican Congressman, by 1940 he had become one of the leaders of Congress's Isolationist lobby lampooned by the Interventionists as the 'Ham Fish–Rome–Berlin Axis'. It was his constantly reiterated view that, by dragging the country into a European war, President Roosevelt would 'plow under every fourth American boy'. He was Roosevelt's *bête noire* (and vice versa).

There was perhaps nothing more typical of the schisms that underlay pre-Pearl Harbor America than the rifts which Uncle Ham's extreme position opened up within the family. On one side were the 'America First' Hamilton Fishes; on another his two unreservedly pro-British sisters; and on yet a third flank the eldest sibling, Janet, who was so passionately francophile as to find it hard to espouse Britain's cause after the desperate, brutal sinkings of the French fleet at Oran and Dakar. (The fourth, Helena, the farmer from Garrison, observed a healthy neutrality by affecting total uninterest in anything outside the cow-barn.) The inter-family friction was bitter, the second generation joined sides with the first, and long years after Pearl Harbor the tragic wounds were still visible. Julia refused to speak to her brother during much of the war. Rossy, partly because Ham's picaresque, buccaneering allure appealed to her, but perhaps mostly because of her love of battle, kept the doors open.

So the war seethed through the drawing room of Garrison, across John Cutler's beloved putting lawn – and even on to the characteristically eccentric wooden tennis court. There, when young Ham Jr, my exact contemporary, came to stay, Rossy would set us up to play ferocious singles against each other, like some scene out of the Trojan War, amid bloodcurdling shouts from the sidelines of 'Up the Limeys!', 'Up the Interventionists!', 'Down with the America Firsters!' Then, in the middle of the fracas, spinster Aunt Janet, matron of Washington's biggest hospital, would arrive and – sitting bolt upright in her chair, hands in her lap in the best matronly manner – cry, 'Pox on both your houses!', heap obloquy upon Britain for letting down the French and declare what a fine, upstanding fellow Marshal Philippe Pétain was. Naturally I could seldom remain silent. It was the beginning of a superb political training, such as I had never known within the solitary confines of Ropley Manor.

On to this explosive scene, just after I arrived, there burst Jack, like a projectile from the front line. The eldest Cutler son, passionate, restless, idealist Jack represented the advanced guard of Rossy Cutler's Interventionist America. Few Americans were to have a more varied and exciting war than Jack, or be granted such a charmed life. With his lean and languid six feet four inches and (very American) good looks that somewhat resembled Hollywood's James Stewart, few had more opportunity than him to turn the war into a source of glamour. But equally few could have been less conscious of that glamour. Not for him the leisurely delights of Harvard and the Porcellian Club – Jack, still aged only twenty-two, had just returned from France with the American Field Service, which had tended the French wounded in the terrible rout of May 1940. I never knew what made him join the Field Service; perhaps he did not know himself. At any rate, the piteous columns of refugees and the stark horror of war had left a searing impression upon him, setting him apart from his carefree contemporaries in that precariously serene American summer of 1940. Beneath a nervous laugh, he was seething with an explosive anger that was easily detonated by those who had not seen what he had seen and did not understand how close to home it all now was. Like his mother, Jack was appalled by American weakness. Did we realize, he would tell us, that, as of April 1940, the US ranked *twentieth* among the world's military powers? 'We have a smaller army than the Dutch had – and Hitler smashed them up in a couple of days.' Uncomfortable though Jack was to have around the house, Rossy Cutler was immeasurably proud of him. He was her personal stake in the war, and I found in him a natural ally – and hero. Increasingly ill at ease and unsettled in peacetime America, within a few months Jack was back in the war.

When Jack was about, the strife with Uncle Ham and Aunt

Janet, sometimes reaching boiling point, assumed a new immediacy, with Rossy Cutler fuelling the flames. The onset of the presidential campaign, between the veteran FDR and the unknown Republican from the Midwest, Wendell Willkie, which was just getting into gear, began to bring the issues of war or neutrality into every American home. Under constant and immense pressure by Churchill to step up aid on the one hand, while beset by Ham Fish and the Isolationists on the other, Roosevelt was having to justify to the US electorate every inch of his progress towards intervention. To me, that menacing summer, the progress seemed far too steady, but, until then, I had no conception of just how rooted in various walks of American life was animosity towards Britain, towards its perceived arrogance, its Royal Family descended from the hated enemy, George III, its history, its customs – and its imperial power. And there were, of course, the Irish, with their potent memories of the Revolt of 1916, their politicians railing against 'shedding their blood a second time to save the British Empire'. From 1918 onwards, so I learnt, the US Navy had even looked on the Royal Navy as a potential enemy, in our (short-lived) alliance with Japan. When Neville Chamberlain declared war on Hitler in September 1939, the US began by maintaining the strictest neutrality, with polls showing that US opinion was then overwhelmingly against intervention on the Allied side. Hamstrung by the 'cash and carry' principle, it was only in the teeth of bitter opposition that President Roosevelt had, in November, managed to repeal the arms embargo. There were intriguing tales of how companies like Lockheed circumvented the strict terms of the Neutrality Act by towing planes across the Canadian frontier with North Dakota using teams of horses. Yet still Britain was having to pay for what few arms it could receive out of its rapidly vanishing dollar assets.

Strident German propaganda found much fertile ground to fall on. It was not, for instance, until a whole year had passed that Americans accepted the British version of the sinking of the liner *Athenia* in September 1939, on the day after war had been declared, rather than Goebbels's claim that it had been torpedoed by the wicked British themselves – to bring America into the war. The six months of inaction during the Phoney War had meanwhile done nothing to persuade Americans that Britain was in earnest about defeating Hitler. Under the imposing figurehead of Colonel Charles Lindbergh – every American boy's hero after his Atlantic solo-flight, and every American mother's hero after the tragic kidnapping and death of his baby – the America First Committee, adjunct to the Isolationists, was an articulate and powerful body. Even as late as Pearl Harbor, December 1941, it could boast 850,000 members. Indeed, polls revealed that, from September 1939 right through to December 1941, about one-third of the American population remained steadfastly isolationist. Inflammatory slogans popped up everywhere. 'Drive the British from Washington again. . . . Close the British propaganda offices.' To an impressionable fourteen-year-old, they were highly disturbing. Perhaps more dangerous, however, were the measured arguments of right-wing Republican leaders like Senator Robert Taft from Ohio, son of President Taft, who declared that Roosevelt 'confuses the defences of Britain with the defence of the United States', and who had come close to winning the Republic nomination over the unknown Willkie. When Roosevelt began talking about Lend–Lease to help out the dollar-impoverished British, Taft fired back acidly, 'Lending arms is like lending chewing gum. You don't want it back.'

Removed from our innocent gazes, a savage propaganda war was being waged underground in Washington and New York. The Purvis Mission was at work telling Congressmen what sort of weaponry Britain required, while, with utmost skill and dexterity, under cover of the British Library in New York and under the aegis of John Wheeler-Bennett, distinguished historian and man of irresistible charm, the British Information Services were helping to create the public mood which allowed the arms to be supplied. Arrayed against Ham Fish and the America Firsters, they had stalwart allies such as Senator Claude Pepper – shortly to be hanged in effigy outside the Senate by Washington women for his support of Lend–Lease – and the energetic William

Allen White, a Midwest republican, editor of the *Emporia Gazette*, who had founded the Committee to Defend America by Aiding the Allies, otherwise simply known as the White Committee.

Of course, the strongest card in the hand of the British Information Services was Winston Churchill. Across the States, in an age without television, women like Julia Breese and Rossy Cutler would be glued to their radios, often on the verge of tears, as that sonorous voice with its studied timing came across the ether. The impact of those two magnificent, defiant speeches of June 1940 – 'We shall never surrender' and 'This was their finest hour' – had been quite incalculable. Followed as they were at the beginning of July by the ruthless sinking of the French fleet at Oran, Roosevelt and the American public recognized that the British were, at last, in deadly earnest about fighting the war to the bitter end, about 'no surrender'. As a first material sign of that recognition, before the summer was over Roosevelt would be announcing the historic deal whereby Britain would be supplied with fifty ancient, 1917 destroyers urgently needed for convoy work in the North Atlantic, in exchange for ninety-nine-year leases on six Caribbean bases. It was a pretty tough bargain. Pete Cutler, the family's naval expert, reckoned that they were 'real old tin cans, top-heavy and roll like logs' – though, had it not been a tough bargain, it seems unlikely that FDR could have got it past the 'Ham Fish–Rome–Berlin Axis' in Congress.

The need for those old destroyers was just one of so many reminders of how desperately the war was going for Britain. With the conquered French ports that now enabled them to burst out of the Baltic, German U-boats were sweeping the Atlantic of British merchantmen. Bringing it all home to those who had safely made it to America came the news, in September, that the *City of Benares*, flagship of the Ellerman Line, had been sunk with the loss of 256 lives, including 77 children, four days out of Liverpool. One of the survivors, Tony Quinton (later Lord, and President of Trinity College, Oxford – and still later my next-door neighbour) had sat at a desk just across Mr Capel Cure's classroom from me only a few months previously. Always a portly small boy, he floated; only eight of the twenty-three passengers and crew in his lifeboat were alive when picked up, after twenty hours in tumultuous seas. But, endowed with an unfailing sense of humour, he always made light of it, claiming that, on returning to his grandmother's house in England, she barely looked up from weeding the flowerbeds, and remarked, 'Good heavens, are you back already?' The London *Times* damned it as 'Another hideous German crime', and it marked the end of the evacuation of the 'Bundles'.

With every hot, pleasant August day that passed in America, invasion seemed imminent. The Battle of Britain was at its height, magazines like *Time* and *Life* were full of spectacular photographs of the vapour trails of dogfights over the Channel, and claims of staggering Luftwaffe losses. Stories of the heroism and brilliance of 'The Few' (adroitly disseminated by Wheeler-Bennett and the British Information Services) were on everybody's lips, and they made one walk tall. But it was agonizing to be so far away from it all, to wake up every morning expecting to hear that Hitler had landed. And – remembering the pathetic, disarmed remnants that Cousin Cecil had brought home from Dunkirk – how could he effectively be repelled? The bad news came from every quarter, even the Duce's despised Italians had overrun British Somaliland, and the fortress of Sidi Barrani inside Egypt.

From home my father's letters, generally just one page written in his sloping, hard-to-read Relief Nib hand, came spasmodically. Though dispatched once a week, many were sunk. Sadly, those for 1940 (I have the rest still) seem to have been lost somewhere along the way, but I remember the gist of them. They were stalwart, always affecting cheerfulness and echoing Churchill's defiance, and often quoting him. They were not, however, overwhelmingly informative, leaving one with a thousand anxieties.

Despite these deep anxieties, however, life at Garrison among those kind, noisy Cutlers, getting to know my strange new family, was happy enough. Far off as those days are, when I close my eyes, with extraordinary vividness I can still see every detail of the furnishings, revive in my mind the human crises, the noises and the very smells of the Post Road Farm at Garrison, the Currier and Ives prints of old New York and carved American eagles upon the walls, the emblematic leather pigs and pewter fishes – and black lentil or cold vichysoisse for dinner, depending on the time of year. Behind the house was the 'swamp', allegedly full of poison ivy, copperheads and rattlesnakes, and to one side of it lay the tennis court, scene of those bitter political matches. I had never seen anything quite like it; it was built of slatted, creosoted wood, and we played with bright red balls. Eccentric in their bounce, often they would leap right out of the court. Then there would be cries of 'Ally, go get it. Limeys don't get poison ivy!' while all round the hummingbirds were pursuing their last helicopter-like flights of the day, darting their tiny needle beaks here and there into the orange blossoms of the trumpet vine that grew up the walls. Finally the sun would sink into a torrid bed behind West Point, behind Rip Van Winkle's Catskill Mountains, to be followed immediately by the orchestra of night sounds, the chanting of myriad cicadas, the ping of the maybugs striking the mosquito screens on the windows, and the accompanying noiseless but magnificent pyrotechnics of the fireflies. And I can see the room I shared with Peter Cutler, full of model schooners, dried and inflated globe-fishes, pocket knives with a hundred and one blades, gadgets for splicing ropes, and shelves crammed with scrimshanks made of walrus tusk, and every sort of book on the sea.

Captain Ahab's soul was no more deeply ingrained with the sea than was Peter's. Even at nineteen, Peter walked with the roll of the practised salt. As soon as he could, he would enlist as an ordinary sailor in the US Navy, with which he spent most of the war on a submarine net-tender in the South Pacific. The war over, he immediately shipped off to sea again as deckhand on a merchantman. No great success in the schoolroom, Peter was one of the best-natured human beings I have ever met. Although he was five years my senior, it was to him I used regularly to pass on the teasing I received at the hands of the other Cutlers, for example placing within reach of his greedy, candy-craving fingers marshmallows laced with laxatives. Yet he never once gave me a well-deserved hiding; on the contrary, we became the most inseparable of allies. It was with him that I used to go fishing for succulent black bass in the nearby Indian Lake, and with him that I used to indulge in the hazardous pastime of taking pot-shots at the snapping turtles which basked on the edge of the lake, with a .22 rifle from a wildly rocking canoe. It was with Peter that I went to the passing-out parades at West Point – carefree peacetime occasions, the chapel bells pealing out 'Jesu, Joy of Man's Desiring', where the cadets in their faintly *opera bouffe* uniforms hurled their caps in the air at the end of a moving ceremony, and where afterwards we would both ogle enviously pretty girls draped upon the arm of each newly commissioned cadet, as they strolled along Flirtation Walk on the ramparts above the Hudson.

Of the other four children, apart from Jack there was Peter's twin sister Pat, who – sadly for my buddy – had grabbed all the genes of both brains and beauty. She looked (and, in advanced years, still does) strongly like Katharine Hepburn, and had cultivated some of the great actress's marvellously cool, patrician manner, with considerable success. Recently graduated from school, she was leading the conventional life of the hotly pursued debutante, rushing off to tennis parties and balls in the ancient family convertible. The war did not affect her, then, perhaps as strongly as her mother, let alone Jack, with whom she would argue vigorously. The intruding 'Bundle from Britain' she regarded neutrally as something sent to try grown-up nineteen-year-olds, and – quite rightly – took to putting me in my place from time to time. Then there was Judy, who at sixteen was my nearest contemporary in the family. But she was temporarily out of town, on a riding-and-fishing trip out west in Wyoming with her new brother-in-law, Dicky Aldrich. Though absent, her name was constantly coming up in conversation, which made her something of a legend to me. I deduced that, as the baby of the family, she was certainly her father's favourite and was doted on by the ancient family retainer, Anna. I also formed the impression that she was something of a hellion, and had inherited much of her mother's talent as a tease. I viewed her return with curiosity – and apprehension.

The Cutler child I saw least of was the eldest, Susan, married and departed the previous year, before I had arrived on the scene. Her husband, Dicky Aldrich, scion of an ancient New York family – and, of course, a Harvardian – was plump and bonhomous, with a fund of anecdotes, and worked with an oil firm. His (second) passion in life was to get dressed up as a duck and sit for hours in a freezing blind on the edge of the Hudson, waiting for flights that always seemed to be heading for the neighbouring promontory. His first passion was something he shared with his father-in-law, John Cutler, and which was strictly banned from Rokeby, the ancestral home, by his terrifying mother – alcohol. Dicky, who always treated me as an adult, invited me to go ice-boating with him on the Hudson (generally vetoed by Rossy Culter, acting *in loco parentis*, on account of the appalling danger from bouncing over rough hummocks of ice at 60 m.p.h.). Later in the war, when he was sent by the US Navy to London to investigate Nazi synthetic rubber production, we became great friends and drinking companions – which, alas, was to lead to his downfall. His wife Susan, then in her late twenties, immensely tall with a mop of curly brunette hair, highly intelligent and well read, was as passionately anglophile as her mother; and was therefore particularly kind to me. But, in contrast to the rest of this rather happy-go-lucky clan, she was very serious-minded, a perpetual worrier (over the years, she had a lot to worry about) and the conscience of both families. If anyone had a problem, even if it was only how to catch the next train from Garrison, she would take it upon herself to resolve it. As far as the war was concerned, whereas her mother was always unfailingly optimistic, Susan tormented herself with dark foreboding. Life, I also felt, never gave her its fair share of fun.

Occasionally we would drive up the Hudson to spend the day with the Aldriches at Barrytown, not far from Franklin Roosevelt's Hyde Park. Here rolling mountains and steep cliffs make it one of the most beautiful sections of the great river. Early settlers evidently (and not unreasonably) saw resemblances with the

Rhine, giving it place names like Rhinecliff and Rhinebeck. But, as far as I could judge, that was about all there was of Germany. The Aldriches and their neighbours along that particular stretch of the Hudson were fiercely and uncompromisingly British – and eccentric. Rokeby, built by one of Washington's generals at the beginning of the nineteenth century, must once have been a magical place. But, already by 1940, it had seen better days – many better days. Over it ruled a formidable, widowed and sternly moralist chatelaine. Susan's mother-in-law, Margaret Aldrich, banned from the house all Catholic (or, for that matter, Episcopalian) converts, remarried divorcees and alcohol (the era of Prohibition lay only a decade in the past). To get a drink at Rokeby, so John Cutler once confided to me, you had to smuggle it inside teapots. One guest, parched with thirst in the middle of a torrid Hudson River night, on reaching out for the bedside thermos-flask of iced water, found himself taking a great swig of bootleg gin. Inevitably, of old Mrs Aldrich's two children, one got divorced and then married a lapsed Catholic, the second – my friend Dicky – died of drink. Instead of doing the decent thing and moving out when her son married, the widow Aldrich hung on until removed in a shroud. In the damage she did, she epitomized the worst king of strong-willed, high principled, God-fearing American matriarch. The life she imposed on Susan must have been, indeed was, intolerable and would never have been accepted by any contemporary American woman less laden with conscience than was she. I rather dreaded the visits to Rokeby, except when one could escape down to the great river with the perpetually good-humoured Dicky.

One August day, in the Cutler's capacious timbered Ford station-wagon, jolting and creaking like an ancient ship, we set off for Martha's Vineyard, with Rossy Cutler at the wheel, peering determinedly through a green eyeshade like that worn by a Hollywood sub-editor, one eye fixed on the road and the other scanning for Antique Shoppes. Julia Breese sat at her side. In the days before freeways, it was a long but leisurely day's drive, through the smiling pretty villages of coastal New England, with their white-steepled churches and clapboard houses. These were the kind of communities that I would shortly be reading about at school, in Sinclair Lewis's highly evocative *Babbitt* and *Main Street*. Their gardens, which were not separated by fencing – so different from the high, forbidding walls of rural England – made me marvel at the trusting, friendly openness of these Americans. At the same (and not the first or last) time, they offended my British upbringing with their lack of privacy.

As we reached Massachusetts, the slow-moving, pretty fishing communities with their grey-shingled roofs and barns of salt-box red, which looked as though they had been asleep since the War of 1812, when their yards laid down the keels of those fabulously fast ships that first established the repute of the American navy, made me think painfully of maritime England, of the Solent – the tempo, if not the architecture. So wonderfully tranquil, this was a world that hardly seemed to belong to the rush and worry of twentieth-century America – let alone of a world at war. With Julia Breese suffering occasional heart-failure as we traversed ungated railway crossings, the drive was interspersed with numerous acquisitive stops, and we arrived at the ferry at Woods Hole, Mass., a minute before it left, the station-wagon groaning with pewter platters in the shape of fish, chunky wooden salad bowls and every variety of symbolic pig. A rainy fog that might have been bottled in the Thames estuary and shipped over for my benefit clung to the whole surface of the sea. But the venerable ferry ploughed on relentlessly, blasting sailboats and small craft out of its way with its throaty foghorn, oblivious of all attendant dangers.

Suddenly the fog began to dissipate, and as a hole formed in it Martha's Vineyard appeared in the distance, turned by evening sunshine into a golden band floating on top of the sea. We all felt a curious sensation of excitement. I still do not know how to account for the magic of Martha's Vineyard, but it must be a powerful one, because, on revisiting it years later, in no other former haunt did I feel quite so strong a nostalgia. A flat island devoid of dramatic cliffs like Cornwall, alternately hot and sticky – or foggy – much of the summer, most of the Vineyard has no great beauty. Yet, for many a year, its peaceful charms continued to draw celebrities like Emily Post, Max Eastman, Katherine

Cornell, James Cagney, S. J. Perelman and van Wyck Brooks. It was (and still is) little more than an overgrown sand-bar, about twenty-five miles long and ten wide, with (in the 1940s) a permanent population of less than 5000, and in those years reachable only by ferry, which often did not sail because of fog. Except for one point, Gay's Head, there are no proper cliffs and most of the interior of the island is covered with stunted oaks. At one extremity is an immensely pretty and isolated fishing village called Menemsha, a mecca for New England artists. There is Oak Bluffs, in the centre of the island's coastline, democratic and bubbling over with uninhibited seaside fun and mild salacity and gingerbread boarding-houses. With its dodgem cars, merry-go-rounds, vulgar postcards and fried-fishy smells it might be Clacton or Ramsgate. Next to Oak Bluffs are the symmetrical promontories of East and West Chop, pointing towards the mainland some six miles away like the udder of a goat. Both are sprinkled with the houses of summer residents, but while West Chop is as lushly vegetated as the Massachusetts mainland, on its more exposed eastern twin little else but scrubby conifers and poison ivy will grow. Nestling between the two of them is Vineyard Haven, the island capital and principal harbour.

But it is really Edgartown that provides the island with its particular mystique, and it was there that the two sisters had rented a house for the rest of the summer. It was one of New England's most exquisite jewels – and still is, little spoilt despite the unwelcome publicity attracted to it first by Senator Edward Kennedy in the Chappaquiddick incident of August 1969 and later by the film *Jaws*. In her architecture she is perhaps inferior only to her sister, Nantucket, some twenty miles further out to sea. From the end of the eighteenth century to comparatively modern times, Edgartown and Nantucket, then two of the finest harbours in the world, became centres of the whaling industry. Those old whaling captains waxed exceedingly prosperous, and between their year-long voyages to the Antarctic and round the Horn, they built singularly handsome houses for their grass-widows. What was even more remarkable than the prosperity of these salt-encrusted Ahabs and Starbucks was the very great excellence of their taste. Their houses still stand on Edgartown's North Water Street, a row of dazzling white villas with dark-green shutters, gazing out over the harbour under shady catalpa trees. Some have colonnaded verandahs like southern colonial mansions, bounded by low white palings and fragrant box-hedges, but the loveliest of all are those with the curving double flights of brick steps that lead up to exquisitely decorated doorways with little rows of window panes set in at each side, and the fan-shaped architraves that are the glory of Georgian New England. And atop every house, just to remind you of its past, sits a balustraded Widow's Walk, where, abandoning the rocking chair on the porch, anxious wives would repair to watch, with telescope glued to the eye, for the return of the whaling fleet. Everything in Edgartown was on a miniature scale, which was perhaps part of the reason for its allure for mainlanders seeking refuge from the hugeness of American life. There was no room for a supermarket, and even the jail had room for only one miscreant.

Those were halcyon, happy weeks at Edgartown in the perilous month of August 1940. The rented house, just off the harbour and up by the tennis courts, was packed with a stream of Cutlers and cousins. There were the Forster children from Garrison: a rather lumpy thirteen-year-old girl who thought only of cows and chickens, and the two seven-year-old twins, who bickered constantly in high-pitched nasal whines. I decided I didn't much care for all-American brats. But Pete, my new friend, was in his element. He would take me down to the harbour and explain the differences between a yawl, a ketch and a schooner, and teach me how to sail a Cape Cod cat-about. He would watch in silent envy as the *Yankee Clipper* glided proudly out of her mooring with a crew of young navy cadets aboard, her magnificent raked masts under full sail. We would chat to the grizzled old swordfishermen, who might have been invented by Hemingway. Wearing comical caps with elongated visors that made them look a bit like their prey, they sat aboard their frail vessels, scraping down with penknife the sword of a recent catch, soon no doubt to be sold in the Main Street curio shop. The tiny swordfishing ketches, with their kind of crow's-nest fixed perilously at the end of a long bowsprit for the harpooner, seemed then – in the days before modern technology threatened to decimate the creatures of the seas – one of the glorious survivals of old New England. They provided the only commercial means of catching the richly succulent fish, an activity which still had its dangers and required as much skill and strength of arm on the part of the harpooners as in the days of *Moby Dick*.

The old fishermen were eager to tell us how they set about it: 'Well, first of all we have to find out where the big fish are lying. And that's darned near the hardest thing of the lot. They're the most mysterious fish in the sea. They only spend a few weeks in the year off the Vineyard. Nobody knows what brings them here, or where they spend the rest of the year. Nobody knows when or where they spawn. They're strange creatures.' When the lookout spotted a school, usually lying basking on the surface, they would cut engines and hoist sail, in an attempt to move quietly up behind them to get within harpoon range, without scaring them away. The harpooner had only one shot. If he wounded but didn't kill, the swordfish, perhaps weighing many hundreds of pounds, would take a run at the boat, as in *Jaws*. So the fishermen would put out decoy barrels; they showed us a firkin-sized barrel that looked as if it had been hit by a sledge-hammer. It was easy to imagine just what could happen to the timbers of a boat.

Occasionally, as a special treat, we would be taken down to the Yacht Club, which stood grandly out in the harbour on wooden piles, for a dinner of swordfish steak, followed by blueberries and cream, deliciously fresh in their blue-green crispness. I thought swordfish then was the quite the best thing I had ever tasted. These dinners almost atoned for revolting squash and pumpkin pie. Apart from the Yacht Club, which was the centre of social life for young and old, sailors and non-sailors alike, Edgartown revolved with engaging simplicity around the tennis club, the drugstore – with its delectable raspberry ice-cream sodas – the cinema and the church, with its traditional white columns and cool, classical interior. I was amazed how, in contrast to home, at 11.00 a.m. on Sunday the streets of Edgartown were empty. *Everybody* – schoolchildren, debutantes, parents and grandparents, no longer dressed in Bermuda shorts but in suits and tidy dresses – was in church. I found the Episcopalian service slightly strange, the hymns cheerful and lively, though some, like 'America the Beautiful' ('thy alabaster cities gleaming from sea to shining sea . . .' etc.), faintly disquieting in their sickly nationalism. (And how dare they pinch the simple melody of 'God Save the King' for 'My Country 'Tis of Thee'! Loudly I used to make a point of singing out the proper words.) Though the family regularly teased Mootsie Cutler for going only for the pleasure of meeting her cronies afterwards and catching up on the Edgartown gossip, I began to take on board just how seriously religious a people the Americans then were.

Then there was the Movie House, a small, intimate affair and almost as much an institution as the church. That summer I seem to remember seeing, among the plethora of Hollywood B-films, *Pride and Prejudice* and *Rebecca* and feeling painful nostalgia at the English accents of 'Mrs Bennett', young Laurence Olivier and the delectable Joan Fontaine. There were the anti-Nazi films like *Mortal Storm*, *Escape* and *Four Sons*, starring 'good German' heroes such as Paul Muni, and Charlie Chaplin's hilarious *The Great Dictator* – all noisily applauded by the Cutlers. So were the Movietone News and *The March of Time*, which depicted the heroism of the Battle of Britain. On one occasion, an oaf sitting in our row booed the King, then promptly got up to go. As he passed I gave him a vicious hack on the shins, tripping him and causing him to fall heavily in the aisles – amid much applause from the Cutler claque. The story, embroidered, went the rounds, in Edgartown and in Garrison: 'Did you hear how little Ally beat up that guy who booed the King?' I blushed, but I suppose felt heroic. Less ennobling was my experience at a charity performance to raise money for the church, when my ticket won first prize in the lottery. It turned out to be a negligée. When I shamefacedly brought the pink and frilly object down from the stage and walked up the aisle with it, the whole audience rocked with laughter, and for a moment I hated all Americans.

The white clapboard rented house, with its hurricane cellar (just in case) which reminded me of *The Wizard of Oz*, surrounded by hydrangeas and rugosa roses with great red hips like ripe tomatoes, and its croquet lawn fringed by the inevitable poison ivy, was commodious and charming. Regularly, every morning at elevenses, a visitor would wander uninhibitedly on to the croquet lawn: a black-and-white dog of interesting ancestry, part Old English sheepdog, part beagle or even bassethound, with an engaging expression and vigorously wagging tail. Salteena (not quite a gentleman), as he was immediately christened by Julia Breese, would pause for conversation, for a game and a roll – and half a dozen crackers. He would then disrupt the croquet by picking up one ball after another and dropping them in the poison ivy, before moving on to his next port of call. Surely the best-fed dog on the entire island inevitably he began to arouse Mrs Breese's anxieties that he must be a stray or had an unhappy private life – until we met him one day attached to the grandest lady in Edgartown. She was astounded that he seemed to know us all so well.

There were picnics and barbecues on wonderfully long, empty beaches at Chappaquiddick, where we would trundle across the bridge that later became so infamous, or at South Beach where we would join the Elliott Cutlers, four exuberant boys my age and upwards who taught me to play touch-football, and an equally noisy father who, strangely as it seemed, was one of Boston's most famous surgeons. I was fascinated by the weird denizens of the lagoons behind South Beach. The hideous sea robins, which had bright orange wings under their fins and great mouths that greedily swallowed up any bait offered, were boiled up into chowdah that I thought tasted disgusting. The even weirder horseshoe crabs, inedible, but now made almost extinct by pollution it seems, were the nearest thing I had ever seen to a prehistoric animal. Completely encased in a smooth armoured shell, sometimes they gave me bad dreams about Panzers and coal-scuttle helmets. Moving away from the jolly, noisy crowd, there were hours when I would lie on the sand at South Beach, watching the waves turn over at their crest and pause with the slow deliberateness of really serious Atlantic rollers before plunging down in an explosion of foam. I would listen to the prolonged hiss of the water drawing the sand back down into the great maw of the next breaker, and reflect that there was nothing but the ocean – empty but for its lurking U-boats – between me and home. I would feel beset by a deep wave of melancholia – which I would try to keep to myself – of homesickness, of helplessness and of worry about my father, Ropley and Terry, and Cecil, and I would wonder if I would ever see any of them again; or if England would survive the war.

Keep it to myself as best as I might, the two sisters seemed to sense some of this, and lavished upon me warmth and affection, sensibly mixed with a great deal of cajolery. Meanwhile, they had their own agreeable preoccupations. Having decided they had fallen in love with the island, they determined jointly to buy their own property there. Accompanied by a venal-looking real-estate agent and a Portuguese builder they would set off on prolonged house hunts. Eventually they 'discovered a dream': a ramshackle stable belonging to a big house right on the end of the point at East Chop, the right half of the bosom in which Vineyard Haven nestled. Treeless, gardenless and unprotected, compared to cosy Edgartown, it looked awfully bleak to me, but Pete was enthralled, reckoning that every yacht and worthwhile ship in the world would round that point. The view over the sea from three out of four sides of the stable was indeed irresistible, so the Cutler–Breese combination bought it, 'for a song' – and set about converting, with maximum excitement and cheerful arguments. I viewed it all with detached interest, reckoning that, by the following summer when it was ready, I would no longer be there, but back home again.

Suddenly it was Labor Day, there was a brief surge of husbands and working folks from the city, and then the summer vacations were over. Among the visitors landed Judy, the mystery member of the Cutler family, suntanned from her ranching summer in Wyoming. Life was never to be quite the same again. Nearly six feet tall, with a heart-shaped face, dreamy green eyes and high cheekbones that gave her a sort of half-Slav, half-Magyar look that belonged more to the Danube than the Hudson, she bore little resemblance to anyone else in the family. There was much teasing speculation (often led by the wayward John Cutler) that impeccable 'Mother dear' – Mootsie – must have stumbled. A Sioux chieftain? Or a Hungarian count? Whatever the genes, it was evident to my untrained eyes that Judy was one of those few American girls who possessed real beauty, as opposed to just great prettiness. She swam like a dolphin, played tennis with a lazily graceful competence, had a thousand friends and bubbled over with vitality, warm-heartedness and sheer *joie de vivre*. And she had a laugh that would stop a tennis match three courts away. In short, she had everything. Wonderfully disorganized, but as passionate about the war as her mother, she was unmistakably Julia Breese's favourite. Swiftly she embroidered my established nickname in the family to 'Hiya, Alleycat'. Then, when her mother teasingly bade her show more respect because one day (quite inaccurately) I would inherit my father's title, it became 'Sir 'orne', finally reduced to 'Sarong'. Then, back in Garrison, there was a family wedding – of Coco and Alix – one of those wonderful American weddings where everyone dances. I watched, admiring the American capacity to have a good time and the capacity of the Cutler men to get legless, and listened to the wonderful dance music that I thought only happened in a Fred-and-Ginger movie. But, most devastating of all, Judy floating like a wraith across the floor, in the arms of one dashing Harvard man after another. I had not the least idea how to dance. The band kept playing the current Rodgers and Hart hit, 'Bewitched, Bothered and Bewildered', and I suddenly realized that – aged fourteen – I was all three. And hideously jealous to boot. The war receded into the background.

CHAPTER SIX

Millbrook, 1940

It must have been shortly after Labor Day, the big American holiday that marks the end of summer in the first week of September, that the Cutler–Breese caravan hit the road again. Leaving behind happy Edgartown and next summer's exciting projects for East Chop, the venerable station-wagon laden down with antique booty, tennis rackets and luggage, headed back to Garrison. After a brief spell there, it was Manhattan again. This time I was based on the Cutler town house at 58 East 80th Street, just off Madison Avenue. It was time to make preparations for school. The decision had been made to send me to Millbrook School, in Upper New York State. The second Forster boy, Bayard, had just graduated from it, with every distinction (into Harvard, naturally). Peter Cutler had been there too, though without distinction – he could not quite make it academically, but had been happy nevertheless. It had an 'almost English head-master', Rossy Cutler assured me, and it was within forty miles or so of Garrison, so she could keep an eye on me. Preparations meant getting kitted up with clothes. Rossy Cutler inspected, in amazement, my Stowe wardrobe, laid out on the dining-room floor. 'My Gawd, Ally, you *can't* take any of *that* to Millbrook.' I looked in dismay at the arrayed white flannels, Stowe's grey suits, the baggy rugger shorts, the chocolate-brown blazer and the school cap which made me look like one of Billy Bunter's mates in Lower Fourth, and which provoked howls of shaming, agonizing laughter from Judy. I shrugged my shoulders helplessly, but Aunt Rossy was never short of ideas. 'Pack them all up, and take them down to one of those shops on 3rd Avenue, you'll certainly be able to sell them . . . all that beautiful English material.'

Obediently I set off, staggering under the weight of a vast suitcase. Even though it was already September, it remained hotter than the most torrid London summer day. In those days, when the famous 'El' still rattled noisily overhead, Third Avenue was a depressed street, where Jewish pawnbrokers and second-hand clothes dealers huddled in the perpetual shade cast by the elevated railway – a far cry from the swinging singles bars and restaurants of the 1970s and 1980s. I may have hoped that the shopkeepers, with their almost impenetrable *Mitteleuropa* and Yiddish accents, would show compassion on a fellow refugee. But I was misguided. The first half-dozen I tried studied with a mixture of disbelief and disdain the 'beautiful English material' on which my poor father must have spent a small king's ransom only the previous September. One muttered imprecations about British policy in Palestine – which I didn't quite understand. Were we not, I thought, all on the same side against Hitler? Finally, as hot as ever I remembered feeling that first sweltering day in New York of two months before, exhausted and thoroughly discountenanced, I met a friend at last. Let us call him 'Honest Abe'. Going through the now much fingered finery, with a sardonic smile, he declared in tones of magnanimity, 'OK. I guess some of it will do for theatricals, or a kid's dressing-up box. I'll give you a dollar for the lot. You got a deal.' I pocketed the dollar, not displeased at my first experience in business, and returned home to 80th Street, via an ice-cream soda counter, with the empty suitcase. Rossy Cutler was appalled: 'You mean to say you sold the whole lot for *one dollar*? What would your father say?' Defensively, I mumbled something about their being soon too small, anyway; and we set off to Bloomingdales. Fortunately for my generous sponsors, the outlay for a 'trousseau' for Millbrook was incomparably more modest than for Stowe, let alone Ludgrove. In the era before jeans were invented, all that was required by way of school uniform was a tweed jacket and a pair of nondescript trousers, and a blue suit for Sunday occasions.

About a hundred miles upstate from Manhattan, Millbrook School was set in magnificent, unspoilt countryside. It was a part of the interior of New York State that the Age of Change had not yet reached. It had not yet been awakened by the roar and whistle of the giant stainless-steel streamliners. Train services, as I discovered on many future journeys back and forth, were slow and depressed. And so was the countryside, wrapped till late spring in the winter slumbers – what a fallacy it was to regard all America as a series of vast scenic entities that remain unchanging over hundreds and hundreds of miles! On the way to Amenia (the nearest village) and Duchess County, within an hour or so of the world's metropolis, one had already entered into a different world. Bleak hills replaced the gentle, maritime prettiness of Connecticut. Gone too were the prosperously sparkling white-frame houses – to be replaced by ugly utilitarian structures, painted drab shades of ochre, grey and faded Indian red, and the red silos of farms, many of them poor-looking, wresting a meagre living from rocky, hillbound fields. If you left the train or strayed off the roadside, you would no doubt hear the broken accents of German, Slav and Sicilian immigrants. It was hard country; already it was the interior of America.

The school sat on a hilltop amid some 500 acres of rolling dairy country, midway between the small towns of Millbrook and Amenia. Years later the neighbourhood was awoken out of its Rip Van Winkle repose by the notoriety acquired when the briefly famous Dr Timothy Leary of the 1960s set up his druggies' paradise there, until the elders finally ran him out (and he himself saw the light – 'Now that I've tuned out / Why is life so dreary, weary? / Tell me, Timothy Leary, deary' went the lamenting refrain). As of 1940, it all centred around an imposing old wooden barn and its inseparable silo. Virtually everything, from classes to basketball and the weekly movie, happened there. Around the Barn had grown up an ever growing cluster of houses in the traditional white clapboard, for faculty members and their families, and some not-unpleasant-looking dormitory buildings in neo-Georgian red brick, symbolic of the East Coast private school and college. With its nearby stream and pond, though obviously it lacked the Palladian grandeur of Stowe, there was a warm friendliness about this close-knit little community, stuck in the middle of nowhere, that immediately imposed itself. Nevertheless, as the two sisters drove me up in the Cutler station-wagon for the beginning of that first term, a terrible apprehension suddenly seized my heart: yet another school (my fifth)! Would it be yet another disaster?

The earliest encounter with my fifth new headmaster, Mr Edward Pulling, was certainly not an auspicious one, recalling all too painfully similar occasions in the past. It set the seal (or at least I always felt it did) on much of our future relationship. As was the custom for new boys, on my first day at Millbrook I sat at the headmaster's table. The dining-room tables at Millbrook were scientifically designed to procure optimum conditions for the flow of intelligent, controllable conversation, each being oval and seating eleven. I was seated at one end of the ellipse's minor axis, Mr Pulling at the other. To my horror we had particularly hard baked potatoes – and, as I had already so often found in America, only a fork to deal with them. To have asked for a knife, thus revealing my alien shortcomings, was more than I dared, so, though still inexpert in the art of forkmanship, I sawed away at the hard skin of the potato. Tragedy occurred. The fork slipped, the plate shot like a discus across the polished table, promiscuously shedding its contents, and, narrowly missing my new headmaster, scudded between him and the rather queenly-looking Mrs Pulling, to shatter itself on the ground.

It certainly did not seem to bode well for the future. Lucy Pulling exhaled a nervous laugh, and turned the conversation with a patrician ease for which we all came to love her. The Boss, as he was known throughout his thirty-four-year reign, in a blend of awe and the nearest that both masters and boys alike could ever come to familiarity with so august a personality, looked grim. I wilted.

When I arrived at Millbrook, the school had been going just nine years and had little more than a hundred boys – no girls, of course. Yet it had already made a remarkable name for itself among America's private (the equivalent of British public) schools. This was perhaps not surprising, for Mr Pulling was a most remarkable man. Born of an English father and an American mother, he had degrees from both Princeton and Trinity College, Cambridge, and in 1917 had rushed back to Britain to serve as a sub-lieutenant in the Royal Navy during the last months of the First World War. Aboard the destroyer HMS *Christopher*, he reckoned to have dispatched at least one U-boat before hostilities ended. The sea was deeply in his blood, his pale-blue eyes reflected it, and he was proud to claim that it had been a Pulling ancestor who brought the news of Trafalgar to George III. Equally he claimed (by the end of his life) to have crossed the Atlantic sixty-one times, while a naval battle was the only subject ever known to distract him from the issue at hand. His accent was, and remained, resolutely – and agreeably – mid-Atlantic. After the war he had taken a job as junior teacher at the blue-chip school of Groton, under the redoubtable Endicott Peabody, who was supposedly the protagonist in Louis Auchincloss's classic novel, *The Rector of Justin*, and on whom it was often felt the Boss modelled himself. While tutoring the wayward son of Franklin Delano Roosevelt (then Governor of New York State), who was in danger of expulsion, he caught the eye of the future President. Having recently been Woodrow Wilson's Secretary of the Navy during the war, Roosevelt was evidently attracted by their mutual love of the sea, urged the young teacher to start his own school and promised to help him if and when he did.

When the moment came, in fact Edward Pulling renounced the backing of this powerful and privileged potential patron, on the grounds that their views on education might not be quite the same. At thirty-three, in the midst of the Depression, it was a courageous moment to start any new private school – especially one in a barn, with half a dozen or so pupils. But Edward Pulling was backed by a host of ideas and an inflexible will – plus a charming and educated wife from an influential (and wealthy) Long Island family called Leffingwell (her father was a senior partner in J. Morgan & Co.), as well as an unstinting fairy-godmother in the form of a railway mogul, one Henry Harkness

Flagler. Under Edward Pulling's determined drive, Millbrook grew at a steady rate and has never looked back. Six foot four inches tall, extraordinarily good-looking with a jaw like the Rock of Gibraltar, and slightly greying wavy hair, at forty-two the Boss, as a personality, was surrounded by an aura of tremendous, though perhaps a trifle chilly, presence which you felt the moment he entered the room. As my future room-mate Bill Buckley wrote of him many years later (when he was in his eighties):

> his light blue eyes penetrated you and, incidentally, the room; his questions were kindly composed, and patient, but there was an instant no-nonsense that prevented you, say, from suggesting impulsively that you both go out together to buy a Popsicle. Anyone interviewed by Mr Pulling was, so to speak, permanently interviewed by him.

This was approximately how I remember feeling after being invited over to the Boss's study for a first interview, following the baked-potato incident. The Pulling House, as it was called, was the only other building – apart from the Barn – at Millbrook when the Pullings bought it in 1931. An old clapboard farmhouse, it discreetly dominated the campus, and from it almost every corner could be observed. In 1940 it served a multiplicity of purposes: its capacious drawing room was where both Sunday chapel and the once-a-term dances took place, where visiting speakers orated and Negro quartets crooned. Yet, somehow, the Pullings managed to find there some modicum of privacy in which to bring up three small daughters, a son and a succession of spaniels. In the Boss's small study, whence the whole school was run, a gilt American eagle and the model of a British destroyer were symbolically displayed.

Across a crowded but orderly desk, he surveyed me at that first interview for a few moments, made some welcoming and sympathetic remarks about Britain, then asked, 'Tell me, do you have a second name?'

'Yes, sir – Allan,' I replied, slightly puzzled.

'In that case, I think we had better call you "Alan" – because it's just possible that American boys might find "Alistair" a trifle effeminate, and I don't want you to be teased unnecessarily.'

I thought I detected what looked like the trace of a twinkle in those Atlantic blue eyes. In his retirement years later, he admitted that he had once accepted a new boy, while his verbose mother rabitted on non-stop about all his virtues, simply on the grounds that the child had had the nerve to wink at him. 'For very important and private reasons' read the acceptant note that he later dictated to the school secretary. But it would have been hard to imagine any small boy actually winking at Edward Pulling, and I decided forthwith that this was not a man to be trifled with.

The Boss was imbued with uncompromising principles, somewhat unbending and not over-endowed with a sense of humour, a man with whom it was not easy to be intimate, which is probably why he was such an outstanding headmaster. Like all strong personalities, he had his idiosyncrasies that were subject to the lampooning of cynical small boys – though always well out of his earshot. There were the pet phrases, without which no address to the school was complete: the exhortative, 'to function with the maximum amount of efficiency'; the cautionary, 'lest there be any ambiguity'; and the deprecatory, 'personal aggrandizement at the expense of others' (signifying anything from financial swindles to petty theft). Then there was the flashlight, at least two and a half feet long, borne about the 'campus' after dark like a sceptre of imperial office. And there was the push-bell on his table on the dining room for proclaiming the beginning and the end of meals. Its tiny tinkle was really quite unnecessary, because the hand which hovered above it for seconds of agonizing deliberation before the decisive plunge had already galvanized the school by the waves of authority it transmitted.

By his own account, it was on one of those sixty-odd Atlantic crossings, while teaching at Groton, that he met 'a tall, beautiful girl' who needed a partner at deck tennis. The following year, 1928, they were on their honeymoon aboard another transatlantic liner. Lucy Leffingwell was a quintessential patrician from Long Island, and regularly rode a very patrician horse to the Millbrook

Hounds, one of America's smartest hunts. Yet she was utterly unsnobbish. Gracefully tall, with prematurely grey hair in her late thirties that always seemed as if it had just been released from a riding net, and the complexion reddened by the wind of the chase that often betrays hunting folk, she had a natural dignity which compelled good manners – but also a wonderful, slightly mocking sense of humour. Though deeply supportive of each other, occasionally it was known for Lucy Pulling to transmit something extremely close to a wink at a senior when the Boss was being excessively pompous. They clearly adored one another, while she held the affection of every boy in the school, of whatever age. If there were (rare) moments when he seemed to ride over her, or cut her short, the silent disapproval of boys present was almost audible. As Bill Buckley admitted to the Boss, in a moment of audacity in middle age, 'Mr Pulling, we tolerated you, but we loved Mrs Pulling.'

There was never any doubt where Mr Pulling's wartime sympathies lay, try as he might, in his official capacity, to hide them. Shortly after I arrived he addressed the school on the subject of the William Allen White Committee. After praising the collective heroism of the Royal Navy at Dunkirk, he remarked,

> I am most hopeful of the attitude of the present administration towards this question of aid to Britain . . . [but] the need for aid to Britain is increasing rather than decreasing. . . . nor must we allow ourselves to be too sanguine about the fact that so far England has held her own in the Battle of Britain.

In devious ways (so as not to offend Isolationist sensibilities), the school was kept miraculously well informed of every major action of the Royal Navy. Seldom could a British cruiser creep in to lick its wounds in Brooklyn Navy Yard before the Boss knew of it and was cornering its commander to come up and address the school. Officers of the navy, the RAF and the merchant marine (promoted by Wheeler-Bennett's British Information Services), and American visitors returning from embattled Britain, all came to Millbrook in a steady stream. The modestly told stories of the

RAF heroes, some of them often badly scarred, recovering from burns, the Richard Hilarys and others, made us Bundles walk tall.

It was that which at about this time, had decided me to become a Spitfire pilot.

Lest there be any ambiguity, however – as the Boss was wont to say – in no way whatsoever did he, or the school, as a whole make favourites of us Bundles. On the contrary. There were seven of us, all newcomers that Fall Term. We were quite a mixed bag; of us the school magazine, the *Silo*, wrote at the beginning of that term: '. . . Alan Horne lived in Hampshire, which is fifty miles away from London. He went to Stowe School. He was not much bothered by the air raids. . . . Brian Larwill watched a submarine sunk from the *Countess of Atholl*. . . .' There was no formality about surnames at Millbrook. Brian (whose father was a bank manager in Essex, and whom the common bond of Englishness made my best friend during those first terms) and I were the two oldest; then there were Keith Williams and his cousin, Bill Cookson, two cheerful and friendly Mancunians from simple backgrounds and with broad Lancashire accents. Their aunts had come over with them, and lived quietly near Garrison – not entirely approved of by Rossy Cutler, who felt they should do more for her Bundles for Britain. Tim Marshall, a little blond boy who looked constantly as if on the verge of tears, had come over with his pretty young mother, the wife of a senior executive in the BBC. Tony Ingles was a Scot with a thick accent, flame-red hair and a temper to match. He had been fostered by a local Millbrook family, the Bontecous, and made his mark by dedicating himself to looking after the strange animals in the Zoo – one of Millbrook's special eccentricities. Finally, there was the Lord Primrose – Neil, at eleven the youngest (and probably most eccentric) boy in the school.

I doubt if any of us would claim that we were brilliant ambassadors of Britain – certainly not when we arrived. We were, in fact, generally odious, supercilious and often arrogant, complaining of American food ('I never had to go to a dentist before I came over here'), decrying American educational standards ('Why, I was doing Virgil before I left England'), and ridiculing their national sentimentality ('That awful hymn, "America, America" . . .'), scorning their apparent lack of toughness ('We don't wear helmets to play rugger, or gloves and masks to play cricket'). It was always a mystery why most of us were not massacred within a week of arrival. We certainly would have been at Stowe – let alone Ludgrove. As it was, there were those who regarded us with pity, and those – when it came to politics and the war – who viewed us with a certain amount of suspicion. But on the whole we were accorded that warm, spontaneous and unquestioning friendliness which only Americans seem capable of. 'After all,' as one very small boy explained to me in my first week, 'I guess you're really just Americans with funny accents.' Gradually we were tamed and became less appalling.

Not, however, all of us. Neil Archibald Primrose, the youngest among us, and the son of a well-known racing peer, the Earl of Rosebery, resisted assimilation with a tenacity that Winston Churchill would have admired. On the football field and in the dormitories, in the classrooms and in the dining hall, Neil fought them. A diminutive creature about three feet tall, Neil's temper, and the invincible whirlwind of kicks, cuffs, scratches and bites that went with it, earned the healthy respect of boys and masters alike within the first week of his arrival. Years later, writing in the *New York Times Magazine*, William F. Buckley Jr described him as 'the most insufferable brat ever exported by the United Kingdom'. When things got too out of hand, Neil would be whisked off to the Infirmary for a couple of days R-and-R by the school nurse, a human tranquilliser called Miss Miller, who was the only person who could control this small fiend. That is, except for Neil's 'sponsor', that great mogul the late J. P. Morgan. When the formidable JP visited Millbrook, Neil was always on his best behaviour.

To my intense satisfaction, I was granted the privilege of having a special locker in which to set up my precious wireless equipment. Later it expanded to half a basement room, shared with an industrious metalworker, an older boy called John Lothrop, nicknamed 'Latherop', who turned and filed away silently at exquisitely accurate miniatures of steam engines, not in the least distracted by the crackles and howls from my loud-speaker. It was possibly not so much a kindness, to enable me to keep in touch with the 'old country' and the battle front, as the Boss's ingenious ploy of legalizing and controlling a potentially insidious black market. At Millbrook, like most schools of the day, private radios (let alone record players) were strictly taboo. I am ashamed to say I cheated, adapting the little radio Julia Breese had given me to use earphones and concealing it in a secret cupboard in the dormitory, so that I could fall asleep to the soothing strains of Tommy Dorsey – and dream of Judy Cutler. Apart from that, the only special treatment meted out to us Bundles proved to be a kind of stigma. As we were, most of us, weedy and deemed to be suffering from wartime malnutrition, we were required to report to Miss Miller's Infirmary to swallow down a daily 'egg-nog'. Concocted out of eggs, cream and sugar, at first it was nectar. Then, gradually, it began to get fulsome and virtually impossible to swallow down without gagging. As often as not, the Infirmary loo would become the secret beneficiary of Miss Miller's precious elixirs. When I thought of what my father would have done with the eggs, each revolting egg-nog a week's ration in England, I felt contrite. But the remarkable thing was that none of us Bundles was ever teased for being accorded such unmanly 'privileges'.

In many ways the antithesis of Mr Pulling was Henry Callard, the assistant headmaster. In my youthful studies of American history, I derived a perhaps naive notion of how two very divergent archetypes were constantly recurring. I named them the Hamiltonian and the Jeffersonian, after those two great Founding Fathers of young America. Like the financial wizard Alexander Hamilton, the Hamiltonian is a down-to-earth pragmatist, an expansionist and a hard-headed businessman. He is the American with whom the outside world is usually best acquainted. The Jeffersonian, on the other hand, is generally a retiring person of some humility, who is deeply sensitive to the unhappy state of his fellow men, a liberal and a reformer, and marked by more than a streak of idealism. His caricature is Graham Greene's Quiet American, but if you search for his true counterpart in European literature you would be most likely to find it among the works of Dostoevsky. As the American historian J. T. Adams said of the two men, 'Hamilton stood for strength, wealth, and power; Jefferson for the American dream.'

If Mr Pulling was a Hamiltonian, then Mr Callard belonged very much to the Jeffersonian stream. Surrounded by a swarm of little red-headed children, he was the Conscience of Millbrook, incredibly modest and retiring, and one of the most kind-hearted and hard-working men one could imagine. As I was to discover in my last year at Millbrook, he was also a great teacher, with a special brand of infectious enthusiasm that led to remarkable results in exams, and remained undiminished long years after one had left school. Yet Henry Callard was obviously at his happiest bouncing about on the school tractor, tending the school vegetable farm and organizing a hundred and one construction 'projects' around the place. There was a strong streak of the pioneer in him. Just as Jefferson longed to creep away from the capital to plan, invent and create with his hands at Monticello, so did Mr Callard cherish the end of classes when he could escape from the schoolroom into his faded and battered dungarees. Although only in his late thirties, Henry Callard's hair was nearly white and he was seldom without a worried look on his face. He was universally adored. In spite of his kind-heartedness, he kept remarkable discipline. If you committed a misdemeanour you felt you were adding to his personal grief, and the worried look would become yet more painful to behold. Yet there was also much laughter in him.

Before Henry Callard took front stage in my life, that first year at Millbrook I had two principal mentors whom I had instantly liked. One was Arthur Tuttle, to whom I had been introduced earlier that summer, on a beach on Martha's Vineyard, and who therefore took a particular interest in my progress. A retired, reputedly well-to-do businessman who had taken to education more or less as a hobby, he was something of an outsider. The term before I arrived, the school had been treated to a very American spectacle. Mr Tuttle, desirous of bringing up his family not entirely encompassed by a hundred juveniles, had set the 'Tuttle Home' on vast rollers and trundled it intact half a mile away down the hill. As might have been expected, mathematics were his speciality. Tough but with a soft streak, he conducted his classes by means of a series of staccato instructions, reminiscent of a stockbroker issuing orders from the floor, interlarded with such slogans as 'can do' (this is the way to proceed), 'will wash, won't wash' (an equation capable or incapable of solution), 'duck soup' (too easy, isn't it?). Tuttle was an alert teacher and expected an alert class. There was no slacking with him, and of all the courses at Millbrook I found my English education gave me the least advantage in maths. But Arthur Tuttle was my first (and last) teacher capable of making that disagreeable subject interesting – and almost comprehensible.

The other mentor was Hank Austin, my dormitory master and English teacher, a new addition to Millbrook. Hank, aged twenty-five, was the type of young master idolized by schoolboys in every country. He was athletic, cheerful and breezy, would not stand on ceremony, and was always prepared to listen to grouses and hear iconoclasm of school gods without resort to pomp of office. He was a thoroughly uncomplicated character. But although Hank was a universal type, he was especially American. With his brisk, rolling gait, careless clothes and two-tone shoes, books carried at the hip rather than under the arm, and a genial, homely face with a pronounced Habsburg lip, he belonged unmistakably and inseparably to the campus. In class he conducted affairs with the utmost informality, his favourite posture being to sit on the table-top with his arms clasped about his knees like a fakir on a bed of nails, interpolating the subtleties of English literature with such exhortations as 'Attaboy, Willy, you're really on the ball today,' or when the class seemed prone to sloth, 'Now get in there pitchin', fellers.'

It seemed, at first, somehow incongruous to hear the all-American Hank extol the subtle virtues of *Silas Marner*, or explain to fourteen-year-olds the deadly seriousness that lay beneath the rollicking, and very English, humour of Barrie's *The Admirable Crichton*. But he succeeded admirably.

Then, soon after the beginning of that first year, Hank announced that we would devote the remainder of it to the study of American literature. Brian, my fellow countryman, and I exchanged sly glances. Was there any such thing? We had not been told. Hank must have intercepted our glances: 'Right, Al, you name an American Romantic of the early nineteenth century.' I couldn't. 'Well then, name an English one.' 'Edgar Allan Poe,' said I promptly. 'That's real neat, Al – I guess that English school of yours taught you Abe Lincoln was a Limey politician too?'

I don't know how good a teacher Hank was, but his boundless excitement about what he was teaching brought the spirit of the American classics alive and pungent into the classroom. In and out of the windows flitted the grim visages of Nathaniel Hawthorne's Puritans of old Salem, mingled with the dust of the hard and endless prairies of Willa Cather's pioneers, and the steamy smell of the muddy, indolent Mississippi of Mark Twain. Before our eyes rose the vicious but fascinating Chicago of Carl Sandburg, the riproaring West of Bret Harte and Jack London, the tragic, wasted heroism of Stephen Crane's Civil War, and the loving nationalism of Walt Whitman that aspired to unite all these things. All this, Hank was able to turn into flesh and blood for unimaginative fourteen-year-olds. It was under his administration that I took Hemingway's newly published bestseller, *For Whom the Bell Tolls*, away with me for holiday reading. (I remember Harold Macmillan once telling me, in his late eighties, when I was writing his official life, how exciting his recent (and first) trip to China had been – not because of seeing the Great Wall or meeting the new leader, Deng, but because he had 'discovered' on the plane a wonderful 'new' novel. It was *For Whom the Bell Tolls*. I thought, then, that it would be worth living to a great age if only to read that particular Hemingway for the first time.) To add spice to my first trip down south, Hank despatched me with Willa Cather's *Sapphira and the Slave Girl*, which had just been picked Book of the Month. As well as expanding my knowledge of the facts of life, they made me reappraise my views on the native literature. Sadly, Hank left us after that one year.

There were two Millbrook teachers on whom I was perhaps somewhat less keen. One was Fred Knutson, a Swede from the Midwest, who was the football coach and taught Latin – later to come into his own when the war brought to all American schools a craze for physical fitness – 'der Führer' was the secret sobriquet that was then appropriately awarded him. There was something sanctimonious – added to the way his Adam's apple rose and fell during community singing – that vaguely irritated one. Millbrook didn't seem to win many football games, but I felt he knew more about coaching than Latin. He taught sixth-form Latin, the top class in school, in which – to my surprise – I found myself, more through the dereliction of American classics education than any prowess on my side. An elite group of three of us, in a tiny classroom up an outside staircase in the barn, studied Virgil under Mr Knutson, but he was unable to make exciting even Aeneas' escapade in the cave with Dido. Yet, when my Latin came to a natural end after that first year, it was a loss that I regretted for many years to come.

Then there was Frank Trevor, who was inseparable from one of the more remarkable of Millbrook's institutions – the Zoo. According to Edward Pulling's reminiscences, Trevor had 'showed up on his doorstep with a battered station-wagon filled with the animals which were to become the Millbrook School Zoo', which, in turn, was, over the course of the next half-century, to become one of the most important teaching zoos in the country, nurturing half a dozen endangered species, a million-dollar affair handed on lovingly from generation to generation, repeatedly capable of raising hundreds of thousands of dollars for its expansion. Frank Trevor was one of those zealous Americans in whom singlemindedness amounted almost to fanaticism. He lived, ate and slept in the animal and vegetable world, and woe betide anyone joining his biology classes who did not also wholeheartedly share his dedication to the Zoo. His empire lay over a wooden bridge across the old mill-stream and at the bottom of the ice-hockey pond. Under his vigilant eye it was entirely run by boys, and its doings regularly received front-page news coverage in the *Silo*, under such earth-shaking captions as 'NEW MONKEY ADOPTS BLACK AND WHITE RAT'. With my Dr Dolittle love of animals, I wasn't keen on the way they were kept in small, smelly cages; nor was I particularly drawn to the bird-banding programme, which – under the aegis of the admirable Audubon Society – banded some hundred creatures a year. One of my rare excursions to Trevor's domain ended tragically. While handling some little boy's tame grass-snake, it slithered out of my hands into the cage of the Brazilian coatimundi, the biggest and by far the fiercest beast in the Zoo. The coatimundi seized the unfortunate reptile in both paws with one swift, joyous flourish, bit off its head and proceeded to chomp down the remainder of its writhing body like some gory banana. I was not welcomed again.

Trevor himself, I thought immediately – and perhaps unfairly – was a faintly sinister figure, an impression which his appearance certainly reinforced. A skull-like face, with eyebrows permanently arched, topped by sleek jet-black hair, like one of his pet ravens, imparted a mephistophelian look, which made him central casting for his perennial role as Grand Inquisitor at the school's Halloween high jinks. Mrs Trevor was dumpy, with an unAmerican figure and heavy bosom that rested disquietingly on the table at mealtimes. She always seemed to be on the look-out for misdemeanours. I joined Frank Trevor's advanced biology class, partly because I had quite enjoyed dissecting frogs at Stowe. Then I discovered that the syllabus was largely dedicated to the sex-life of the *Drosophila Melanogaster* – fruitflies to the unscientific. Kept in milk-bottles, and fed on the school porridge (which, surprisingly, seemed to make them even randier), these dreary animalcules were staggeringly fecund – producing, as I recall, roughly a generation a day. All of their prolificity then had to be recorded in genetic tables. It was too much like dreaded maths rather than biology. Then my *Drosophila* escaped one day and got into a friend's bottle, where they copulated merrily, wrecking weeks of careful experimentation. The débâcle led to my first and only academic setback at Millbrook (though it also opened the door, inadvertently, to a major breakthrough in life – and the beginning of a coldness, if not a feud, with Frank Trevor.

Among the other masters about whom I felt strongly neither one way or the other was my French teacher with the marvellous name of Hargraves Joyous Bishop, or 'Bish'. With Dickensian spectacles and frizzy grey hair that rose up, startled, like Mr Pickwick's, in our youthful estimates Bish's age was put at sixty-five. To our amazement one day he turned out to be under forty, and a recent graduate of Princeton. An avid francophile from days in France with General Pershing's US Expeditionary Force he was thrilled by the French diplomats and artists inveigled (in the Boss's ineffable way) down to speak; he would sit uttering '*Tiens!*' every third second, to signify that he had understood everything. Against another Europhile sophisticate, the newly arrived Austin Johnson, he would vie, gently, for the attention of Miss Sally Frankenstein, the much abused (secretly) school dietician – a lady with sallow features and hair like steel wool (and another sexagenarian who later turned out to be in her thirties).

The other, marginal characters of importance at Millbrook were wonderfully cosmopolitan. There was Ralph, the school gardener, a Sicilian who looked like Chico Marx and whose English was just as rudimentary; the ever smiling school chauffeur and mechanic, George Telfer, whose parents had come over from Scotland in 1909; and Mr Fritz, the janitor and overlord of all the boilers. Mr Fritz had served in the Kaiser's army, had a square head and a strongly guttural accent. He looked like a Prussian *Feldwebel* and reminded me of the taboo toy-shop proprietor in Winchester. His sense of humour (or lack of it) was considered typically Teutonic, but given the rising passions provoked by the war, his life cannot have been much fun. Yet no one ever thought of him as being anything but American. Down below the pond, a salt-box red building that had once been the old mill housed – on the top floor – the art school, run by a talented water colourist, Grant Reynard, who was of French extraction. On the ground floor was the carpentry shop. Here presided Fred Blownstine, of Scandinavian descent. The Mill, as it was called, was – certainly by comparison with the workshop at Stowe – superbly equipped with all the latest American technology: jigsaws, planers and sanders such as I had never seen before. A big, fair-haired, easy-going man, Fred always had time to instruct and help, no matter how busy he was turning out fitments for the school. I loved the smell of the sawdust, of hot oak on the lathe, and I set to – hour after free hour – constructing an elaborately inlaid console, to house a home-made radio (no longer were they to be called wirelesses) as a small token of gratitude for Julia Breese. It was barely completed before I graduated three years later.

Apart from the great enjoyment and satisfaction it provided, the Mill was also a welcome refuge – whenever possible – from the ardours of the football field. My fellow Bundle, Brian, a burly fellow, took to American football like a duck to water, and eventually became a stalwart on the school squad. More angular, despite the derided armour, I didn't enjoy being painfully buf-feted, 'blocked', when I hadn't even got the ball – which didn't seem to be sporting, or accord with the rules of rugger. It was a long time before I understood the subtleties of the game. Later I came to love its tactical intricacies, the intense drama of the well-executed deception play, end run or elegantly arcing long pass, the good-natured excitement of the crowds, and all the razzmatazz of the cheerleaders and bands – even the foolish majorettes. But never (in contrast to ice-hockey) as a player.

Perhaps like schools anywhere, each of the six classes at Millbrook seemed to have its own special character. The sixth form, who virtually ran the school, hand in glove with the Boss, seemed to have a quality of high seriousness that was beyond their years as American seventeen-year-olds. Perhaps it was in part because of the encroaching menace of the war, which was increasingly likely to impinge on their lives. Nevertheless, the majority – as I recall – were Interventionists, to one degree or another (if not quite as out-and-out as Rossy Cutler). Without exception they went out of their way to be sympathetic to us Bundles. Their juniors, the fifth-formers, were by and large rather academic; several were keen Zoo-ites. One of them, John Foster, an extremely bright boy but, as a spastic, cruelly affected both in walk and speech, was the first handicapped person I had come across. He was enormously determined and good-humoured, but what struck me most at the time was how – in what was not a caring age – at Millbrook boys of all ages went out of their way to ensure that John was enabled to lead, not a favoured, but a normal life. Our form, the fourth, initially numbered some fifteen, but, through the course of normal school attrition, lost three or four on the way (two, to the distress of Coach Knutson, were potential football heavyweights, but they were short on brainpower), and later picked up one – Bill Buckley. All, without exception, were congenial and fun. Among the brightest was Phil Jessup, son of a famous academic and (later) Democrat statesman of the same name. Somewhere at the other end of the spectrum was Ferris Hamilton, a thickset midwesterner. Ferris was fundamentally not interested in academic matters. To Hank Austin's exhortations to get inside the characters of J. M. Barrie, his standard response would be 'Gee, gosh, I'm just a simple farmboy from Illinois!' – a refrain that would run round the class. His younger brother, Fred, baby-faced and equally bucolic, who was perhaps even less academically inclined, and who might then have been described by the uncharitable as a fat slob, fell foul of the Boss and finally left under a shadow. In the years to come, the hugely successful Hamilton Brothers became one of the first pioneers to open up North Sea oil. Ferris, sadly, died; but Fred – tall, lean and good-looking – was reckoned by some to be the prototype for Blake Carrington of *Dynasty* fame. Their total presumptive wealth could have bought up all our class, and Millbrook too, many times over. On the only occasion I ever heard him admit error, just two years before he died, the Boss confessed he might have been 'hard on Fred'. His remorse, just possibly, I reflected, was compounded by the thought of all those millions that might otherwise have flowed into the ever eager alumni funds – had poor Fred stayed the course.

Below us, the school tapered away into younger generations, comprising – at the very bottom – the noisy and plaintive small-fry, idolatrous of such heroes as Bugs Bunny, Dick Tracy and Jack Benny, all-American brats with whom one had little traffic. But immediately beneath us came the third form, a bunch of rowdy, football-playing extroverts who enjoyed taking the micky out of our Englishness. Egregious among them, however, was a shy, studious fourteen-year-old, with front teeth in braces that gave him a rather rabbity look, and who always looked as if the school food suited him not very well. Identified by his class, nervously, as something of an aesthete, somewhat priggish, Bill Buckley was already an accomplished pianist and swiftly became the anchor of the school orchestra with his energetic renderings of, alternately, *La Cumparsita* and the *Appassionata*. His two elder brothers, John and Jimmy, had been to Millbrook previously – John too long previously to have made a lasting mark; Jimmy, who had just left, had been a pillar of the Zoo and generally much loved.

The Buckleys lived at nearby Sharon, Connecticut, eight miles away, where William Buckley Sr was viewed as something of an eccentric, held in respect, fear or dislike by his neighbours – depending on their point of view. Among his rather conservative views was the opinion that the last non-communistic President of the United States had been Teddy Roosevelt; and his tenets on education were equally distinctive. Remarking to his wife, in the later 1930s, that at least five years had gone by since he had understood a single word uttered by any of his ten children, he sent five of them off to be schooled in England. So, at twelve (when I was somewhere between Ludgrove and Le Rosey), young William found himself at St John's Beaumont, a Jesuit prep school near Windsor. A year at Beaumont left him with the smattering of an English accent, plus a rooted dislike (though he revered Father Sharkey, his headmaster) for many things English – for reasons that, to me, remained always somewhat obscure. He had not suffered anything like the indignities of a Ludgrove – or a Stowe. Perhaps it was the food, or perhaps it was because he had arrived even at Beaumont preceded by a certain reputation, having reputedly written – aged seven – to King George V, demanding that his country pay back its war debts to America. On returning to the US just before the war, Will Buckley decided, with utmost reluctance, to send Bill to an American boarding school. Recognizing a strong character when he met one, he had settled on

Edward Pulling and Millbrook. But, in his mistrust of the anti-Christian ethics of institutional education, he was able to bend even Mr Pulling to accept his own special terms: namely that the boys 'would be his until noon on Saturday, after which they would return for one and one-half days at home' – for, presumptively, what today would be called debriefing, or brainwashing.

Though his sharp wit soon proved that he was more than capable of looking after himself, this unique privilege ensured that young William was regarded both with envy and as something of a special case, something out of the crowd. Three years previously (and therefore a year before Hitler's *Kristallnacht* would have augmented the outrage of the deed), local reports had it that four of the Catholic Buckleys had been among seven children who lit – in the style of the Ku Klux Klan, but more as a childish Hallowe'en prank – a fiery cross outside a nearby Jewish resort. (Bill had not been among them, simply because – as he admitted with painful honesty many years later in his *National Review* – he had been considered too young. But the episode, and what it was held to signify, never ceased to haunt him.) This was compounded by Bill's inheritance of his father's strong views about the war in Europe, which were, in simplest terms, that – for a devout, ultra-conservative Catholic – Hitler's Nazism represented a lesser evil than Stalin's communism, and that Washington's Farewell Address eschewing foreign entanglements should be rigorously heeded. On his return from Europe shortly after the outbreak of war in Europe, speaking to the school, Buckley Sr had delivered the kind of pessimistic message that Ambassador Joseph Kennedy was filing from London: there was no enthusiasm for the war in Britain, and America had better keep out. There had followed a lively debate, the school then being fairly evenly split. A school poll, which was fairly representative of East Coast schools at the time, showed that 93 per cent wanted the Allies to win; but only 8 per cent wanted America to join in the war, rising to 14 per cent if the Allies were losing; while only 15 per cent would send war supplies to the Allies and *not* to the Germans. By the time young William arrived the following September, France had fallen and the school was more Interventionist-minded. But it was no coincidence that he had christened his first sailboat *Sweet Isolation*, and the moment the first school debates began he never missed an opportunity to speak up fearlessly – and effectively – in support of America First.

After my Fish family indoctrination of the summer, I had come to regard the Isolationists as the deadliest enemy of Britain, in league with the Devil, and compared with whom Hitler was only marginally worse. I therefore instantly regarded this precocious intellect with gravest suspicion and distaste. As soon as I had found my feet, I challenged him on every occasion in the Forum, the school debating society. He invariably won, on forensic skill, but lost the ensuing vote from an audience that had already made up its mind. Then as later, however, defeat and unpopularity only seemed to sharpen his appetite.

Preceded by weeks of ominous warnings about what it would signify 'for youse new guys', accompanied by the slitting of eyes and noses bizarrely into great orange pumpkins, Hallowe'en descended on Millbrook, followed shortly thereafter by the half-term dance weekend. The warnings suggested that, by tradition, in the course of 'Initiation' on Hallowe'en Night, terrible retributions would be exacted – by the whole school, led by the sixth form – from those perceived to be particularly bumptious among the new intake. A cold hand gripped my heart as I wondered whether, despite the previous cordiality of my fellows, something like a reincarnation of Ludgrove was about to manifest itself. On the appointed night, to the accompaniment of chilling banshee noises, we neophytes were marched blindfolded and trembling through swamps and other unsavoury places, then led into the gym, before the presence of the Grand Inquisitor, who was, of course, Frank Trevor, his face painted white to resemble a death's-head (this, in fact, contrived to make him look only marginally more sinister than in real life). Next to him stood a regal Queen of Sheba (Mrs Pulling, of course). Reblindfolded, we were then condemned by these two personages to various minor indignities, such as a shampoo concocted of flour; the worst was having to drop a coin off one's forehead into a funnel stuck into one's trouser top – into which was then poured a jug of icy water. The most painful part of the whole evening, however, came at the end of it all: being treated to disgusting pumpkin-pie. Even the odious Lord Primrose was submitted to nothing more injurious than a mild biffing about, and having to eat three dry crackers and then whistle 'The Star-Spangled Banner'. It was all very innocent, very childish – and very American.

What this innocuous 'hazing' signified, in effect, was one of the more salutary features of Millbrook, one which I believe was also true of most American private schools. Beyond Hallowe'en there was a complete absence of bullying, or ganging up on nonconformist or wayward boys. On the sole occasion when there was a brief but obnoxious outbreak of bullying, the shocked repugnance of the sixth form was such that they trooped off *en masse* to obtain official sanction from the Boss to punish the offenders. At morning prayers the following day, he announced dramatically to the assembled school that he would rather close its doors than tolerate any such behaviour. Nor was there any of that petty snobbery or the frantic sucking-up to boys with opulent parents likely to produce the most delectable sweets on 'grub days', which I remembered so vividly as being one of the less agreeable features of Ludgrove. At Millbrook we were totally oblivious to the rank or wealth of our fellows. Professor Higgins's famous line – 'It is impossible for an Englishman to open his mouth, without making some other Englishman despise him' – could never have been applied there. Indeed, a regional accent, southern or midwestern, was generally a source of pride. At Millbrook, you were accepted purely at face value; civility was actually encouraged.

The informality of masters like the beloved Hank Austin was typical of Millbrook school-life. There was no uniform. Provided your hair was brushed and your nails clean at meals, and you put on a blue suit for chapel on Sundays, nobody minded what you wore. Equally relaxed were relations with the faculty, though, by English standards of those days, discipline might have seemed lax. In fact it was effective. The American system, and mentality, shunned corporal punishment, and thus at Millbrook punishment for the most heinous offence was exacted through an institution popularly known as the Jug. Each Saturday a Judgment Day was held, when those who had erred during the week were weighed in the balance and sentenced to periods in the Jug proportional to the gravity of the sin: that same night the condemned would convene in the Barn to copy out vast chunks of the *Encyclopaedia Britannica*. Meanwhile, in the gymnasium above, the good and the crafty enjoyed the movies, the high spot of the Millbrook week. Such were the structural frailties of the old Barn that the noisiest and most exciting parts of the films, together with the audience's applause, would seep down to the unhappy miscreants below, making it a punishment that might have been dreamed up by Dante. The weekly movie was carefully selected by the sixth-form Movie Committee, guided by the Boss, and was kept a deadly secret, so that would-be malefactors would never quite know whether it was worth committing a crime that week. They were a carefully chosen blend of thrillers, like *The Maltese Falcon*, war dramas like *Casablanca* and Hitchcock's *Foreign Correspondent*, and the inevitable Errol Flynn action movie such as *The Sea Hawk*. For the younger school, there was a larding of Westerns (*Stagecoach*, with a young John Wayne) and comic turns by Abbott and Costello, plus the occasional daring bedroom farce, with William Powell and Myrna Loy, magnificently unprurient, played strictly according to the Hay's Office rulings – under which, if a couple were in bed together (regardless of marital status), one of them always had to have a foot on the floor. Just to make sure that there was no barracking, no off-colour commentary, the Boss inevitably sat unobtrusively in the back row, armed with his enormous flashlight to pick out any offenders and pack them off down to Hades below. On retirement he reckoned he had watched over one thousand movies – good and awful – in the course of his stewardship.

Scholastic discipline was maintained more by carrots than by sticks. The studious were rewarded with occasional weekend leaves to get away from school. Nor were 'high grades' rated the only academic distinction; there was also an insidious system known as 'effort marks'. Thereby a boy not over-endowed with brains could still earn a weekend by a first-rate effort: E-1 (failed but tried hard). Needless to say, the swaggering nonchalance afforded at the other end of the scale by an A-5 (full marks, but made no effort at all) – the sort of grade Bill Buckley frequently got – gained far more envy from one's contemporaries.

In addition to the faculty, the sixth form also had disciplinary responsibilities. But they had none of the imposing powers of their opposite numbers at a British public school. Their weapons were the rebuke and the report, not the cane, Hallowe'en being the only time they were permitted physically to impress neophytes with their authority. Recently a consumer research revealed that, whereas in 1990 the 'top problems' in US secondary schools were 'Drug Abuse, Alcohol Abuse, Pregnancy, Suicide, Rape, Robbery, and Assault.' In 1940 they comprised simply, such devastating heinous sins as 'Talking Out of Turn, Chewing Gum, Making Noise, Running in Halls, Cutting in Line, and Littering.' Millbrook ran true to form; despite the apparently happy-go-lucky disciplinary system, there was remarkably little serious crime in the 1940s. Lateness, scruffiness, blasphemy, disobedience, idleness and the illegal possession of radios or food composed the usual run of offences that kept the encyclopaedias in constant use. Smoking was the most serious crime (drugs, of course, were simply unheard of then), and warranted either the sack or suspension for a term, depending on the flagrancy of the offence. Eventually (in my last year), wisely acknowledging the almost irrepressible urge of American sixteen-year-olds and remembering what the principle of Prohibition had done to the morals of adult Americans, the Boss decided to control the vice rather than attempt to repress it. A 'smokehouse' was set up where sixth-formers could smoke once a week. All the foul accessories of nicotine had to be kept there, and any further law-breaking was treated ruthlessly as a 'capital' offence. Inevitably, it all reminded me of Le Rosey and the distressful saga of Knatch-bull's nose. Unlike most English public schools, there was not even a nearby town to present temptation; thus a roadhouse called the Tollgate Inn was the main objective of any illicit breakouts from school. But the furtive glass of beer and the dim prospects of finding a pretty girl there to gaze at from a distance were small recompense for a ten-mile scramble across thorny hills and marshes.

The next excitement that was upon us was the school Dance Weekend for the Upper School, the culmination of weeks of feverish letter-writing and telephoning. The girls who came were alarmingly sophisticated creatures, ranging from fourteen to seventeen, mostly from the 'smart' day-schools of Manhattan, to be put up in the school Guesthouse or parcelled out around the married faculty members. I looked on sadly, and with envy, knowing no girl to invite; but fantasizing that, one day, I might summon up courage to ask up the goddess Judy Cutler. The weekend included a barbecue and a ball game, where the 'dates' shrieked out encouragement to their armour-clad heroes and hurled abuse at the visiting team. Millbrook generally triumphed on these days. In one of her most memorable *obiter dicta*, the great Dorothy Parker once observed that if all the girls who went to the Harvard–Yale Football Game were 'laid end to end . . . I wouldn't be a bit surprised'. But surely *nothing* like that ever happened at Millbrook. Under the watchful eye of the Pullings, and the beam of that enormous torch, it would have been a lucky man who got more than a chaste peck. Anyway, kept clean-minded by the Hay's Office rules, we were all sublimely innocent. To have as your anointed guest the prettiest, liveliest girl lent vast kudos; perhaps that was partly what it was all about.

During my three years at Millbrook, I cannot recall a single case of theft, and only one where there was a suggestion that perversion had contributed to a boy's dismissal. Looking back on how the United States, since 1945, so swiftly became the gay centre of the world, embracing with such abandon what Americans derisively used to dub the 'British disease', I am amazed at how straightforward we all were then. Was it, perhaps, partly because our youthful libidos were kept in a healthy state by those regular Dance Weekends? Why was it all so different to what went on, avidly and incessantly, at Stowe? And what changed it all?

Despite the congenial atmosphere at Millbrook, it was hard for any of us Bundles – and especially that first term – not to be

distracted from our new, comfortable and perhaps slightly parochial world by the distant clamour of the war, growing ever
closer and more sinister, and creating daily more anxiety in all
our hearts. We arrived at school, walking tall in the knowledge
that the Battle of Britain was being won, in the air, by the heroic
Few. But the threat of invasion persisted. Each night we went to
bed half expecting the morning to bring the dreaded news, but
each time there was a daybreak tang of frost in the air at
Millbrook, we realized it must also be bringing the safety of
winter a day closer at home. Then came the news – particularly
anguishing for those with homes in or around the capital – that
the Luftwaffe had switched its main assault to London. On 7
September 1940, nearly a thousand German planes took off,
watched by Göring, for the heart of Britain, in the greatest raid
of the war to date, setting the whole of Poplar and East Ham
ablaze. With pride, we joined the school listening to Churchill's
great speech of 11 September, likening the challenge to Drake and
the Armada, the resonant cadences hurling defiance at 'This
wicked man':

> now resolved to break our famous Island race by a process of
> indiscriminate slaughter and destruction. What he has done is to
> kindle a fire in British hearts, here and all over the world, which
> will glow long after all traces of the conflagration he has caused
> in London have been removed. He has lighted a fire which will
> burn with a steady and consuming flame until the last vestiges
> of Nazi [always with the long-drawn, scornful pronunciation,
> 'Naasi'] tyranny have been *burnt* out of Europe, and until the
> Old World [and here came the direct message to America, to
> our companions at Millbrook] – and the New – can join hands
> to rebuild the temples of man's freedom and man's honour,
> upon foundations which will not soon or easily be
> overthrown.

It was all great stuff, and we knew as we clustered around the
radio in Hank Austin's rooms, or over at the Pulling house (or on
my own illegal receiver), that we were listening to history – and

literature – being made. One may now forget the exact words, but those gruff tones filled all of us with resolve and courage – yet also with sadness and deep anxiety. For it was clear that the news from London was grim, the casualties and damage appalling. Despite censorship, America's finest correspondents, Quentin Reynolds and Ed Murrow, finding a cause and rising supremely to the occasion, in their nightly accounts of the Blitz fired US imaginations with the flames that Hitler was lighting in London. At the same time, their tales of Londoners' heroism could not help but fuel our own apprehensions.

The weekly letters from my father, brave and uncomplaining, but amazingly uninformative as they were, hardly helped. Ritualistically, the first paragraph would be taken up by acknowledgement of letters received. He fussed if, like every good English schoolboy away at boarding school, I did not write religiously every Sunday. The second paragraph would consist of comments on my handwriting and school reports; the third would be a sentence on Terry's state of health; then would follow a couple of guarded sentences on the war, terminated by a note of rather formal affection. Once, in that autumn of 1940, he revealed casually that the favourite pub of Saville, his major-domo in London, had 'disappeared'. I shuddered, recognizing, between the lines, that it must have been the one on the corner of Lees Place, barely fifteen yards from my father's house. (When I returned, in 1943, he shook me by showing me the hole, observing mildly that the bang had blown the shaving-brush out of his hand. I was glad I had not known at the time.) Another letter reported that the beach hut at Titchfield had been destroyed 'by enemy action' (how the news would have pleased Madame Scap, hiding out from the Occupation down on the sunny Riviera!) – and his Scotch delight that he had received £25 compensation. When those immortal films appeared on American news screens of St Paul's lit up by fire all around, I knew that the area near where my father spent his days in the City must have been devastated.

As I heard that parts of London I was just beginning to get to know, and love, as a teenager were being destroyed, from the Wren churches – one after the other – to the scruffy little shops selling wireless bits-and-pieces in Holborn, I hated the Germans with a passion that I had never felt before – and sometimes Roosevelt's America only marginally less for its inaction. The image of Theo, the Good German, had all but disappeared into oblivion. After a blazing bonfire on the school farm, quite irrationally I suffered a series of hideous, holocaustic nightmares. One day, on smelling burning bacon in the dining room, I retched. It was silly.

As the attack spread from London, Coventry was shattered, while, from the comfort of his White House office, Roosevelt was calling upon Churchill, bloodthirstily, to 'bomb the Germans everywhere' (towards which end, had we Bundles known of the call, we would have felt – instinctively, but privately – that he was doing precious little to help). Nevertheless the Blitz began to galvanize American opinion like nothing else, not least among the boys of Millbrook. 'You burnt the City of London in our homes,' wrote the American poet, Archibald MacLeish, 'and we felt the flames.' Overnight the character 'Mrs Miniver' became the symbol of brave, embattled Britain. Wheeler-Bennett's British Information Services were swift to parade its engagingly under-stated author, Jan Struther, across America, making her a Book of the Month Club choice and instant bestseller, and launching a somewhat romanticized film version (with Greer Garson and Walter Pidgeon), which was to sweep the box offices the following year. Declared FDR, 'Mrs Miniver has done more for the Allies than a flotilla of battleships.' It was all grist to the mill of the Cutler–Breeses, Pullings and FDRs of this world. Through Rossy Cutler's British War Relief, private subscriptions were raised across America to purchase planes for Britain – $100,000 for a new bomber, a bargain $20,000 for a Spitfire.

Apart from the passive heroism of the Londoners that winter term, there were other straws to give us comfort, to make us proud, and to help persuade America that Britain did indeed mean business. Although a joint effort to grab Dakar was thwarted by those indiscreet Gaullists, two new stars had arisen in North Africa and the Mediterranean – Admiral Cunningham and General Wavell. In the first major aircraft-carrier action of the war, and with the daring of a latterday Drake, Cunningham attacked Mussolini's fleet, safely tucked up in its lair at Taranto on the heel of Italy. Using ancient Swordfish biplanes that looked like something out of the previous war ('stringbags' as their crews derisively called them), Cunningham managed to torpedo three Italian battleships, thereby changing, in a matter of minutes, the whole naval balance of power in the Mediterranean. Then, with equal surprise, out of the desert wastes struck a new, one-eyed general with the face of a gentle St Bernard, Archie Wavell, sweeping the Italians out of Egypt and plunging deep into Cyrenaica, with the capture of thousands of demoralized prisoners. Though they were not Germans, it supplied Britain with its first land victory of the war, providing an immense boost to morale, in America, as well as in Britain. Wavell and Cunningham duly made their appearance on the cover of *Time*, that great yardstick of fame. In America that winter it was, quite unmistakably, Britain's finest hour. On top of all this, in the savage Epirus the Greeks were inflicting another, even more unexpected humiliation on Hitler's ally. To the Führer's disconcertion, in the autumn Mussolini had launched his troops out of Albania into northern Greece. But, fighting under appalling winter conditions in the Pindus Mountains, and with little more than First World War rifles, the Greeks counterattacked, routing crack Italian troops that somehow seemed to lack what 'Private Angelo' later described as the *dono di coraggio*.

Yet still, in our eyes, when it came to participating, to joining in the war, Roosevelt's America continued to stand on the sidelines. We smirked when told that FDR (never renowned for his table) generously sent Churchill a whole crate of brussel sprouts. Obviously, in our tender years and from our fastness at Millbrook, we could not gauge just how menacing and finely balanced were his problems in Congress. The devilish power of German propaganda in the States remained strong, coupled with the work of the fifth-columnist German-American Bund, and comforted, aided and abetted by the clamorous and influential Isolationist press of William Randolph Hearst and Colonel McCormick in Chicago – and, of course, by Ham Fish in Washington and Bill Buckley at Millbrook. According to *Silo* polls taken that December, 83 per cent of the school was convinced that British morale would stand up over the winter; though, in a debate with the neighbouring school of Hotchkiss, the Isolationists were recorded as having won.

From September onwards, the importance to the war of the forthcoming presidential elections gripped the nation. As, so it seemed, could only happen in America, the Republican candidate was an unknown quantity. Wendell Willkie from midwestern Indiana proudly let it be known that he owned neither a watch nor a car. He had never been elected to any public post. He had embarked with no campaign headquarters, no manager, no organization and no funds. What he did have was a hoarse, gruff and rather attractive voice, ideas and the ability to express them. He also had a mistress, Irita van Doren; but this was not known in clean-minded 1940, where the private lives of American leaders were not subjected to the obsessive spotlighting of later years. (On the other hand, we are now told that FDR also had a girlfriend – and so did Eleanor. Had the public morality of the 1990s prevailed then, we should today no doubt all be provinces of Germany or Japan.) Defeating (to most people's surprise) the Isolationist candidates, Senators Taft and Vandenberg, at the Republican Convention in the summer, Willkie had stood out for intervention. After his victory, one of Roosevelt's top Cabinet members wrote, 'Thank God. Now we can go on helping Great Britain during the next four months.' But, when it came to the crunch, Willkie found himself forced to make all kinds of electoral promises to keep the country out of actual involvement. He flinched over the fifty-destroyers deal ('the most dictatorial action ever taken by any President', he called it), and when Roosevelt, trying to steal his clothes, declared under pressure to the all-important American Moms, 'Your boys are not going to be sent into any foreign wars,' Willkie raged, 'That hypocritical son-of-a-bitch! This is going to beat me!' He was right. Traditional Republicans like Julia and Billy Breese voted for Roosevelt, and I long suspected that Rossy Cutler did, too – though, years later, she hotly denied it ('What a terrible thing to say!' she wrote me).

In those weeks preceding the presidential elections, possibly the most important in American history, at Millbrook the flurry and frenzy parodied the nation at large. As I had already discovered, American schoolboys were by nature politically conscious to a high degree. Hot and furious the arguments waxed over the merits of Roosevelt versus Willkie. Small boys ran about sporting campaign buttons in their lapels as the febrile atmosphere of the Convention spread around the school. Boys wrote home to their parents begging for yet more buttons with even more virulent slogans. 'WE WANT WILLKIE' was superseded by:

NO THIRD REPUBLIC

NO THIRD REICH

NO THIRD INTERNATIONAL

AND NO THIRD TERM! ! ! !

which in turn gave way to 'WE DON'T WANT ELEANOR EITHER' and 'I HATE WAR: MY WIFE HATES ELEANOR'.

We aliens kept (fairly) quiet – with a certain barely muffled superciliousness. How could you elect any *serious* government to the accompaniment of all that razzmatazz, the drum-majorettes and so on, of the Conventions! Yet the salvation of Britain, if not of mankind, turned on it. But there could never have been any doubt whom in our hearts we wanted to win: FDR, the man who was (we hoped) bringing America into the war on our side.

In the event, the veteran campaigner and incumbent won an unprecedented third term with 27 million votes to 22 million – in itself a record for the Republicans created by the dark horse from Indiana, and including the 'business vote' of thousands of New Deal haters like John Cutler. But, though tragically removed by a prematurely early death before the next presidential elections in 1944, Willkie then lent Roosevelt maximum bipartisan support on war policy. All the talk now became of Lend–Lease, the great new concept FDR was trying to push through Congress, first outlined in a quite informal post-election speech on 17 December:

'Let me give you an illustration – suppose my neighbour's house catches on fire, and I have a length of garden hose four or five hundred feet away. . .'

Once the fever of election had passed, FDR safely re-elected, Thanksgiving was upon us. Ever since the 1940s I have felt that it was, fittingly enough, one of the happiest of American public holidays – if not of almost anywhere, combining as it does the brightest features of Britain's Harvest Festival and Christmas. The last Thursday in November, it comes at a time when one most needs a holiday, in the long span between the ending of summer and before winter begins, but when the leaf is often still sere and yellow. It is celebrated with cider and doughnuts, turkey and cranberry sauce, but with none of the pagan pressures and vulgarization of the modern Christmas. Thanksgiving 1940 was a good introduction – according to the impeccable *Silo* columns, it was 'the warmest and sunniest in many a year'. A hallowed holiday, Millbrook celebrated it with a colourful hunt meet, and a treasure hunt (I note that I was on the winning team, together with the resourceful school dietician, Sally Frankenstein, and her admirer, Austin Johnson of the language faculty). For the week-end, the school, bar a few miscreants, closed down, and I was scooped up by Rossy Cutler for a joyous reunion at Garrison, glowing under the autumnal sun. Jack had, I recall, already set off to join the RAF, but Judy, mischievous, funny and beautiful, was there. My heart skipped a beat or two when she asked if I could help translate her Latin homework, currently causing her sleepless nights in her last year of high school in New York. Rossy herself was in wonderful, ebullient spirits, rejoicing in the good news that Britain still stood, and glued to the radio news hour by hour, overwhelming in her praise of Churchill. I went back to school, thoroughly warmed by it all, and perhaps understanding a little why, with so good a life, the Isolationists should want to preserve American innocence, away from it all.

Swiftly on the heels of Thanksgiving came the end of term. It was dignified, as of tradition, by Mr Pulling reading the whole of *A Christmas Carol* to the entire school. 'To the graduated dismay of all who had heard the story once, or twice, or three times', commented Bill Buckley in years to come. But Mr Pulling read it with such personal enjoyment, so mellifluously with that agreeably mid-Atlantic accent, that it never failed to make me feel nearer to home. In 1940, Dickens was succeeded, in the last chapel of the term, by the Boss choosing as the text of his sermon King George VI's famous Christmas broadcast of 1939: 'And I said to the Man who stood at the Gate of the Year . . .'

And so the first term at Millbrook, in a strange – but not unfriendly – American world, ended for me. But could I truly say that I was *happy*? No, at least, I thought I was not. I was too unsettled, too torn by all that was happening 3000 miles away, feeling more than a bit miserable to be away from it all. Unkindly, I must have intimated as much to the saintly Julia Breese in my letters from Millbrook. I cannot recall what I may have said, but suppose I expressed less than total enthusiasm for the food and customs – and indicated that I found the education somewhat lacking. At any rate, it evidently distressed and worried her greatly, provoking from her son Billy a pages-long letter of reproach. It must have cost him, one of the world's worst, most strained and painful letter-writers, hours of anguish and outpouring of life-blood ('Took Nora and me weeks to prepare,' he told me many years later). It made me feel terrible, quite rightly, which was the proper object of the 'rocket', and it also taught me something useful, and fundamental, about Americans – 'When in doubt, *enthoose*. If you don't actually *enthoose*, that implies criticism.' Some years went by before I got – and relished – the message, growing to feel that the ability to enthuse was perhaps one great advantage Americans had over us inhibited Brits. It was a prime lesson.

CHAPTER SEVEN

Dolls and Guys

Even now, fifty years on, though the great stainless-steel Stream-liners are long since gone, I find it impossible to arrive in New York by rail without a tingle of excitement and anticipation. There is the melancholic hooting as the train sweeps round the curves alongside the majestic, oily Hudson; the transit through the bombed-out slums of the Bronx and Harlem (bad enough even in the 1940s); the disappearance, after the 125th Street halt, into the long, black tunnel beneath Park Avenue. That sombre forest of pillars, apparently holding up the whole of Manhattan's great skyscrapers, always struck me as one of the wonders of the modern world – reminding me, later, of the endless Cisterns of Constantinople, where one half expected to see blind fish swimming among them. Then you suddenly emerge into throbbing life and light at very grand Grand Central, with its Oyster Bar, shoe-shine boys, Wall Street prices, Horn and Hardart Automat cafeterias, and every other kind of emporium – the heart of New York City. Depressing as the other is exciting, the return journey is possibly even more dramatic, as if descending into Hades. But when you emerge at 125th Street you are never quite sure whether you have really escaped from Pluto's dark territory.

Beneath the mock baroque building, with its massive gilded finial, standing athwart the world's richest avenue (until Pan Am ruined the whole effect by erecting a vast concrete tombstone behind it), Grand Central to me always symbolized the whole wealth and bustling energy of America. In the early 1940s, at Christmas time an electric organ above the bustling concourse greeted commuters during rush hour by belting out carols and the Hallelujah Chorus (Irving Berlin's great hit, 'White Christmas', had not yet, happily, become top pop) – all of them, male and female travellers, seemingly wearing hats of some sort, but few, if any, uniforms. From Grand Central that first school holiday of Christmas 1940, I hastened with an eagerness I couldn't recall from days at home – and couldn't quite define – up Madison Avenue to 58 East 80th Street.

The Cutler house on 80th Street was a typical New York brownstone family house, steeply straight up and down, nestling quietly away from the hubbub of central Manhattan, just above the grand Society Library on 79th Street, a socially acceptable but relatively inexpensive address in those days. Like any house inhabited by Rossy Cutler, it was a place of life, merriment – and a good deal of confusion. The family lived sandwiched between a series of half-demented Irish cook-generals, with an unnervingly rapid turnover, in the basement, and up in the attic the constant, unchanging and always harassed person of Anna McCabe, the retired faithful retainer. Reminiscent of a Peter Arno *New Yorker* cartoon, the head of 'Onion-Bunion' (as she was nicknamed) with its plaited bun of hair and tiny gold-rimmed spectacles, seemed to be a fixed embellishment to the façade of the house, framed in the attic window, crying out after an oblivious Judy speeding down 80th Street on her long legs: 'Jude, what about your homework – you haven't finished it, have you?' 'You should have been out to lunch half an hour ago!' 'You've forgotten your key – your bag – your overcoat – your gloves . . .' These cries would reverberate down the street. The last to leave the nest, Judy as of 1940 was the hub around which the house revolved. She was Onion-Bunion's favourite, the special cross she had to bear and for whom she provided the memory and engagement book indispensable to so exquisitely and irreproachably vague a person.

The principal reason for my haste and excitement that December day was practising the piano, in the rather dingy dining room that led straight off the front steps. She was playing Brahms's *Hungarian Dance No. 5*. It was, I suspect, the only piece in her repertoire, and clearly she had some way to go before arriving at Carnegie Hall. But still I can never hear *No. 5* and its exuberant

Magyar tempo without thinking of Judy, her elegant fingers pounding the ivories, the dreamy green eyes and heart-shaped face that could so easily have come from somewhere exotic like Budapest. At the time, it was – quite simply – devastating. She threw down her music, got up and gave me a tremendous, noisy greeting – that of an elder sister. 'Why, Ally – welcome home!' I was installed in Jack's room; he was currently back in Egypt, now a Yank in the RAF. That evening we all dined together, almost certainly Boston black-bean soup in which floated a slice of hard-boiled egg, so thick you could stand a spoon in it, and I was never made to feel more like coming 'home'. The talk was, of course, all about the war. More even than before, in the Cutler household Britain – its endurance through the Blitz and Wavell's exploits in the desert – was the flavour of the month. 'The British must be really knocking hell out of Göring,' said Peter, ever the ineffable optimist. 'That Wavell,' said Rossy Cutler, 'what a great general! And he looks so modest.' 'Don't you feel so proud for your Mr Churchill, Ally?' Judy chipped in. '*We* all are.' I felt thrilled that she shared my pride; but then, with the prickliness of the teenager in love I wondered whether I detected just a note of condescension, of the elder sister. At this point, John Cutler would arrive, flushed and a little late for dinner. The accepted view at the time was that he had made a detour via one of the taverns down on Wall Street, but it was revealed when we were all much older that he had almost certainly been sojourning with a lady-friend. An invariable ritual would ensue, with Mr C. exclaiming, 'Mother dear, it's too hot in here!', and throwing open every window within reach. After a discreet interval, Rossy Cutler would get up and quietly close them again; and so on, merrily, through the evening.

Hardly was I settled, in the absent Jack's room, before Rossy Cutler announced, 'We've a busy schedule lined up for you, Ally. There's a ticket for you to go to the Middle Holiday Dance, at the Plaza. You'll have to go rent a tuxedo.' I started. A *dance*? I had never been to one in England, and I didn't know *how* to dance (it was considered 'soppy') – and what was a tuxedo, anyway? Hopeful, I asked if Judy was going too. 'No, I'm too old!' The

Middle Holiday was for fourteen- and fifteen-year-olds; she was going to the Senior Holiday. In torment, I envisaged her being swept around the room, endlessly 'cut in on' by handsome Harvard freshmen. My heart sank. 'But we've got the *cutest* little girl to go with you. She's called Libby . . . as *cute* as a bug's ear!' Judy assured me. In a fury, I decided I would certainly hate the 'cute' Libby, and thereafter every time I heard that particular adjective of condescension, I wanted to reach for my revolver.

Nevertheless, I set off for my friend of the summer, Honest Abe, to whom I had sold all those white flannels, in pursuit of the magic tuxedo. Complete with a dress-shirt and made-up elastic bow-tie, at a rental cost of several times what I had got for the Stowe trousseau, it made me feel magnificent – and immeasurably grown-up. I paraded before the mirror. Pat gave me some rushed lessons on the foxtrot and rhumba, and even the waltz, just in case. All duded up, in the words of the immortal Fred Astaire, I collected my date, Libby. She was indeed cute, a fourteen-year-old like a blonde doll, with a sweet smile. We arrived at the Plaza, that wonderful gargantuan French château on the corner of the park, surrounded by the fiacres, with their elderly top-hatted charioteers hunched over their braziers, blanketed horses and the strong odour of dung and horse-piss that always gives that elegant hotel its special flavour as you enter. There were hundreds of other schoolboys, looking immensely important and self-possessed, with their primped-up dates – and a good sprinkling of be-diamonded chaperones and dowagers. Previously, with many a giggle, Judy had initiated me into the secrets of that amazing black and orange volume, *New York Social Register*, something so barefacedly snobbish that it might even have brought a blush to the cheeks of my old headmaster, Ali Barber of Ludgrove. There, on a gallery overlooking the great ballroom, was every grandee in the *Register*, pointing and exclaiming, 'There's my Harry . . . That's Evvie – isn't she cute?' I averted my gaze for fear of seeing, and being spotted by, Rossy Cutler. 'Why that's our little Bundle from Britain!'

In the centre of the room was the vast 'stag-line', the pool of unattached singles (male, of course), milling around and brazenly studying the form with loud comments, for all the world like the paddock at Ascot. It was a nightmare system. If one happened to strike it lucky with a pretty girl, every ten seconds a stag would come up, tap you on the back, cut in on you and remove your dance-partner. On the other hand, you could be stuck without relief all evening with some unhappy prune. One would quite often see some boy desperately waving a dollar bill behind his plain partner's back. It was an easy, though risky, source of income for the impoverished stag, caddish enough to make frequent impromptu escapes to the men's room.

I took all this in, realized I knew not one soul in this vast assemblage and was about to lose all courage. Just at that moment, a friendly hand descended on my shoulder. It was Brad Mills, one of the football jocks of the third form at Millbrook, something of a blade. Alas, his grip on my hired shoulder was just a shade too jocular, and something terrible occurred. The whole sleeve of Honest Abe's rented 'tuck' came away from its parent body. I stood aghast among the gorgeous creatures of the *Social Register*, and wanted to turn and flee. My date's 'cute' doll's face began to melt. Suddenly, out of nowhere, a rescuing angel appeared in the form of a little old lady – presumably the hotel seamstress. She led me up to a tiny room atop one of the château-style turrets of the Plaza and, with amazing dispatch, sewed up the collapsed jacket without so much as my taking it off. I returned to the dance and to a relieved partner, and – in a manner of speaking – had a ball for the rest of the evening, though very little of it was actually spent with Libby. But the real trouble came when I returned to a darkened 80th Street at pumpkin time. Getting undressed, I discovered that the sweet little old lady had sewn on to the shoulder of the jacket, not only its sleeve but the (rented) shirt too. Handing it all back to Honest Abe the following morning, with fragments of shirt still adhering to the 'tuck' lining, it was definitely not quite the same garment. To avoid dispute, the sainted and burly Peter accompanied me.

The rest of that first Christmas-time in New York was sheer delight. Exploring New York on my own, I swiftly – and permanently – fell under the spell of its extravagances and crazy eccentricities: the electric atmosphere that set off sparks when you touched a door knob, and made you feel marvellous and full of vital energy; its multiplicity of noises; and its fantasy architecture, alternately imposing and ridiculous. I gazed up in awe at the Empire State Building, and at the alarmingly sharp point of the Chrysler Building, decorated with what looked like stainless-steel wings and automobile parts. I was fascinated by the exotic absurdities of the apartment blocks that soared forty floors, with Ye Olde Tudor half-beamed roofs perched improbably on their summits, and of the great hotels, the Pierre with its mansard roof and its neighbour, the Sherry Netherland, with its gothic spires thrust hundreds of feet up in the sky. My favourite view was the great panorama of distant skyscrapers, observed from a granite hillock in the centre of Central Park, a great holiday snap framed by lakes and weeping-willows. In that Age of Innocence when muggers and rapists were unknown, Central Park was a joy to ramble in, watching in winter for the big red ball which meant it was safe to skate on the ponds, or rowing in summertime. I used to love striding across it, from 80th Street, via the Giant Panda pacing around its cage in the Zoo, to the Natural History Museum on the West Side. I roamed, much of the time on foot, from the sleazy warehouses downtown, where a magical mail-order emporium called Lafayette Radio held sway, to Harlem and its jazz clubs in the north.

There was virtually no such thing as a no-go area in those days. To save money, as well as for the excitement of discovering the city, I used to walk great distances, intrigued by the glitter that came from some substance in the sidewalks – symbolically like diamonds. But it was a thrill, also, to be whirled at 70 m.p.h. by Express subway down to the Battery, for a nickel, and return slowly in a progression of jerks and roaring accelerations in a bus up Madison, with the strange machine by the driver's elbow that jingled as it digested its coins, and the cacophony of equally strange languages as the bus cut through Manhattan's different ethnic stratas. Occasionally, with one of the Cutlers there would be the treat of a taxi ride, all new, shining yellow and surging with silent power, with the modern luxury of a radio in the rear, to drown out the non-stop commentary, on every conceivable subject in fluent Brooklynese, from the driver. (In those days, unsurly, and uninhibited by the presence of the intervening panel of bullet-proof plastic, most of the drivers spoke English – of a kind – and actually knew where they were going.)

In the hundreds of times I have been back to New York since, it always struck me as a city poised, excitingly, on the brink of catastrophe. There was always a drama; a drought, with the sedate *New York Times* urging 'share a bath with a friend'; thunderstorms that cut the city off from the outside world by blocking the tunnels; sudden blizzards that choked the streets; heatwaves that reduced them to molten tar; power breakdowns that locked people for hours in the subway or in elevators. The first thing that intrigued me in 1940 (and has done so ever since) were the smoking, steaming manholes in the middle of the streets. What lay beneath? Were we all living on top of a volcano? It wouldn't have surprised me. Peter assured me that the steam came from underground Chinese laundries. Convinced of the Yellow Peril, he was sure they were plotting one day to blow up the city. I never discovered whether he was pulling my leg, or whether he too had been taken for a ride. With the sense of drama went the noise. It wasn't just the constant hooting of the taxis, but – whether it was the bagel-sellers, the men in ear muffs crouched over their braziers of wonderful-smelling roasted chestnuts, the hawkers and the drunks – somebody was always shouting at somebody else. On street corners, the New Yorkers always seemed to converse at the tops of their voices. In the half minute while you waited for the lights to change, you could hear the stories of their lives, of their financial problems, of their wives and girlfriends. How different it all was to sedate London, where I remembered everybody speaking almost in hushed, shy whispers!

As a teenager, I loved it all – especially the focal hubbub of it all down at Times Square, gazing at the modern wonder of the *Times* 'Motogram', which provided the latest headlines in letters five feet high, and politely wished the revellers good-night at midnight. With equal courtesy (and noise), the diminutive mayor,

Fiorello ('Little Flower') La Guardia, who had presided over the whole of this mad city for the previous six years, would broadcast on Sundays: 'Ladies, I want to ask you a little favour. I want you please to wear your rubbers when you go out in this weather.' Half-Italian, half-Jewish, he seemed to symbolize this curiously unAnglo-Saxon Tower of Babel, of which he was the ninety-ninth mayor. As a good Republican, Rossy Cutler approved of the way he had broken up the Democratic machine in New York, but just wished he could carry his fellow Italians to be a little bit tougher on Benito Mussolini.

The days passed happily. With Pat I went skating in the pocket-sized ice-rink that nestled beneath the great concrete tombstone of Rockefeller Plaza, where Julia Breese had taken me – gasping in the heat – for tea those first days only a few months previously. With greedy Peter, I was introduced to the joys of hamburgers (surely the best in the world) and lemon-meringue pie at Hamburger Heaven (sadly, long since extinct). Or we would go up to the 86th Street movies in German Yorktown, growling together at the propaganda news features put out by the Bund. With Rossy Cutler and Judy, I would go down to the British War Relief centre, also in Rockefeller Plaza, now adorned with bits of shot-down Luftwaffe bombers, where I would be made to blush on being paraded before the legions of adulant, anglophile ladies, before spending the morning quietly folding abdominal bandages – wondering with dread what hideous British wounds they would shortly be covering. In the evenings we would sometimes go to a dance at the English-Speaking Union for visiting British servicemen. These were generous, warming affairs, but also sometimes hideously embarrassing for poor Judy, prodded shamelessly towards the first soldier, sailor or airman ('It's Mrs Cutler's war work, darling . . .'). At times her will to 'do something for those British boys' caused all of us fearful embarrassment; even a walk posed a danger. Having discovered that British pay was only a tithe of what the Americans received, Rossy Cutler formed a covenant with herself to give a dollar to every Briton in uniform she met on the streets. And she was by no means a millionairess. Sometimes, on the way out to a cinema *en famille*, when her evening's bag had been so high as to leave her penniless, she would then offer some able-bodied seaman, flabbergasted at his good fortune, the services of the beautiful Pat, or Judy, to take him around New York for the evening.

The astonishing thing in all this was that Rossy Cutler was never rebuffed nor ever taken advantage of. There came a time, however, when Judy and I formed a kind of alliance. The moment one of my fellow countrymen hove within range of Mrs Cutler's unerring vision, I would engage her in animated conversation, while Judy beat a hasty retreat round the block. In return, she would cover up for me when air-gun pellet holes appeared mysteriously in the mosquito-screens at Garrison (they made such an engaging, guitar-like pinging sound, to one who had never before seen doors and windows so clad). Equally I rejoiced in the quiet evenings at 80th Street, when, as a very special privilege, I would be allowed up to the sanctuary of Judy's room, to translate, or scan, her dreaded Latin for her. She may have been the most popular member of her class, but it was clear that she was *not* Miss Stringfellow's foremost academic at the Chapin Day-School – certainly not in Latin. Then would follow the inevitable clustering round the radio, for the evening news. One came to know all the commentators with their funny names and odd idiosyncrasies of speech: Raymond Gram Swing, and his clipped monotone; Elmer Davis, calm and detached; Gabriel Heatter, always sounding as if he had just come from his mother's funeral, full of the gloomiest prognostications. Yet there were many moments when I would forget all about England. Deplorably, I remember giving hardly more than a thought to how my father would be spending his Christmas: in the Blitz, sojourning with the old bores in the Oriental Club – and alone.

After the razzmatazz of New York and the constant drama of life with the Cutlers, I passed the remainder of that first Christmas vacation in Washington, which came as something of an anti-climax. Julia Breese's little apartment being too small to house me, I was farmed out to her son Billy and his Nora, with their newborn baby girl, Belinda (who cried rather a lot), in one of those charming garden suburbs that still surround what was then a small, very provincial capital. There was no one of my age – and, above all, no Judy. I pined, quietly. Of Billy, languid and full of those high ideals that I could never aspire to, I was just a little nervous after his rocket about enthusiasm.

I passed much of my time whizzing round the Chevy Chase ice-rink, working up my ice-hockey turns for the coming term. Although in the early 1940s Central Washington's white population was still, just, in the majority, it was the first time that I, an unworldly Bundle, had found myself in a truly black city. Mrs Breese took me round Washington and out to Mount Vernon, to improve my scant acquaintance with American history. Never having been to Paris, I was instantly awed by Washington's spacious splendour. Charles Dickens, visiting in the wake of the war of 1812 and finding little to like about America, unkindly dubbed it the City of Magnificent Intentions, complaining that its vast avenues, still without buildings on them, 'begin in nothing and lead nowhere'. To my constant, and continuing, surprise, non-Washington Americans as often as not were no less impolite about their capital than Dickens was. Its great eponym, they told one, wanting to insulate himself from the rowdy and drunken soldiery in Philadelphia, as well as to be conveniently adjacent to his beloved estate at Mount Vernon, selected a wilderness of woods and malarial swamps, with an appalling climate in summer, to be the capital of the first great republic founded since ancient Rome. Not so many years ago, the British Foreign Office classified it a 'hardship post'. (Equally, one should recall that General Eisenhower's medical corps in the Second World War had the Thames Valley rated as a malarial area!) Even as late as the 1960s the New Englander John F. Kennedy sneered at it as 'combining northern charm with southern efficiency'.

I disagree. Coming back to live there for a long spell in the early 1980s, despite the drug and crime horrors of its gutted, no-go centre, I always found it a warm and friendly city, with an easy-going tempo more like Europe than New York, and an agreeably gentle climate (except during its horrendously humid summer months) – always exciting, and unfailingly one of the most beautiful cities in the world. I look back with lasting joy on recollections of the glories of the alabaster white Jefferson Memorial, floating in a mist of cherry blossom in springtime; of the hazy pink and gold of the glassy Potomac in early morning; of the blazing azaleas and dogwoods amid the city's vast greenness (it must encompass more trees than any other city in the world); of the light filtering through golden leaves, and the cigar-like dryness of the crisp leaves underfoot along Rock Creek in the balminess of fall; of the staggering colours of the Blue Ridge in nearby Virginia in its extraordinary luminosity (it is so easy to forget that Washington DC lies on the same latitude as Tunis); of the maritime prettiness of the ancient soft-crab fishing villages along Maryland's eastern shore – not to mention Jefferson's enchanting, cosy stately home at Monticello crowded with all the domestic inventions of that Leonardian genius.

As of 1940, Washington undoubtedly was a rather parochial place. It had no proper theatre (was Ford's, where Lincoln was assassinated, the last one it had?). It was a bourgeois town that had sprung up around a bourgeois government – despite the influence of the Hudson Valley patrician who now resided in the White House. Its agreeably small-town ambience had, apparently, survived almost intact from the previous century – until FDR. But I found the glistening white symmetry of the Capitol, standing up so portentously on its hill (where the Interventionists were currently locked in ferocious debate with Ham Fish and his bad men over Lend–Lease), with the great sweep of the Mall down to the Washington Memorial, totally breath-taking. Having Buckingham Palace at the back of my mind, however, I could not believe how tiny was the residence of America's all-powerful leader, with the homely baseball diamond only just beyond the railings of its modest grounds. Explaining to me, pointedly, why it was called the White House (painted to hide the humiliating burn marks left by the wicked British in the war of 1812), Julia Breese took me inside. Even then, it struck me as extraordinary that one could (then) wander into the White House, without any formality or identification – typical of this great, open and unthreatened country.

Wandering round it, this small country house, not much larger than Ropley, in the middle of town, I kept on hoping – with burning curiosity – that we might bump into the Great Man in whose hands now lay the future of my country, of the world. How extraordinary it was, I reflected years later, that, although we all were told how he had contracted polio, supposedly swimming in the icy waters off Campobello Island, in common with most Americans I had no idea that the President, newly re-elected for that unprecedented third term, was in fact a cripple. In that televisionless age, we only heard his vigorous voice on the radio, this titan in whom all our hopes resided, or saw him photographed discreetly just head and shoulders – or else comfortably sitting down.

As I arrived in Washington, the British community was still reeling from the shock of the sudden death of the Ambassador, Lord Lothian. Hyper-energetic, and enormously popular in Washington, he had been considered a major card in the struggle to gain support for Britain's cause in the White House and Capitol, and had literally worked himself into an early grave. Almost his last utterance to the US press had been, as recorded by his subordinate and great admirer, John Wheeler-Bennett, 'Well, boys, we're broke; it's your money we want.' It was nothing less than the truth. Under the edict of Congress, Britain up to that moment had paid, in cash, for every gun and shell it had received. A month after Lothian's untimely death, the Lend–Lease Act was passed in Washington – later described by Churchill as 'the most unselfish and unsordid act of any country in all history' and clearly then a turning-point in the war. After some delay, Lothian's successor, Lord Halifax, arrived. As Julia Breese relayed to me, Washington was not immediately impressed. The new Ambassador was preceded by his reputation as a pre-war appeaser, and was soon known by the Churchill family's nickname for him, the Holy Fox, or, yet more uncharitably, as 'the Praying Mantis with an umbrella', on account of his appearance, which contained much that was not entirely to American tastes. Word swiftly ran round (as it does, pre-eminently, in that capital of 'government-by-leak') of his initial gaffes – like accepting an invitation to go fox-hunting. Presciently, however, Julia Breese reserved her own judgement. 'He's a very spiritual man,' she said. 'That must mean something.' In the end the Holy Fox proved to be a notable success for Churchill, and for Britain.

We listened raptly, and encouraged, to Roosevelt's Inaugural Address of January 1941, with that curious American upper-crust pronunciation of the word 'war' ('*wauh*') – and indeed a far more warlike tone than anything he had said hitherto, now that he was safely ensconced for another four years. 'Give us the tools, and we will finish the job,' declared Churchill, during the passage of the Lend–Lease Act, and it was on this note that the new term began at Millbrook. British fortunes were at an all-time high. *Time* magazine had selected Churchill as its 'Man of the Year' – 'Blood, Toil, Tears, Sweat – And Untold Courage'. No praise was too excessive for the man who had, at last, stood up to Hitler and fought him off. After the terrible injuries inflicted on the City during those December nights – perhaps the worst days of all, culminating in the tragedy of 11 January, when one single bomb killed 111 people sheltering in the Bank tube station – the Blitz seemed to be petering out. Lavishing praise on London's heroism, the American correspondents echoed the words of Elizabeth Bowen in *The Heart of the Day*: she had noted 'a diffused gallantry in the air. . . . Everybody in London was in love.' In the desert, Wavell seemed unstoppable, capturing Tobruk and sweeping right round the great bend of Cyrenaica, to El Agheila, mopping up Italian prisoners of war at an ever increasing rate – at one point ten divisions surrendered to part of one British division. At the same time, in East Africa General Alan Cunningham, brother of the Admiral already a household name in America, was relieving Mussolini of last remnants of his ill-gotten empire, including Ethiopia. In the Epirus, the valiant Greeks were registering more and more triumphs against the demoralized Italians; while, before the term was over, Admiral Cunningham had scored another triumph by destroying an Italian battlefleet in an old-style naval engagement off Greece's Cape Matapan.

Britain's growing band of friends and admirers in the States were jubilant. It was a school term during which we Bundles justly felt good. Might not Mussolini, after so many humiliations, now be forced out of the war? And then what? For a few wonderful weeks, even months, the optimists of the US press even had us fantasizing that Hitler, curiously passive, was at the end of his tether – his Luftwaffe smashed over England, the country rebellious and starving from the effects of the British naval blockade. Perhaps I would be back home by the summer?

At Millbrook a dramatic metamorphosis had taken place. North American winter, crisp and sometimes ferociously cold, had descended on Duchess County. Boys clattered on to the train taking us back to school, excitedly clutching skis and razor-sharp hockey skates, taping up their brand-new sticks with electricians' tape, and clad in the warm red-and-black-checked lumberjack shirts that I have worn all my life all over the world ever since. There was the statutory halt outside Wingdale Asylum, as the cheerful loonies waved at the train, and the inevitable comments passed round: 'What, Millbrook already?' Around the school campus, the stately maples were covered with a dusting of snow, and teams of boys with snow-scrapers and shovels were soon, with frenzied eagerness, clearing it off the pond, which shortly began to resound with the pleasurable swish of skates, the clicking of pucks on sticks, the thuds on the boards. There was always an exhilarating sensation of the dry cold freezing stiffly in one's nostrils. Football was behind us – the raucous exhortations of Coach Knutson a thing of the past. I began to feel, at last, in my element as far as sport was concerned – Le Rosey had prepared me well.

At the end of the Fall Term, squads of boys on Community Service, led by the industrious Henry Callard, had been busy, with extraordinary efficiency and good humour, laying down boardwalks and putting up storm-windows. At that time the

Community Service system was the feature of Millbrook life that most set it apart even from other American schools. *'Non sibi sed cunctis'* was the well-chosen school motto: Not just for oneself, but for the good of all. It was a sacred concept for Edward Pulling. It worried him that, by and large, boys who went off to American private schools were a privileged lot, out of touch with how the community functioned. 'If we want to maintain the privileges we so richly enjoy as members of a free, democratic society,' he declared with force, 'we must be willing to shoulder the obligations they entail. Privilege and responsibility must go hand in hand. You cannot have one without the other. Responsibility cannot be learnt only by hearing about it; one must actually experience it.'

Community service was Mr Pulling's pet brainchild; although it was, in fact, an extension of the Dewey philosophy of education. There was hardly any aspect of modern American education in the 1940s that did not bear the stamp of John Dewey, then regarded as both America's foremost philosopher and its foremost educationist. Dewey was an integral product of the great age of American material growth. Steeped in traditions of practicality and pragmatism, he reacted strongly against the classical approach to education. 'Children are people' was his favourite slogan, and he urged that school be made as much like real society as possible, emphasizing the importance of man in his community as against man the isolated individualist.

In line with Dewey's teachings, nearly all American schools in the 1940s had some form of 'training for citizenship', their own 'student government'. Mr Pulling's system carried it one stage further. Under Community Service every boy had his job or jobs which contributed to the school's administration. The jobs ranged from menial tasks like cleaning out the school buildings to running (very professionally) such vital school functions as the post-office (where I would rush, anxiously, at lunchtime to collect letters from my father, or new electronic components from Lafayette Radio), the bank, the shop, the cinema projection booth, the milk bar, the library and the fire department. One small boy would be detailed off to raise and lower the flag each day: a delicate task, for it was a mortal sin to allow any part of the hallowed Stars-and-Stripes to touch the ground. There was virtually no task around the campus that was not carried out by the boys, and planned and supervised by the 'student council'.

With very little interference from the faculty, the scheme ran with astonishing smoothness. There were the occasions when the school's slumbers were undisturbed after the Boy of the Day had forgotten to toll the awakening bell. There were the inevitable dramas, such as when rats got into the School Store in the cellar and ate the Hershey Bars, while mould destroyed the rest. The store was then moved above decks into the all-purpose, over-loaded Barn. In addition to the routine jobs, members of the school also ran such special projects as the greenhouse, the observatory, the school meteorological bureau and, of course, Trevor's Zoo and bird-banding station – all of which had been constructed *in toto* by past generations of Millbrook drones. As the war came closer, more and more jobs were to devolve on the boys, including waiting on table and dishwashing, as the domestic staff were gradually drained away into war work.

Dull, humdrum and faintly smug it all may sound – and how we used to moan among ourselves that our labour was being exploited, that we were saving the school thousands of dollars that should have been deducted from the fees of our wretched parents and sponsors. But it did help instil in us all a certain sense of Emersonian self-reliance that was (and maybe, to some extent, still is) lacking in British public schoolboys of similar ages. Certainly working afternoons side by side with Henry Callard on the farm helped create a sense of camaraderie, and enabled us inhibited Bundles really to get to know, and like, our strange schoolmates. It gave us too, perhaps, a sense of belonging.

In my first year the Boss thoughtfully gave me as my Community Service duty the job of school electrician. Hardly challenging, the responsibilities involved checking and replacing the hundreds of light bulbs throughout the school, and checking the fuses when they blew. Occasionally an unintentional disaster would occur, and the school would be plunged into darkness. Awareness of the immense potential for mischief did present itself from time to time – particularly of fusing the movie-projection circuits in the gym during the dread Saturday evenings when one was oneself condemned in the Jug down below, working away on the *Encyclopaedia Britannica*; or of plunging Trevor's biology lab into darkness at the ticklish moment when the *Drosophila Melanogaster* were being transferred from their bottles; or even of a more general power cut at a critical time. But an equal awareness that the Boss's vast torch would soon identify the obvious culprit, plus perhaps the more benign consideration that a power cut would also strike at the saintly Callards and their flock of tiny redhead children stayed one's hand on the fuse-board.

A much subtler form of mischief was at hand through the services of my new friends in the downtown slum area of New York, Lafayette Radio. For a few dollars, I contrived to assemble a tiny and highly portable transmitter, with a range of only a few hundred yards – enough to cover the campus on the broadcast band. Constantly shifting our site, like the best French Resistance operators, we set ourselves up as Radio Revolution, with a network of small spies who would discreetly ascertain what wavelength our target of the evening was tuned into. We were then able to broadcast subversion on that wavelength. We would urge the school at large to revolt against Führer Knutson's new scheme for a toughening-up 'assault course'; as a precursor of Animal Lib we wanted to alarm Frank Trevor with the threat that a group of local anarchist animal lovers were coming to open all the cages in the Zoo (alas, it turned out that the Trevor House was just out of range of my transmitter). But the best wheeze was to tease the Pickwickian French master, Hargraves Joyous Bishop, with German accents affecting to be a group of Nazis from the Bund, threatening to sugar the gasoline of any francophiles. We chuckled to think of the poor man, muttering '*Tiens!*' and sweating in front of his radio. It was all very childish, and harmless; needless to say, we never dared interfere with the Pullings' evening listening. However, although I was never allowed to speak on the air myself because of my give-away English accent, sooner or later the Gestapo were on our tracks: the famous flashlight appeared round the corner and the transmitter was confiscated. Standing rigidly to attention in the Boss's study I was accused of 'taking advantage' of my privileges (momentarily I thought of the Merch's strong right arm that would certainly have accompanied such a misdemeanour at Stowe), and phlegmatically faced yet more Saturday-evening work on the *Encyclopaedia Britannica*.

Radio Revolution did, I suppose, establish me as something of a local hero, for the first time. Among our small groups of 'revolutionaries' I made some good new friends. One was called Jack Hemphill, who remained a close buddy for the rest of our time at Millbrook. Very bright, he had an agreeably eccentric way of looking at things, and was a natural rebel. In his room he had a formicary in a glass box which, squatting cross-legged, he would study for hours on end. From his reveries he would emerge occasionally to announce, lugubriously, 'There's no doubt about it – the ants are going to take over the world, and soon! They work so damned hard, and they're so *organized*!'

As the new year progressed, life at Millbrook showed signs of getting better and better. I was, as they say, beginning to fit in. On top of the accustomed run of British heroes, there was the eclectic flow of other outside speakers, inventively corralled by the Boss, to widen our horizons. There was an eminent Indian, and close friend of Mahatma Gandhi, who went into great detail as to why the Indians hated the Raj ('a very valuable experience', wrote a student reporter in the ubiquitous *Silo* afterwards, with perhaps just a dig at us proselytizing Bundles: 'after all we have heard about the persecution of the British by the Nazis . . .'). A dear old man called Mr Marcy, cheeks of wrinkled apples like Thomas Hardy, who was the neighbouring farmer, came in as the temperature sank through the floor to tell us about the great blizzard of '88, which he had experienced as a boy at this self-same Millbrook. Trapped by drifts forty feet high, he had had to melt snow for his thirsty oxen and himself for days on end, sleeping between the animals for want of firewood. A Negro dean from a college in Washington, with a saintly face, came and told us about an unknown man called Albert Schweitzer, 'building a hospital in Africa for its poor natives'. He left us with a quote from Stephen Crane: 'I saw a man pursuing the horizon – the man pursuing the horizon was after something larger . . .' It rather seemed to epitomize Millbrook's idealism in those noble 1940s. And then there were regular visitations from a wonderful group of Negro spiritual singers, the Golden Gate Quartet, an art form made popular by the famous Inkspots. There always seemed to be a bass with a voice way down in his boots who was invariably round, jolly and very black. No less invariably, the tenors were what Willa Cather's southerners would have called 'high-yaller', lugubrious ectomorphs. I loved their marvellous harmony, and longed to know more about the deep south, where their melancholic and evocative songs came from.

Spring came, and with it a dread innovation of the Boss – Spring Speeches. Every boy in the school had to stand on his legs after lunch each day and speak, without notes, on a topic of his own choosing. It was agonizing for the victim, deadly for the rest of us – three minutes for the Bennies (as the smaller boys came to be called), and so on upwards to a massive ten minutes for the adult sixth-formers. To a yawning school, I delivered an exposition on 'British Schools' (it was later published by the *Illustrated London News*, in a symposium of essays by Bundles); my compatriot, Brian, one on 'Changing Conditions in England' – what bores we must have been! Jack Hemphill, predictably, told us about 'Ants'; Bill Buckley, no less predictably, orated 'In Defence of Lindbergh'. War subjects were strongly represented, with one Senior making our hair curl with his scenario for 'The Nazi Conquest of the United States'.

Young Buckley, however, was – as his subsequent career evinced – not readily deflected from what he believed. In the Forum he spoke up for the Juniors versus the Seniors against a motion 'That the German-American Bund be Abolished', on the principle that such measures would be resorting to the Nazis' own methods. The 'Affirmatives' won; nevertheless WFB Jr, aged fifteen, gained the laurels of being judged easily the best Junior speaker of the year for an anti-British polemic on 'Our Debt to Britain'. He claimed, according to the authoritative *Silo*, 'that, since in the past Britain had often been our worst enemy, we

Above Left: Rossy Cutler; in a mischievous mood.

Above Right: Peter Cutler, aged nineteen, in Martha's Vineyard, 1940.

Left: Jack Cutler, in French uniform as member of the American Field Service, 1940.

Connecticut Avenue, Washington, DC, 1940; 'Bundles for Britain' and 'America First' in adjacent windows.

Millbrook School; Edward and Lucy Pulling, dispensing hospitality in the last year of their long reign.

Millbrook School; typically, Henry and Clarissa Callard, true American pioneers, build their own house.

HMS *Rodney*, in Boston Navy Yard, being repaired after the sinking of the *Bismarck*, 1941 (note the scaffolding on the main gun-turrets). I took the photograph.

The 'Four Freedoms', Newfoundland; first meeting of Winston Churchill and Franklin D. Roosevelt, on board HMS *Prince of Wales*.

'Washington's Phoney War', shortly after Pearl Harbor, December 1941.

Millbrook girds itself for war:

Left: Führer Knutson leads the physical training programme.

Below: Frank Trevor in his biology lab, constructing model aircraft for the US Navy.

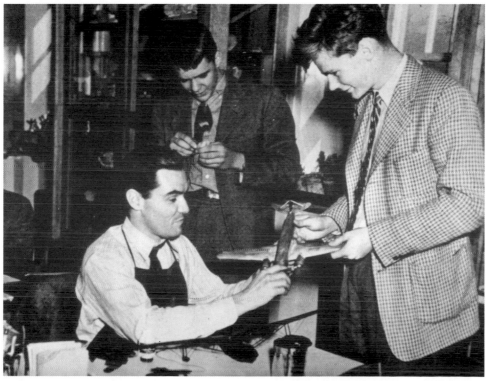

The Cutler wedding in the old German consulate, February 1942. *Left to right*, Bob Fowler, Pat Cutler, Harry Fowler, maid-of-honour Judy Cutler gives the toast.

The Buckleys at Great Elm, 1940. Bill is perched on the right arm of his mother's, Aloise senior's, chair.

Top: Millbrook. The graduating class of 1943. The author left rear, Bill Buckley seated second from right.

Above Left: Young airman; the author, Moncton, NB, Canada; 1943.

Above Right: Old airman, the 'Skew-Leader', Squadron Leader Brian Nixon, in retirement.

should *not* now help her out of a dilemma in which we have no concern. This controversial comment,' noted the *Silo*, with some shock, 'provoked much interest.'

For several weeks we glared at each other, more intensely than usual. Nevertheless, the precocious young orator was on a loser. Interlarded with such items as 'THE ZOO HAS LATELY BECOME A MATERNITY WARD FOR DOVES', polls – both intra-mural and inter-scholastic – were reported by the *Silo* in the aftermath of Lend–Lease that showed steadily mounting support for Britain. 'Should the US send over to Britain larger quantities of the tanks, guns, planes and other war materials originally intended for our army?' *Yes, 66.25 per cent.* 'Do you think that our present policy of "all aid to Britain short of war" will lead us to war?' *Yes, 66.25 per cent.* 'Do you think we will have to fight Germany within the next two years?' *Yes, 56.25 per cent.* But: 'Would we be justified in risking American ships to carry material to Britain to ports in Neutral Ireland?' *Yes, 38.75 per cent only* (this was an inter-scholastic poll). A few months later, however, 62 per cent of Interventionist Millbrook was favouring deployment of the US Navy to convoy war supplies across the Atlantic. Fierce leaders in the *Silo* over Lend–Lease endorsed 'giving dictatorial powers to the President' with the assurance that 'he will not misuse his power; he is as much a loyal American as you are'. America should stop feeding conquered France: 'Our job . . . is to feed the free people of the British Empire.' A letter was published from a Senior at Exeter School, calling for the creation of a Defence League among schools, with a manifesto 'Britain is democracy's first line of defence, and America her second and last. . . . Aid to Britain and her Allies short of war.'

Then there was a new topic, far removed from our British visions: 'Should the US take a firm stand against Japan and her ambitions?' *Yes, 87.5 per cent.*

Meanwhile, however, the most immediate impact on school life was to step up the grisly tempo of physical training. The *Silo* menaced us with a rather crude cartoon which depicted America as a small boy lifting dumbbells, confronting a vast Hitler, his feet planted on Europe, with the defiant caption: 'We'll be ready,

Mr Hitler.' Readiness was symbolized by a disagreeable new innovation in the shape of a 'Tiger' assault course, over which we had to charge in full football kit. Führer Knutson was in his element. In resisting, and dodging it, Bill Buckley and I at last began to find a first cause to share.

I was, as I said, coming to terms with school in America. *We* were. My coeval, the extrovert Brian, had become totally assimilated, losing most of his British accent, and was very popular. Even my prickly self was accepted in a way I never recalled in previous schools. 'Acceptance' seemed very much a virtue at Millbrook. I found I had virtually no foes, no bullies or bother-boys, nobody (except possibly the distrusted Buckley) whom I even disliked – nothing but friends. About the only letter I recall getting from a chum at Stowe made me feel few regrets. Life was, he wrote, 'carrying on without any interference. . . . We have to watch cricket matches all afternoon when we have a free day, and there is a Settler taking down names of those who do not turn up to watch.' Like my father's letters, fear of the censors removed all reference to the actual war.

I sometimes wondered how the education would compare with what one might have expected at Stowe. Where would it leave me? After little more than two terms, I found myself moved straight up into the top form at Millbrook in Latin (giving me that extra kudos in the eyes of the adored Judy), above average in French and German, about level with my contemporaries in English literature, rather behind in maths and distinctly – and disastrously – behind in Frank Trevor's advanced biology. On the whole, Millbrook was probably stronger than its British counterparts in maths and the sciences: but that was the American tradition. Its weakest subject was geography; this was only taught the youngest classes in the school, and in a fairly rudimentary fashion. By the time I was ten years old at Ludgrove, I recalled having a pretty good idea of where all the pink-marked countries in the British Empire were situated and what their staple products were. I also knew something of how they were governed and what sort of climate they had (dreary as was the study of isobars and isotherms at Ludgrove). By comparison the young American's geographical knowledge seemed abysmally poor. I shall never forget one fourteen-year-old Millbrookian being intensely worried just after Pearl Harbor that the victorious Japs were any minute going to invade his home-state, Florida, because he had heard they were occupying the islands of the *East* Indies! This weakness in geography also seems to have been rather rooted in the American tradition, I reflected years later – wondering whether perhaps some of America's most incomprehensible past blunders in the arena of foreign affairs may not have stemmed indirectly from this lack of basic training.

But compared with other American schools, Millbrook's academic standards were high, and we were thus more fortunate in the education we received than were some of our fellow Bundles. In the college entrance exams (we used to plod off to the girls' college at Vassar, in Poughkeepsie, to take them), Millbrook always came out well above average. These exams, incidentally, always struck me as one of the poorer aspects of American education – indeed they were fairly ridiculous. They were mostly of the order where you simply had to put an X against one out of four or five possible answers. An unprepared candidate could often pile on marks by intelligent guesswork. Sometimes the wrong answers were no less obvious than the written driving test I once had to take in Washington DC. One of the questions read: 'You are parked on a hill. You wish to move off again. Would you? 1. pull out as quickly as possible, and step on the gas; 2. let the automobile roll back to the bottom and start again; or 3. look in the mirror, put out your indicator, and pull slowly out when you have seen that nothing is coming?'

Edward Pulling's pragmatic approach to learning, however, undoubtedly had its great merits in other directions. My intellectual growth was not entirely being stunted, I felt it commendable to tell my father. And, proof of the pudding, when the war was over I found myself with an offer of scholarship entry into Harvard – and acceptance into Cambridge, England, even after four years' stultification in uniform.

With that intense rush of the North American seasons, spring and almost immediately summer was upon us. The boardwalks and storm-windows disappeared; Henry Callard's battered farm truck came out of the shed; the grass abruptly turned from brown to green; the crack of baseballs replaced the click of pucks. In the longer evenings there took over one of the harmlessly silly, but pleasant, traditions that Millbrook had acquired in its brief life – the softball Twilight League, for the younger boys. Letting his hair down (one of those rare occasions), the Boss would open it as the 'Mayor of Lithgow', the neighbouring hamlet, all duded up in top-hat, white tie and tails, chewing at a foot-long cigar – with Lucy P. as his 'doll' in a sleazy costume, and carrying a bouquet of assorted vegetables. Nat Abbott, the gentle music master and Latin teacher of the lower school, would then take over umpiring – in Latin. It was his way of demonstrating that it was far from being a dead language. A strike was *directa*, a ball *divia*, a home-run *circuit circum stationes*, a foul *turpis*. But baseball and its languors never grabbed me the way that fast and exciting ice-hockey did, enthralling me marginally less than cricket. The best thing was that baseball games ended more quickly than cricket. I opted for tennis instead, no doubt in order to impress Judy in the hols.

And so, in the comforting warmth of early June, that first year at Millbrook ended, with the paradoxically named ceremony of Commencement. We took leave of the departing sixth-formers (almost all of whom had got into the colleges of their choice, to Edward Pulling's delight) – rather sadly. Devoid of any rifts of rank or swank, they had all been our good friends. For me, undeniably – at least scholastically – *qua* school, it had been a good year, despite all the external vicissitudes, possibly the best in my undistinguished career to date.

CHAPTER EIGHT

Black Dogs of War

After nearly a year in America, no matter how much I had enjoyed it, I still felt terribly unsettled, suffering bad bouts of what Winston Churchill identified as the deadly 'Black Dog' – feeling dark shame about being away from it all for so many months, and simply longing to get home. With spring, too, the war had suddenly gone bad again, all the hopes and optimism of the 1940/1 winter turning to ashes in our mouths. Like a coiled snake that had been lying dormant through the winter months, Hitler was on the move again. Despite – or perhaps because of – Lend–Lease, sinkings in the Atlantic had reached a new peak. Many of my father's letters sank with them (I knew just how many, because he had efficiently begun numbering them). I felt shame about the brave sailors dying to bring them over. At home, the diet deteriorated to the poorest of the entire war. In London, the Blitz had flared up again with a final ferocity. While officers on leave and London's 'smart set' danced deep underground in Coventry Street's Café de Paris, a bomb burst in their midst, causing terrible carnage. Details of it were not spared by *Life* magazine, and later I learnt that friends of Uncle Newt and Aunt Ursie had died in the explosion – which they themselves had narrowly missed. A cutting sent by my father revealed that disaster had overtaken Wicked Uncle Henry too:

> Fine old house at 19 Buckingham Gate, once the residence of Emma Hamilton, burned out recently. . . . Where Henry Horne dispensed hospitality to men famous in politics and journalism, commerce and sport. . . . Hardly anything salvaged

from the ruins. . . . Once, Mr Horne recalls without pleasure, Ribbentrop was entertained there. On the night he lost his house, Mr Horne was dining out and helped to put out flames in his host's house, while his own home was blazing.

Windows in Aunt Ethel's little house in Park Street had also been blown out. In May, our eyes were moistened by pictures of a lone Churchill, clad in that curiously extended Homburg hat of his, standing grimly among the ruins of his beloved House of Commons. That fiercest night of the entire Blitz had, it turned out, cost 1400 civilian lives; a total of 90,000 casualties had been inflicted over the eight and a half months that the Blitz had lasted. Word came through the American correspondents that nerves, understandably, were beginning to fray. Londoners, Constantine Fitzgibbon was to write in *The Blitz*, 'no longer looked at one another with that instant sympathy which Miss [Elizabeth] Bowen called love'. 'Don't be distressed,' Josiah Wedgwood comforted Churchill after the bombing of the Commons. 'Such ruins are good assets . . . especially in America!' True, but hard to grasp at the time. Then, with ominous suddenness, the bombing ceased.

In March the Wehrmacht moved into Bulgaria. Brave Greece's imminent peril attracted our attention. Field Marshal List made his appearance on the cover of *Time* – 'BALKAN MEANS MOUNTAIN AND HE KNOWS MOUNTAINS'. After a brief interlude in praise of Bing Crosby, it was Hitler once more – 'SPRING IS HERE'. Then it was Simovic̆ of Yugoslavia, who in a sudden coup of utmost courage had swung his country on to the side of the Allies – 'MEN DIE FIGHTING, BUT NATIONS DIE ONLY IN YIELDING'. Within days, the Luftwaffe had reduced Belgrade to ruins, the German Panzers sweeping relentlessly through the country, with Britain utterly unable to lend a hand. To us it looked like the tragic tale of Poland all over again. Then, almost immediately, it was Greece's turn. Under strong pressure from Churchill, a reluctant Wavell was forced to dispatch some of his victorious troops from Libya to support the Greeks – the first time since Dunkirk not quite a year before that British troops had landed on the European mainland. They were not there long. Within days they were already evacuating Salonika; by the end of April they had been forced to abandon Greece altogether, withdrawing their battered remnants to Crete – minus 12,000 men. They had been there less than a month.

Was there absolutely no stopping these irresistible Germans? Almost immediately, the war in the desert took a severe turn for the worse, a weakened and discouraged Wavell suddenly finding himself up against Germans for the first time, with the appearance of a new player on the scene – General Rommel and his Afrika Korps. By mid-May all the brilliant gains of the winter had been wiped out: British forces were back across the Egyptian frontier, the garrison at Tobruk encircled, three generals captured. A letter from my father about this time sounded unusually depressed:

> Your letters, and hearing that you are doing well in every way, are about the only cheering thing I have now. Life here very difficult for all now and we have been having a rough time with the bombing. I am beginning to feel my age a bit as I shall be 66 years next month. . . . Business is very difficult now and the taxation is frightening. Also so many firms have had their offices destroyed. . . .
>
> . . . Terry is very well and happy. . . .
>
> PS At the end of the summer term, get the Matron to take your weight and height and let me know. Also ask her if your weight is normal for your age.

It was, by his standards, a very long and chatty letter. Nine days later came another: '. . . I don't believe in saying much about the War [indeed, something of an understatement] because of the censorship, but I am sure you get it all in your wireless and press. In fact more than is good for any of you.' But he went on: 'your cousin Cecil will soon I hope be a Major General. It is not spoken about, but I believe he has gone overseas – probably Middle East.' Thus, despite all my father's caution, the most half-witted German agent could have worked out that Cecil's 50th Division must now be in the desert. I felt a cold clutch of apprehension.

The letter contained the statutory reproach about my hand-writing: 'Your epistles . . . quite *pain* me at times, and they make me wonder if you have ever left the nursery!'

The very day my father wrote that letter, German paratroopers were fluttering down on Crete, cocking a snook at the British fleet beneath, the all but unopposed Luftwaffe wreaking terrible damage. It all seemed like an exact repeat of what we had watched happening to the Dutch and Belgians from Stowe that previous May. But these were *British* troops. Had we then learnt nothing over the past year? A week later Crete had fallen; another defeat, another evacuation. What was wrong? Then, as Crete was succumbing, we learned the terrible, inconceivable news that, out in the wastes of the North Atlantic, HMS *Hood*, Britain's mightiest warship, had been sunk, after a few salvos fired by Hitler's newest battleship, the *Bismarck*, with the loss of all but three men. I remembered having seen the great battle-cruiser in Portsmouth, its fast raking bows and giant fifteen-inch guns. How could the pride of the world's greatest navy be destroyed like this, in a matter of minutes? The ensuing hunt for the *Bismarck* and her annihilation by a vast superiority of units were hardly compensation. Suddenly (and not for the last time in my life), I wondered why a German piece of equipment should seem so massively indestructible and enduring, the best that we could set against it so frail and ephemeral. On the wall of my room I had a huge chart naming every ship in the opposing navies. Grimly I would cross off ships as they were sunk – and after the *Hood* and all those cruiser losses at Crete the black crosses began to look menacingly numerous. All that brave 'Run, Rabbit, Run' talk at Stowe of the early war months, about how Hitler's Reich was a structure of tinsel built on sand, seeped out of my body like water. With Russia still its ally, and our American hosts *still* sitting on the sidelines, how on earth were we going to avoid losing this war?

I felt desperately depressed, unhappy – and alone. Somewhere about this time, I wrote to my father, crazily proposing to come back, just for the summer. Could I not get a job on a merchant-man, as a wireless operator? A fatuous hope, at the age of fifteen and a half, and it produced a round ticking off from Aunt Ethel, currently evacuated to Devon's Exmouth, in her almost inde-cipherable hand: 'You really are a very lucky boy to be where you are and with people so very kind. Don't worry your father saying you want to come home. You *can't* and he can't get to see you. It does worry him and you are so lucky.' She complained that my father had driven her out of her house (borrowed from him) in Park Street, where he was now intending to live after the war, now that Madame Scap had left Lees Place. She apologized that she was unable to go on sending me the *Sphere*, because of the paper shortage. Accompanying her letter was an equally illegible note (why did they complain about *my* handwriting?) from her daughter, Cousin Eve, my one and only first cousin, describing jauntily how her mother had got caught up in a barbed-wire entanglement on the beach, and had had to be liberated by the army:

> I don't know where Cecil is – I think Libya. He is living in a tent by the sea and is fairly near the fighting. The flies he says are too terrible. I hear fairly frequently airmail. It is dreadful to think we shan't have seen him for years. But there it is, and we have got to get on with it. . . .
>
> We are sending you a sample of the government lavatory paper! It is too awful for words.

Thoughtfully a diligent censor had removed it, attaching a note to that effect (though he missed the reference to Libya).

Amid all war gloom, there had been an interlude – of joy intermixed with stress – down in Aiken, South Carolina, over the spring vacations. Though it was not quite the same as going out to Le Rosey on the plushy, romantic Orient Express, I do remember being wildly excited by that first trip down to the deep south out of Penn Station, aboard a twin to the legendary Chattanooga Choo-Choo immortalized that self-same year ('pardon me, Boy . . . Track Twenty-Nine, Boy, you can give me a shine . . .'). It was one of those green-curtained sleepers encapsulated in history by Marilyn Monroe in *Some Like It Hot*. All night the train loped along, through the endless sand and pine flats of the eastern seaboard, down through Virginia and the Carolinas, making one appreciate just what a vast country this was.

After a still wintry New York, Aiken was sparkling and welcoming with dry sunshine. Subsequently, alas, ruined by the building of a vast A-bomb plant near by, it was then an inordinately sleepy, sweet town of wide streets flanked by avenues of live oaks, beneath which were sand tracks exclusively for horses. Aiken existed for such gentlemanly pursuits as polo and golf – and elderly people with chest problems. Instantly I felt wonderfully well there. Everything moved at half-speed, and everybody seemed to smile. Despite the archaic segregation laws, which had endured unchanged since the Civil War, in those distant days the southern blacks almost always seemed more at ease with the whites than their surly northern brothers were, full of fun and jokes – and great courtesy. No doubt, in later years, these gentle and friendly people would be written off as Uncle Toms. But I loved the languid southern drawl, black and white, and often the tempo of life, its old-fashioned courtesies, made me think achingly of England. And they loved us, with a bizarre sentimentality dating back to the Civil War. 'If only you-all could have given us just a little more help,' they would murmur wistfully. God knows, with our blockade runners, we-all gave little enough, but if we had actually *made* the south win, then, I often speculated later, that delightful southern indolence would almost certainly have lost the war against Hitler – if not the Kaiser before him.

Julia Breese had a small bungalow hidden under immense, live oaks festooned with Spanish moss. Pine Breeze Cottage it was called. The garden was full of magnolia and brightly coloured birds, flashy red cardinals, orioles and robins. The robins were very much bigger than their British cousins, a Cadillac to a Baby Austin. But, Mrs Breese would say reprovingly, 'They can't sing like the British birds – everything in America's only for show!' There was a steady flow of prosperous dogs, affecting to be strays, but knowing that they were on to a good thing. When she was not working away at her dogs' home or knitting her bandages in the British War Relief, we would at regular intervals go to lunch with one of her favourites, a splendid and very old Scot, who had come out just after the Civil War and made a vast fortune. Mr Young was stone deaf, but – unlike the supposed norm of the deaf – was always bursting with fun and good humour. Conversation (hard word) consisted of writing him diverting notes, to which he would reply with *fortissimo* bellows of laughter, even if you had just told him about the sinking of the *Hood*, and even when, as occasionally happened, with an excited motion of his cigar he would detonate a large bowl of matches just in front of him. He was a dear man; rather less of a favourite was a grand Swedish lady, Miss Wolstenholm, with whom Julia Breese used to make up a bridge four. She was a neutral. About the time of Crete, she rashly remarked, 'The British can't have many ships left.' Thinking of that grim chart on my wall, but bridling, I was recorded as having remarked, pompously, 'But we have a *very* big fleet.' Mrs Breese was delighted. I was definitely flavour of the month.

Then Judy arrived. My cup was full. She was looking more beautiful, more full of life, than ever – and, at seventeen and about to graduate from Chapin's, distressingly grown up. The talk was all about coming-out parties (though she didn't really care, and tossed it all aside lightly), and what she was going to do after school. Once again I felt an intolerable anguish. There she was, about to spring out of the chrysalis a ravishing debutante, with every eligible Harvard man clogging the lines to 58 East 80th Street, the birds of prey of the stag-line all poised to descend. And there was I, not even yet into solid geometry. Would I never catch up? We had fun together, cantering down the soft dry 'sand river' beds in the tangled swamps around Aiken, laughing uncontrollably as the divots flew on the elitist golf course. She was a wonderful companion, but I was always 'Ally, my adopted little brother', squarely (and properly) put in my place if I showed signs of getting out of my basket. I couldn't bear it. And Julia Breese adored her. Without any sort of obsequiousness, Judy never hid the proper admiration she held for her aunt's high moral character, together with a deep compassion for all she had suffered in life. Mrs Breese returned it in undiluted love and support for the daughter she had never had. Judy only had to flash those green eyes to get away with murder. They were very close. Spoilt, displaced teenager that I was, craving affection, I must have showed my jealous disturbance that sunny holiday in Aiken. A letter followed me to Millbrook, overflowing with praise for her adorable niece – then: 'you don't seem to appreciate her or be very courteous to her, but . . . nevertheless she is always very kind to you. Don't you agree?' Well, of course.

Then, suddenly, it was the three and a half months of summer vacation again – at least a month longer than ours in Britain. After a few happy days at Garrison, canoeing and fishing on Indian Lake, an expedition I wanted to mount on the Hudson with my schoolfriend Eric Stevenson having been vetoed on grounds of extreme danger, I went down to New York. It was there that, on the radio at 58 East 80th, we heard the staggering news that Hitler had invaded his ally, Russia. It was the launch of the long-planned Operation Barbarossa. The world seemed to be spinning on its axis. Rossy Cutler almost exploded with excitement.

But, after the initial exhilaration had passed, I remember being plunged into deepest gloom. I recalled the terrible ineptness of the Red Army against the courageous little Finns, whose struggle we had watched from Stowe the previous winter, and the ridicule of movies like the hilarious *Comrade X*. How could these incompetent, slovenly Bolsheviks and ludicrous political commissars conceivably stand up to Hitler's invincible hordes? All our fears were compounded over the next days, as it became apparent that Stalin had been thoroughly taken by surprise. The *New York Times* showed maps of staggering advances which made Hitler's slicing through France look like the halt and the lame by comparison. A buffoon-like figure, straight out of *Comrade X*, appeared on the front pages, that old-style, ex-NCO cavalryman with the Cossack handlebar mustachios called Marshal Budenny, who lost the whole Ukraine in one of the greatest encirclement battles of all time. But I also remember all of us going off, that evening of 22 June 1941, to cheer ourselves up with a comic movie, and in the street John Cutler remarking to me in that quiet, clipped Bostonian accent, 'You know, Ally, a fellow called Napoleon once invaded Russia. It's a big place . . .' John Cutler was to prove a wise man, wiser than most of the glum radio pundits.

Every night the gloomy monotones of Gabriel Heatter would announce fresh catastrophes, new staggering advances. Within the month, the Germans were surging across the Berezina, where Napoleon's nose had been so bloodied, taking Smolensk and heading irresistibly for Moscow. By the end of the holidays, Leningrad was encircled, the mighty Dnieper crossed and the third great Soviet city, Kiev, captured. Was there no stopping these terrible grey Panzers? But at least they were heading even further from Britain. The whole of the Luftwaffe had deployed to the Russian front, giving London a respite – and my poor tired father some peace in which to celebrate his sixty-sixth birthday. Soon, his letters were bouncing back with something like his old exuberance.

Yet what would happen to Britain, once Hitler had vanquished the Russians – which now looked like a matter of weeks away, not months? In the way Americans have of switching or losing interest with rapidity, Britain began receding into the background. Rossy Cutler's good New York ladies began drifting away from sewing bandages at the British War Relief to running up valenkas, those great felt boots, for the heroic Red Army. Suddenly Stalin became cosy old Uncle Joe, a benevolent pipe-smoking patriarch with a happy family life. One magazine (it may have been *Time*) even discovered that the new Soviet Supreme Commander, Marshal Timoshenko, was a natural-born Irish-American – his real name O'Shenko. I even caught Judy reading *Crime and Punishment* one day, and teased her mercilessly. Copies of the Soviet Constitution popped up everywhere, making it all sound just as benign and democratic as that framed by the Elders of Philadelphia. Later, amid the post-war excesses of McCarthyism, it was amusing to recall that, by the end of 1941, we were all willing fellow travellers.

As the Germans plunged on, ever deeper eastwards, we set off once more for Martha's Vineyard, green visors and all, antique-hunting all the way – just like the previous year. But, before we left, I had to return to Millbrook – not to the school, but the town – for some disagreeable days at the hands of the school dentist. Mr Mahoney had contrived to find no less than fifteen cavities in my head, one for each year of my life. He was Irish, and as I sat in his chair hour after hour, pure agony without the modern comforts of novocaine, I pondered on Julia Breese's pronouncement of the previous summer about the Irish and the English. 'What was with that British dentist of yours?' he asked disparagingly. 'Actually, he was American,' said I coldly, thinking of a brute in London with hairy forearms. Mr Mahoney gave the drill an extra twist. Had I truly got fifteen bloody holes? Or could it be the American food?

Arriving at the Vineyard, the humid air was trembling with human excitement. The new house, the now converted ramshackle stable bought for a song the previous summer at East Chop, was ready for habitation. At least, more or less. After the Capuan delights of elegant Edgartown, my heart sank. It was uncompromisingly austere and bleak – not a tree, and barely a blade of grass, the structure sitting on a point surrounded by water on almost three sides, buffeted by every wind and tide, impossible to swim in the heavy current. But the view over the sea from those three sides was, undeniably, irresistible. The sitting-room-cum-dining-room had great plate-glass windows facing out to sea without a trace of land in the foreground. The bedrooms were unplastered, redolent with the smell of the raw white wood, resin and cedar shingles, mingled with the sea air. But the big attic room I shared with Peter also lacked any insulated ceiling, and the heat could be – and usually was – stifling. Within a few weeks of occupancy, we discovered why no trees grew on the East Chop. One night a wind got up that made the whole house creak and sigh, and a formidable sea began tearing at the shore that was little more than ten yards away from the verandah. The following morning we found that the brand-new dock, designed for swimming off and as a mooring for a sailboat, had been uprooted and hurled in small fragments on to the shore. A second dock was erected, then a third, each more robust than its predecessor, but they too were devoured by the unappeasable sea. At breakfast, the discovery that the big windows had been glazed with salt water from a storm the night before was nectar to Rossy Cutler, in her insatiable quest for drama. She thrived on the uncertainty produced by each new storm, on the sheer excitement of it all, on the ever changing spectacle presented by the lean grey warships and noble barquentines heavy with sail that slipped past our windows.

For my big friend, sailor Peter, too, it was all sheer magic. Hour by hour, he would stand on the end of the short-lived dock, his powerful body naked from the waist, the palms of his hands resting on his buttocks, clad in khaki slacks and a long-peaked swordfisherman's cap, inspecting the ceaseless marine activities like some old salt on the bridge of his merchantman. Pete was a walking combination of *Jane's Fighting Ships* and Lloyd's Register. He was, I think, almost infallible. No East Chop day would have been complete without Pete pointing out, unassisted by glasses, some distant speck on the horizon: 'That's the *Boston Clipper* out of Salem, square-rigged, last of her class,' or 'That must be the *Manxman*, biggest yawl afloat. Jeez, what a ship!' or else 'There goes the Guggenheim yacht, just been converted into a hospital ship,' or as a battle-weary destroyer flying the White Ensign limped by, heading for repair at New London, 'There's an old American flush-decker, three four-inch guns, commissioned 1917 – one of the original fifty tubs traded to Britain last year.'

One of the most commendable features of American life, it always struck me, was the system of holiday jobs, whereby, during those three-month summer vacations, children of all ages took themselves off from under the feet of their harassed parents. Life was superbly geared to it. Older children went to be 'counsellors' in summer camps somewhere in the wilderness, looking after younger children; others helped pay their way through college by delivering newspapers, or working on farms or in the woods. Accordingly, for one happy and profitable month, Pete and I took a summer job at the Vineyard Haven Lobster Pound, a bicycle-ride down the road. The Lobster Pound was a rough-and-ready seafood restaurant, started by an enterprising local shipbuilder inside his yard. It had been an immediate success and Pete and I were taken on as waiters for three or four hours every night – at the princely wage of seventy-five cents an evening, plus as much lobster and lemon-meringue pie as we could eat. Pete's appetite was legendary, and the proprietor would stand by anxiously after closing as his profits disappeared. It was fun. The regular waitresses, working girls 'as corny as Kansas in August, as normal as blueberry pie', were merry and always supportive.

Yet I always associated the place with a certain amount of physical pain. Amid the trestle tables, set up right among the hulls of the boats in the shipyard, was a large tank filled with live Maine lobsters. Customers, generally of the blue-rinse brigade, would select the lobster they favoured and I, as the most junior in the establishment, had to catch and fish out the giant crustaceans. They were all supposed to have had their claws immobilized with strong elastic bands or wooden pegs, but many was the wily one that managed to wriggle free, and their nips were no laughing matter. To this day I wince when I see the crusher claw of even a cooked Maine lobster. Another frequent source of pain was the quahog (pronounced 'co-hog'), a giant clam with an armour-plated shell at least a quarter of an inch thick, and it could only be prized open with the point of a kitchen knife. The number of times the knife slipped is too agonizing to recall. I soon discovered I was allergic to lobsters and all the shellfish. Nor did the supplementary wages we received in the form of delicious blue-berry and lemon-meringue pie at the end of each working night ever quite atone for the frenzy and pathetic squeaks of the lobsters as they were dropped into the boiling vats, and it was a long time before I could bring myself to raise the heavy chopper to bisect a living lobster that some customer had ordered 'broiled'.

Knowing the anguish it caused Julia Breese to hear of the least animal suffering, Pete and I agreed to draw a veil over our activities at the Lobster Pound, telling what I am still convinced was a lie, that lobsters don't feel a thing. But the excitement of being a wage-earner, for the first time, and of working alongside one's big hero, made it somehow possible to repress these qualms.

East Chop, however, was not a place that left me with happy memories. I could not share Pete's enthusiasm. I missed the cosiness and beauty of Edgartown, the laid-back life that gravitated round the drugstore, the harbour and the movie-house. The nearest place at East Chop where, in the teenage vernacular, it all happened (and that was not much) was the tennis club, presided over by a rather surly tennis pro called Joe Crimmens, and full of preppy hearties from Massachusetts schools, among whom I didn't find many friends. The bleakness entered one's soul. It was so stickily humid that a table I shellacked for the sisters was still tacky two summers later. Jack was now in faraway Rhodesia, training to fly with the RAF; Pat was working; Judy (oh jealous agonies! – 'those green eyes with the soft lights, promise of sweet nights' went the tantalizingly seductive song of the moment) was pursuing the deb season, and being pursued all round the eastern seaboard. The war news was terrible, the Germans getting ever further down the road to Moscow. Life was pretty boring, and joyless. The heat was at its most sultry. But none of this could excuse the inexcusable (and inexplicable) episode that was shortly to occur.

It was towards the end of the summer of 1941. The heat was stifling in our uninsulated loft. I had slumped into the blackest fit of the Black Dog, of which sheer homesickness, the worst to date, was a major ingredient. I was irritable and bloodyminded.* From causes I cannot recall, I had had a row with the endlessly good-natured Peter, something that was virtually impossible – and about what? Feeling that the whole house was against me, I flounced off to our loft, slamming doors, and, in a fury of self-pity, knotted a sheet and flung it over a rafter. Of course, I had not the slightest intention of committing suicide, then or at any time since. It was nothing more than a crazed teenager's protest, but it was a wicked, cruel and heartless thing to do. Julia Breese came in, presumably to cajole me out of my ill humour, saw it and left silently. Years later, Rossy Cutler, with her earthy instinct about people, told me she knew I hadn't meant business – to her, with her five children, it was just one of the oddities of

---

* Among us Bundles, I read many years later, American psychiatrists found themselves geared to dealing with all manner of stress-related bed-wetting, tantrums and other forms of attention-seeking, including stealing and even self-inflicted injuries.

growing up. But her less worldly sister had been stricken. I was, after all, *her* responsibility. I could never quite forgive myself the pain that I had so thoughtlessly caused this sweet, saintly lady. She never referred to it, but, patently, she never quite trusted me again. At least a year later, when I had all but banished the dismal episode from my mind, I discovered one day that my prize weapons, the knuckleduster and the virtually ineffective tiny pistol, good only for scaring rabbits and alarming the pigs at Ropley, which I had bought at Le Rosey for a few francs and which I suppose I had been imaginatively saving for the day when, shot down in my Spitfire, I would heroically use them to dispatch the first German coming to round me up, had inexplicably disappeared.

Immediately following the episode at East Chop, I was aware that there were long night sessions between the two sisters, accompanied by much mysterious and secretive telephoning. Were they going to send me off back home? I half hoped they were. Then one day Julia Breese sprang the surprise that she and I were going to Boston for a few days. It would be good for my history studies to see Bunker Hill, to learn about Paul Revere, to discover why the wicked Lobster-Backs had been thrown out, and to see a very old, English-style city that might make me feel at home. I swallowed the bait – hook, line and sinker. Aboard the ferry we passed close to HMS *Rodney*, our most powerful battleship, quite unmistakable with its three huge sixteen-inch turrets all mounted forward of the bridge, anchored off Boston Navy Yard and still being repaired – under FDR's new measures to help Britain – after the battle with the *Bismarck*. To see the great guns on one of the turrets all askew, surrounded by scaffolding, brought tears to one's eyes.

Then, suddenly, I found myself in a Boston psychiatrist's waiting room. Within minutes I realized that the man was a charlatan, a total buffoon. I also realized what many a true psychotic must surely grasp with deadly speed – namely, that here was a situation and a man over whom, at least temporarily, I possessed astonishing power. As he gazed knowingly at my ink blots, I spun a fantastical tale of Arabian proportions. He would, I knew, believe anything I told him (of course, I never once mentioned the name of Judy Cutler, the cause, as I readily, but secretly, accepted, of much of my turmoil). As we left, I overheard him say to Julia Breese, '. . . serious case of schizophrenia . . .' She was devastated. But somewhere along the line, the influence and common sense of Rossy Cutler must have prevailed. Otherwise I might still be locked away behind bars in some Bostonian bin. (On the other hand, perhaps the diagnosis was correct? Whoever knows.) Nothing more was ever heard about the shrink or his verdict. I don't think my father was ever told. Nevertheless, since then I have never much liked Boston, a cold, crabbed city full of knotted-up people trying to be more English than the English. Nor, having had to consult them on behalf of others over the years, have I ever found much good to say about shrinks – a breed of self-enthralled people, with a few distinguished exceptions, disturbingly prone (in my limited experience) to exteriorizing their own bizarre hang-ups upon the syndromes of their unfortunate patients.

From Boston, joined by Rossy Cutler and (oh bliss!) Judy, recovering from her season, we went off on a trip to Canada, to visit Billy and Nora Breese in their summer hideout at St Andrews, New Brunswick, just across the US border. 'It'll be good for our little Bundle to see a few Union Jacks,' Rossy Cutler told every amazed Canadian. 'He's fed up with us noisy, vulgar Americans.' She had a point. Canada in 1941 seemed like a strange sort of halfway house. Compared with its affluent, wasteful neighbours, it was an austere country. In some ways it reminded me a bit of Norway in 1939. In the backward Maritime Provinces, it was not unusual to come across carts yoked to two bullocks. Lots of things were rationed, the Canadians were a reserved people, and there was manifest resentment that they were at war and Americans were not. Equally there were the occasional raised eyebrows: what was a privileged *English* schoolboy doing here? There were Union Jacks and pictures of the King and Queen everywhere, and much loyal sentiment, and sympathy, for the Old Country. Before such costly disasters to the Canadians as Dieppe had occurred, Britain's stock was high. Response to the call to the colours had been remarkable. Men in British-looking uniforms abounded – including a sprinkling of much decorated young RAF officers recuperating from the Battle of Britain, whom I studied with idolatrous looks. Rossy Cutler's handbag was seldom closed.

One day we drove up through Nova Scotia, to the port of Halifax, the western terminal of almost all the Atlantic convoys. Judy and I climbed up a hill overlooking the great basin concealed behind the port, and an extraordinary sight met our eyes. There must have been a hundred merchantmen, forming up for the dread crossing, the little grey destroyers bustling bossily about like nannies, looking so slender and frail as if one big wave would break them in two. For quite a few minutes, we sat, in silence, just looking at them. Once again I felt a terrible pang of self-division, half wanting to be on one, bound back for Liverpool; and I noticed Judy had tears in her eyes. I suppose we had the same thought in mind: how many of those storm-battered ships and their courageous but perpetually frightened crews would ever get to the other side?

It must have been while we were in Canada that the astonishing news came out that Churchill and Roosevelt had met, for the first time, at sea only a few hundred miles further north, off Newfoundland's Placentia Bay. The Movietone newsreels of the two great men ('Emperors of the West and East', as Harold Macmillan later dubbed them) seated on the deck of the mighty *Prince of Wales* for Sunday service, surrounded by all the brass of both nations, as the sailors bellowed out lustily 'Onward Christian Soldiers', surely one of the most moving moments during the entire war, suddenly brought home to one how the earth had tilted on its axis over the past few months. What further proof was needed that the Americans, at last, were now with us – soul if not body? Could it be more than a matter of weeks, now, before they were really in the war altogether? All that had been hidden over the past year from the sight of the US public – and fifteen-year-old British schoolboys – was now out in the open. I felt a tinge of guilt that I had become so critical of Roosevelt and his apparent lethargy. Julia Breese, however, sounded a note of caution: 'You do realize, don't you, Alistair, that Mr Churchill has had to pay a price? "The Four Freedoms" must mean the end of the British Empire.' She was referring to the Atlantic Charter, the joint declaration issued by the two leaders following the Placentia Bay meeting.

It was on this note that the new year began at Millbrook. I was glad to get back (not a feeling I had been familiar with in the past). I felt I knew my way around, I wanted to see my friends again. There were new quarters, new faces, new teachers and new stories to listen to, and, above all, a magnificent new building – courtesy of Edward Pulling's tame railway mogul, Henry Flagler, before whose annual visit painful weeks would be spent by the Community Service slaves 'bulling up' the campus with comb and nail-scissors. The New Building housed a superb, walnut-clad library, new classrooms and a super-modern science basement (largely tenanted by the empire-building Trevor). Somehow, leaving the cramped but cosy old Barn and its irrepressible rat population changed the whole atmosphere. Millbrook had almost become smart. Two new woodchucks (reported the *Silo*) had joined the Zoo. The bumptious William F. Buckley Jr, skipping the fourth form (where he should never have been anyway) joined us in the new fifth – not entirely a matter of rejoicing among us ardent Interventionists. But even more lamented was the departure of the beloved Hank Austin, who had left to join the Navy Air Corps. Among the new masters was a rotund Luxemburger, Xavier Prum, whose impressive girth was exceeded only by his unshakeable ego ('Sir, do you know the answer to Problem Five?' 'I know zee answer to oll zee problems!').

Instead of Hank Austin as English teacher, we had a swinger called Jack McGiffert, a dapper and sophisticated Irishman who sported a bow-tie and the sexiest wife on the campus (she ended up – after my time – in a torrid affair with the art master). In a very different way to the rough-and-ready Hank, he too was an inspirer. He introduced D. H. Lawrence to us, making us read

The Prussian Officer, which certainly imbued me for one with a feel for that strange, tormented genius that I never lost. When we did *Macbeth*, Jack took the whole class down to Broadway, to see the classic performance by Maurice Evans and Judith Anderson. Wearing a titian wig, she made me think forever more of Lady Macbeth as a redhead. They were, to our perhaps inexperienced minds, magnificent; and – thanks to Jack McGiffert in the Upper State New York – Shakespeare became a thing of living excitement, rather than baffling drudgery.

As fifth-formers, in our penultimate year, we lived in semi-autonomous comfort in the dining-room block – which was to have certain venal advantages in the year ahead. By request, I found myself sharing a room with fellow Bundle Brian Larwill, but it was not a success. We had moved in different directions. In the way that some Brits do, one of two extremes, I felt that he had become excessively assimilated, and I certainly did not then share his enthusiasm for American football. As in any school, the first days were dominated by excited chatter about holiday events. Professor Jessup, Phil's father, had miraculously walked away from an air crash, one of three survivors, in the middle of the Brazilian jungle, engaged on some mysterious mission for President Roosevelt, and had been given the Southern Cross for bravery by the Brazilians. Eric Stevenson's father came to tell us how he had been recruited to plan Manhattan's air defence. Not long afterwards we were treated to another memorable lecture about the Royal Navy from a Commander Dickinson, of the light cruiser HMS *Dido*, badly damaged by German Stukas during the Battle of Crete. Packed with twenty-one tons of gold belonging to the fleeing Greek government, she had been combing the Aegean for caiques filled with German invasion troops, when a heavy bomb struck forward, killing a hundred men and doing appalling damage. Limping into Alexandria, her bows were temporarily patched up with concrete, and she then made her way through the Suez Canal to Aden. From there she helped capture the Italian stronghold of Assab, though able to fire only with her after turrets. She then sailed round the Cape of Good Hope, always stern first in the heavy seas, so as to preserve her temporary bow. *Dido* just made it into Brooklyn Navy Yard, where her commander was picked up by the sharp eyes of the Boss. (Forty-eight years later, aged ninety, Ed Pulling was able, vividly, to remind me of the saga: 'Do you remember *Dido*, backing all the way round the Cape with her concrete bows?')

Russia was the flavour of every month; the inter-scholastic poll showed 55 per cent calling for the British to launch an immediate Second Front to aid the Soviets. The Forum trekked over to Vassar, to observe a debate with Harvard on the motion 'That the United States Should Declare War against Germany Immediately'. By a majority of two to one, Harvard won over the less belligerent women. In terms of how opinions had shifted since I had arrived at Millbrook the previous fall, the result was significant. At the same time, the *Silo*'s political correspondent attending the debate, one William F. Buckley Jr, noted fears expressed by the Vassar ladies that Japan would declare war on the US first. 'Girls' nonsense' was I expect how we dismissed this.

All eyes were on the enormous, heroic Eastern Front. Britain had largely disappeared from the headlines. After FDR's election triumph just a year before, it had seemed impossible that America could stay out of the war more than another few months. But here we were a year later, and, although the President had pursued his policy of 'all help short of war' to the utmost extreme against Germany, there seemed no sign yet of his taking the final plunge. In fact, even as recently as September Congress had passed by only one solitary vote a new bill extending the draft. Such was, still, the sense of national urgency: and in October only 17 per cent of the American populus was polled as favouring a declaration of war on Germany. One day, we Bundles felt sure, there would be another *Lusitania*, and America would be committed. But how many desperate years might there be yet ahead for Britain before that day came?

That was the way it would almost surely happen. None of us for a moment suspected what was afoot on the other side of the world. Did we worry about Japan, like those timorous ladies of Vassar? Not much. When that impenetrable envoy (or rather decoy), Mr Kurusu, arrived in Washington in November 1941, even sceptical *Time* magazine commented, 'That jittery, encircled, embargoed Japan proposed to follow months of Washington conversations with still more conversations was a clear sign that Japan still did not dare to follow its sword-brandishing with sword-play.' *Time* did, nevertheless, go on to quote Mr Kurusu as telling his son before leaving for the States, 'Maybe I will not be able to come back.'

There were more immediate topics of conversation at Mill-brook. High on the hit parade was a tune with a refrain lauding 'Joltin' Joe DiMaggio', who had just gained immortality in what the history books were to rate the best baseball season *ever*. The odds-on Yankees had started it glumly, stricken by the death of the legendary Lou Gehrig (he gave his name to a rare but terrible wasting disease to which, four decades later, the great David Niven tragically succumbed). The unlikely Brooklyn Dodgers, the 'Bums', operating out of unfashionable Ebbets Field, so matey then that fans in the front-row seats could chat with players, had come within a hair's-breadth of winning the World Series. The battles were fought and refought in the fifth-form dormitory. Exotic names like 'Fat Freddie' Fitzsimmons, and the great 'knuckleball' pitcher, 'Pee Wee' Reese, 'Ducky Wucky' Medwick and 'King Kong' Keller flew around, while DiMaggio was god. I was able to contribute little – not my sport. But when it came to the world-shaking news that Fred Astaire had a new partner, the devastating, long-legged redhead Rita Hayworth, then I had something to contribute.

Of course we repeated our elders' anxieties. After the Japanese had moved into the former French colony of Indo–China earlier in the year, Roosevelt had slapped on a paralysing oil embargo. How could the Emperor's war machine go on in China without new sources of raw materials? The names of Nomura and Matsuoka and Kurusu, the smiling Japanese 'peace envoy' with the Chamberlain-style Homburg hat currently negotiating in Washington, were known to us. There were two fifth-formers from the West Coast, Bill Rheem and Al Chaney, who told horror stories of how the little yellow men were penetrating

California, everywhere, disguised as market-gardeners. But none of us could take them seriously. We all had a healthy Wasp schoolboy contempt for the little men out of the trees, reinforced by their bestial treatment of the Chinese, of which the media were constantly reminding us. And there were the 'Don Winslow' serials that always ended with lines of star-spangled battleships, with their peculiar basket superstructure, guns and 'Anchors Aweigh' blazing forth, thundering down to the rescue as Jap battleships slid beneath the waves. Rumours ran round that the Japanese, renowned even then as great copyists, had pinched the blueprints of the latest US warships – but Edgar Hoover's smart G-men had doctored them, with the result that two of the latest Japanese battleships had recently turned turtle. We chortled. To us Bundles, Japan was incredibly remote. If I thought of the Japanese at all, it was as the ingenious little people who made clever shells (non-military) that opened in water, releasing strings of beautiful aquatic flowers – and costing nothing. They were surely not to be taken seriously.

Anyway, of much more transcending, immediate gravity was the football dance and the agonizing issue of finding a partner. With consummate ingenuity, I conspired for room-mate Brian to invite Judy. Alas, predictably, she already had other, bigger fish to fry that weekend. Instead I received a big-sisterly letter (I still have it!) which drove me into a minor paroxysm of jealous rage:

> we are all very worried about you neglecting that cunning [synonym in Judy language for 'cute'] Sylvia Montgomery. You simply *must* write her immediately and ask her up to the dance. After all she was nice enough to ask you to dinner last Christmas and the very least you can do is to ask her back.

It wasn't precisely what I had in mind. Poor Sylvia, another pretty mammiferous blonde, came. I was, I suspect, an aloof partner.

It was only a matter of days after we were licking our wounds from the dance weekend, that, huddled round the radio in the rooms of the fifth-form dormitory master, Austin Johnson, on a

Sunday afternoon, we heard the unbelievable news of Pearl Harbor. Bit by bit, over that appalling day of 7 December 1941, stunned radio commentators read out the news that one great American battleship after another had been sunk in Hawaii, like so many sitting ducks – by those despised little Japs.

CHAPTER NINE

All In The Same Boat Now: Pearl Harbor

Dismayed, dumbfounded and all incredulous, we – sixteen-year-old fifth-formers of Millbrook School – sat huddled round Austin Johnson's radio that Sunday, as the successive items of dire news came in. By the hour it got worse. At first, it was conceded that 'one old battleship, used for training', and a destroyer had been lost. Bit by bit the full extent of the disaster that had struck America over a space of two hours emerged. Out of ninety-six US Navy ships (half as many again as the whole Royal Navy of the 1990s) that were moored at Pearl Harbor, eighteen had been sunk or damaged. Seven of these were battleships, the pride of the US Navy, but not designed to withstand aerial attack from bombs and torpedoes. All, we learned in the months to come, had been moored close together, some in pairs, like so many private yachts lined up in a marina – an irresistible target for practised Japanese airmen. *Oklahoma* was the 'old battleship' that had capsized; *West Virginia* and *California* had sunk at their moorings; *Tennessee* and *Maryland* had been knocked out by bombs; so had *Pennsylvania*, in spite of lying in the comparative safety of dry-dock; *Nevada* alone, temporarily commanded by an inspired ensign, had managed to make it out of her berth, only to be beached in a sinking condition near the harbour entrance. Most tragic of all was the fate of *Arizona*, ripped in two by a hit exploding its magazines.* Among

---

* In fact, miraculously, all the battleships with the exception of *Arizona* and *Oklahoma* were refloated to fight again. What we also did not know that day, but which the Japanese did, was that the supreme prize of the aircraft carriers *Lexington* and *Enterprise* were out of harbour that day. Their survival alone was to turn the tide of war against the Japanese, with quite remarkable speed.

the details kept secret until after the war was the fact that no less than 1100 of her crew died within her – among the nearly 3000 killed at Hawaii that day. No US battleship, so the shell-shocked commentators reminded us, had been sunk since the *Maine* had blown up in Havana Harbour in 1898 – and that had instantly led to war with Spain, even though the exact cause of its explosion was never determined.

In the American style, but more particularly in the chaos of those first hours when news was all but uncensored, little secret was made of the actual horrors of the attack, and pictures of squadron upon squadron of burnt-out warplanes, parked – just like the battleships – wing-tip to wing-tip on Hickam Field, were soon in all the papers. There were the occasional deeds of extraordinary heroism, such as men firing from the hip with .30 cal. machine guns at the Jap bombers, later made much of by Hollywood. But, even to us schoolboys, it seemed unbelievable that there seemed to have been no attempt by this great base to defend itself. How could they have been caught napping like this? How could anything quite so shameful have happened to this great country, to the navy of Don Winslow? Over the past few months, there had been a surfeit of news coverage on Hawaii, with an endless flow over the radio of that tedious 'Aloha' music, that still sounds to me like someone pissing into a tin pot. Did not this all presuppose some state of alert? Excuses later came out that radar had mistaken the Japanese attackers as a flight of B-17 bombers due in from the mainland.

Nevertheless, our class-mates were totally thrown down that day, in shame and incomprehension at what had happened. As we sat in silence, we tried to avoid each other's eyes. The silence, so uncharacteristic of America, is what many foreign observers most remember of that day: British visitors to Chicago recorded Union Terminal as being 'silent as the grave, silent as a cathedral in the middle of the night, everybody not speaking, silent. . . . It was like visiting a drugged nation.' Yet soon it was the turn of us Bundles, of Brian and myself, to blush, as with terrifying rapidity British bastions like Hong Kong and the impregnable Singapore also fell. Within days of Pearl Harbor, the mighty

Prince of Wales, victor of the *Bismarck*, and the battle-cruiser *Repulse*, sent to Malaya inexplicably without air cover, would be sunk by Japanese bombers with over a thousand of their crews. On 'that day of infamy', we were soon listening to the grim tones of the President, damning the treacherous Japanese in a statement of extraordinary brevity and calling upon Congress to declare war forthwith. With an unprecedented display of unanimity, Congress did so in thirty-three minutes flat. There was only one dissenting vote – Republican Representative Jeannette Rankin from Montana, who had also voted against America's declaration of war against Germany in 1917 – amid shouts of 'Sit down, sister!' Of that powerful Isolationist lobby only one Congressman, Senator Nye of South Dakota, still struck a discordant note, blaming the administration for 'doing its utmost to provoke a quarrel'. One of the first to call for unqualified support for Roosevelt that day was Congressman Hamilton Fish, so recently his bitterest opponent, who declared vigorously, 'There can only be one answer and that is war and final victory, cost what it may.' At a stroke, wounds within the Fish family were healed. I could now play tennis with my contemporary, Hammy, without it being transformed into a kind of single combat from the Siege of Troy. It was symptomatic of what 7 December did for the US at large. As Roosevelt said to Churchill, 'They have attacked us at Pearl Harbor. We are all in the same boat now.'

With terrifying speed, the news got worse and worse. The Japanese were attacking, and landing in the Philippines, Malaya, Hong Kong and the Dutch East Indies. They seemed to be on the move all the way across the Pacific. Any moment now an invasion of Hawaii was expected as a natural follow-up to Pearl Harbor. The only good news the papers had to offer was 'NAZIS GIVE UP EFFORT TO TAKE MOSCOW TILL SPRING'. In between lessons and news bulletins, we sat listening to records – I remember the tunes so well – of Gershwin's 'Embraceable You' and Stan Kenton's 'The Nango'. Somehow the latter, with its big-band pounding rhythm, sounded rather more appropriate background music than the comforting lyrics of Gershwin, as the little men in their strange, scruffy uniforms hopped irresistibly from island to island.

As they went, raping British nurses in Hong Kong and disembowelling (so we were told) our captured prisoners of war in live bayonet practice, there was something peculiarly and alarmingly sinister about these little people, copyists and manufacturers of paper flowers, whom until so recently we had been taught heartily to ridicule. Momentarily, they looked, to us, even more frightening than the Germans – and, through American eyes, more immediate. I calculated that the US must have lost over half its battlefleet at Pearl Harbor, leaving it with roughly half the number of battleships the Japs possessed. And, looking at my *Illustrated London News* chart, now covered by ugly black crosses, the loss of the two British capital ships had left an ugly hole in the British lines.

Though there was lots of noise, and much excited talk, there was no hysteria or panic in America – except, perhaps, when it came to rumours about spies and fifth columnists. On the West Coast, the Japanese fifth columnists our Californian class-mates had been warning us about were rounded up, some 60,000 of them, their market-gardens taken away for ever, in what was subsequently to be recognized as one of the great injustices of democracy at war. For a while, whether in New York or Washington, spy-mania ran rampant. On holiday in sleepy South Carolina that Easter, I had my camera confiscated by a cop while photographing a friend, who unfortunately had chosen as background a run-to-seed 'Baby Doll' cotton mill that happened to be on some kind of war work.

Young Americans flooded into recruiting stations in every city across the land. Not unnaturally, America was suddenly obsessed with the Rising Sun: Moscow, the desert, Hitler, the Battle of the Atlantic, and Britain – all else was momentarily forgotten. I remember voicing my fears, very quietly, to room-mate Brian. What if . . .? Supposing the United States were now, understandably, to throw all its might against Japan, turning its back on Britain and Europe? Just where would *we* be? Roosevelt had *not* specifically asked Congress to declare war on Germany, too; it had not attacked America. Hitler was in no way bound by his loose alliance with Japan to do so. One tends to forget that it was, in fact, not until four days after Pearl Harbor that he obliged by declaring war on the United States, in the maddest act of arrogance he ever committed, his most fatal error of the whole war. For the very strong US lobby that had resisted war with Germany now supported influential Pacific First elements in Washington, headed by no less a personage than the redoubtable Admiral Ernest J. King, Commander-in-Chief US Atlantic Fleet, subsequently Chief of Naval Operations – and an articulate anglophobe. It was for this reason, as we all learnt later, that Churchill, in a cold sweat, hurried over to Washington that Christmas for his first post-Pearl Harbor meeting with Roosevelt, to offer America full British participation, but in turn urging that Europe and North Africa be given first priority. To the eternal benefit of subsequent history, he triumphed, against very considerable resistance. On his return to England and in patent relief, Churchill memorably cabled his new ally (on his sixtieth birthday), 'It is fun to be in the same decade with you.'

At just sixteen we were quite old enough to share Churchill's cold sweat of apprehension in those first days, followed by immeasurable relief at Hitler's declaration of war on 11 December. I remember going for a long walk, by myself, to conceal from my stricken American school-mates the awful feeling of exultation that I felt my face might betray. The suddenness of the Japanese treachery, succeeded by Hitler's blow, was numbing. Perhaps among the whole school, the older of us English boys had the clearest idea of what it really meant. Through adolescent minds passed incoherently the same thoughts that Churchill later made coherent: 'We had won the war. England would live; Britain would live; the Commonwealth of Nations and the Empire would live.' But at the same time it was impossible not to feel a small tinge of shame that the cause of one's exultation had brought unspeakable tragedy to the people who had taken all of us, so unreservedly, into their homes, and their hearts, during the past year and a half.

Like the sudden blow which cleanly removes a limb, neither the shock of Pearl Harbor nor its devastating injury to the US Navy was felt in full until some time later. The American schoolboy had no high regard for Japanese ability. His history taught him that the yellow races' standard of living was so low that laws had to be passed to prevent their immigration to the States. Therefore in a war the Japs would not be able to stand up for long against the technical might of the USA. Meanwhile, the US could resurrect its navy behind the powerful shield of Britain's battleships in the Pacific, invincible Singapore and the experienced divisions of the British army in the east. Then in a few months its might would reassert itself like a compressed spring, pushing the Japanese navy off the face of the Pacific. So we all thought. Thus the sinking of the *Prince of Wales* and *Repulse* on 10 December – rapidly followed as they were by the terrible American losses in the Bataan death march and the inexplicably swift fall of Singapore – came as even more of a shock than Pearl Harbor.

From that moment of the sharing of disaster in the Pacific, relations between the Bundles at Millbrook and the rest of the school underwent a subtle but distinct modulation. Such barriers of suspicion, of mutual reserve, as still lingered on now fell away. The sense of proud loneliness, sometimes also of frustration, that one used to experience when listening to the voice of Churchill, fading and swelling over thousands of miles of short waves – that too now disappeared. We were, as Roosevelt declared, all in it together now, and our distant, embattled country was the respected senior partner.

The metamorphosis throughout America was sudden and astounding. Admiral Yamamoto, the reluctant architect of Pearl Harbor, is recorded as remarking somewhere, 'I fear we have only awakened a sleeping giant, and his reaction will be terrible.' His prediction was unerringly accurate: Pearl Harbor proved to be a major blessing for the United States – and the free world. Never before or since had the country been so united in war, even during the glorious Revolution of '75 against the British. It is quite impossible to exaggerate the incalculable depth of the effect that Pearl Harbor had (and still has) upon the American mind. 'It couldn't happen to us' was the immediate reaction. America in war and peace had, one had been taught, always fought and played fair. Yet here was war being made upon it in the foullest of foul, most treacherous, ways. What hurt far more than the crippling losses was the outrage of national humiliation. The hatred that every American, down to the smallest boy at Millbrook, felt for the Japanese because of the style of this attack was beyond words. And this hatred was constantly fanned as the fighting in the hell-hole of the Pacific atolls grew dirtier.

Hardly had we at Millbrook settled down to the implications of being at war than the Christmas vacations were again upon us. At 58 East 80th Street all was, predictably, turmoil and excitement. With Rossy Cutler torn between delight that America was at last in the war on the side of the British and horror at the disasters striking America in the Pacific, there was hardly a moment of the day when the radio and the newscasters were silent. Gabriel Heatter and his doom-laden tones thrived. The war had already come close to the family. Jack was nearing the end of his advanced pilot training with the RAF in distant Rhodesia, ready for battle. At home, Peter, predictably, was trying to enlist in the navy; Judy was looking for a war job in Washington. In Boston, Uncle Elliott Cutler, the surgeon, had joined the army, though he was in his fifties – and would soon emerge as a general, in charge of all the medical officers under Eisenhower. One of his four boys was off to Annapolis, another to West Point. The good news was that beautiful Pat was engaged, to a handsome and charming twenty-two-year-old Harvardian, Bob Fowler, who had already joined up in the US Navy and had just been commissioned. The Fowlers were a distinguished old New York–Boston family, the parents close friends of the Cutlers, while Bob's younger brother Harry was one of the anglophiles who had joined the British Army pre-Pearl Harbor, to serve with gallantry in the King's Royal Rifle Corps.

Because of the hubbub at 58 East 80th (and perhaps, not unreasonably, to keep me out of Judy's hair) that holiday I was farmed out to one of Rossy Cutler's close bridge-playing friends, Mrs Tucker. 'Ant Marcia Tucker', as the family called her, lived in great splendour in a mansion on 71st and Park, which filled about half the block's frontage, one of the last grand private houses of Manhattan. Although the almost blind Mrs Tucker was a truly gentle soul, I was unaccustomed to – and alarmed by – such grandeur. At our first breakfast alone together, across the vast dining-room table, I was trying to make polite and intelligent conversation, my eyes fixed on the hostess, as the butler offered me porridge (a special treat, 'Ant' Marcia having discovered me to be a Scot). Quietly she interrupted me to say, 'But wouldn't you like a plate, Mr Horne?' I looked down in horror at the pile of porridge that lay steaming on the place mat.

To most of us Bundles with some memories still of the bitter realities of wartime Britain, there seemed a lot about America's early war effort that made us smile, privately. In this country of boundless plenty, in emulation of a Britain constantly on the verge of hunger, or worse, because of the stranglehold of Hitler's U-boats, food rationing was brought in – though there was very little necessity. There were 'eggless' and 'meatless' days (alas, I thought, why not 'squashless' and 'pumpkinless' *weeks*, too?). Occasionally, a panicky local newspaper would print such a headline as 'FAMINE LOOMS IN AMERICA', but what shortages there were were caused largely by dislocation of labour and food demands of the gigantic expansion of the armed forces. Soon, in this country where the automobile was king, if not god, there was gasoline rationing, though the use of a private car was more restricted by the condition of its tyres (as a consequence of the acute shortage of rubber that followed the fall of Malaya) than the fullness of its gas tank. Like Lord Beaverbrook stripping British housewives of their precious aluminium saucepans to make Spit-fires (eventually production lines had got to work replacing the pans), everywhere there were zealots appealing for the surrender of rubber mats, shoes, girdles, hot-water bottles, hoses, even baby-bottle nipples. Roosevelt's much publicized Scottie, Fala, was reported donating his rubber bone to the war effort. 'We accept anything made of rubber, except condoms,' proclaimed patriotic gas stations. Leon Henderson, the official responsible for gasoline rationing, had himself photographed riding a bicycle to work with his secretary on the handlebars, to prove that 'even bicycle rides could be pooled'.

There was, inevitably, much abuse of the gas-rationing

system, the A, B and X (privileged for those on special war work) cards, which 'those in the know' considered quite unnecessary. One of these was John Cutler, in whose household rationing became a source of bitter strife. Discovering that he had applied for, and received, an X card for the 'farm' (half a dozen acres of 'swamp') at Garrison, an outraged Rossy Cutler promptly sent it back. There followed a prolonged silence in the house. Eventually the system was abandoned. Even that next most essential American apparatus, the telephone, was 'rationed', with appeals to long-distance callers: 'The War Needs the Wires'. Then it was the turn of typewriters, needed by the million by Washington's newly inflated war bureaucracy. Radio stations played merry little jingles like 'An Idle Typewriter is a Help to Hitler'.

In New York, war precautions introduced a 'dim-out', which at night turned the skyscrapers into a truncated black shape above the fourteenth floor, an undiminished blaze of light below. Atop the Empire State Building, elderly guards kept there to dissuade suicides were replaced by fire-watchers and air-raid wardens. The ever thoughtful Mayor, 'Little Flower' La Guardia, urged that air-raid shelters be equipped with playing cards to help people pass the time. But the blazing, affluent glow of New York, and much of the eastern seaboard as well, silhouetted merchantmen disastrously a hundred miles out to sea. Now permitted to sink US ships without restriction, the delighted U-boat commanders, one learnt after the war, called the resultant massacre within American territorial waters the 'second happy time' or the 'American turkey shoot'. For Britain the sinkings of the first months of 1942 nearly spelt disaster, and brought forth howls of rage against their partner – so my americaphobe Uncle Newt hastened to inform me.

Trains began to run twenty-four hours late, hostesses wondered whether they ought to call off next summer's deb parties. The old First World War patriotic songs of Irving Berlin and George M. Cohan were resuscitated, and a new one called 'Praise the Lord and Pass the Ammunition' was played on the radio every few minutes, pushing aside the schmaltzy former favourites out of Britain, like 'Blue Birds over the White Cliffs of Dover', 'A

Nightingale Sang in Berkeley Square', and even 'There'll Always Be an England', and even the 'Volga Boatman'. Instead, increasingly we heard those jaunty marches, 'From the Halls of Montezuma . . .' and '. . . Into the Wide Blue Yonder'. At training bases, rookies were given broomsticks to train with, because there were not enough rifles to go around, and at Madison Square Garden crack armoured units of the regular army gave recruitment demonstrations of tanks, fired upon by wooden guns, and breaking through anti-tank barries composed of potted palms.

Colourful topicality made its way into the industrial ads of all the magazines: 'No use, Adolf, you can't shut out that hum,' 'I'm fighting for my right to boo the Dodgers', 'Electric furnace steels will build a better world tomorrow.' Clattering away at her Liberty ships, 'Rosie the Riveter' became overnight the heroine of the hour. Factories proudly proclaimed they had been awarded the 'Army–Navy E-for-Excellence' pennant. In the windows of countless American homes red-and-white pennants with a blue star in the centre went up to denote that a member of the family was on active service. Gradually, as the first casualty lists appeared, and steadily lengthened, many of the blue stars were replaced by gold ones, and just as gradually one began to perceive beneath all the moonshine the earnest rippling of America's gigantic muscles. Each month there were reports of some new monster 'Willow Run' war plant that had been erected. After twelve months of war, aircraft were already coming off the assembly lines built by the Fords, the Reuben Fleets and the Henry J. Kaisers at a rate of 60,000 a year, ships at a rate of three a day, compared with four a month in July 1940. By April 1943, it was proclaimed that the previously almost defenceless US would have an army of 1 million men, ready to invade Europe the following year.

'How are those noisy Cutlers now?' Julia Breese asked with an affectionate smile when I went down to Washington to stay with her. I gave her a résumé of the war fever sweeping 58 East 80th and New York, and told her of my disgrace chez Mrs Tucker. She was much amused, and asked if she could relay it to my father: 'It would give him so much pleasure!' Anglophile though she was, knowing all too well herself what war meant in practice, her enthusiasm for America's involvement was more sober, and tinged with anxiety. She was deeply disapproving of the revelry and frivolity that had suddenly beset this new boom city, the non-stop cocktail parties at the Mayflower and the Shoreham: 'How could they?' she wondered, when the seriously burnt and wounded from Pearl Harbor were just arriving in the city hospitals.

By early 1942, sleepy, provincial Washington had suddenly woken up with a vengeance, to become a frenzied metropolis of well over 1 million. Endless rows of 'tempo' buildings were soon to clutter the beautiful Mall (especially designed by Roosevelt, supposedly, to fall down within ten years, so that the architectural horrors that had survived since 1917 would not be repeated). Across the river a gigantic new military command complex, to be called the Pentagon and offering three times as much floor space as Manhattan's Empire State, was being rushed up at phenomenal speed. Presiding over it was a new Under-Secretary of State, Judge Robert Patterson, old friend and neighbour from Garrison of all the Cutlers, and father of a recently graduated sixth-former at Millbrook. But there was no accommodation for the vast inflow of personnel and secretaries, many of them dossing down in hideous discomfort on benches in Union Station. In the hotels and public buildings, officers paraded, looking uncomfortable and self-conscious in uniforms that had not been worn since 1918. To show that it, the Nation's Capital, was also ready for the worst, and was not going to be caught asleep like Pearl Harbor, anti-aircraft guns appeared on top of public buildings, and air-raid wardens were hastily trained in the use of gas-masks by the DC fire department. But, during an early air-raid drill in December 1941, the best the city's single warning siren could do was to emit a squawk like a distressed chicken.

Experiencing it all, this fervour and sudden release of energy, as well as the nonsense, which surged so amazingly across America in the immediate wake of Pearl Harbor, it was hard to see – despite every successive disaster on the battle-fronts, East and West – how we could conceivably lose the war now.

Anything was possible, in the mood that now possessed America. Admiral Yamamoto is supposed to have told an unheeding Japanese War Cabinet, 'I have seen the oil wells of Texas and the factories of Detroit.' If that untravelled little Austrian corporal had also seen them, how much misery might the world have been spared? Many a time in years to come, I reflected what a tragedy it was that, in 1950 for instance, Stalin and his ugly North Korean minion, Kim Il Sung – and still later Saddam Hussein – could not have shared some of that which we Bundles had seen of America aroused, and its quite astonishing power.

Abruptly, the war swept away the depression, destitution and boredom. By the end of it, the US would have built 50 million tons of merchantmen, compared to Britain's 8.3 million, and 8.2 million tons of warships, to 2.4. So great was the unused strength called forth by the war that, by 1945, the overall standard had also been raised to the point where the average American was eating far better than in 1941. Meanwhile, within nine months of Pearl Harbor, US Marines were already hitting back hard at Guadalcanal.

Was December 1941 the time when we at Millbrook all grew up? Returning to school after those dramatic Christmas weeks, I found that, echoing the rest of the country, Millbrook's war effort had a similar admixture of moonshine and earnestness about it. The *Silo* printed a rather boy-scoutish editorial, urging, 'We must be calm at all times. We must rebuke those who spread wild tales of victory or disaster. . . . Our main contribution to our country is preparing ourselves for the future. Should we enter the Army or Navy, physical fitness is most important.' There was something ominous about the last sentence which I for one did not fancy. The *Silo* then went on to print in full the US Bill of Rights. As a first practical measure that January, the dining-room waitresses were packed off to more lucrative war work. We missed them, in more ways than one. They were a jolly lot. There was sparky Ida ('sweet as apple cider') and a bashful nineteen-year-old, Olga, who excited our youthful libidos, with her tremendous, thrustful bosoms – it was almost more than one could bear as she leant over to place a milk pitcher on the table, and it must have been intolerable to her, poor girl, as dozens of lascivious eyes followed her entry into the dining room each breakfast, eager to see if there were any fresh splits in the overtaxed gingham apron. We boys took over waiting at table, sometimes with disastrous results.

Progressively more and more jobs joined the Community Service lists. Soon the boilermen and the vegetable gardener went too. Mr Fritz remained – treated, apart from a few ill-judged, private remarks about his secret transmitter to Berlin, with more studied respect than heretofore – telling us all how much he hated Hitler. Amid much grumbling, the winter dance weekend had to be called off, because of lack of fuel oil to keep the sweet things warm. Hardly less serious was the threat to ice-hockey, because of a sudden shortage of rubber for pucks. Adopting the new Daylight Saving time (it being argued that Millbrook's electricity saving alone would be the equivalent of purchasing two more machine-guns), we were made – growling – to get up an hour earlier, at 6 a.m. Masters went on war courses in the holidays and returned full of weird and wonderful ideas. There was no OTC, because the democratic US forces assumed that a 'private school' education did not of necessity produce a good officer. We were taught not to lead, but to 'pitch in'. Doubtless the different systems had their faults and their advantages. We had Morse-code instruction and that great character, George Telfer, the school driver, now become a star, dug up the motor of an antique car and tried to teach us the principles of internal combustion. There was also a course in elementary seamanship – needless to say its mentor was Mr Pulling. Mr Prum put Millbrook on the map as a registered US Meteorological Station. There was an Observer Station for spotting German bombers (100 miles upcountry from New York City!), while an experimental blackout all over Duchess County showed that, so the *Silo* proclaimed, 'Millbrook is ready.' Less successful were map-reading endeavours, too taxing to young Americans' bumps of geography, with stragglers rolling in half an hour late for Mr Tuttle's maths class.

There was a Defence Committee to save paper and food, and first-aid courses were organized by the valiant school nurse, Miss

Miller, instructing us how to pound each other's rib cages by way of artificial respiration, on the floor of the Study Hall. Constructing scale model aircraft for use by the US Navy, Frank Trevor introduced aircraft-recognition courses into his biology labs. Though, by capitulating before the horrors of advanced biology, I had only just escaped from Trevor's clutches, together with all those of us who reckoned on an air-force future I found myself back in his domain, carefully studying the features of the exquisitely modelled little black aircraft his team turned out.

The new school motto became 'Be on the alert all the time!', and accompanying it the most arduous feature of Millbrook at war, undoubtedly, was the Physical Education Programme. Some official in the Pentagon with a perverted sense of humour had suggested that this was the most useful way schools could prepare their graduates for the armed services. Coach Knutson, the Führer, took up the hint with gusto. A Commando Course was erected, and every afternoon before the discomforts of football we were made to torture ourselves, diving through barrels and over walls, and swinging across rivers suspended from a rope. We were made to tear each other's arms off in wrestling contests and beat each other's brains out in the boxing ring. Somehow we survived – as often as not subsesquently to be turned down by the recruiting officers for fallen arches, incurred by jumping off high walls on the Commando Course. The war films and the lecturers (with a special British bias) selected by the Boss continued. We had Noël Coward's epic *In Which We Serve* (I am not sure the Jug was not abandoned that night, so none should miss it), and I remember how struck my class-mates were by the scene where the bedraggled survivors from Dunkirk are marched off the destroyer by a sergeant-major, arms swinging, to the admiration of a young seaman, John Mills. 'Well, gentlemen,' Mr Pulling declared afterwards, looking into the distance, 'you have just seen a great movie . . .'

I had already decided definitely that I was going to join the air force on leaving Millbrook the following year. I was just sixteen. In his letters, my father showed himself profoundly shocked by the notion. He wrote in one:

candidly, I should be rather unhappy . . . because I think it is a somewhat dangerous service, especially for a youngster who is not too robust. I should preferably like you to join up in a good Guards or Cavalry regiment here when the time comes, because the discipline and training is so good. . . . With regard to what I said about the RAF, please remember that you are my only child, and the only person who will be able to carry on the name.

Another letter urged me to put aside all thoughts of joining up, because the war was clearly going on for a long time, and to think of going on to Harvard, to study economics: 'When I leave this Earth, your inheritance from me will be business interests and accompanying responsibilities, and therefore you should bear this in mind. Moreover *there is more prospect of earning good money in business.*' As usual he closed with: 'What about your present *weight* and *height*? I would like particulars.' Thereafter, in both his and Uncle Newt's letters, the exhortatory phrase (perhaps a somewhat drole conceit, given the exigencies of war) 'a nice quiet Guards regiment' reappeared with regularity.

In America it was, for all of us, still an age of sublime innocence, an innocence which perhaps ended only with the assassination of John F. Kennedy, and which even Pearl Harbor could not dent. Idealism, always the life-blood of America, what has made it great, and what also from time to time threatens to isolate it from the rest of the world when disillusion sets in, coursed through our veins like fire in those days. Once America found itself plunged into war, such humdrum motives as the honouring of treaties, the independence of Poland, the matter of national survival – and even the avenging call of 'Remember Pearl Harbor' – were dumped in favour of far more cosmic conceptions. This time America was fighting, we were told, not merely to 'make the world safe for democracy', but to ensure 'a pint of milk a day for every baby in the world'. The noble defeated presidential candidate of 1940, Wendell Willkie, left his secluded Midwest to make a lightning tour around the globe. On his return he announced the startling discovery of 'One World', whose 2 billion inhabitants surprisingly enough had the same need of food, drink and sleep, the same basic fears and desires as his native Indianans. In those early months, all America came to look upon the war as a glorious thing, a final panacea to all the world's social ills. The war merely had to be won, and lo and behold 'One World' would become reality. We schoolboys, being younger and more naive, were even greater idealists. We saw the Grand Alliance of Russia, Britain, the US and the agglomerate 'United Nations' as enduring to eternity – a symbol of humanity's return to its senses. Bill Buckley (to whom, after Pearl Harbor had administered the *coup de grâce* to America First, we listened with new respect) led a debate on 'Freedom of Speech' – even in wartime. Censorship, he declared, was useless, as the enemy would undoubtedly know already whatever the press might divulge, while free dissemination of the news would nip any rumours in the bud. He won the debate, and was judged best speaker.

Our idealism was unquenchable. We clung with rapt interest to every successive blueprint that emerged for tomorrow's brave new post-war world. The Beveridge Plan, and the monumental Lutyens scheme for rebuilding a fabulous, Phoenix-like London, we took as pledges of the wonderful new England that was to arise from the ashes. But it was Stalin's Russia that began to play an increasingly important part in our idealism. When, to everybody's surprise, it showed that it was not going to be knocked out of the war in one brief *Blitzkrieg*, America's imagination was increasingly captured by the titanic battles being fought on the Russian front, whose immensity so completely dwarfed any other. At Millbrook we crowded around the newly installed notice board where the daily communiqués cut out of the *New York Times* were pasted up. Progressively the heroic Red Army tankmen had begun to take over in American sympathy from the Battle of Britain pilots and the sun-lashed veterans of the Eighth Army. An alarming female called Lieutenant Ludmilla Pavlichenko, said to have personally killed 309 Germans, made the rounds – displacing those Battle of Britain heroes. (One noted, marginally, the inability of the US public to maintain love or hate, or even interest, for too long.) Politically we at school (at least some of us – never Bill Buckley!) began to imagine a new agreeable and co-operative Russia that would teach us all so much. The New Dealers told us that the staggering industrial accomplishments of communist Russia were simply the logical extension on a vast scale of organization like the Tennessee Valley Authority. Even Willkie, the Republican, exhorted on his return from Omsk and Tomsk, 'Put aside your thoughts about communism, godlessness.' We did. We were ready to swallow any propaganda that gave glorious news of Russia.

No one was more vulnerable to the pro-Russian wave than I or more outspoken in debate after debate in the school forum. Looking back at some old issues of the *Silo*, I find (with some dismay, now, fifty years on) that I am recorded as upholding the affirmative in the following debate: 'Resolved: Russia should be allowed a free hand in determining her political boundaries after the War.' Happily, I lost that debate. Had I been twenty-six instead of sixteen at the time, I might not have found it quite so easy to get a visa to return to America during the McCarthyite 1950s. At least, later, it helped me comprehend what produced Alger Hiss, and a little of the subsequent disillusion that set in motion the swing of the pendulum of which McCarthy was the result.

Early that winter term, in January, I was given special permission to go down to New York for a singularly exciting event – Pat Cutler's wedding to Bob Fowler. The family finances being habitually over-stretched, and in her normal generosity determined to spare no expenses for what was bound to be one of the first post-Pearl Harbor major society weddings, Rossy Cutler had hit upon a brilliant idea. After the actual wedding down in the historic old church of St Mark's-in-the-Bowery, they would hold the reception in the now abandoned German Consulate on 77th Park Street. The building had long been a Fish-owned property, its leasing to the Germans yet another bone of contention within the family. Now that the unwanted tenants had departed, it stood empty and devoid of any furniture that could be damaged by carousing wedding guests, and – presumably free of any rent or hire charges – it seemed an ideal place to throw a party. With the war now come so close, it was indeed a glamorous, if not wild affair. Bob, an ensign in the navy, and many of his friends were in their sparkling new uniforms, already bound for the Pacific. His younger brother Harry had somehow wangled special leave from the British army to be best man, and Judy, tall and elegant and breathtakingly beautiful in a dark-green satin dress was maid-of-honour. After some initial misgivings – She always seemed so grown-up – I had come to be very fond of Pat and was made to feel importantly part of it all.

For the first time, I felt grown up enough to be Judy's equal and her accomplice in merriment – and a very merry occasion it was. We got into appalling trouble tipping champagne over the banisters on the excessive hat of a stuffy aunt. There were many toasts, and more toasts – and still more toasts. I had hardly ever drunk champagne before, or anything for that matter. Suddenly, to my horror and shame, I found the circular staircase in the German Consulate beginning to rotate, slowly. I realized that, for the first time in my life, I was hopelessly drunk, but sober enough to be determined that, under no circumstances, should Judy see it. So I crept up to the top of the building, in search of somewhere to retreat. Eventually I found what must have once been a caretaker's or housemaid's bedroom, with just an iron bedstead in it. Gratefully I sat down on it, momentarily to collect myself.

The next thing I knew, waking out of a merciful slumber, it was two or three hours later. The party was over. Every last person had left. The building was firmly locked. When I tried to telephone 58 East 80th for help, I found the line had been disconnected. Suddenly the full horror of my predicament struck me. In the prevailing spy-mania, what would the New York police make of a bedraggled youth, with an unAmerican accent, caught breaking *out* of the vacated Nazi Consulate? Spectacles of Ellis Island, of Sing Sing, maybe even of the firing squad (shortly to deal with two groups of Nazi fifth columnists), swiftly ran through my mind. But, amazingly enough, there appeared to be not even a single sleepy cop guarding the old Consulate, and I was able to climb my wobbly way out of a window, unchallenged, in a manner that remains incomprehensible to me, and make my way home. There was Peter, in the later stages of conviviality, with a French girl on one knee, his pious cousin Henry Forster murmuring prudence in his ear, 'Take it easy, Pete, you know what those French are like!' Preoccupied, no one asked me where I had been, nor did I come clean for a long time afterwards.

That happy, carefree wedding party in the German Consulate, I reflected later, had something about it of the ball on the eve of Waterloo. For one of his later wartime novels, that enjoyable chronicler of Massachusetts, J. P. Marquand, chose the apt title of *So Little Time*. It suited what we – or our elders – were already beginning to sense, echoing what warring Britain had known for several years already, a hectic urge for *carpe diem*. Wartime exigencies were moving in fast. After only a brief honeymoon, Bob Fowler was off to 'somewhere in the Pacific', to join a destroyer, the USS *Duncan*.

Despite the overtones of war, schoolboy life at Millbrook, with its pressures and priorities, went on much as usual. To the sympathetic delight of the anti-Trevor faction there was the continuing saga of Joey the woodchuck, repeatedly digging herself out of the Zoo. Meanwhile, my urge to escape (like poor Joey) from the clutches of dread Trevor opened a new door rich with future significance that I could certainly not foresee at the time. In order to give up hated advanced biology, yet still gain the required number of credits to qualify for college, I discovered that I could make up the deficient half-credit by taking typing. Twice a week a lady, Miss Louise Durkin, would come up from Millbrook town to coach us in the joys of touch-typing. What could be more boring, of less obvious consequence to the war effort, than to tap out endlessly on taped-over keys, 'Now is tje time fir all godd men to come to tje aid of . . .'? But many were *tje* years to come when, hunched over a machine in a newspaper office – and especially now that I have (at last) graduated to a word-processor – that I bless the name of my admirable typing teacher. It was surely the most useful thing I ever learnt at any school, and it never ceases to amaze me that, in this age of the computer, touch-typing is not automatically on the syllabus of every school in the world.

One day on a stroll through the 'swamp' which bordered old Mr Marcy's farm, Jack Hemphill and I came across a magnificent great maple. With mighty forked branches jutting out twenty feet above the ground, it was absolutely designed for a tree-house. We collected together a team of half a dozen classmates, and with utmost secrecy humped down to the swamp stacks of timber scavanged from an old barn which had been recently demolished, although aware that beloved Henry Callard had earmarked it for the 'root cellar' (for storing vegetables and fruit) which he and his Community Service team were building for the school. To avoid detection, we took elaborate detours, lugging the heavy planks miles over hill and dale, pushing ourselves to exhaustion every half-holiday for several weeks. Then, when bringing in the very last load we needed, who should we run into but Henry Callard. Escape or subterfuge was out of the question, so we stood there, perspiring and awaiting the worst. But Henry Callard merely remarked with a kindly smile, 'That's a tough way of spending a Saturday afternoon – you should have told me and I'd have brought the truck down to help you out.' He had known about the 'project' from the word go. There was no retribution. It was just his way of instilling a sense of original sin, whereas the Boss's more frontal technique would have chiefly evoked fear.

We felt momentarily ashamed. Nevertheless the tree-house went on. It was watertight and snowproof, boasted a large window, an oil lantern and (supplied by Sears Roebuck for $1.25) a wood stove, keeping us snugly warm over the winter months – and occasionally, when over-stoked, setting fire to the roof. Fortunately, for dousing the flames, a few yards away ran a stream, which in summer we dammed up to make what Huckleberry Finn would have called a 'swimming hole' – disgustingly muddy, but wonderfully refreshing. Occasional midnight forays into the school kitchen would provide pilfered eggs and bacon. Fried in rebarbative old grease on our lethal stove, they tasted better than any fried egg before or since. By mutual consent, smoking was banned, so as not to tax Henry Callard's gentle omniscience too severely. Of the Tree-House Committee, I suppose Jack Hemphill and I used it most, reorganizing the future of the world there (hand in hand with a benign Joe Stalin), and, rather less frequently, perusing banned magazines of soft porn – very 'soft' indeed in those days. It was an idyllic retreat, rigorously kept secret from the rest of the school.

Jack's inquisitiveness was boundless. One afternoon, when the rest of the school was watching a football game, it took us into exploring the inner sanctuary of our dormitory master. To our horror, through the half-open bedroom door we saw him, beneath a print of Rodin's *The Kiss*, similarly intertwined with Sally Frankenstein, the school dietician. Unseen, we fled to the tree-house without stopping, to consider the full offensiveness of our discovery. Our appreciation was identical and censorious: 'How appalling – surely people no longer made love *at that age!*' Investigation revealed that the miscreants were in their mid-thirties, but that hardly affected the issue in our eyes. Like seventeen-year-old Marianne Dashwood in *Sense and Sensibility*, shocked to discover that her admirer Colonel Brandon was thirty-five, and therefore unmarriageable, the thought of antique bodies making love was to us so disturbing that, there and then, we formed a mutual euthanasia pact, to take effect from the age of thirty-five. After that age, judging from the affront to nature we had just witnessed, life could not possibly be worth living. (Years later, both of us rising forty, Jack visited me in London – with his attractive Norwegian wife, Wenche. Joking, I asked, 'why didn't you?' He didn't understand; I reminded him of our pact. He appeared offended, assuming – I imagine – some slight against his wife. We never met again – until our 50th Anniversary reunion in 1993. He was forgiving.

The annual torture of the Spring Speeches was upon us. Even more than the previous year, the majority of topics had something to do with the war. I chose 'Peace for the Axis', laying down the terms which should be imposed – principally by Britain and America – upon a defeated and flattened Germany. In the original that survived the war, I find myself pre-empting Nuremberg and declaring ferociously, 'We must try their leaders, who have been the cause of all this bloodshed, and execute them.' The judicious and literal Jack McGiffert was outraged, sidelined the offending sentence in red and wrote in: 'BRITISH JUSTICE??!' The highest mark he would give me was a B−. 'Utopian,' he snorted. 'Aren't you assuming infallibility on the part of Britain and the USA?'

Among the visiting lecturers, that commander from HMS *Dido* had perhaps been the beginning of the end of the British heroes to address us. After 7 December, progressively they gave way to the daring operatives of the brave little American torpedo boats that had done their best, suicidally, to keep the Japanese navy at bay in the Philippines. Meanwhile, in each successive issue of the *Silo* there were now reports of more alumni joining the armed services, of new jobs devolving upon the Community Service, of long-unused fields being brought back to growing potatoes, carrots, onions – and oats, for the Pulling hunters. We smiled. The expanding school farm, run by Henry Callard, announced that it would like *paid* volunteer workers for the summer. After efforts to join an RAF cadet radio course in Montreal proved abortive, pushed by the Cutlers and enticed by the fact that it would be run by Henry Callard, I signed on. My father praised me for deciding to work on the school farm that summer. It would be good for my health, and he commended the 'intelligent tone' in my latest letter: 'It seems that you are now taking a responsible view with regard to your future career.'

As the months passed, the war news still had little enough of comfort to offer. To 58 East 80th Street there arrived in April an alarming communication from the RAF. Jack, who in 1941 had rejoined the American Field Service in the Middle East, on reaching Cairo had changed his mind and had volunteered for the RAF instead. From distant Rhodesia, where he was just completing his advanced pilot training, Rossy Cutler now received the news that he had had a terrible accident. While doing aerobatics, the RAF trainer which Jack was flying had gone into a spin from 2000 feet, following which he remembered nothing more until he awoke in hospital the next day. He had been amazingly lucky to be picked up by Africans in the bush, but the RAF medical report, at that distance, sounded grim – as if, apart from his other extensive injuries, Jack had been all but emasculated. Though worried stiff, Rossy Cutler showed none of it. She was sure the intrepid Jack, indestructible, would come through.

In the world at large, it was a time of continuing disasters. The East Indies, Burma and Singapore were all swallowed up by the Japanese, infiltrating their way through the supposedly impenetrable jungle. India looked threatened, as did Ceylon, with task forces of the Rising Sun ranging far and wide into the Indian Ocean. In the Philippines, the last heroic bastion at Corregidor fell, and the American public – unaccustomed to such humiliations – were treated to films of the Bataan death march. Nearer home, equally unbelievably, Hitler's crack battleships, *Scharnhorst* and *Gneisenau*, broke through the Channel right under the noses of the heavy guns at Dover. It was the last straw, and for a moment, in what he later reckoned to have been his lowest ebb in the war, Churchill looked like falling.

In April, there came a brief but amazing morale-booster for Americans: flying apparently out of nowhere, Colonel Jimmy Doolittle and his sixteen courageous B-25s bombed Tokyo. (He died, aged ninety-six, in 1993.) Only a pinprick, but it was a foretaste of what the infuriated, humiliated Americans would do to the Japanese homeland. The following month, again in a foretaste of what was to come, the RAF devastated Cologne in the first thousand-bomber raid of the war. Then, just as Millbrook was about to celebrate Commencement, 1942, at the beginning of June came news of the first great US naval victory of the war. At Midway, planes from those US carriers missed at Pearl Harbor fortuitously discovered, and sank within five minutes, four Japanese aircraft carriers. It marked – though who could see it at the time, after such a run of disasters? – the turning point of the war in the Pacific. Yamamoto's mighty battlefleet, intent on seizing this island bulwark vital to America, swung about and headed for home.

Along the great Russian front, however, the Germans – having recouped their setbacks of the winter – were plunging ahead with renewed ferocity. This time it was clear that all their efforts were staked on the south, in an all-out attempt to grab the Caucasus oilfields and sever the supply to the Western Allies via

Persia. But, meanwhile, the headlines from Libya were the worst ever. Yet another British general, Ritchie, had been poised to thrust westwards, once again – but, in the words of Winston Churchill, 'the bear blew first'. The redoubtable Rommel, moving with utmost skill, struck a deadly blow at Ritchie's armour. In that most fluid of campaigns, the British front reeled precipitately backwards. At a place called Ain el Gazala, a key position forty miles west of the fortress of Tobruk, a British infantry 'box' was reported to have been overrun and completely wiped out on the first day of June. Though isolated the previous year, Tobruk, which had held out for nine months, surrendered with shocking speed. The whole British front seemed to have collapsed, with the Eighth Army falling back to El Alamein, just sixty miles from Alexandria, farther east than the Axis forces had ever reached before. It sounded as though, with one more heave, Rommel would be at the gates of Cairo, and master of the Middle East. Then what? A thrust to link up with the Wehrmacht already reaching out towards the Caucasus oilfields, or to join hands with the victorious Japanese on the plains of India?

Not since Dunkirk had the war news looked bleaker. I wondered how, in all this wretched shambles in the Western Desert, Cecil was faring. A letter from Uncle Newt said, uncharitably, 'I do not know where Brigadier Cecil is – I expect he has reached the limit of advancement in his military career – he is not a Wellington or a Wavell.' A week or two later my father wrote, with the bald news: Cecil, commanding the 150th Infantry Brigade that had been holding the key point of Gazala, was missing in action. His whole brigade appeared to have been overrun around the beginning of June while the 8th Army retreated before Rommel; there were no further details. I had never really liked Cecil, yet held him in great respect – and a considerable amount of awe. And, in the terrible, prolonged uncertainty now besetting her, I felt miserable for Eve, who had been the closest family ally of my childhood, and was now horribly far away. I was also rather shocked by the dry, detached way in which my father had given me the news, as impersonal as when he had written about the bombing of the beach-hut at Titchfield. Eve was, after all, his only niece and he had always treated her more like a daughter. That was, however, the impersonal way of all his numbered letters – now dictated and typewritten following my complaints about *his* handwriting. Perhaps it had something to do with Britain's general war-weariness, which, after three years of unrelieved harsh tidings, must have led to a numbing of the senses.

Months later my father wrote, again in that matter-of-fact way of his: 'Cousin Evelyn is much thinner and . . . rather worried about her husband with regard to no definite *official* news having reached us.' For over a year, there was no news, but the omens were not good. It was not difficult to imagine the combination of hope and despair in which poor Eve, with two young children, lived during those long months. Then, later in 1943, information came via escaped prisoners of war, the only surviving members of Cecil's brigade headquarters, who confirmed that he had been killed at Gazala. 'The final morning, 1st June 1942,' his former intelligence officer reported,

> the artillery was reduced to less than a dozen rounds for such guns as remained. We were and had been attacked on all sides by tanks and I like to think that, like the Captain of a ship, the Brigadier went down fighting. I imagine he must have been hit about 11 hours on 1st June. A few hours before, he had realized that in effect the battle was over and had instructed his staff to try and get out while they could and lie up in the minefield until nightfall, then to make their way north, to try and get to the rest of the Division. He remained at his post until the last. It is believed that Cecil's last stand had held the enemy for five days, during which time reinforcements had landed in time to hold the enemy at Alamein.

His divisional commander, Major-General Ramsden, spoke of Cecil's 'outstanding courage and efficiency'. There were further reports, later, that Cecil had been killed by a shell while making a last attempt to break out, and there was serious talk after the war that he should have received a VC for his heroism. But no one survived who had been with him at Gazala at the very end, so there was no one who could have supplied first hand the obligatory official citation. In his *The Second World War*, Winston Churchill eulogized the 'devoted tenacity' of the 150th's stand at Gazala. (Later it became apparent that the disaster should never have been allowed to happen.)

All this, however, could have done little to assuage Eva's grief. She never really recovered, withdrawing after the war more and more into herself and dying at an early age. Meanwhile, it was in the wake of the Gazala disaster and the fall of Tobruk that Churchill narrowly survived the first vote of censure against him in the Commons. Americans like Rossy Cutler and Julia Breese, all compassion and sympathy about Cecil, were profoundly shocked that – at this time – Britain should contemplate dumping the hero–leader. His survival of the vote, at the beginning of July, eclipsed the news of a few weeks later that two new, unknown generals had been appointed to take over in the desert, with Churchill himself flying out to Cairo, presumably to give them a major pep-talk. Alexander and Montgomery – would they simply become two more names in the long list of defeated British leaders? We had all become thoroughly pessimistic about the prospects of beating, or even holding, the Desert Fox, Rommel.

About this time in 1942, after America had been at war for six months, one began to detect a gradual changing of attitudes towards Britain – and us Bundles. No longer were we the embattled 'heroes' that we had been in 1940 – that is, if we ever had been. Now we were no longer *different* to the rest of our school-mates. Most of us (though one could not vouchsafe for Master Primrose) liked it that way. There were reports that, with the onset of food and gasoline rationing, some Bundles – as guests that had perhaps stayed over-long – were feeling slightly less welcome than say a year before. I for one certainly did not sense that. On the one hand there was the feeling that we were now 'all in the same boat', with all the psychological advantages which accompanied it. On the other hand, it was steadily becoming America's war, especially after the heady news in the summer that US Marines had landed at Guadalcanal. Following the notable naval victory at Midway, America was now hitting back hard at the loathed Japanese. There were those Americans who left one in no doubt that they thought that their country, with its vast human and material resources, would soon be the boss in the Grand Alliance, and that, with more than a touch of arrogance, they would be teaching the British how to win battles. After the retreat to Alamein, while the novice US forces were winning points in the South Pacific, British repute was at an all-time low, and – after all the disasters on land, against the Germans, since 1940 – perhaps those critics had reason. Nevertheless, there were times when this boastful attitude was difficult to bear, especially coming on top of the news about Cecil.

On the reverse side of the coin, Americans were increasingly irritated by the sniping directed at them and their war effort, as reported by correspondents back from Britain. There were no Stars-and-Stripes flying in the whole of London, Rossy Cutler had heard. Far from being thrilled, and grateful, for America's entry into the war, and the arrival of the first US troops in Britain, as many Americans somehow expected, there was little jubililation evident. That idealism which was sweeping America very evidently did not entirely strike a harmonious chord in war-weary Britain. Too little, too late? – the old slogan was trotted out yet again. A visiting British clergyman who came and spoke at Millbrook, in tones of moral superiority conveyed implicitly much of the criticism of the US currently rife in Britain – and we Bundles resented that too. A poll taken in the following year revealed that the Americans were only marginally more popular than the Italians, Hitler's (by then former) ally, and came well below the Poles and the French.

The same theme was echoed, in his letters to me, by Uncle Newt, who, truly a blood-brother of Nancy Mitford's as yet uninvented Uncle Matthew, had never managed to conceal his dislike of America and Americans. He wrote (in one of the letters I kept), 'I think it was a great mistake letting you go to America, you were too old and should have stayed and seen the show through. . . . No doubt you find the Americans nice – they are the kindest, most hospitable, most simple and ignorant people in the world. Their lack of knowlege of world affairs is abysmal

. . .!' I suppose I had provoked him by sending him a letter in the US press declaring that Americans were not at war to 'hold the British Empire together'. In return, he would pass on to me the latest anti-American joke: the arriving US troops were 'over-paid, over-sexed – and *over here!*' or – much worse – they were 'like bananas – some green, some brown, but *mostly yellow*'. In retrospect, most of the wisecracks were neither funny nor clever, but rashly – as a counter-tease to Rossy Cutler – I jokingly passed on one of his letters. It was a foolish thing to do. She, predictably, feigned mock outrage, but sent it on to her sister, Julia Breese, who was deeply offended. She winged the unfortunate letter back to my father, together with a sharp note of her own. He reproved Uncle Newt, and the circle was completed with a stinging jeremiad from the chastised uncle to me, about the virtues of discretion.

Taking the load off those over-burdened foster-parents, among the seven or so who volunteered to work on the school farm that summer, the Bundles made up a strong faction. There were Brian and myself, Keith Williams from Manchester and his cousin, Bill Cookson. It was hard work, from dawn to late afternoon, often in torrid heat hoeing the melon fields under supervision of Ralph, the analphabetic Sicilian who so closely resembled Chico Marx. By evening we all flopped down lifeless, almost too lifeless even to turn on the radio and listen to the Jack Benny Show. We were well fed by a circular lady called Ethel Sweeney, the deputy school cook, who identified herself proudly as Pennsylvania Dutch, just to ensure that no one could mistake her for *German*. Those five or six weeks were among the happiest I spent in America. Osmotically, I felt I learnt a lot more about (literally) its grass-roots. There was that deep satisfaction of working on the soil in the summer warmth, coupled with the even greater satisfaction of over $50, a Croesan treasury, rustling in my pocket at the end of it all. But, above all, I discovered that, for the first time in my life, I had made a true friend and ally of a teacher – Henry Callard.

On leaving the farm, enriched, bronzed and muscular, I followed the now familiar holiday track of Garrison, East Chop and Canada. It was hardly a routine that any schoolboy, British or American, could have complained about. There was the same long drive up from New York in the rattling half-timbered station-wagon, with the sisters in front, peering determinedly through their green eyeshades, one eye fixed on the road and the other three scanning for Antique Shoppes. There was, sadly, no Peter, but the house at East Chop still smelled of resin and cedar shingles, was still as bleak and storm-tossed as ever. There were sweltering days when it seemed even more unbearably hot and humid than the previous year. 'Think of the boys in Burma, Ally!' Rossy Cutler would exhort me if I complained too loudly.

But this summer my mind was distracted: Jack McGiffert had allotted me, as my summer task, the whole 1500 pages of *War and Peace* to wade through. In view of the gigantic struggle on the Eastern Front, where the Germans were already lunging forward yet again and the Russians once again resisting as heroically as the previous summer, it seemed singularly appropriate. Soon I could not put it down. I lived and ate with the Rostovs, dreamt of great cavalry charges at Borodino, and wept for Prince Andrei. Even Judy uttering Indian war whoops from the other end of the verandah could not always rouse me out of this heroic new world I had entered. I was, I suppose, still stricken with hopeless, unrequited calf-love, but now, puberty having raised its ugly head rather late, the fifteen-year-old adolescent translated into a spotty sixteen-year-old prurient youth, Dante had been trans-muted into Boccaccio. I had moved down from the attic of unpleasant memory to the room alongside Judy's. Unplastered like the rest of the house, in the dividing wall one day I discovered conveniently located knot-holes to peer through lasciviously – which did momentarily take my mind off Natasha. But, to my acute embarrassment, no sooner did I unknot one knot-hole than it would suddenly be covered over with a war poster. I returned to the reality of Natasha. Poor Pierre Bezukov – that was me.

That summer the Vineyard was all abuzz with a staggering piece of war news, so alarmingly and effrontingly close to home that it intruded upon all else. Four German saboteurs, landed from a U-boat, had been rounded up in Long Island in June. Their instructions, so Edgar Hoover of the vigilant FBI warned the country, were to cripple the American war effort. A few days later, a similar group of four were caught near Jacksonville, Florida. (Two months later, while we were at East Chop, they were summarily executed.) What possible material results their mad Führer thought these wretched men could have achieved is hard to conceive. But the alarm they created was out of all proportion. Enemy agents had actually landed in Fortress America! What next? The whole country was visibly shaken by the news. Even at the time Operation Pastorius, as it was called, sounded like a suicidally desperate venture of Hitler's. But just supposing these two teams that had been rounded up were but the tip of the proverbial iceberg, that there were other, more accomplished groups of spies and saboteurs roaming this wide-open and extremely vulnerable country, with its own large groups of indigenous Germans, Italians and Japanese? Rossy Cutler was agog with excitement, manifestly longing to get her own hands on a Nazi spy.

There was even talk about doing what the most recent storm had failed to do: demolish the dock at East Chop, so that no Nazi saboteurs could land *there*.

Meanwhile, in Europe, the tentacles of the still unbeatable Wehrmacht had reached the outskirts of Stalingrad, within what looked like easy reach of the Volga, and were poised to seize the whole Caucasus, cutting Russia in two. The funereal Gabriel Heatter had much to maintain the melancholy of his evening broadcasts. But, on going up to stay with Nora and Billy Breese in their tranquil hideout at New Brunswick's St Andrews, I found the sober-sided Canadians much more stirred up by news of the recent disaster of the Dieppe Raid (out of 7000 officers and men landed, they had lost 5000). Alternately described as an attempt to take the pressure off the failing Russians (which it didn't) and as a dummy run for a full-scale invasion (which was not to take place till nearly two years later), what outraged the Canadians about Dieppe was that the great majority of the troops pinned down hopelessly and slaughtered on the beaches of Dieppe were Canadian – but the plan was British, and so were the commanders. Worse still, rumours had it that the 'Canucks' had been chosen for Dieppe 'to give them something to do', to keep them out of mischief, instead of beating up the pubs in southern

England. So, understandably, compared with what I recollected the previous summer, the prevailing view of the Mother Country among the summer residents of St Andrews-on-Sea was not exactly at its highest.

Of Nora Breese's Scottish brother-in-law, David Walker, who had been captured with the Highland Division at St Valéry in 1940, and now languished in Colditz after several escape attempts, there was little news, except that he was involved in further, regular escape attempts. It was a tragic story: after David's capture, his wife Willa (Nora's sister) had given birth to their first child. It had died a cot death, but for many months they kept the truth from David, in Colditz. Willa, a pretty, dark-eyed brunette still in her twenties, had now suddenly appeared resplendent in the uniform of a wing-commander in the RCAF, head of the whole women's air force of Canada. I was profoundly impressed. In the house there was a wind-up gramophone with, as far as I can recall, only two records: 'The Dance of the Sugar-Plum Fairy' and 'The March of the Royal Air Force', equally sugary but – to me, engrossed by thoughts of the following year – deeply stirring. In and out of the house trooped much decorated young RCAF, and RAF, officers on leave, or from the Empire Training Scheme in nearby Moncton. I gazed at their beribboned uniforms with unquenchable longing. Next year! Every Saturday there were dances (dry, of course, because puritanical New Brunswick was that way) in the great Canadian Pacific Algonquin Hotel, which dominated the little harbour. There was a hardly veiled censoriousness towards the war-widows, and grass-widows, who seemed to go possibly *too* far in their enthusiasm to entertain the visiting heroes. But it didn't affect me, and I found myself unexpectedly being attracted by girls other than beloved Judy, and *even*, apparently, being found attractive by one or two of the blonde Canadian teenagers. It was fun. For all their seriousness and hypersensitivity, I liked these Canadians – who were not quite English, not quite American – and their great big, beautiful, brave and empty land, and hoped I would return to see more of it one day.

Surreptitiously, life was beginning to change – for the better.

Emancipation was on its way. Perhaps I was even growing up. And the summer was at an end – already, against all expectation, my third as a Bundle. Instinctively I knew, now with some genuine regrets, that it had to be the last: either the war would be over, or I would be back home in the sky-blue uniform of the RAF.

CHAPTER TEN

The Last and Best, 1943

Most schoolboys, I suppose, find – or should find – their last year at school, *aetat.* 17, to be a year of take-off. For me it was certainly that, at last. I soared, I flew (that is, alas, only figuratively). Life seemed to be speeding up dramatically. Looked at even through the rose-tinted spectacles of the time, 1942–3 remains one of the happiest, most fulfilling years of my life.

There were a number of factors combining to produce this year of hyper-exhilaration. For one thing, I was growing up. I felt I had come to terms with America. It no longer seemed a strange country; I felt at ease there. I had made some good friends. I had a new 'family', whom – despite the constant teasing – I felt affection for and at home with. And America had, quite surreptitiously, given me a new self-confidence. Although not entirely liberated from that lunatic infatuation with 'an older woman', at least I was finding that I could – in the modern jargon – handle it. Though, of course, Judy Bayard Cutler remained in a class beyond compare, gradually there seemed to be other options, promises of wider horizons. Then, unmistakably, as the new year at Millbrook began in September, the war seemed to be going better – or, at least, not quite so badly. And, at school, for the first time in my hardly distinguished career I found myself beguiled into learning, motivated and orientated by at least one outstanding teacher, if not two.

The Millbrook year started full of hope and expectation. At the end of it there would be graduation, and beyond – the RAF. Returning that September, we suddenly found ourselves an elite, sixth-formers, at the top of the school, vested in responsibility, respect and even a little power. We were a tiny, rather closely knit class of only thirteen. The two West Coasters, Rheem and Chaney, had dropped out – returning home, no doubt, to keep at bay the menacing Japs. I can still remember not just the names, but the faces, voices and personalities of all thirteen. There was the hard core of the tree-house group – rebels, but by modern standards only to the most restrained extent; the journalists, who ran the *Silo*, the *Mill* (a magazine dedicated to literary endeavours) and *The Tamarack Yearbook* (which we proudly started); and the administrators, on whose good-humoured loyalty the Boss depended for the running of the school.

We began the year comfortably at ease with one another, in our different factions, and were to end it all close friends. Assimilated into the American Way as we had become to different degrees, Brian, my fellow Bundle, and I had rather drifted apart; and now, quite unexpectedly a new star entered my firmament. Through the infinite wisdom of Edward Pulling (and, with subsequent gratitude, I came to recognize that it *was* infinite), I found, with some initial concern, that I had been put down to share a room with my former political arch-adversary, Bill Buckley. Or, rather, it was an apartment. Up on top of the third-form dormitory there were attic rooms (close, by my reckoning, to where in the movie of *The World According to Garp*, shot at Millbrook in the 1980s, the wayward child Garp fell off the roof). In them we were allotted two rooms, and our own private bathroom, with only three younger boys in our charge – that is, exactly one and a half charges each. Our other classmates were each responsible for a dormitory of some twenty boys; none had our enviable quarters, or lack of responsibility. But at the beginning of a long (and critical) school year together Bill and I looked at each other with considerable apprehension. Would it end in blows?

Of my putative misgivings at the time, Bill Buckley was to write elsewhere in retrospect:

He must have felt a singular revulsion at the prospect of spending his final year in such close quarters with a student who argued against US participation in a war whose outcome could mean liberty, or Nazism, for his people. But then of course Pearl Harbor came, and the issue became moot. I doubt, as it turned out, that we'd have ended other than as we have done, which is as closest friends, if the Revolutionary War had come up at about that time.

Years later I asked the Boss why he had thrown us together, so improbably, that last year. With a twinkle in those Atlantic-blue eyes he replied, 'Because I thought you would be good for each other!' There must also clearly have been an element of self-interest involved – he reckoning, I suppose, that, as the least reliable of all his new sixth formers, Bill and I, stowed away in our garret, would also be least trouble; and, who knows, perhaps even lend our talents to getting down to some serious work? Our awesome headmaster and Bill had already established a stand-off of mutual respect and a certain mutual wariness. His father liked to relate (taking some historical liberties, Bill always insisted) how early in young William's career at Millbrook he had suddenly appeared, uninvited, in the midst of a faculty meeting, to report that 'a member of the faculty had deprived him of the right to express his political views in class', and had then proceeded to expound to the stunned faculty the virtues of Isolationism, the dignity of the Catholic Church and the political ignorance of the school staff.

How, though, can one begin to explain in a few lines the rationale of what was to become the longest and deepest friendship of a lifetime, let alone describe one who in later life was to emerge as one of the most renowned – if not notorious – Americans of his generation, founder of the American Conservative Party, profound influence upon Ronald Reagan, and one of chief among the intellectual architects of the fall of the 'Evil Empire'?

Perhaps the foundations of this friendship were rooted, pragmatically, in little more than a certain adolescent resistance to discipline. Our attic suite swiftly became a haunt of undisturbed disorder, plushy high-living (the instinct for which, regardless of our respective means, was to stick with us both for evermore) and modest corruption – by which I mean, in those happy, innocent times, nothing more venal than doughnuts and non-alcoholic cider. (I tried smoking corn-silk in a corn-cob pipe, but it made me as violently sick as when Knatchbull had twisted my arm at Le Rosey. Bill had not yet taken to cigars, thank God.) From our eyrie, we could spy trouble coming from whatever quarter in the campus. We were generally left alone. I constructed for him an illegal radio and record-player; he typed my essays – with far greater speed and accuracy than I had yet mastered. At $1 a thousand words, and eighty a minute, Bill – who had somewhere along the line taught himself to touch-type and, with his usual adroitness, could already outpace most professional typists – had a good racket going to help swell the family coffers, until it was put into liquidation on being denounced by the Boss as 'self-aggrandizement'.

By the beginning of that new school year Millbrook's 'war-preparedness' programme had really got into top gear. In the fall, there was apple-picking and corn-shucking. The orchards and the seven-foot-high corn jungle provided an ideal retreat for the smokers – or shirkers; while the corn husks, with leaves twisted back to act as fins, made deadly mortar bombs for Guadalcanal-style battles. As a result of the terrible bout of torpedoings off the eastern seaboard, school heating had been reduced by 60 per cent. Gasoline rationing meant fewer parental visits and weekends, football matches and dances reduced to a painful minimum, and the disappearance of bananas from the school menu (we Bundles doubtless reminded our school-mates that many British children had forgotten what they even looked like).

A new job had been added to Community Service: that of the War Map Boy, whose duty it was to pin up the latest bulletins from the *New York Times* and move different-coloured flags about on a vast map of the world. We studied it gravely over the milk-and-crackers break each morning. Thirty-three graduates, the *Silo* informed us, had now joined up. Some came back and told us what it was like, with all the exaggeration of the 'old sweat'. Judy's cousin, Bayard Forster, training with the army in Mississippi, swore that the temperature 'never fell below 125 degrees', men died by the dozen: 'I never saw the flag at anything but half-mast.' We, of course, believed it all. Within a few months Bayard was in Guadalcanal. John Buckley, Bill's eldest brother, glorifying his army life, was introduced by the Boss as someone oddly chosen as a cavalry officer, given that he had previously not known which end of a horse to approach – to which he replied, with spirit, that he had 'carefully studied pictures of the things'.

A father of one of the boys, William S. Gibbs, designer of the first Liberty ship, came to tell us all about it, while the flow of outside lecturers and our Forum debates were now almost all war-related. Still the Boss invited a few British veterans. An officer off an RN minesweeper diverted us with how he had come close to demolishing Dover Castle, with the Admiral inside, during gunnery practice. An RAF wing commander excited me greatly with an account of the latest, agile Mosquito fighter-bomber, built out of plywood, but upset native sensibilities by observing that the much vaunted USAAF Flying Fortresses were not 'proving practical' for air raids on Germany. The Boss regaled us with his 1918 experiences aboard his British destroyer in the Channel. Hargraves Joyous Bishop, possibly trying to chalk up points in the losing battle for the favours of Sally Frankenstein, told of his daring exploits with the US Medical Corps in France. Frank Trevor returned from having inveigled his brother into letting him participate in armoured manoeuvres as co-driver in one of the latest Sherman tanks; some of us uncharitably wished in secret that the army had hung on to him. In the Forum, I found myself recruited to support a motion that called for retaliating in kind, atrocity for atrocity, against the Germans and Japanese. This would, I declared ferociously, do no end of good for civilian morale. I was defeated resoundingly. Speaking out against 'Social Reforms for Negroes Now', my reactionary new room-mate (blaming 'northern agitators who were pushing the Negro question at this time when our country had so much else to do') also lost his cause.

But what truly united us was a certain iconoclastic distrust of the pompous and over-earnest, of authoritarianism. This found its expression especially in resistance towards the latest physical excesses (as they seemed to us in our Capuan indolence) of Führer Knutson, who had returned from the vacations stuffed with enthusiasm for paramilitary bodybuilding, which some smart-arse down in Washington had assured him would win the war. Records of push-ups and pull-ups, were duly recorded on the notice-board. A Senior Ranger Run, or assault course of bone-shaking difficulty, was constructed. Worst of all, the Führer – so Bill recalls – 'was so carried away by the military spirit of the World War that he took to marching his athletes to the playing fields, in accents so martial they could be heard in West Point'. Once, through inspired mimicry from our third-floor eyrie, an order of 'Reverse, march!' caused the oppressed student column to turn about in total chaos, all but trampling down the Führer, who conducted a vain search for the impostor.

Our other shared *bête noire*, of course, was Frank Trevor, he of the Zoo and mephistophelian features. Bill's antipathy dated to the pre-Millbrook summer of 1939. W. F. Buckley Sr had decided to move to Europe – to 'improve' his three eldest children, leaving the remaining household of seven children (plus one governess, two nannies, two music teachers and seven servants) in the charge of Frank Trevor – under whose spell animal-loving Jimmy had fallen at school, 'to teach us about nature', wrote Bill:

> My father returned to find – somewhat to his chagrin, we were pleased to note – that our property now harboured probably the largest zoo this side of the Bronx. The entire summer had been given over to making leaf impressions in white clay, building pens, feeding snakes. And dinner conversation was usually on some such theme as how horses were actually responsible for more deaths than snakes, the poor little, misunderstood creatures. It was not until much later, when I sat opposite him [Trevor] in class at Millbrook, disembowelling a pig, that it occurred to me that, unlike horses, no one attempted to ride snakes.

Doubtless Bill had not refrained from passing on this interesting observation. Unlike me, with no leanings towards the air force, he had shunned Trevor's war-programme aircraft-recognition classes, currently celebrating construction of their 190th model.

As of that September 1942, the sinister little swastika flags on Millbrook's new map board stood frighteningly deep inside bleeding Russia, reaching the Volga at Stalingrad and spilling far south into the Caucasus. Still the question was fixed in all our minds – how much longer can the Russians hold on? In the desert, the flags still sat where they had in June, at El Alamein, perilously close to Cairo, though those two new, unknown generals, Alexander and Montgomery, appeared to have checked Rommel in a fierce battle at Alam Halfa. In the Pacific, things looked brighter. Far out in the ocean, a single Stars-and-Stripes was stuck heroically on tiny Midway Island, while southwards the impetus of the Japanese towards Australia seemed to have been halted in New Guinea, within walking distance of vital Port Moresby, and in the Solomons. On Guadalcanal another solitary US flag showed the precarious toehold gained by the Marines, in the face of some of the fiercest fighting of the war. All around the approaches to the Solomons, tremendous naval battles swayed back and forth.

Then suddenly, in early October a blow fell which brought the distant clamour of battle tragically close to my adopted family. Two furious naval battles for the approaches to the Solomons, off Cape Esperance and Santa Cruz, to preserve that tenuous lifeline to Guadalcanal, left the Americans without a single aircraft carrier in the Pacific (as one learnt much later), and forced them temporarily to withdraw. To 58 East 80th Street then came the grim news that Bob Fowler's destroyer, the *Duncan*, had gone down in the Cape Esperance battle, a confused night action, on 10/11 October. Bob had been picked out of the water mortally wounded. Posthumously he was awarded the Navy Cross, for sinking a Japanese warship with his torpedoes. Later in the war a destroyer-escort was named after him; still later, evidence suggested that the *Duncan* had almost certainly been sunk by 'friendly fire' from a US cruiser. Pat, at twenty-one, was expecting a baby in a few months. Coming so soon after Jack's narrow escape from death in the RAF, it was a devastating blow for the Cutlers. To me, the proximity of their loss weighed almost more heavily even than had the news, with its still hanging question mark, of Cousin Cecil. The shock to their world of the death of this good-looking, bright and attractive young American, so full of promise, prompted me to wonder – as I began to study the First World War many years later – whether this was just how those families in England had been stricken by the deaths of the Grenfells and the other brilliant stars extinguished early in that war. I cannot recall what I wrote to Pat at the time, but I am sure it was inadequate.

Barely had we got over the shock of Bob's death than there came the stunning news of Montgomery's thousand-gun barrage at El Alamein. For ten cliff-hanging days the maps on the Millbrook board stayed put. Would it be yet another desert fiasco? Then they began moving forward as never before. An ecstatic letter from my normally pessimistic father described how all the church bells at home had pealed out – for the first time since it had been the established warning of a German invasion. The movie news showed USAAF Mitchell and Liberator bombers in action over the British Eighth Army for the first time, and equally telling was the news that the breakthrough had been achieved with the help of 300 brand-new Sherman tanks diverted from the US Army. A sign of the times. As Churchill wrote in his memoirs, up to Alamein the Allies had not won a battle; afterwards they would not lose one. For the first time in the war, the Germans – even though led by the legendary Rommel – had been trounced by a British and British-commanded army. Every magazine, every movie-house was full of that cocky little sparrow of a general, with his sharp nose and funny hat with two badges, who had at last brought us a victory. At Millbrook, eight of us walked especially tall as stock in the home company soared again.

Then, so hot on the heels of Alamein that one could hardly regain one's breath, came the news of Operation Torch, the Anglo-American landings at the other end of North Africa – occurring, by an amazing piece of coincidence, at the same time as the release of that all-time Bergman–Bogart classic *Casablanca*.

On the board, Union Jacks and Stars-and-Stripes stood side by side for the first time in the war; there were even a few French tricolours – though the Community Service Executive Council found some difficulty instructing the confused Map Boy which way they should be pointing. Within days of Torch, the giant Red Army trap at Stalingrad was sprung, encircling General von Paulus and his whole Sixth Army of some 100,000 men. It did not take much youthful imagination to recognize that we were witnessing one of history's decisive battles. All this had happened within the month of October/November. The Map Boy could hardly keep pace. Suddenly the whole tide of the war had turned. Would there still be any need for a gangly seventeen-year-old in the RAF?

As one of the 'deals' imposed on the Boss by the remarkable and exacting William F. Buckley Sr, because of gasoline rationing Bill was now permitted to keep a Mexican moped at school, to transport himself home every weekend to Sharon, Conn. One day in our first term of cohabitation, he invited me to accompany him. Off we sputtered, over hill and dale, the fifteen-odd miles to Sharon. Arriving at Great Elm, a sumptuous white mansion almost overshadowed by the elm that lent its name, I could hardly believe my eyes – or ears. If immersion in the Cutler family had been a culture shock for a British only-child, it was nothing to that first taste of the Buckleys. On the first page of *Northanger Abbey*, Jane Austen remarks with her usual sharp irony that 'a family of ten children will always be called a fine family, where there are heads and arms and legs enough for the number'. With their forty assorted limbs, the Buckley children would certainly have qualified: six girls and four boys, so well planned that, with intervals of a year or eighteen months, boy alternated with girl, almost all the way down. Bill came bang in the middle and was discreetly the apple of his father's eye (after whom he had been named). One's first impression was of a vast gaggle of smiling, brilliant children, all chattering – in several languages – at once, playing the piano, but, above all, laughing with each other.

Everything centred around a spacious, glassed-in patio, filled with plants and creepers, wicker furniture – and children. It all seemed somewhat out of place in New England (as somebody once remarked, 'It was like taking Concorde from New York to Cuernavaca'). Off it, from an upper-level gallery supported by cast-iron columns festooned with creepers, led all the children's bedrooms. In this great big happy family, no Buckley could be out of sight of another for very long; and, manifestly, they liked it that way. Nor, in the Mexican icons and religious statuary that adorned the house, was the Catholic Church ever far away.

Perhaps recalling the panic which had seized me when staying with that other grand lady of Park Avenue, *Ant* Marcia Tucker, I had apprehensions about meeting the matriarch of this imposing clan. They were unnecessary. Hard to find at first in the throng because she was so tiny, Aloise Buckley greeted me (as indeed she did every other spotty and shy friend of all her ten children) as if I were the one person she had been waiting all her life to meet. Just over five feet tall, she had the delicate ankles of a racehorse and five-inch heels on doll-sized, delicately turned shoes. She had never completely lost that accent of the south from her native New Orleans, but the inseparable 'y'-all' shibboleth seemed to be directed to you, and only you. That first lunch, when she seated me on her right at a vast table along which rippled effortless conversation, she appeared to know all about me and to want to know more. I was not the alien, anti-America Firster, but the most honoured guest. Immediately I knew what was meant by southern hospitality, and, for the rest of her life, like countless others I remained in thrall to this tiny lady who radiated so much sunshine and sweetness and such boundless affection. She was unshakeably, unquestioningly devout. Having children, she thought, was a huge 'compliment from God. God forgive me my pride in my children.' She had a lot to be proud of. All were brilliant in their own ways, happy and fiercely devoted to each other. If the neighbours did not always like the Buckleys, it was not necessarily out of anti-Catholic prejudices, or because of their politics or their conspicuous wealth, but possibly because they were so self-assured, so self-reliant, within the spacious, gracious empire of Great Elm – and so damnably, egregiously talented.

To my regret, I never came so close to Will Buckley, Bill's father – although he shared many of my own father's characteristics. Both self-made men, Wm F. Buckley Sr was also well over forty when Bill was born, of a certain eccentricity and a retiring nature (which was perhaps why I never really got to know him before his early death in the 1950s). Like my father, he was given to sending his children (and Mr Pulling) fierce letters about their handwriting (ironically, they both produced probably the two most illegible authors on either side of the Atlantic). Like my father in India, early in life he had amassed a considerable fortune from oil in Venezuela. But that was about where the similarities ended. Rumour had it that WFB Sr had even been offered the presidency of Mexico, but – in those turbulent times of Pancho Villa – he had backed the wrong revolution and had had to leave in a hurry, barely escaping with his skin. It was the Mexican influence that explained the unAmerican atmosphere of Great Elm, and the fact that many of the children (like Bill) had grown up speaking Spanish as their first language.

Politically, WFB Sr was of course the deepest shade of blue – which he passed on to all his children. His rimless, Woodrow Wilson-like pince-nez and his quiet shyness, on top of his somewhat awesome local reputation, lent him (quite unfairly) an air of rather forbidding aloofness. As Bill wrote in an obituary note in 1958, he worshipped 'three earthly things: learning, beauty, and his family'. About his views on education, renowned in the neighbourhood and daunting even to Edward Pulling, there was (as Aloise Jr, the eldest sister, recalled), 'nothing complicated'. His children were to be brought up 'with the quite simple objective that they become absolutely perfect'. To this end, they were 'at one time or another given professional instruction in: apologetics, art, ballroom dancing, banjo, bird-watching, building boats in bottles, calligraphy, canoeing, carpentry, cooking, driving trotting horses, French . . . [and so on down through the alphabet to] tennis, typing and woodcarving'. As a result, in addition to the ten gifted children, Great Elm constantly bulged with every manner of tutor. It was, of course, Will's quest for perfection that brought Will Buckley and Edward Pulling together, and, consequently, Bill and myself into cohabitation at Millbrook. But unmistakably, for all Will Buckley's potent influence, it was Aloise's delicate frame that ran the show.

After that first introduction to this extraordinary and exciting household, I returned to school feeling I had found, almost joined, a new family, made a dozen new friends. And so it was. As the year at Millbrook progressed, so our mutual affinity blossomed. Bill was a hugely stimulating room-mate, never boring, always (like his mother, and something rare among teenagers) deeply courteous. I respected his devoutness, but never once over the ensuing half-century did he try to convert me, though whenever I showed some feeble sign of becoming a slightly less bad Christian, I would inevitably receive a congratulatory note. With the demolition of America First, Pearl Harbor had of course removed the major ideological barrier, yet we still argued vigorously over the good intentions of international communism, as exemplified by the Soviet Union. We would give each other corrective books to read. Otherwise we simply agreed to differ – and have done so ever since. On the Soviet Union, as history was to prove, Bill was right, I in my idolatry was wrong.

I gradually came to admire his extraordinary speed of thought and his capacity for swift footwork. The example acted as a constant pacemaker, shaking me out of my instinctive lethargy (would I ever have followed the course of life I did, but for that pacemaker always in the distant background? Sometimes I wonder). As one of those rare people claiming never to have known more than a moment of despondency, let alone self-doubt, in his life, he was a marvellous anti-depressant, cajoling me out of Black Dogs. I even ended by tolerating what had irritated me so much initially, that infuriating certainty of being right about everything. (In later years it ranged from ski runs to sailboats to computers to peanut-butter.) I envied the clear-eyed ability he demonstrated in almost everything he did, whether it was debating, running the school bank or playing the piano in Al Hunter's orchestra. I responded instinctively to his irrepressible (and often irresponsible) sense of humour, and the mischievous smile that preceded some devastating sally. I find myself quoted by one of his (critical) biographers as saying, 'The outstanding thing about Bill, as I remember him at age sixteen or seventeen, was an unashamed ability to show affection and to *care* about his friends.' As a lapidary epitaph, I would not wish to alter a word. Certainly it was the nearest to an *affectionate* friendship that I had yet known.

As Millbrook closed its doors for the Christmas vacations, I headed once again for 58 East 80th Street – this time not with high spirits. In the window was one of those gold stars that were already beginning to proliferate across America, indicating the loss of a loved one. It reflected the tone of life, so changed, inside. Painful it was to see Pat, the glamorous and carefree deb of just two years before, gaunt and desperately thin, clad in the black that she would wear to the end of the war, and now expecting Bob's posthumous son. Pete was already away in the navy as an enlisted man. Jack was recovering from his injuries in some RAF hospital, trying – now that America had entered the war – to transfer to the USAAF. Judy, seeming to grieve almost as bitterly as Pat over Bob's death, had lost (at least temporarily) much of her old spark and had taken on board a new seriousness; she was away most of the time on war work in Washington. I still have on my shelves a book (*'Paddy' Finucane*, a memoir of an RAF Spitfire hero, wing commander at twenty-one, shot down in the Channel on his twenty-first birthday the previous July), bearing an inscription by Judy, a present from her to mark that sombre Christmas. But Rossy Cutler would permit no excess of mourning. Still indomitable, outwardly as exuberant as ever, she was a tower of strength. Refusing to show her grief or be downhearted, a little fatalistic, she was a kind of American Mrs Miniver at this time. Still teasing, still playing bridge mightily, glued to the radio commentators, she was only full of talk about Alamein and Monty pursuing Rommel round the Gulf of Sirte and towards Tripoli for the first time: 'He must be quite something, that little man. How wonderful for the British, at last!' I respected her with renewed affection that Christmas.

Left, consequently, more frequently to my own devices in New York, I took to exploring its more sophisticated aspects of life with chums from Millbrook. Making a Cuba libra or rum-'n'-Coke drag out all night, I went to my first nightclub on 52nd Street to hear the live jazz. Feeling immensely depraved, several of us ascended the joyless long stairs of a Taxi Dance Hall (the famous Roselands, I expect), the walls plastered with posters of exaggeratedly mammiferous ladies, in the vogue of the 1940s. Inside it was, disappointingly, all decorum and synthetic pleasure. 'Ten cents a dance', in the words of the immortal Cole Porter. We ogled, but didn't quite dare purchase a ticket. Impassive custodians prowled the floor to see that there was no cheek to cheek, and at the end of each session, when the music stopped, the 'hostesses' were whisked away behind a wooden barrier, segregating them from their customers. No mileage there.

Much more fun were our excursions to Harlem, not yet a no-go area, taking the A-train – the Express Subway up to 125th Street that had given the 'Duke' his famous theme song. There we would hunt out the legendary bands and performers like Cab Calloway and Count Basie, the great Fats Waller and wonderful Ethel Walters, and watch the seemingly boneless jiving of the blacks (which was, incidentally, then *the* bad word) in the amazing baggy zoot suits of the time, 'the Shaped Drape, with the Stuffed Cuff, and the Reet Pleat'. The atmosphere, even then, was not always friendly, but it was never menacing, and an evening's entertainment came incredibly cheap. (Alas, within the year, sparked off by gross anti-black discrimination in the armed forces, Harlem and Detroit erupted into the worst race riots known in the US until Los Angeles 1992. That was the end of those wonderful musical nights in Harlem.) Like most of my contemporaries, I had become addicted to the jazz, blues and boogie of the time – classic, vintage years that they were. I could never quite make up my mind which 'sent' me most: the smooth, sophisticated 'licorice stick' of the incomparable Artie Shaw and his Gramercy Five; the trendy self-confident melodies of Glenn Miller and the excited, simple anticipation of 'Chattanooga Choo-Choo'; that trumpet of Harry James which would surely have shaken the walls of Jericho; the exotic, off-key harmonies of Duke Ellington (even today I can never hear 'In My Solitude' – 'you haunt me with memories of days gone by' – without a frisson), or the long-drawn-out woes of 'Blues in the Night' ('My Momma done tole me . . .'). I think the laurels went to Artie and the Duke. It was a heroic age to be alive and listening in. Somehow when you switched on 'A String of Pearls', with its supreme professional competence that trumpeted forth like an irresistible march of American optimism, you felt for a moment that all was going to be all right in the world.

Our judgement was not always infallible. There was, for instance, a spring day at Millbrook when something curious happened to the Pullings. After a rare jaunt down to New York, they – even the austere Boss – came back dancing on air. They explained that they had been to see a new musical, called *Oklahoma!* None of us, of course, had ever heard of it (it was the first of the great Rodgers and Hammerstein musicals). Nor were we hugely impressed when they sat down at the piano and sang us duets from the score. Could anything be sillier than cowboys warbling about a 'Surrey with a Fringe on Top'? We listened politely, but with boredom and amazement, and deduced that senility must be setting in.

More often, however, on our restricted pocket money, in vacations we would stick to the movie-houses off Broadway. Sometimes we would spend the whole day there, shuffling from one to the other; sometimes we were able to economize by creeping into a free seat as the crowds returned after the intermission. At seventy-five cents, however, they were nevertheless fantastic value: a double-biller movie, interleaved with a mighty blast of brass as the curtains rose, and there, on the stage, in person, would be one of the great orchestras, quite possibly the Duke himself, or that young newcomer just making his way up the ladder with his swoon-croon, Frank Sinatra. How they did it, at the price, defies imagination, when one thinks, in today's terms, of £50 tickets for the Rolling Stones alone. And what about the movies, Mrs Lincoln? There was *For Whom the Bell Tolls*, with the ethereal Ingrid Bergman and Gary Cooper, gripping and tear-jerking despite the little models all made in California; *The Constant Nymph*, with Joan Fontaine; *Thousands Cheer*, introducing a sexy new discovery, Lena Horne (no relation, alas!); *This Is the Army*, a recruiting extravaganza by Irving Berlin, with the glum-looking little maestro himself, looking singularly unmartial. There were the war movies, by the hundred: that British classic, *49th Parallel* (with every imaginable star, including Leslie Howard whom my mother had launched in the twenties), and *Five Graves to Cairo* (with Erich von Stroheim as Rommel), rapidly being outnumbered, as American war-heroes took over, by *Guadalcanal Diary* and *Destination Tokyo* – all of which had us jumping in our seats as Jap baddies finally got their come-uppance. There was Betty Grable of the legs, a new diminutive blonde bombshell of the hair, Veronica Lake, and a new B-movie actor of honest but puzzled looks called Ronald Reagan. I avoided the sentimental, escapist movies like *Lassie Come Home* and *My Friend Flicka*, but rushed to see – several times over – Fred Astaire in *You Were Never Lovelier*, with his new leading lady, the ravishing Rita Hayworth, legs that went on forever, every American schoolboy's pin-up, not so great a dancer as Ginger, but infinitely more erotic, and dancing to magical tunes.

My eyes a-swivel from all those double-billers, I took off – for the last time – to Aiken, South Carolina, for the rest of the vacation. I found Julia Breese as kind and welcoming as ever, but she seemed sadder, quieter and perhaps a little older. The death of her niece's husband had manifestly affected her very deeply, no doubt causing her to relive all her own pain from the previous war. She tacked gently around my own intentions, after graduation from Millbrook. I would still be so young; might not my father wish me to go on to college? I understood the point she was making. Doubtless my 'poor father' had been getting at her. I appreciated her tact. We had some very happy days together, perhaps the happiest of all those three years, and I realized just how fond I was of this sweet lady who had been my foster-mother all that time, what a bulwark she had been in the background, and just how much she had had to put up with. I felt terrible guilt about the silly episode at East Chop. There were glorious gallops down the sand rivers of Aiken. I thought I had fallen in love with a sexy girl called Smoky with a devastating South Carolina accent, until a certain episode in the woods indicated, to my wide-eyed discountenance, that she preferred a fellow rider – a rich girl with cropped hair. Life in all its facets was slowly beginning to reveal itself.

Waiting for me at Aiken was a letter from Bill, the first of many hundreds. He gave me all the news of the wedding of his eldest sister, Aloise Jr, the first to leave this tightly integrated family. It had left him feeling deeply 'in the dumps'. He urged me to come over to Camden, site of the second Buckley home some ninety miles from Aiken. I went. Also staying there was another class-mate, Jerry Franks, from New Jersey (who later joined the US marines). He and Bill were conspiring to launch Millbrook's first yearbook, eventually called *The Tamarack*. One of the few pre-Civil War plantation houses missed by General Sherman on his scorched-earth march to the sea, Kamschatka (a curious name for a house about as unRussian as you could imagine) was even more enchanting than Great Elm. Nestling among the live oaks, with its giant magnolia tree, a terraced brick path leading up to the house past a rippling fountain, in superb symmetry, it at once opened the imagination to Scarlett O'Hara sweeping down its great double staircase – with poor, mad Empress Carlota of Mexico's magnificent chandelier hanging above. There was some teasing about how, at sleepy Camden (which, until recently, still bore signs on its side-streets that read 'NO HORSES ON THE SIDEWALK', and 'MOTORISTS WILL SHOW EVERY COURTESY TO HORSEMEN'), George III's disastrous General Cornwallis had won his last battle before going on to final defeat at Yorktown. Reid Buckley, Bill's young brother, once bemoaned the fact that 'In the north, we were the southern Catholics and the new rich; in the south, we were Yankees.

Our experience was always that we had to hold together our-selves.' As the years went by, it always seemed to me that the family were rather divided in their natural orientations. Reid himself was the only one to end up living in South Carolina; Jimmy was very much the northern Senator; Bill had a bit of both cultures, but was essentially Yankee; while Aloise Jr totally belonged in that leisurely, gracious setting of live oaks and Spanish moss.

Once again, the Buckley hospitality was unstinting. It rounded off the picture of my new friend to see him in the other half of his natural habitat, and I returned to Millbrook for the final furlong happy, fulfilled and full of vigour symbiotically acquired. There were letters from my father, decisions that had to be made. After our conversations in Aiken, Julia Breese had written to me: '(as I really should write your father something definite), if you do want to go back to England and he does not want you to, let me know *exactly* what *you* want to do . . .'. She went on to suggest my going on to college for 'some military training' when I was eighteen, but it was plain to me that she would have been disappointed if I had not gone back to fight. My mind had long been made up anyway, and clearly she had interceded with my father, for Letter No. 19 of 24 February 1943 (which enclosed the usual – to me, totally uninteresting – *Times* clipping about the new term at Stowe: 'Head of School' and so on) revealed him acquiescing with the view that college was 'washed out for the time being', and that he was no longer averse to my joining the RAF (though expressing the pious hope that my eyesight might keep me 'on a ground job').

There followed some helpful information, the tenor of which suggested that military realities might possibly be just slightly remote from the Oriental Club:

> you enrol as a private to start with and thereafter if you are found suitable, you qualify for a commission. Privates, I under-stand, get all their uniform and other clothes, board and lodging free from the Government, and pocket money at so much a day, which enables them to more or less keep themselves.

He ended with one of his favourite expressions: 'This is all to the good.' I often wondered, later, what rank-and-file would have said to this rating of their hard-earned pay as 'pocket-money'! He closed his letter with the report that there was 'no definite news about Cecil yet', and expressed his customary obsession about my weight and height, which he claimed he now shared with Mrs Breese. Another course of dreaded egg-noggs?

Three weeks later Letter No. 20 enclosed copies of a sheaf of letters to the Permanent Under-Secretary for Air, to an imposing assortment of air marshals and to leading Canadian businessmen. Each contained a memorandum on the family's military distinctions (apart from Cecil, not a great deal), mentioning of course JAH's First World War appointment as Controller of Munitions in Bombay ('a stiff job, I can tell you!'), and the following note on me:

> QUALIFICATIONS: A well-grown lad [weight and height, however, not supplied] with a special knowledge of French and Wireless which latter he has taken a definite interest in and studied for some years. I rather feel that these two subjects should be found useful if he joined the RAF.

I groaned. The covering epistle contained the sensible caveat:

> Remember, however, that the letters from the Air Marshal and Sir Arthur Street [the Permanent Under-Secretary] should be used in a discreet and modest way, for if the Authorities on your side felt by reason of your connections you were trying to get some advantage over other boys it might prove detrimental to your interests. . . . Remember we are all living nowadays in a *very* democratic age!

I groaned again, but that Spitfire did seem to come a fraction closer. On instructions, aged seventeen, I wrote for advice to Air Vice-Marshal L. D. Kean at the UK Air Liaison Mission in Ottawa – 'My dear Marshall [sic]'.

The following month there came a sad note of the death, from a heart-attack, of Aunt Ethel, aged sixty-five. My father deemed that that was a pretty good age to go. I grieved momentarily, and felt how hard it was for her daughter Eve, coming on top of all the anguish over Cecil – and was a little shocked that the impact on me was substantially less than the news of Bob Fowler's death. Aunt Ethel and my *real* family had become very distant. The previous year, my mother's grand-hostess aunt Maggie Greville had died, aged seventy-five, and had been buried next to the dogs' cemetery at Polesden Lacey. Had I known, I think I should have felt no more than curiosity. My father's next letter (all of them, thankfully, still typewritten by his secretary, and formal), on 14 May, was much more cheerful, commenting on the news that Monty and the new American star, General Dwight D. Eisenhower, had, between them, finally swept the Germans out of North Africa, with the surrender of some quarter of a million men. In marked contrast to his habitual pessimism, he added, 'We are all well and cheery at present and endeavouring to take care of ourselves.' He urged me to do some more farming over the summer, for 'the extra pocket money it brings'.

For Millbrook, 1943 had opened on an unhappy note, with the sad news of the death of the much loved Hank Austin, my first English teacher, killed on active duty in a trainer aircraft crash. Everybody mourned him, though it was two years since he had left the school. 'I never knew a better example of Christian manliness,' declared the Boss. A scholarship was set up in his name. The February temperature hit the all-time low of minus 24 degrees Fahrenheit. With oil short, pipes cracked and we froze; even ice-hockey was suspended.

But, otherwise, the last few months at Millbrook were a constant upswing. Those little flags on the map board went surging forward as the Allies moved from success to success. New heroes appeared weekly on the covers of *Time*: Generals Dwight D. Eisenhower and George Patton, US Admirals Halsey and King, Russia's General Zhukov, Monty and the RAF's 'Bomber' Harris. In January, Monty had captured Tripoli, depriving a battered Mussolini of the last remnant of Italy's once grandiose African empire. Tunisia, after the dread German 88s had inflicted a nasty reverse on over-confident and inexperienced Americans at the Kasserine Pass (thereby giving some fuel to Uncle Newt's undiplomatic crack about 'green bananas'), had been cleared, the number of German prisoners taken exceeding that of Stalingrad. By July the Allies would be back in Europe, for the first time since Dunkirk, invading Sicily and bringing with it the fall of Mussolini, the first Axis leader to bite the dust. The Russian steamroller was surging westwards, now quite irresistibly. From England came news of the heroic attempt of Guy Gibson (for which he was awarded the VC) and his Dambusters to flood the Ruhr, while the nightly sorties of Bomber Command were bringing the revenge bombing of Germany to new peaks (which, in our bloodthirstiness, we all lauded uncritically). With victory coming ever closer, there were reports of more restiveness among British parents, wanting an accelerated return of their Bundles, and more indications that some American foster-parents were only too willing to comply. Some did return in 1943, though none from Millbrook.

In the classroom, I began to discover how much I could enjoy work. The one class taken by the Boss was sixth-form English, and all at once he became transformed in our minds from the rather remote, icy disciplinarian who ran a remarkably tight ship, into an outstanding pedagogue. His demand for the highest standards in written work was uncompromising. Many times in the years to come he would confess that Bill Buckley had been the first of his pupils ever to get an A for an essay – which, he reckoned, entitled him for the rest of his life to criticize each successive Buckley bestseller, picking out unerringly the odd solecism or misplaced comma.

Whether it be *Hamlet* or *Ethan Frome*, that stunning novelette of passion in frozen New England by his favourite, Edith Wharton (long before she was relocated on the map by the feminists, he had recognized her tremendous stature), he brought home to us precisely what each writer was trying to say, and how. At regular, appropriate intervals, and with profound effect, he would recite in that sonorous mid-Atlantic voice W. A. Henley's 'Invictus':

Out of the night that covers me,
Black as the pit from pole to pole,
I thank whatever gods may be
For my unconquerable soul.

In the fell clutch of circumstance,
I have not winced nor cried aloud:
Under the bludgeonings of chance
My head is bloody, but unbowed. . . .

He was a great debunker of the phoney, the meretricious and the pompous, but at the same time he impressed upon us that we were, in the words used by Churchill on another occasion, 'walking with destiny'. He made us ('You gentlemen', as he would address us, with new courtesy – the rest of the school being just 'boys') read books like Herbert Agar's contemporary clarion call, *A Time for Greatness*, opening our eyes to the challenge of the times. We were, as I remarked before, tremendous idealists – and 1943 was a great year to be coming of age in.

To me the true star, however, was Henry Callard. Though he had always seemed at his happiest bouncing about on the school tractor – which was how I had really got to know and appreciate him, that summer working on the school farm – it was his sixth-form class on American history that made its particular impact. One of the best of teachers, his infectious enthusiasm inspired a fascination leading to remarkable results in exams – and remaining undiminished long years after one had left school. In itself a subject super-abundant in colour and interest, American history as taught by Henry Callard came to life in a way that was quite magical, that I would never have believed possible. Under his particular genius, history ceased to be a dreary recitation of dates and kings. To him it was the interaction of personalities and events that mattered. As he manipulated them, those bearded heroes of the Civil War – the majestic Robert E. Lee (his hero) and the brutal, drunken but victorious Ulysses S. Grant – leapt out of the pages into the classroom. Effortlessly he led us from First Bull Run to Shiloh and Appomattox. It needed but a small effort of the imagination to hear the roar of the cannon and the whistle of the grapeshot, to see a flicker of dark blue from that trench a few yards ahead, and the answering shot over the hill from the tired, outnumbered grey-clad figures, inspired only by the knowledge that they were fighting for their homes and had the best generals. From there it was easy to become absorbed in the complex chain of cause and effect. Out of little William Jennings Bryan and his 'Cross of Gold', Henry Callard managed to create a romantic figure; while even the most tedious details of labour wranglings, or farm bills, or the dullest President, became invested in flesh and blood. I have often wondered over the intervening years what was the particular genius of this modest, unassuming man; perhaps it was that, in his total lack of arrogance, he was able to look at history through the eyes of seventeen-year-old boys, as opposed to pressing adult appreciations upon us. Whatever it was – and allowing for the rosy distortions of time – it was Henry Callard more than any other influence in my life that enticed my footsteps towards history. When I wrote *The Price of Glory* (some thirty years ago), and my eyes were first opened to the devastating impact of personality upon that terrible World War I Battle of Verdun, I kept thinking of his teaching of two decades earlier. I owe him an incalculable debt.

'War Subjects Dominate Boys' Spring Speeches,' declared the *Silo* once again, unsurprisingly enough. With some embarrassment, I am reminded that, in the Forum, I had declared how, in the post-war world:

> 'Russia should be granted her territorial demands. She is entitled to Latvia, Lithuania, Estonia, Bessarabia and part of Finland. . . . We must not antagonize Russia,' Horne said, 'by forcing her to accept territorial boundaries dictated by the United Nations. . . .'

Uncle Joe's mouthpiece! I can hear Bill Buckley growling in the sidelines. Once again, I lost the debate . . . Nevertheless, encouraged by Henry Callard I put myself up for the *Time* Current Affairs Prize – and won it. The award was a book entitled *Generals and Geographers*, by Hans W. Weigert, a study in the arcane philosophy of geopolitics, which had achieved fame through the shadowy Professor Karl Haushofer, Hitler's evil genius behind the invasion of Russia, and through his British opposite number, Sir Halford Mackinder. The subject, with its arguments about whether, in the world of the future, sea-power would prevail over land-power ('he who controls the Heartland, controls the World', predicted Sir Halford), fascinated me, and, again coaxed on by Henry Callard, I chose it for my final Spring Speech. I predicted that, after the defeat of Germany and Japan, the USA and my Soviet pin-up would rule the world. With hindsight, it was perhaps not very original thinking, yet it was not bad judgement for early 1943, and on re-reading it half a century later I felt almost smug. Typed by William F. Buckley Jr (at $1 a thousand) it won the school Blaine Prize, was bound and printed for the Millbrook Library – my first tome. Recognition this time was a book called *We Cannot Escape History*. In my case, the title certainly proved portentous – to the perennial delight of dear Henry.

We were, however, as the summer term drew on, all thirteen of us, beginning to feel restive, ready to leave school and get on with life – or what, in 1943, passed for life. Our restiveness against all that we had come to dislike as the governessy attributes of Millbrook manifested itself, finally, in a superbly orchestrated coup, worthy of a commando raid – if not of responsible prefects of Millbrook School – to dismount and hide the school bell, the thief of so many years of early-morning sleep. With no means of transmitting the Boss's iron will, for a whole day we the villains permitted the school to stumble around disorientated. 'Maximum Efficiency', that potent slogan to which we had all marched for three years, slumped. With icy aplomb a messenger from the Boss requested at breakfast that 'the gentlemen who borrowed the bell' should return it 'at their earliest convenience'. Clearly that Olympian order must have been slightly shaken, aware that his chosen elite were, in all probability, the culprits. I was accorded the great honour of 'writing up' the infantile, but heady episode in the *Silo* – our last. It was never alluded to. The Boss it was, of course, who won.

At last there came the great day of graduation, the end of school life – curiously, as I have noted, always labelled Commencement. All available Cutlers came up to celebrate. It was, inevitably, a moment intermixed with jubilation and sadness. I wondered if I would ever again see Henry Callard, to whom I had so much to be grateful for. My father wrote:

> I should naturally have been very pleased to have been present
> . . . but this is impossible because I could not get priority for a
> passage either by air or sea. Also at the present time, I don't
> fancy a trip overseas at all nor do I want to incur the expense it
> would involve. However, I will send you a congratulatory wire.

As I realized later, in no way could he have come over; but poor old boy, I thought, why did he have to spoil it all with that penultimate sentence? I felt sad. Another letter followed, containing the usual cutting about the long-forgotten Stowe: 'there will be no Speech Day this year'. There came confirmation (copy attached) that he had, at long last, received the information he had so ardently and persistently pursued: 'Height, 6 foot ¾ inch. Weight, 138½ lb. Flat feet, yeast – four pills three times a day, Ovaltine at night . . . in the infirmary a total of 15 days during the year.'

Some time during these last months at Millbrook there ensued a curious and disturbing exchange with Frederick, my father's old secretary at Ropley, now retired to Smuggler's Cottage, Burnham-on-Sea, about his beloved Theo Henning, my old German tutor – hero from pre-war days. Theo had evidently become a riproaring Nazi and had written some savage letters to British friends, from the US, before Pearl Harbor, and had then fallen silent. Most of the correspondence is missing, and my memory sketchy about exactly how it all developed in the first place. Just possibly it may have been sparked by a letter I had evidently written the previous year to my father reporting the arrest and execution of the fifth columnists landed by U-boat (he had responded: 'Yes, it must have been somewhat exciting catching that saboteur . . .'). At any rate, in May 1943 Frederick wrote:

> I have lost Theo Henning's address, and as he changed it so often, cannot remember it. I last heard 1940, about the time of Dunkirk. Tho' I never mentioned politics when writing, he expressed his opinion that England and America would be taught to mind their own business. That was the last I heard of him.

That I obviously *had* heard more, and was not just driven on by the spy-mania which had gripped the US in the early days of the war (and especially following the rounding up of the saboteurs the previous summer), is suggested by the evidence that I had somehow tracked him down to an address in Newark, New Jersey – and by some diary notes, which resurfaced during the writing of this book:

> *15.6.'43* . . . the Henning business. I am extremely suspicious and I believe my suspicions are well founded. I haven't done anything yet, because I fail to know where to start. All the proof I have amounts to very little; yet every day I fear time is slipping away, and he may be doing something terrible against us. It is a real problem for me to decide whether to investigate myself, or let the FBI deal with it. I would hate to seem like a suspicious old woman.

With it preying on my mind, I contacted Jack Hemphill, who lived near by in Princeton (and who had a certain affinity for intrigue), and we two seventeen-year-old gumshoes set off to the then rather seedy city of Newark. Terrified of our own shadows, we tracked down Theo's last address, but there was no trace – only suspicious looks. Having drawn a blank, on the way back to New York we stopped in at the FBI headquarters at the bottom end of the island. When asked by a tough-looking agent at the entrance what our business was, we panicked and simply came away, sheepishly, with a pamphlet (I have it still!) entitled *The Story of the Federal Bureau of Investigation*. That was about the end of the Hunt for Henning. A few days later, feeling something of a funk and a failure, I took a deep breath and related the whole story to an attentive and most sympathetic John Cutler (Rossy, I feared, would have treated it as a huge joke and told the whole Colony Club). His last words were 'I'll handle it.' In the distractions of that last summer, and preparing to join the RAF, I thought no more of it. But, whenever I fly through Newark Airport these days, I think of Theo, the super German tutor, and wonder whatever happened to him: was he a Nazi agent? Was he arrested, imprisoned – perhaps even shot? Or had I inflicted terrible damage upon an entirely innocent man? Hero of my childhood, what had I done to you?

The Henning business was swiftly overlaid in a fluster of activity that last summer – beginning with the happy/sad farewell parties in the company of my twelve class-mates, all of us heading off to the armed forces, or college, in our different directions. Naturally, I endeavoured to see the maximum of Bill, either at Sharon or on return visits to 80th Street – though Rossy Cutler, sturdy Wasp that she was, didn't entirely approve (at least, then) of 'those Buckleys, religious fanatics, I hear', whose Isolationist stance and support for brother Ham Fish had not been forgotten. 'Can't understand why you like those pro-Germans Ally!' she would tease me. Those summer days of 1943 at Sharon were quite magical, the duets at the piano strumming out Fats Waller (the great man turned out to be first cousin to Ben, the Buckleys' butler), the singing and laughing, the twilight barbecues, the plethora of pretty girls brought down from Smith College by the elder Buckley sisters, the midnight games (all amazingly innocent) around the swimming pool. Momentarily I decided I had fallen in love with Bill's immediately elder (why this constant passion for older women?) and very pretty sister, Jane.

Then Bill took off with the family to Mexico, to do a course in Spanish literature before joining up with the US Army at the end of the summer. I succumbed to a terrible Black Dog as one by one the rest of my class-mates drifted off in their different directions that last summer. A series of letters followed over the course of the summer: Bill described with excitement his first bullfight, and with equal excitement he wrote of going to see the 'tremendous new volcano, Paricutín'. It had been discovered in February 'by a small farmer who noticed smoke coming out of the ground'. Now 'what used to be a flat field is a furious volcano 2000 feet high. It is a most gorgeous sight.' (It now stands 9101 feet high.) I couldn't help wondering how that poor, surprised Mexican *peón* must have felt. Bill added, 'I miss you very much, and do wish we weren't five thousand miles apart.'

There were farewell visits to Garrison, which I parted from with greatest nostalgia, and various days in New York before the summer heat set in. As often as possible, I saw Judy when she came on leave from her new work in Washington. Recovering from the shock of Bob's death, much of the old spirit had returned. My infatuation, now sublimated, was no longer searing but soaring. I found myself at last accepted as an equal, as a grown-up. I walked on air. We had several happy evenings together, either down at Nick's in Greenwich Village, where what remained of the college crowd congregated, or at Café Society Uptown, which had the wittiest chat-show in New York at the time.

I went up to St Andrews, New Brunswick, to spend the rest of the summer with Julia Breese in Billy and Nora's house, building them a garden shed, which, to the amazement of all, survived many decades. Faced by those gallant, snooty airmen on leave I felt a new sense of self-esteem – in only a matter of weeks, I said to myself, I shall be one of you! Meanwhile, day in, day out, I gnawed away at the raw carrots (trusting the old wives' tale that they were good for eyesight) until I began to turn orange, and exercised my eyes hourly on the oculist's chart at the bottom of my bed. '20/60' was what was required. On a good day, I was just about on the line, otherwise round about 20/70. Daily I agonized over it. But at least I hadn't been plagued with the asthma for months. I began to feel a yearning, the first in a long time, to get back to England, to my father, to poor deserted Terry. It was a yearning mingled with a great deal of apprehension. What would I find?

Then, suddenly, it was all over – that last summer in America as a Bundle.

Postscript. The sinking of *USS Duncan* [see p. 271]: Following first publication of this book, I received this poignant confirmation about the end of Bob Fowler's destroyer from his posthumous son, Rob, now a fifty-year-old film producer in Hollywood. Bob's younger brother, Harry, was serving with the British Army in Egypt early in 1943. While in Alexandria he ran into a college classmate of Bob's, aboard an American cruiser, the *Boise*. He told him that Bob had just been killed in the Solomons, to hear: 'We just got in from the Solomons. What ship was he on?' When Harry replied 'the *Duncan*' the naval officer went white. 'Oh my God, I sank the *Duncan* . . .' . . .

In the confusion of battle, many died in the Second World War from 'friendly fire', but few by the unwitting action of a classmate. For years Harry kept the story to himself.

CHAPTER ELEVEN

The RAF: Canada to England

It was time to take the plunge. The summer of 1943 had passed its glorious zenith, and I had reached the magical age of seventeen and a half, at which I could volunteer for the RAF. Rejecting one more plea from my father and Uncle Newt to join 'a nice quiet Guards regiment', all I had to do was to report to the British Consulate in New York, and they would dispatch me to Canada, to the Empire Training Scheme. It was as simple as that – except that, before the Consulate accepted me, I would have to pass a medical. Despite those weeks of carrots and eye exercises, I was as nervous as a cat. The consular official who received me was friendly and paternal, then passed me on to a doctor. He had the rich aroma about him of having had rather too good a lunch, and seemed slightly unsteady on his feet. Halfway through the examination, he left the room. I could hardly believe my luck. Before he returned I had rushed up to the eye-chart and memorized that elusive third line from the bottom. When the doctor returned, surprise, surprise, I qualified with a spanking '20/50, correctable to 20/20'. I lied convincingly about the asthma (and, the strange thing was, for the next four arduous years in the services, I never once suffered from it). The Consul gave me the long-coveted golden pass to the RAF, a one-way train ticket to Moncton, New Brunswick – and a *whole* one-dollar note 'for expenses'. I was over the moon.

There was a great send-off – congratulations, but no sadness – from 58 East 80th, Anna fussing, 'Sure you got enough warm clothes, Ally?' Rossy Cutler, still grieving a son-in-law and worried stiff about Jack – just recovered from his injuries in the

RAF, but now flying again with the USAAF – gave me a big hug and said, 'Come back soon, Ally, you're a member of the family.' Judy grabbed the morning off from her war work to take me in a taxi to Penn Station. As it drew up, quite unexpectedly, she kissed me full on the lips. I can't recall what she said – I suppose the 1940s equivalent of 'Take care'. My head swam as I climbed on to the train. Was the world ever a more exciting place?

As the train rattled its long way up through the sparkling white clapboard houses of New England, I began to feel a little sad, and lost. Would I ever see those wonderful Americans again? At the border, Calais, Maine (pronounced Callus – I remembered it so well from past summer jaunts up to St Andrews, New Brunswick), I switched trains to St Stephen on the New Brunswick side. There a jaded Canadian customs officer asked me my business. 'To join the air force,' I said proudly. 'Oh,' he replied crushingly, and somewhat disbelievingly. At Moncton, the tiny provincial Maritimes city that acted as the transit station for the whole vast Empire Training Scheme, there was an amazing scene as I stood on the railway tracks waiting for 'transport'. In the late summer sunshine, also on the tracks, waiting, were dozens of those legendary gods, flight lieutenants, squadron leaders and wing commanders, mostly in their early twenties, plastered with DFCs and DSOs, wearing that enviable gold VR pin of the Volunteer Reserve on their lapels and chattering away like magpies – all on their way for a quiet spell as instructors, away from ops. I gazed at them in awe and envy.

Up at No. 1 Manning Depot, as I think it was called, a vast agglomeration of hangars and barracks on a bleak hilltop on the fringe of Moncton, through which funnelled all of the 50,000 odd trainees and instructors of the grandiose (and war-winning) Empire Training Scheme, I found myself in a remarkably diffuse group. All of us were volunteers who had joined up on that side of the Atlantic, for which reason we were honoured with the romantic title, the Western Hemisphere Squadron. It sounded only a whit less noble than the glorious American outfit of the First World War – the Escadrille Lafayette. But we were indeed a comically bizarre group. Most of us were conspicuously young;

several were Bundles like myself. Faithful to our tryst to join up together there was Ian Cole from Ottawa, my friend from two summers with the Breeses in St Andrews. There was George, a clergyman's son, quiet but a natural leader among us. Among the elders, there was also Bob, a self-proclaimed American rapist on the run from New York State, and Geoff, an ageing Californian lothario, all of twenty-six, distinguished by a receding hairline and Clarke Gable moustache, with enviable tales of nocturnal picnics on Laguna Beach. There was a self-contained group of seven or eight Newfoundlanders. The sons of isolated, poverty-gripped cod-fishermen and lumberjacks in what was still Britain's oldest Crown Colony, they were sad people. To them the air force offered huge prospects of social and economic betterment – but they were backward and appallingly ill-educated, and I doubt whether any of them got their wings. Unkindly, we nicknamed them the Neanderthalers.

The largest group, and the most impressive, however, was comprised of about a dozen blacks from the Caribbean – mostly Jamaican. Looking back on them, shivering in the Canadian winter, I remain filled with respect and admiration. They had absolutely no reason to volunteer for the Mother Country, so many miles away, which hardly treated them well on their home islands in those days and was to show them little welcome in post-war Britain. I often wonder how they made out, how many became aircrew – or survived the war – and what happened to them afterwards. One I do know about, Arthur Wint, MBE, FRCS, became famous: Olympic Gold Medallist of the 400 metres in both 1948 and 1952, and Jamaican High Commissioner in London, 1974–8. (He died in 1992.) Older than most of us, he was the elder of one of two pairs of Jamaican brothers who had volunteered for aircrew simultaneously. Highly educated, with that wonderfully melodious West Indian lilt, his athlete's six foot five inch frame filled me with encouragement: for if they could cram Wint A. into a Spitfire canopy – he indeed became a fighter pilot – then there would certainly be room for my meagre six foot two and a half. (Little did we know, alas, that the magical Spitfire – or even the equally glamorous Mosquito light-bomber – was not what we, any of us, were going to be trained for, at that point in the war.) We all got on famously well together, teasing the West Indians about their dialects and impenetrable slang, and bowing before the natural authority of the well-named Caesar, a huge Jamaican black appointed squad-leader. It often makes me sad, when I think today of the surliness of present-day race relations both in Britain and back in Jamaica.

Our immediate lord was a fair-haired, kindly and easygoing RAF corporal with the amazing name of Windebanks; the name of the sergeant and of our officer I do not remember – perhaps they were just too grand. Everybody, whether striped or ringed, in air-force blue seemed to belong to the Great and the Good in those days, so Corporal Windebanks regularly rebuked me for saluting and sirring him. And there were the *real* grandees – among them the legendary Wing Commander Guy Gibson VC, on well deserved R-and-R after the Ruhr dams raid, before his tragic death the following year. There were also the non-com VCs, whom one was expected instantly to recognize across the tarmac and salute – as was their right. 'Watch out for Flight Sergeant Hannah, he's a real terror,' I remember Corporal Windebanks cautioning me.

Oh, the pride when we got fitted up in our uniforms. As we somehow came under the Canadian RCAF, they were a brighter shade of blue than the poor RAF's, and almost as well cut as an RAF officer's. Cole, son of a regular British colonel, struck an admirably martial figure (which was undoubtedly to help him at the next stage of our careers), whereas I seemed to be all knees and elbows in my uniform, certainly too elongated for that coveted Spitfire. But with what swank we marched around the parade ground, to the strains of the stirring, evocative 'Royal Air Force March', which I had listened to so often on the Breeses' wind-up gramophone over those St Andrews summers! We were, after all, aircrew elite (or so we thought), all of us. There was lots of drill, in those early days: to teach you how to fly in formation, they told us. There was Morse code (hellish!), lots of high-speed mental arithmetic (which, thanks to Millbrook's excellent Mr Tuttle, I found somewhat easier than the unhappy

Neanderthalers). But, oh Lord, the aircraft recognition! Frank Trevor's exquisitely made little models in no way prepared one for the quick flash on the screen, a twenty-fifth of a second, of a black silhouette. How could one possibly tell a Spit from a 109? In my most private thoughts, it re-aroused those anxious twinges about my eyesight.

Nevertheless, it was – in the popular jargon – all absolutely wizard. A letter came through from Bill Buckley, in Mexico, waiting the call to the US Army, and seemingly taken by surprise that I was already in the RAF. Possibly stifling the innate instincts of a southerner, he admitted that our West Indian friends did 'sound like pretty exceptional people'. We all felt we were on the way somewhere, somewhere important. Even the food seemed fabulous (compared with rations in Britain, it undoubtedly was – as we subsequently discovered). And, being under the affluent Canadians, we – as Temporary Leading Aircraftmen – also received vast pay packets, some 50 per cent higher than the RAF.

The only trouble was that there was absolutely nothing to spend it on. If we hadn't been so exhausted by the training, so inspired by higher aspirations and the sheer novelty of it all, spare time and weekends in dear little Moncton would have hung round our necks like the uranium that was being mined further east. It was a real dump. Canadians used to say of wartime Toronto that, of a Sunday, its Presbyterian elders 'locked up the sidewalks and threw away the keys'. But it was Babylon, Sodom and Gomorrah compared to Moncton, the dreariest little provincial town that ever crept out of the backwoods Canadian Maritimes. There was certainly nothing resembling an English pub, and there was both liquor-rationing and semi-Prohibition. You were, as I recall, allowed a case of beer a month. But – here was the good news – without a prescription you could also buy from the drugstore 100 per cent pure grain alcohol. The Neanderthalers (their abiding claim to fame) brought with them a secret recipe for converting it into passable bathtub gin, with a dash of juniper essence and a tablespoonful of glycerine – to help it slide down, and stay there. A winter in Moncton, and we would all have become serious ginnos.

Much of our free time would be spent in the soda fountain halfway down the hill, run by a devastating redhead (whom Laguna Geoff swiftly made off with), who served us, future heroes, glutinous, non-alcoholic sundaes and ice-cream sodas (not as good as those of Martha's Vineyard), while we endlessly played the poignant 'Paper Doll' on the juke box. But oh for even a Paper Doll in those long early winter nights in dreary old Moncton. There was something about the ardours of air-force life that made one long to investigate the soft, unknown mysteries of a real-live woman.

Every Saturday night (or was it Wednesday and Saturday?) there was a dance in the main hangar at Moncton. As the sergeants deftly swooped to the sugary strains of 'Charmaine', inside this thirty-foot-high chasm with the Canadian winter beginning to whistle through its numerous chinks, on an unyielding concrete floor and unfortified by strong drinks, the odds could hardly have been more heavily tilted against romance. As it was, diluted by the thousands of itinerant airmen, this quiet little backwater town, with its population of 5000, found the hospitality of its women-folk stretched to breaking-point. To acquire a dancing partner for more than one old-fashioned waltz was no mean achievement. To the envy of all of us, the ancient and experienced Californian, Geoff, amazed our immature ears with unexpurgated accounts of his success with the redhead queen of the soda-fountain, thereby establishing himself as uncrowned king of the squadron. For the rest of us, longing to lose our virginity and prove ourselves, it was just uphill all the way – as indeed it was on the long walks back to camp after escorting a girl home.

One Saturday night in the hangar, I managed to pick up a girl called Irma. She was sitting down at a table, displaying an imposing superstructure. But when she stood up to dance, she came to somewhere between my navel and my chest. *Neverthe-less . . .* ! Irma, daughter of (I think) Polish émigrés, and herself an older woman of nineteen, became my regular Saturday-evening date. The only other Irma I had ever come across was Bulldog Drummond's villainess, which must have added to the allure. The lonely and unconsoled Newfoundlanders regarded me with new respect – and I felt pretty pleased with myself. As each hangar soirée closed down around ten o'clock, I would walk Irma back on her short legs, down to her lodgings in Moncton, then walk back up again.

It was worth it. For the first time in my life, I kissed a woman on the lips, lasciviously. Each Saturday my fumbling hands became a little bolder. Irma seemed full of wordly knowledge – and acquiescence. She made free with her magnificent bosom (well, most of it – as I recall; did I know then that bosoms had nipples? I'm not sure). I could hardly bear it. Time was beginning to run on; we were imminently due to leave Initial Training Wing to head westwards – and then the battlefield. It was now or never! On the dwarf-like Irma's sofa I made a determined lunge for paradise. She grasped my inquisitive wrist firmly, rising to her full five feet, and, in that Canadian burr I had come to find so beguiling, declared, 'Oh, *no!* I'm keeping it for an officer!'

As I crept up the long, icy haul to the camp, defeat was total – no thought that there might be other fishes in the sea, one day. It was failure. In my blazing Spitfire, I would meet my young hero's death still a virgin.

The next day, passing out at Moncton, we set off westwards, heading for places with exotic names like Moose Jaw and Medicine Hat. Then, in the midst of euphoria, came the second blow. Somewhere along the line, before serious flying training began, another medical caught up with me. In my innocence, I had fondly hoped that what I had passed at the British Consulate in New York had been the end of it. But now all of us were ushered into an impressively professional RCAF check-up, with an eye-chart menacingly illuminated at the end of a long tunnel. By screwing up my eyes I could just about make out that decisive third line, bottom. The Canadian medical officer, a real swine, said, 'OK, now try it *with* your glasses.' I did, realized that I hadn't got it quite right before, and memorized that line. 'Now try again, *without.*' I did, rattling off the line I had memorized. But the fiend, unobserved, had somehow pressed a button and switched up a whole new chart. He looked at me, icy and unsparing: 'You're barely 20/70 – at best. I can't think how you got this far' – as if I had somehow been wasting the valuable time of the combined RCAF and RAF. I stammered, 'Well, surely if you wear corrected goggles, anyway, what's the difference between 20/60 and 20/70?' He muttered something about 'risking the lives of the rest of crew', stamped my form 'UNFIT FOR AIRCREW', appended, as a final insult, the handwritten observation 'No evidence of malingering', and called, 'Next!' I have the vile form to this day. Cole went in and came out white. He, too, had been ploughed – because of astigmatism. And there were several others of us . . .

It was, quite simply, the worst day of my life. I still remember every detail of it. Somehow the defeats of *aetat* seventeen seem inconsolably graver than those of later life. I think of other bad moments, like getting sacked from my job as a foreign correspondent, many years later, with a new wife, a first child on the way, no house and not much cash – but it was never as bad as November 1943, perhaps because, at that age, there seem to be no alternatives. And, indeed, what alternative *could* there be? What was the point of soldiering on in ground-crew, servicing the planes of the Guy Gibsons, denied the opportunity to play any active part in the war? It seemed like the end of the world. I felt rejected, disgraced and – once again – on my own. (And what would Judy say? Would she take back that immortal kiss?) I felt I had let down the Breeses and Cutlers, not to mention Mr Pulling. Shamefacedly, I wrote to my father, to my 'family' in the States and to Bill Buckley, relating what had happened. Eventually there caught up with me a sweetly consoling but fairly predictable letter from Julia Breese, saying it wasn't the end of the world and 'how happy your dear father will be to get you back safe and sound – he never really wanted you to go into the RAF – but we're all still so proud of you.'

Sadly we said goodbye to the Western Hemisphere Squadron, to our friends – Caesar and Wints, Geoff and the Neanderthals, and Corporal Windebanks. A forlorn little group of failures, we set off to Toronto where, for a week or two with absolutely nothing to do, we awaited transshipment back to England. We were lodged, thousands of mixed Canadians and Brits, in double bunks in the vast Bull Pen of what in pre-war days had been the National Agricultural Show grounds, on the shores of grey Lake Ontario. It was one immense concentration camp of men on the move. Regularly our kitbags were rifled, our paltry private possessions disappearing. For the first time we were made to feel, by the RCAF NCOs in charge of us, just how much, by this stage in the war, many Canadians had come to dislike the British, who demanded so much of them, and to resent the Empire Training Scheme that had so overloaded and dislocated their country. I thought that cold, unfriendly Toronto, with its hideous Victorian buildings of bleak purple granite, must be the most unpleasant city in the world (a view which, despite Toronto's amazing post-war transformation into the pride of Canada, subsequent trips have had scant success in modifying). How I began to long for New York City and all I had left behind me on the other side of that unwelcoming frontier! I wondered whether there would be any way I could sneak down for a leave, before being shipped off home.

But no! Abruptly one day, a vast mixed squad of us were entrained for Halifax, Nova Scotia. There in the great basin, where three summers earlier Judy and I, crouching down on a forbidden hilltop, had observed the mighty convoy of British merchantmen assembling, was the ancient leviathan, the *Mauretania*, with its four perpendicular funnels, painted grey and stripped down as a war transport. As with that other transatlantic crossing of July 1940 on the now perished *Britannic*, we set off out of harbour with a comforting escort of destroyers and Coastal Command Sunderlands; and, once again, they disappeared after the first day. Yet how different were the circumstances, in every other way. Instead of the few hundred passengers it would have carried on the pre-war Atlantic routes, it was now ferrying an entire Canadian division, some 15,000 strong, plus a large contingent of those RAF officer–gods returning to the fray, plus a miscellaneous riff-raff incorporating ourselves. We, the lowliest, were quartereed in hammocks strung on what would have been the Third Class after-deck, rudely screened off from the winter weather. There we slept, ate (revoltingly greasy pork mostly) and

302

had our being. It was incredibly cold and uncomfortable, and soon stank of sick. Just beyond us, right on the stern, was the comforting bulk of a six-inch gun – comforting, that is, until, on inspection after reaching Liverpool, we found it was dated 1895.

Each morning, after breakfast, we were turned out on deck for exercise. But, such was the crush, it was never possible to complete more than one circuit before lunch. What would have happened had a torpedo struck that horrendously overcharged liner defies the imagination. I doubt if one single lifeboat, most of which looked well and truly painted into their davits, could have been got off. It was zigzagging and streaking full-speed – just like the *Britannic* – for home when a New Zealand subaltern, larking in the rigging, fell overboard just off Halifax. But there was no way the *Mauretania* was going to stop to pick him up. We stumbled into massive storms, and everybody was appallingly sick. My lasting recollection was of an elderly major groping for his false teeth in an overflowing lavatory. Yet still the pork chops kept coming. Somehow I survived seasickness, principally by the good wheeze of volunteering to help man a Bofors anti-aircraft gun, which at least kept one out in the fresh air. Suddenly, after the best part of a week, the seas abated, and we were in the Mersey. An air raid was in process over Liverpool. We could see the anti-aircraft puffs, but not the German planes (why they didn't turn and have a go at the rich target we presented, I shall never understand).

So this was Britain, still at war, just three years and four months after I had set sail on the *Britannic*. It was good to be back – or was it?

The air raid over, we found ourselves humping our heavy kitbags down into the Liverpool docks tube to head for the next stage in our destiny: RAF West Kirby. As we waited endlessly for a train, I noticed on the platform one of those marvellously elegant pieces of cast-iron workmanship of pre-war England, an automatic chocolate machine. It was the first happily familiar reminder of home. I put in a couple of large round pennies, and tugged the drawer. Nothing happened. Thinking it was jammed, I tugged a little harder, then bent down to find out what was wrong. It turned out to be sealed up, as it doubtless had been since the early days of the war. Suddenly I felt a tap on the shoulder, and there was an RAF military police sergeant looking at me with utmost suspicion. 'Right, name and number. Where've you been all these years?' Clearly he thought he had captured an important spy. It was with difficulty that I explained myself. When I mumbled out the word 'evacuee', he looked at me with undisguised loathing. 'Dodging the war, eh?' he said, and moved on. It was hardly the most auspicious home-coming. Sometimes the image of that sealed-up chocolate machine and the MP comes back to me over the years, each time I encounter in frustration an example of the upraised Nanny hand of British bureaucracy, saying 'No, it can't be done!'

Nor, for that matter, was one to find any warmer welcome at RAF West Kirby, perched on a bleak hill in the Cheshire Wirral, miles from nowhere. I cannot remember what was the point of West Kirby. It had no planes and no obvious function – except perhaps as just one more vessel for retaining the masses of wartime servicemen whom nobody quite knew what to do with. We were unemployed and apparently unemployable. While some unknown bureaucrat decided our fate, they set us to work on the vital war service of fumigating officers' blankets. I can still remember the smell, of rather ancient plum pudding. What a wastage of all that bursting teenage energy! What a loss for the war effort! We were the dregs, the failures combined with the men of no ambition, the motley ground-crew returning on posting from Canada, the cooks, the clerks, the sweepers, the general-trades, the jankers-men, as they derisively called them, whose sole and not unadmirable desire was simply to survive the war.

Our own little group, survivors of the glorious Western Hemisphere Squadron, was reduced to a dispirited handful. There were Cole and myself: a Jamaican called Fielding, the younger of one of the two sets of brothers, physically so feeble and lethargic that one wondered how he had ever passed the aircrew physical in the first place, and quite lost without his big brother; Bob, the rapist (why he was with us I can't quite think, as there seemed to be nothing particular wrong with him – perhaps he was on the run again): and another Jamaican, an immensely bright accountant called Smith, whose eyes had ploughed him too. The weather and boredom of West Kirby rapidly got into poor Smith's soul. He was always grousing, gained the nickname 'Binder' Smith and became resentful and chippy. For the first time racial stresses began to appear. We were glum and thoroughly demoralized: even Bob talked about getting back to America, face the rape charges and try to join the US Army. Gradually our little group fell apart. New friends came along. In the bunk next to me was a wizened little fellow called Plummer, who was indeed a plumber in 'civvy street' and who kindly sold me a French letter. I had never seen one before and carried it around my person at West Kirby for weeks, hopefully. Prospects were even worse than in Moncton. In the biting, dank cold of north Cheshire, we huddled gloomily around an evil-smelling coke stove, which gave out the feeblest heat, in the NAAFI – consuming our weekly ration of one Mars Bar and making desultory passes at two NAAFI girls with lank, greasy hair who promised prospects of future pleasure down in the damp and unheated air-raid shelter. And we *waited*.

I began to think that maybe I didn't really care for this dilapidated, war-weary, small-thinking bleak country that seemed to have so little use or purpose for me, where the answer to everything was no. I began to pine for America, for all those jolly, big-hearted Cutlers, for Judy, for Millbrook, for Bill – now in the midst of officer training with the US Army. I did not feel very English.

Then, suddenly, on to this unpromising scene there burst a remarkable figure. The commanding officer of the dismal holding unit that had us fumigating blankets at West Kirby was one Squadron Leader Brian Nixon. He was unlike any RAF officer I had met before, or since. By 1943, he was approaching sixty – therefore well over the age of retirement. Almost all the blue had faded out of his ancient greatcoat. His ill-fitting false teeth clicked and clattered in the mean Wirral wind as he spoke, or – more often – growled. He walked slightly hunched from having broken almost every bone in his body playing polo in India between the wars. He had nearly died of pneumonia, and there was virtually no tropical disease he had not had. On his chest he wore the half-winged 'O' emblem of an observer – something relatively rare by the latter part of the Second World War – as well as a string of 1914–18 ribbons. From the Indian Army he had fibbed his way into the infant Royal Flying Corps so that he could fight in the Mesopotamian campaign of 1915. There he had flown as an observer, in a primitive, open two-seater. (Among his belongings when he died a few years later was a scribbled note from his one-time pilot: 'GET OUT AND TICKLE THE KARB [sic]' – which had meant just that, crawling out on the wing to fiddle with the engine when it conked out.) He was Irish and, every inch of his battered body, a fighter. Returning from retirement in 1939, he had served (on the ground, in admin, to his frustration) at one of the big Battle of Britain fighter stations. But what misdemeanour, what act of indiscipline, what affront to air-force order or hierarchy had relegated this pugilistic old warhorse to such a dump as No. 1 Wing, RAF West Kirby, can only be guessed at. He was clearly bored out of his mind by the post – not to mention by the unpromising human material that passed through his jurisdiction in an unending stream.*

Shortly after our arrival at No. 1 Wing, he got us new intakes out on to the parade ground and gave us a ferocious harangue about the war, fighting spirit and courage. He more or less told us that we were a lot of cowards, to be standing there as ground-crew. The war was going to continue a long time, casualties in Bomber Command had been rough, and replacements were badly

---

* I came across these details of the old Squadron Leader through one of those extraordinary coincidences that life so often effects. When I was just beginning work on this book, and trying to focus my memory on the West Kirby interlude, I was invited to speak at an Oxford college, St Peter's. Out of the blue there followed a letter from the wife of the Master, Gerald Aylmer: did I by any chance remember her late father, Squadron Leader B. Nixon? She had just been going through his papers, of forty-plus years ago, and come across some letters I had written him, in 1944–5, and had wondered whatever had happened to me. Now she knew! We met, and I am indebted to her for giving me access to this old correspondence and for refreshing my memory of her remarkable father.

needed. For those of us rejects who wanted to 'have another go', there was a newly created slot as flight engineer, and he would move heaven and earth to help us get accepted. For the rest . . . he scowled menacingly. There was much grumbling in the NAAFI afterwards. Cole and I looked at each other. To be a sort of aerial mechanic, running round a great lumbering bomber, with an oilcan in hand, was hardly romantic – and certainly not what we had joined up for. At best we would be like the madly heroic Sergeant Ward VC, crawling out on the wing of his Wellington with the fire extinguisher. And did we even still really want to fight? Why not just settle for trying to get a commission in some cosy technical ground trade like radar or electronics? The temptations were not inconsiderable. But at least 'flight engineer' would be aircrew. We marched into Squadron Leader Nixon's dreary office: Cole, Binder Smith, Fielding and myself – two dispirited British Bundles and two gutsy Jamaicans. The old warrior greeted us with warmth and encouragement, and arranged a fresh aircrew interview – and medical – at nearby Warrington.

For a brief day or two, our spirits picked up. Then he packed us off on leave.

I raced up to London, to see my father – or, more precisely, I was shunted and jolted up to London, as the wartime trains from Liverpool were then taking an erratic seven or eight hours. Other Bundles, returning after three or four years in America, were to admit that they simply did not recognize their parents. I was prepared to see my father changed, to be older; nevertheless, I was shocked. Now sixty-eight, he had visibly aged, and seemed so much smaller. His whole world had got smaller, too, shrunk within itself – and poorer. Ropley was long gone, sold to a family who had promptly let part of it (my nursery wing) burn down; preceded by the others, Terry had been put down – probably a long time before. The reassuring references to the merry terrier in his letters had been intended to save my feelings. My father was living in a tiny two-bedroom house that I remembered as having once belonged to Aunt Ethel, in the posh area of that small triangle of Mayfair off Grosvenor Square where he had always lived. It was a Queen Anne gem, 74 Park Street, but age and the Blitz combined seemed to have strained its joints. The floors sloped so much that a golf ball would roll from one end to another, and its natural pine panelling made it dark and, frankly, depressing. To my surprise, I could find only one book in 74 Park Street, a copy of Arthur Bryant's recent bestseller, *The Years of Endurance*. It appeared to be on loan from the well-read Uncle Newt.

Gone was the vast, under-employed back-up staff of Ropley. Mrs Saville, the wife of his faithful London retainer, mobilized for war work (making cardboard boxes for gas-masks, almost certainly more useful to the war effort than I was) would pop in to leave him a few, fairly inedible, scraps of food from his tiny single-person's ration for his evening meal. Or, more likely, he would potter off to one of his clubs, the International Sportsmen's, just round the corner in Grosvenor House, or, more often, to the Oriental, a half-mile walk there and back in the blackout, where he would hobnob with his old pukka-sahib friends from Indian days. Occasionally his rations would be supplemented by a food parcel from Wales, from a new (and determinedly pursuing) lady-friend.

His nose seemed as rubicund as I remembered, his complexion perhaps even a little more florid, suggesting that the lonely evenings had encouraged him to become an enthusiastic, possibly even heavy drinker. At sixty-eight, though long nominally retired, my father could never quite give up the City life (indeed, how otherwise would he have kept his mind occupied?), and remained chairman of both Seager's Gin and Sorbo Rubber. Both were clearly sinecure posts, but he would trip weekly to Seager's in bomb-battered Deptford, where shortages and rationing had reduced production to a mere trickle, and to Sorbo in Woking, now on vital war-work. Otherwise he kept a modest office down in Lombard Street, where he played around with figures that bore little relation to the war around him. Occasionally, in earlier years, he would put on his air-raid warden's helmet, but, like so many of the elderly in Britain, the war passed him by and flowed around him, making him feel an encumbrance and one more useless mouth. Compared with the vast majority of Britons after four years of war, he was still pretty comfortable, but I was stricken by what I now realized must have been the drabness and empty loneliness of his life all those past years. Never once had he complained in any of his letters to America – and now I suddenly felt a total rat at having deserted him.

What should I call him? Here was an immediate problem. When I had left, in 1940, he was 'Daddy' and had remained so in our letters. But that was the language of a child, and now I was a grown-up airman, Second Class. I tried 'Father', but that sounded awfully formal and slightly ecclesiastic. I never quite resolved it. So, for the short time there remained to us, I tended to resort to that very English vocative of a noncommittal grunt. It illustrated how great a chasm had been opened by those three years apart.

But there was – all at once – a great, implicit and unspoken warmth between us. He affected great pleasure in the simple presents I had brought him from Moncton, including a rather tatty Canadian trapper's beaver-fur hat, complete with earflaps, which he wore proudly to the Oriental Club. I was older; I could appreciate his droll, dry sense of humour and could understand his quaintly old-fashioned formality, which wasn't in any way coldness, but which made it difficult for him to put an arm round me. Yet he was so unmistakably, touchingly proud to have me back, in my gawky AC2's uniform.

Our relationship started again, where it had left off, on board the *Orion*, in that particularly happy summer of 1939. I had grown up, and now could begin to see him as a companion and friend. On my side, I felt immeasurably proud of him too. We talked cheerfully about the past, about Ropley, and Kenyon and Hall and Frederick and Mrs Bufton. He asked warmly about Julia Breese and the Cutlers and my life in America. He hoped it wouldn't be too long before we could pay them back, and they could all come over and visit us. There would be no more Ropley – that was the past. We would have a cottage somewhere in post-war Britain. The essence, now, was what he still called the simple life. He had sold, or given away everything – to stop Hitler burning it or grabbing it. We talked about the future. He wanted me to go to Cambridge, then into the City, become a chartered accountant ('That's where the future will be – but I don't think you've got the maths, poor old boy'), or maybe a diplomat ('Hard exams, but I think your mother would have liked that – all those foreign countries'). And we talked, imperatively, about my more immediate future. He was plainly relieved that I had failed aircrew, but looked unhappy when I told him about the bellicose Squadron Leader Nixon and said I was going to have another go, as flight engineer. There was more talk about 'nice quiet Guards regiments' – just in case the aircrew interview at Warrington failed too.

I was touched by his manifest pride in me, his pleasure in having me back. He introduced me to all his old club-mates, to his new lady-friend, Mrs Rennie O'Mahney, principal of a smart girls' finishing school, the Cygnets, that had been bundled off to Wales. I wasn't immediately impressed. To my eyes, adjusted to transatlantic glamour, she had bad legs, like a grand piano's, and didn't seem particularly appealing. But she was all over me. She would introduce me to her prettiest girls when I was next on leave. Meanwhile parcels of delicious, black-market Welsh food began to make their way to West Kirby.

Proudly, my father took me, through the battered and desperately seedy-looking East End, down to Seager's at Deptford. He showed me the gin, flowing through great copper stills that might have existed from Dickens's day, carefully supervised by Customs and Excise officers to see that wartime rationing was not exceeded, nor the gin watered down. He was amused when I told him of our humble efforts at bootlegging in Moncton. We lunched with elderly gentlemen with Yorkshire accents (all described by my father as 'salts of the earth'), porty noses and melancholic anecdotage of the trenches in the First World War, sitting at Bob Cratchit desks – clearly not very inspired by the priority of their war work either. I sympathized, silently. We went down to Woking, to visit Sorbo Rubber. In a small factory that had once turned out multi-coloured balls and rubber flooring, slow-moving middle-aged ladies with hair in kerchiefs were working, manually, on self-sealing tanks for aircraft. 'My boy's in the RAF,' my father would say, proudly. To my America-tinted vision, accustomed to *Time/Life* accounts of Kaiser's mammoth new war plants, it all seemed a bit of a cottage industry.

There was a gathering of the clans, to meet the returned prodigal son. Wicked Uncle Henry was still away in Cape Town, where he had spent much of the war on some mysterious work, lodged comfortably in a suite in the Mount Nelson Hotel. But Cousin Eve, my godmother and only first cousin, came up from Exmouth, where she had been evacuated to a rented house after Cecil had been reported missing, when her home in Camberley had been requisitioned. Her mother, Aunt Ethel, and her father had also died during the war, and she was struggling on war rations and a widow's pension to raise two small children. It distressed me to see her, even more than had the first sight of my father. She had become prematurely white-haired and old. Any reminder of Cecil, whose death had just been confirmed after one agonizing year of uncertainty, caused her to fight back the tears. I sensed unspoken criticism of my having 'run out' on the war; her questioning about my life in America was perfunctory. We went to a light-hearted musical, *The Lisbon Story*, about lovers finding haven in neutral Portugal. I hadn't seen Piccadilly Circus since 1940. It was awash (more or less literally) with raucous, drunk and puking – and, by British standards, vastly overpaid – US servicemen. It wasn't hard to detect what Cousin Eve was thinking: had Cecil been killed for all this? Where had the Americans been when he was dying at Gazala?

A year later, when I was in a poor state lying in a miserable military hospital at Pirbright, she was marvellous to me, bicycling over from Camberley (where she had returned) a hilly seven miles, bringing pots of delicious home-made gooseberry jam, concocted from her own precious sugar ration, and nearly getting crushed by one of our own Guards Armoured Division Churchills crossing a bridge on the way. She was good to me in the rough times that lay ahead, yet we never managed to establish any true rapport, never had much in common, my one and only cousin and I. Perhaps it was those three years in America that had got in between us.

Rather more vocal in his criticism of America was Uncle Newt. The war seemed to have changed him, and Aunt Ursie, perhaps least of all the family. Ursie had had white hair ever since I could remember, since her thirties. Newt, with his drooping moutaches, looked, rather as he always had done, like a retired colonel from the Crimean War. He rejoiced in the latest anti-American jokes. Had I heard about the GI being quizzed by an English lady about his row of medals? 'Well, that one's for being in the European war theatre, that's for having left Mom, that's for learning how to shoot a rifle.' 'And what's that one?' 'Oh – that's for saving an Englishwoman from rape.' 'How did you do that?' 'I changed my mind!' I sizzled inwardly, thought of Pat Cutler's husband Bob, killed in his destroyer off Guadalcanal. Newt and Ursie were, both of them, crashing snobs. Their talk was all about 'Bert' and 'Bobo' and 'Maureen' – people I didn't know, and didn't really want to – 'attractive gels', who seemed neither attractive nor 'gels' to me, and about who had said what to whom at the Carlton Club.

It was clear that Uncle Newt harboured misgivings about Mrs O'Mahney and her intentions. He had quite a fixation about women's legs and how they betrayed their characters. Women with very thin legs were, almost certainly, all nymphomaniacs. Then there were 'good, sensible *Cart*holic legs' – they were all right. But, he confided to me, after my father's death, Mrs O'Mahney had 'a *disastrous* undercarriage . . . must belong to the criminal classes. . . . We all had a lucky escape . . . your poor father!' In years to come, I grew to be rather fond of Uncle Newt and his dry sense of humour. But, at the end of 1943, I couldn't quite see the point of either him or Aunt Ursie. He was, predictably, scathing about the RAF, socially speaking. He respected my desire to fly and fight – but, if I couldn't, there was no future. I might find myself ending in the RAF Regiment, guarding airfields, with a lot of former convicts – and what sort of friends for later life would you make there! I remonstrated that the war was not, surely, about making the right sort of friends.

Talking about the latest proposition of the excellent Squadron Leader, Uncle Newt remarked that, if it failed, I should try to switch to one of those 'nice quiet Guards regiments'. Of course, he knew most of the Regimental lieutenant-colonels by their first name, or at least knew someone who did. And Ursie had a cousin, a lord, who was a serving major in the Coldstream, nicknamed Gilly and recently back from North Africa (where, so Uncle Newt reminded me, his battalion had had – twice – to recapture Tunisia's bloody Longstop Hill, after those hopeless, over-sexed and ill-trained Yanks had lost it). And there was 'Bunnic', now Regimental Adjutant of the same Coldstream Guards ('he knew your mother'). If I wanted, they would press some magic buttons. I thanked them, not very enthusiastically.

Meanwhile the war rumbled on, and great deeds were in the offing. By the end of 1943, the Russians, sweeping relentlessly forward after Stalingrad, had recaptured Kiev. The mighty *Scharnhorst* had been sunk by Admiral Fraser, off the North Cape. In the Pacific, US Marines had retaken most of the Solomons. In the Mediterranean, all North Africa had been cleared, and Monty – plodding up the long leg of Italy – had captured Naples and was battering at Monte Cassino. Some of those 'quiet' Guards regiments were there, suffering dreadful casualties. Night after night RAF Lancasters were pounding Berlin, while American B-17s devastated Germany by day – both with heavy losses. The Luftwaffe retaliated, with desultory but nasty raids on London. Fascinated by the novelty, Cole and I watched the fireworks from a balcony, until a large piece of ack-ack shrapnel whizzed down between us. Would it, the war, suddenly, all be over, before either of us could play any part in it? All Britain was bulging with freshly arrived US and Canadian troops. Round Park Street, US troops from Ike's headquarters in Grosvenor Square seethed like a beehive, drawing up the plans for D-Day. It, the big battle, could not be far off. And what were we doing, AC2s Cole and Horne? Fumigating officers' blankets at West Kirby! Oh, the wastage!

It was glum, returning to West Kirby, to that bleak camp, back to the blankets, after that first leave, at home, with my father. But, for a brief time, there was a glimmer of light at the end of the tunnel: the good Squadron Leader had got things moving. The four of us survivors from the Western Hemisphere Squadron were shipped off for our flight-engineer tests at RAF Warrington, a vast establishment in Lancashire. But it was the same sad story all over again. Once more the eye test showed me up to be just over the top. I lost my temper. To be a mere flying mechanic, why in hell did one need 20/60 (or 6/18, as I think the RAF in Britain rated it)? Oh, but you might drop your glasses or have them broken in action. Well, what about those newly invented contact lenses? Oh, they might fall out, and then where would the rest of the crew be? I stormed out, threatened with insubordination charges, my heart back in my boots again. The other three had equally failed. I remember the long uphill walk, in the dark, from the station back to West Kirby, utterly demoralized. Jamaican Fielding, forlorn and half-frozen, dragging behind, got lost. We tried to cheer ourselves up with shrieks of 'Fieeeeelding!' All the poor fellow could think of now was getting back to his sunny island, as quickly as possible.

Squadron Leader Nixon was all sympathy. He sent for us – Cole and myself – to enquire how we now saw the future. As ex-public schoolboys, we could probably get commissions in a technical branch. If that was what we wanted, he could set the wheels in motion. Or we could join the RAF Regiment – he didn't sound enthusiastic. But if we really did want to 'have a crack at the Hun', why didn't we both get out of the RAF altogether and transfer to a combat unit in the army? His moustache bristled, his teeth clattered. He'd never heard of anyone doing it before, but why not try? Perhaps family 'pull' at the other end might help. Cole's father, after all, was a full colonel of the regular army.

Uncle Newt, I suddenly realized, was right: there was no future in my beloved RAF. It simply didn't want me. Looking back on it now, from the very different standpoint of the cynical and worldy-wise 1990s, I am faintly amazed at how utterly devastated I was, at my mad ardour, at how truly brainwashed we had all been – and I am more than a little relieved that things turned out as they did. By the end of 1943, the RAF no longer wanted those glamorous Spit pilots, the Douglas Baders and the Cocky Dundases of three years previously. So the Lancasters, plodding gamely over Germany, night after night, losing an average of one in ten planes each time, would have been our fate. If I hadn't been shot down, there was a fair chance that I would have survived the war with a hideous guilt complex at what we had done to those German cities and their inhabitants. As a foreign correspondent in Germany in the 1950s, I made friends with a former bomber pilot, DFC, with whom I did numerous stories in the Ruhr. He never travelled without his old logbook, to remind him of which pulverized city, and on what dates, he had visited it. It never ceased to haunt him; years later he committed suicide. There were many, like him, who – become aware of just how little the indiscriminate mayhem did to hasten the end of the war – ended as psychological wrecks.

With the enthusiastic connivance of Brian Nixon, invisible wires began to be pulled. Uncle Newt had been as good as his word. One day Ian Cole and I found ourselves summoned to Birdcage Walk, London, for an interview with the Regimental Lieutenant-Colonel of the Coldstream Guards, M. F. Trew. Looking as smart as we possibly could, nevertheless, in our somewhat bluer-than-blue Canadian RAF uniforms, among all those rigidly drilled, shorn-back-and-sides, stamping and saluting Guardsmen, with their peaked caps crammed down over their eyes, we must have cut the most incongruous of figures. From the stares one might have concluded that no aircraftman Second Class had ever dared cross the threshold of Wellington Barracks. The Regimental Sergeant-Major, with fierce handlebar moustaches, who ushered us – one by one – into the godlike presence, looked faintly disbelieving. Colonel Trew was warm and encouraging, but – well – godlike. (One was soon to learn that the highest deity in the military hierarchy was not the Chief of the Imperial General Staff, nor the General Officer Commanding, but the regimental lieutenant-colonels of each regiment of the Brigade of Guards.) Like the Squadron Leader, he didn't think such a transfer had ever been done before, but he couldn't see any reason why it should not – was that what we really wanted? Nervously, only just eighteen (and wondering apprehensively what lay behind all the shouting and stamping, and the terrible tales we had heard of the parade ground and assault courses at Caterham), we assured him – yes. With the technical and mechanical training we had already received in the air force, he thought we would be well suited for the new and as yet unblooded (it was waiting for D-Day) Guards Armoured Division. But, after the RAF, it might be hard going. Ho, ho!

We left proudly, though perhaps a little white around the gills, with two slips of paper. Mine said, 'I am prepared to accept this man for potential officer training.' Cole's mysteriously contained the enhancement 'without hesitation'. We were now ranked equally as 'Guardsmen Recruits', and had two new regimental numbers which, as in the RAF, were consecutive, because we had both signed on the same minute of the same day. But what had he done, I asked, that I hadn't? 'Oh,' said Ian, 'I told him I liked cricket.' In the post there followed a little placard, emblazoned with the State Colours of the Coldstream, to inform 'relatives and friends' that I was 'serving King and Country as a soldier (No. 2666732) in the Coldstream Guards'.

The Birdcage Walk procedure gave me the opportunity to sneak a couple of days' leave more with my father. He was, of course, delighted by this development, though, I suspect, out of the same protective motives that had caused him to dispatch me to America, he would have been still happier had I been found a non-combatant role digging potatoes. We got on famously. As a great treat he took me round to the neighbouring Connaught Grill, where we saw the American Ambassador, Gilbert Winant, dining quietly in a corner. My father introduced me: 'My boy, just back from America – did him so much good.' I watched with greedy expectation as the head waiter, among that august panelling, unchanged half a century later, with great ceremony whipped off the silver covers to reveal 'reconstituted' American dried egg, scrambled on toast. Nevertheless, the conversation flowed. I felt a warm happiness. Amid all the bitter disappointment of the RAF, I had found a new friend. Whatever grim passages may lie ahead, one day the war would be over, and, with him, one could look forward to that bright new world we had all thought so much about, back at Millbrook.

Cole and I returned to West Kirby, in a state of limbo, to await summons to the dread Guards Depot at Caterham, and to thank Brian Nixon for all he had done for us. Blanket fumigating no longer seemed quite so intolerable. Then, one grey December day, there came an urgent summons for me to report to the CO. I blanched. Had I committed some misdemeanour? Had Colonel Trew and the Coldstream Guards changed their mind? Squadron Leader Nixon looked upset, but treated me with more than usual friendliness. He asked me to sit down and offered me a cigarette. A signal had just come through from the Air Ministry: my father had been knocked down by a car in the blackout and was in St George's Hospital. Nixon didn't know the details, but from his face he clearly thought it sounded bad. He was kindness itself, arranging for me to hurry back to London on immediate compassionate leave.

Uncle Newt took me to the hospital and filled me in. It seemed that my father had been dining at the Oriental Club, celebrating my return home with some cronies. He was walking home from Hanover Square in the funereal dark of the blackout. Very probably he had had one too many. They took him to St George's. His skull was fractured and he had not recovered consciousness. The surgeon, a natty figure wearing a pink bow-tie, could not offer any encouraging prognosis – at his age . . . I went and sat with him, in the accident ward, every day. His poor old head was swathed in bandages, and he seemed peacefully asleep. I longed for him to open his eyes, smile and say something. Once he seemed about to wake up, murmuring something unintelligible about 'ginger wine'. But he never came to, never spoke again. With great determination, though getting visibly frailer, he lingered on unconscious for another six weeks. He died on 4 February 1944, in St George's. He never lived to see me in that 'nice quiet Guard regiment'.

And so I lost him, my new friend, before I had really ever found him. Not until half a century later did I discover that my mother had worked at St George's during the First World War, little knowing that her future husband would die there during a second great war.

That Christmas of 1943, in austere, battered London, was the cruellest and loneliest I ever remember. Uncle Newt and Aunt Ursie did their best, but we were not close and I felt no warmth. The redoubtable Mrs Rennie O'Mahney disappeared overnight, and so did the black-market food parcels from Wales. From distant America the letters were wonderfully consoling. Poor Julia Breese was stricken. She wanted to come over at once, but the exigencies of war forbade it. (Years later I often speculated, had my father survived the war, might they have got together, and married? Rossy Cutler had thought it possible. It was always a lovely fantasy, and would certainly have been a fairy-tale ending.) They, those wonderful Cutlers and Breeses, Judy and Pat – and Bill – were so far away, and I missed them terribly. But the slender thread never broke: they were always there, and I knew they always would be. Regularly the incredibly generous CARE parcels arrived, the wonderful rich home-made plum cakes, to be scoffed by greedy Guards recruits at Caterham and Pirbright. Even blessed Mrs Saville came to be embraced with their bounty. Then they began to come over themselves – first Dicky Aldrich, Aunt Rossy's son-in-law, dressed in the uniform of a US Navy lootenant, then Pat, still mourning but working in some highly secret capacity with the Office of Strategic Services, forerunner of the CIA. And there were the old Millbrookians, like Captain Bob Patterson, two classes ahead of me, navigating a group of Flying Fortresses on the regular route to Berlin, and thoughtfully inveigling me into the South Audley Street PX to buy a sumptuous pair of US pyjamas.

While waiting in London on extended compassionate leave, waiting for my father to die, I started trying to write about those three years in America. I got as far as Ludgrove only, in the preface. Then the war intervened, providing a blessed distraction in the shape of a summons to Caterham for Gdsmn No. 2666732.

It was hard, harder than either Gdsmn Cole or myself had ever anticipated. To begin with, arriving (with no other option) in those bluer-than-blue Canadian uniforms before trading them in for khaki battledress and stiff peaked cap, we inevitably became marked men, and the remaining traces of transatlantic accents hardly helped. 'So you've come back to 'elp us win the war, 'ave you now – like Errol Flynn, eh?' was the standard NCO's friendly quip that followed the invariable parade-ground reproaches of 'dirty rifle', 'idle' (that is, just plain bloody exhausted) or 'dirty flesh' (a couple of whiskers that missed the matutinal razor). Though, at eighteen, we felt older hands than the others – some, hot out of school, were entitled to 'extra milk', much to the derision of the Trained Soldier (a rank unique to the Brigade of Guards, an old sweat who was the barrack-room nanny) – in fact our RAF training availed us naught, or worse than. It was a bit like hoping that a passing acquaintance with Ancient Greek at prep school might help you with Demotic Greek.

But the two of us, Cole and I, were experienced enough – just – to recognize that the shouting, the terrible 'chasing' (changing, in three minutes flat, from one 'kit' to another, six times a day), the endless pointless 'bulling up', painting the hearths white and the coke black for Company Commander's inspection, were all part of survival of the fittest, breaking down the unfit, and – though sometimes hard to perceive – basically good-humoured. We lost a few. One passed out in the medical officer's introductory lecture, accompanied by gory 'visual aids' on VD; another following the statutary harangue by the second-in-command, a much decorated veteran of two wars, on the theme that Guardsmen die but don't surrender; a third went berserk when having painful anti-tetanus injections, chased around the room by the sergeant orderly, syringe in hand ('Only nancy-boys are frightened of pricks,' observed Gas-Sergeant Crabb, the company wit). An encouraging note arrived from Bill: 'you would annoy me more than I can say if you should go and get yourself killed one of these days.'

Somehow, like a foster-father over those tough weeks, the

old Squadron Leader, to whom I owed so much, kept in almost paternal touch (finally, by special invitation, he was to attend my passing-out parade at Sandhurst) and I wrote back:

> Dear Sir [the formality, always, of those days, as if he were the bank manager!] . . . The rigidness of Guards' discipline came as a bit of a shock to us at first, but once we got used to it, it didn't bother us much. The PT is very tough and consists of assault courses, but it makes you feel marvellously fit. Altogether we like the life very much indeed, although it is much harder and stricter than the RAF.

It must have been the understatement of all time.

CHAPTER TWELVE

... And Ever Afterwards

The war ended, in 1945, victory was achieved, the victory we had all awaited for so long, which some of us had almost despaired – though never the Rossy Cutlers. Surprisingly, the Coldstream Guards ended up appearing to want me more than I wanted them. It was not until summer 1947 that I was demobilized, as a twenty-one-year-old captain working with MI5 in the turbulent Middle East. The moment I returned to Attlee's austerity paradise, those wonderful CARE parcels started up again. Was there any limit to American generosity? Tenuous as the lines of communication had been, in correspondence we had – like the famous wartime boast of the Windmill Theatre – 'never closed down'. The news arrived that Judy was getting married that autumn. It made me decide, whatever the cost, to go over for it. In October, still on demob leave and playing hooky from my first term at Cambridge, I hitched a lift in an unconverted hospital plane. In an America still deliriously intoxicated by the ending of the war, all the clan had gathered for the wedding. It was the happiest of family reunions, and I was made to feel I had never left. Shedding the formality of adolescence, those two inimitable foster-parents at once became 'Aunt Julia' and 'Aunt Rossy'. Judy was as beautiful, as funny and as disorganized as ever. Fortunately she still had the faithful, ever fussing Anna, 'Onion-Bunion', to ensure that she got to the church on time. So much water had passed under the bridge, I was long since over my teenage woes of infatuation, and I could only feel delight that Judy had found such a 'great guy' as Jackson Shinkle from St Louis, formerly a USAAF pilot in Burma, and one of the most laid-back men I ever met. (Aunt Rossy's first reaction, predictably, had been one of mock horror: 'Why, how could my Judy ever have met one of *those Germans* from the Midwest?') Anyway, they lived happily ever after, and Jackson – as well as Judy – became my friend for life.

Fortunately, all the immediate family (with the exception of Bob Fowler) had survived the war. Jack, that professional survivor, had had one more remarkable escape. Recovering from his nearly mortal injuries in Rhodesia, he had transferred from the RAF to the USAAF, as an enlisted man aboard a bomber. Shortly afterwards, he was shot down while on a raid against the Rumanian oilfields. With other surviving members of the crew, he bailed out over Sarajevo, landing in the middle of the Germans' crack Prinz Eugen Division. A boy claiming to be a Serb Chetnik helped him escape, only to lead him into an ambush. On its way to prisoner-of-war camp, the transport was waylaid by angry Balkans, who wanted to settle accounts with the American airmen who had been bombing their homes. Rescued, this time by the Germans, Jack then spent the next six months between a series of Hungarian and German POW camps. Finally, in January 1945, in the confusion of the Russian advance through East Prussia, he escaped. After hiding in a barn for ten days, he procured a French slave-labourer's uniform (which, he said, came barely below his knees) and set off across Germany, concealing his ignorance of French by pretending to be shell-shocked. After walking for four months, and covering some 400 miles, his war ended on 2 May 1945, when he met up with the British 11th Armoured Division. 'What a day, I'll never forget it,' he wrote home to his mother. 'I rode right behind them with the Royal Engineers, and together we took Lübeck that night.' Still Jack could not quite shake off the dust of Europe and the war, and after a short rest at home he was back again – this time with UNRRA, trying to sort out the legacy of chaos and misery presented by the hordes of Displaced Persons. Unable to sit at a desk, as of 1947 he had decided to enter the hazardous profession of tree-surgeon.

Pete had left the navy, after a long stint in the Pacific, and – still in love with the sea – had joined the merchant marine as a deckhand. His twin, Pat, had spent the rest of the war in her

highly secret work with the OSS in London, and then Spain.
When, after a long time, she recovered from the death of Bob,
she would eventually marry an engaging, talkative Harvard
history professor, 'Shot' Warner, and produce five more children.
The eldest Cutler, Susan, remained wedded to the beautiful but
unprofitable Aldrich manorial home among the eccentrics of the
Hudson Valley.

At Judy's wedding in 1947, I found Aunt Rossy quite
unchanged. The epicentre of the family, revelling in the excitement, she was as full of mischief as ever. Again and again, she
would retail – a little more embroidered on each occasion – those
anecdotes of my youthful indiscretions ('Don't you remember
when little Ally beat up that Fifth Columnist who booed the King
. . . ?'). An unwary trout, I would always rise; but protests were
of no avail. Her brother, Uncle Ham Fish, the old Isolationist,
though still as ingratiating as ever, I found rather a sad figure.
Finally defeated in the 1944 elections, after twenty-four years in
Congress, he seemed like a stranded whale left by a tide that
would never return (albeit he would live to 102 – marrying, for
the fourth time, at the age of 100!).

I journeyed down to Washington to see Julia Breese – and
Billy and Nora. I had had no idea just how stricken she had been
by my father's death. She was enormously sweet about how
much it had meant to her to have me during those war years, as
if it had been I who had done her the favour. I was a little
amazed. Still she tormented herself over the plight of dogs across
the world, and I sensed a growing, weary disillusion with the
Grand Causes that had meant so much to her during the war.
Later, when she made trips to England there was unvoiced but
unmistakable disappointment. Perhaps it was because my father
was no longer there, at Ropley. But England was no longer the
country she had so loved. In one of her last letters to me she
observed:

> I am sorry that I do not feel that most of my country's people
> mix very well with the Old World peoples – they do not seem
> to have enough patience and tact, and most of us I think lack

that Christian quality of humility. . . . For so many years of war we have tried to mix with foreign peoples and look at the result. Might as well face it. Few foreign peoples like Americans, and I don't think they ever will.

Her letter made me wonder how many thousands of other generous-spirited Americans, in their craving to be loved, had, over the years, felt the same kind of rejection?

As soon as I decently could, following my father's death, I set about trying to repay at least the material debt of my Bundle years. In the period of Attlee austerity and strictest currency controls, it was not easy and – inevitably – took time. In the midst of negotiations I was just a little shaken to receive from that gentle Jeffersonian, Billy Breese, an enquiry about precisely how much the 'compound interest' on the sum (totalling, as I recall, inclusive of the Millbrook fees, somewhere between $5000 and $10,000) would come to. When she, eventually, heard of it, Aunt Julia was mortified. Billy's attitude to money was frequently a source of merriment within the clan (though, to his children, more often of dismay), but to me it was a reminder that within the most generous-hearted Jeffersonian American, there might sometimes be a hard-nosed Hamiltonian financier trying to get out. When I reflected, however, on how much I owed him – not least for impressing upon me that vital art of 'enthusiasm' – what little resentment I might have felt swiftly passed.

A top priority, of course, during that trip was to see Bill again. He had last written on his discharge from the army: 'There is something about an organization as largely impersonal and regimented as the army that forms within me a very natural aversion. I can subject myself to the discipline, discrepancies, inconsistencies for only so long and then I think I will go stark, raving mad.' It was a very personal creed, a dislike of regimentation that would constantly mould his political philosophy. Accompanying his letter, from Mexico he had sent me an exquisite leather folder, with my initials on it. As a repository for all those treasured letters from America, it had travelled with me to the Middle East (and I still have it). Arrived at Yale, Bill was already making a reputation as the stormiest petrel the *Yale Daily News* had ever had as editor. Together we went to the Harvard–Yale Football Game, after which I got appallingly drunk on a disgusting concoction called milk punch. Rashly (possibly showing off, but also with little else to wear) I went in uniform, and came to to discover that most of it had been removed by female trophy-hunters.

From Yale we went over to Millbrook, where Bill's younger brother Reid was now a sixth-former. The warmth of my welcome from the Boss was, alas, somewhat chilled when – while we were all attending chapel – the Pulling spaniels consumed, cardboard boxes and all, dozens of the famous illegal doughnuts which Bill had intended smuggling in for Reid, but which he had incautiously left concealed in the Boss's study. We returned to a terrible scene of canine regurgitation. 'Oh you dogs, you have been sick,' murmured Edward Pulling, for once guilty of tautology, and looking us both in the eye with the same distant, mid-Atlantic look we remembered so well from the bell-stealing episode of four years before. I was at once reduced from Coldstream captain to the ranks of the Jug offenders. So it was to remain.

I tried to catch up on my old class-mates and teachers. Three I had particularly liked in the classes immediately above ours had been killed in the war. Of our tiny sixth-form of thirteen, there had been only a single casualty – Whit Landon, who had lost his leg in the Battle of the Bulge, 1944. Henry Callard was no longer at Millbrook. He had become headmaster – a kind of American Mr Chips in his own time – at the famous Gilman school in Baltimore. Over the year whenever I went to Washington to give a lecture or attend a think tank, Henry would come over, bringing with him that indefinable encouragement, which always left one feeling expanded and reassured.

As I packed up to return to England and a freezing, hungry Cambridge that November, Aunt Rossy presented me with a handsome coffee-table history book, entitled *The American Past*. In it she had written, 'We all feel you belong to our American Future – so don't fail us.' It gave me a wrench, not for the first or last time. I was leaving to go back to a world of virtually no family and a broken romance, where, for a long time, I would still feel slightly alien. But I had made the choice. My essential Britishness, aided by those years in the Coldstream, was progressively asserting itself.

The 1940s became the 1950s. Truman gave way to Eisenhower. Bill married a tall, beautiful and strong-minded Canadian, Pat – fortunately with an advanced sense of humour. Against every probability, we all got on famously together. John Cutler died. Beloved 58 East 80th caught fire, and with it went all those emblematic pigs and fishes I remembered so well. Only one of the numerous second generation of Cutlers went through Harvard, or joined the chic Porcellian Club. The Post Road Farm at Garrison went too. Left poorer than expected, but never complaining, Aunt Rossy moved into a long, narrow apartment described by a son-in-law as a *wagon-lit*, but from which she continued to radiate hospitality – and controversy. And, one by one, the Cutlers, Breeses and Buckleys would descend on me in England – often, in that most infuriating of all American diseases, ringing unannounced from Heathrow with a cheery 'Hi! We've just arrived,' but hugely welcome, nevertheless. Then there were their children, and, eventually, grandchildren too. The chain never broke. Our lives remained constantly linked, and relinked.

In 1956, I made a three-month voyage of rediscovery, visiting all those clansmen, but also heading out to St Louis and the West Coast and all those distant parts of the States I had read about, but never got to. Sailing with Bill and Pat, we literally cruised over the bubbles of the *Andrea Doria*, the great Italian liner sunk that same morning, on our way to visit Aunt Rossy in Martha's Vineyard. When I read in a British newspaper of some new hurricane ravaging the Massachusetts coast, I used to have ghastly visions of her sitting in the hurricane cellar as the house was reduced to matchwood above her head, or being swept out to sea, her ample frame clinging to the top of the dining-room table. To Julia Breese, though, torn between adoration of her nephews and nieces and a longing for peace and quiet, life at climactic East

Chop presented just too much excitement. As soon as she tactfully could, she sold her share in the house to her sister. Aunt Rossy sold hers, too, a short while later, and was now summering in rented rooms in delicious Edgartown, of much happier memory. Any minute, a deluge of grandchildren was expected, and meanwhile life continued for Rossy Cutler at exactly the same excited tenor as thirteen years previously: bridge (at which she usually won) till the small hours of the morning, and during the day a steady stream of elderly admirers coming to bring tidings of the world and leisurely, entertaining conversation – and arguments.

One day we drove over with Aunt Rossy to see East Chop. I knew the embarrassing and embroidered memories of my childhood delinquencies that would be conjured up out of the visit, but I was nevertheless curious. The family that had bought the house were in residence, but that did not deter our hostess from insisting that I re-explore every last room. I thought of Pete, standing at the end of the latest dock, spotting for the *Yankee Clipper* and flush-deck, four-stackers. I looked down at what had once been our valiant attempt at a croquet lawn, remembered Judy's cries of 'Let Alleycat get the ball out of the poison ivy. Limeys are immune to it!' But there was little of the croquet lawn left. Despite the huge breakwater boulders set all along the shore, a great chunk of it had been gnawed away by the hungry Atlantic, and the sea was even nearer the house than it had been fifteen years back. Rossy Cutler had been wise to return to Edgartown. Another family would now grow up in that house, be stimulated or frightened by the storms, have their dramas and fights, sadnesses and ecstatic moments which throughout the rest of their lives they would associate with that house. And then, one night, perhaps there would be a truly horrendous hurricane, and then . . . But that was America. You never quite knew what nature was going to do to you, and it was only daring it that really made life worthwhile.

By this time, Bill had made something of a name for himself, with his first book, *God and Man at Yale*, which attacked the very foundations of that venerable establishment, for failing to live up to its Christian mission. He then went on to confront liberalism,

in all its woolly aspects. With considerable courage and persever-
ance, he then founded *National Review*, a still small voice in the
liberal wilderness, allocating all his patrimony to it, so that, for
many years to come, he had to work like half a dozen maniacs to
keep it and himself (in his extravagant, generous lifestyle) afloat.
Most of his friends thought him mad. I saw him from time to
time, here and there – but never enough. Then, in 1958, a happy
miracle occurred. I had flown down from Canada to Stamford,
Connecticut, to be with him after the death of his father. After a
bibulous dinner one night we decided to share a chalet that winter
in Switzerland. With two wives and three tiny children, we did
just that, and wrote a book each, at either end of the dining-room
table, at Saanenmöser high above the valley of Gstaad. It seemed
rather like the good old days in the attic eyrie at Millbrook –
which showed that, as someone said, there is a silent music
between friends – and it launched an annual skiing tryst that still
persists almost beyond the age when serious men hang up their
skis and take to curling.

The 1950s moved into the 1960s. Kennedy took over from
Ike, and was replaced by LBJ of the ears; McCarthy was forgotten, Vietnam began to fill American television screens. One day
Bill announced he was going to run for Mayor of New York in
1965, on a Conservative ticket against the wealthy and attractive
liberal Republican John Lindsay – at least partly as a joke. I raised
my eyebrows when I heard of it. Yet it was a joke that put him
squarely on the map. When asked by a reporter what he would
do if he won, he retorted, 'Demand a recount!' He collected only
13.4 per cent of the votes, but his remark caught the fancy of
Americans who had previously regarded him as little more than a
humourless right-wing maverick, author of rather dry books. In
no time at all he was on the cover of *Time* magazine (in 1967), in
the slot which, at Millbrook two decades back, had been filled by
Olympians like Churchill, Stalin, Hitler, Monty and Ike. The
mayoral race (about which he wrote yet another book) for the
first time truly lent respectability to all that Bill stood for and
believed in – as well as revealing him as a man of wit and warmth.
As a kind of endorsement, five years later brother Jimmy was

elected Conservative Senator for New York, in succession to the assassinated, liberal Bobby Kennedy. But he remained the same old warm companion with the highly developed sense of the ridiculous.

One day there came the dread news that Aunt Julia had cancer, and almost before I had time to think about it she was dead. She was barely in her seventies. I was shattered, reflecting on how much of her life had been encompassed by sadness, and I wondered whether I had ever shown proper gratitude for all she had done for me. It was a first, grievous break with those war years.

About the same time, the Boss retired from the school he had created three decades previously. But (though long predeceased by the universally loved Lucy) he survived another quarter of a century, until the ripe old age of ninety-two, with two successive pairs of new hips, living – the patriarch that he always was – in a small feudal empire in Long Island's Oyster Bay, surrounded by some sixteen children and grandchildren. From Oyster Bay he kept up an amazingly close contact with all the many hundreds of boys who had passed through his hands. Every Christmas would bring unfailingly his annual bulletin of the year's doings, with a handwritten personal note recalling exactly the name of every wife and child – and even dog: 'Bowser sends his Christmas Greetings to Bumble.' Though constantly mellowing (even with a perceptible sense of humour), he remained forever the Boss. For all the warmth, by the time I parted on my final visit to him aged ninety I was back to where I had left off in 1943, still with the same awe and respect. We, none of us, ever left our places. Eventually I managed to call him 'Ed', but Bill never could. To Bill, the arch-iconoclast, it signified an unacceptable step, almost, towards *lèse-majesté*. In later years, by which time he had become one of the most eminent men of his generation in America, the only time I ever recalled my old room-mate showing signs of total discomposure was when the Boss, now in his eighties, came for lunch. Within minutes of that imposing figure reappearing before us, we were both reduced once again to being fifth-formers, and suddenly, to my horror, I heard the *éminence grise* to the President of the United States embark upon, in his disarray, the most puerile of dirty stories, about a 'Mr Rabbit'. Pat Buckley ran choking from the table. I froze, aghast, expecting a sentence of no movies for at least a month. In icy silence the Boss sat as if he had heard nothing.

Following the Boss at Millbrook, three or four headmasters came and went. Under the menace of a new broom, threatening cuts for his beloved Zoo, our old foe Frank Trevor went berserk, arriving at a faculty meeting one day with a loaded revolver. Nevertheless, not only did the Zoo survive but, bearing his name, and lavishly supported by alumni, it became a multi-million-dollar affair, one of the most important teaching zoos in the country. Despite the lean years, the Boss's overall creation doubled in size, opening its doors to girls. Meanwhile, among its distinguished alumni, *inter alios* the mid-Atlantic Boss's creation was to produce the first career ambassador ever to be sent to the Court of St James – the brilliant Ray Seitz, Class of 1959. Edward Pulling, dying in April 1991, just lived to learn with delight of the appointment.

The 1970s, dark years for America, of the humiliation in Vietnam and Watergate, opened with Nixon and closed with Carter. Worse than at any time since 1940 (or, perhaps, ever) families divided bitterly down the centre. Rising eighty, Aunt Rossy – still following a new generation of newscasters as avidly as ever, and now able to lambast their physical appearances as well as their voices on the screen – began as a hawk, but ended a dove. With Nixon in the White House, Bill became a regular visitor and was appointed to the President's Advisory Committee on Information, in which capacity he set out, with me, on an exhilarating trip to South America, to see if the alarming Salvador Allende, the first (and last) Marxist president to arrive via the poll booth, really presaged a Soviet foothold in the Western hemisphere even more dangerous than Castro. Out of it (for me) came a book, *Small Earthquake in Chile*. Our room in Santiago's Carrera Hotel – constantly filled with excitable Chileans – came, once again, to resemble that old disorder of our Millbrook eyrie. It was a happy time.

One of the last occasions I saw Aunt Rossy was on the way out to Chile. Then the telephone rang. It was Judy with the news that her mother – like Aunt Julia – had contracted cancer. She was rising ninety. Before her voice became too weak, we spoke on the telephone. She told me exactly about Walter Winchell's (or was it Drew Pearson's?) latest commentary on Vietnam – what did I think of it? Typically, always the complete extrovert, there was not a word of concern about herself. Just as when Bob Fowler had been killed, she would allow of no mournful thoughts. I was reminded, later, of Milton's:

> Nothing is here for tears, nothing to wail
> Or knock the breast; no weakness, no contempt,
> Dispraise or blame; nothing but well and fair,
> And what may quiet us in a death so noble.

We said goodbye, as if I would be seeing her again in a few weeks. For a long while I could hardly bear to go to New York. A great light, a spark of energy had gone out of the world. To her large family (of which I proudly counted myself one), the centripetal force binding them all together had been switched off. For me, with her and Aunt Julia passed the only childhood I had ever had.

The leaves were falling thick and tragically fast. Though we had all survived the war, five out of our tiny Millbrook class of thirteen died, or were killed in silly accidents. In the mid-1980s Henry Callard was paralysed by a stroke. For months he lingered on, a total invalid, tended night and day by the devoted Clarissa, mother of all those little redheaded children at Millbrook. From Washington my class-mate Eric Stevenson and I drove over to Baltimore to see him. It was painful. With appalling injustice, the stroke had rendered this most articulate of teachers unable to speak a single word. Clarissa insisted that he could take in everything, so in front of him we artificially chatted about what we were doing, and reminisced about the good old days. He sat in his chair, silent, just smiling the same gentle smile that had us all his willing slaves at Millbrook. Afterwards, Clarissa assured us (how she knew was an eternal mystery) that he had understood everything and that it had 'made him so happy'. I hoped it had. He died a short while later; within a few months Clarissa joined him.

In 1980, I had the opportunity to go to work in Washington for the best part of a year, at the Smithsonian's Woodrow Wilson Center. It was my longest spell in the States since those wartime years. I went apprehensively. Had I romanticized too much? Would I find the realities of day-to-day life, not just as a tourist, unrecognizably altered? Would I find that friendships had worn thin? The answers were no, no, no. In New York, I wandered up to 58 East 80th Street. The steep front-stoop had disappeared and it had been turned into condos. Cowering between a new Pentecostal church and the Chemical Bank, it looked small, narrow and vulnerable. *Ant* Marcia Tucker's mansion on Park Avenue had vanished, to make way for yet another great glass skyscraper. A few more people get mugged and raped each year, the potholes on Fifth get bigger, the public buildings seedier, new graffiti like 'FUCK IRAN' regularly replace the old, the taxi drivers – from Liberia, Georgia, Afghanistan and Ethiopia – speak less and less English, making those interminable conversations of yore a regrettable anachronism (even if you *could* speak between the armour plate between passenger and driver). But otherwise New York constantly seems, to me, less changed than any city I know in the world.

At Millbrook, in what used to be Trevor's advanced biology course, fifteen-year-old girls were being taught how to unroll a condom on to a dummy penis, as anti-AIDS education. Otherwise, it was all happily recognizable. At Sharon, Dutch elm disease had long since removed the eponymous tree, and the house had also been turned into condos. But two of Bill's sisters, Priscilla and Jane, had cleverly managed to keep its core, the old patio of such happy memory, creating their own apartments around it. Each last Thursday of November, ever increasing hordes of Buckleys would roll up in the patio, to play the traditional Thanksgiving game of touch football. At Garrison, I revisited Post Road Farm. It too seemed small and run to seed;

the wooden tennis court had disappeared, consumed by the jungle of poison ivy. The old, *Hello Dolly*, railway station, falling apart again, still bore on its wooden slatted platform the warning 'NO BARE FEET'. Down by the grey stone church, I stopped at the modest graves of Aunt Julia and Aunt Rossy, so close to each other in death, looking across three yellow rose-bushes, and near by the grander triple grave then waiting for their centenarian brother, Ham Fish – flanked by two deceased wives.

Whenever repeated, on visits to recharge my batteries, all these memories, smells and sensations make me feel 'America, I never left you.' Of course, distance lends enchantment, rendering invisible the everyday flaws of friends, not to mention places. But it is, I hope, not just the nostalgia, the hankering after an America long since gone, but, also, continuing fulfilment and joy, and renewed delight in a country where the art of the possible, the 'yes we can' instead of the 'no we can't' attitude, the enthusiasm and a special warmth of friendship reign. Perhaps best of all is the knowledge that, as one fades, a second generation is taking over the 'special relationship'. Each of my three daughters had a Cutler, Breese or Buckley as godparent, each godparent exhibiting from the start the zestful devotion which the dear Red Duchess has shown to me only when I was already an undergraduate. One has produced for me an all American son-in-law, settling into the bosom of a new generation of Cutlers in Cambridge, Mass. When that wonderful, American, invention rings, it is Judy from St Louis saying, 'Why, Alistair [the 'Ally' finally disappeared], you sound next door!' And so, for all the years that pass, that is where I feel I am.

And, in a funny sort of way, did it perhaps all help me – all of us Bundles who went – to appreciate our own country just that much the more?

Thank you, my other country.